INTRODUCTION TO PROGRAMMING USING FORTRAN 77

GLENN A. GIBSON

Electrical Engineering Department
The University of Texas at El Paso

and

JAMES R. YOUNG

Storage Technology Corporation

D1377098

CONTENTS

7 FORMATTED INPUT–OUTPUT 291

8 FILE PROCESSING   343

9 PROGRAM DESIGN   384

Contents

PREFACE

This book is designed to be a text for a three-semester-hour introductory programming course; however, by covering only selected sections of the first seven chapters it could be used for a two-semester-hour course. The instructional philosophy used in organizing this book could most accurately be described by what many refer to as the spiral approach. The spiral approach first provides a brief introduction to computer systems and this is quickly followed by sufficient basics of a computer language to permit the readers to write simple programs. Then, with some programming experience behind them, they are taught the fundamentals of problem formulation and programming procedure. This is followed by a detailed study of the language and, finally, by a more thorough discussion of programming techniques. This approach permits the student to begin programming early and to mix the study of the details of the language with topics such as program structure, testing, debugging, and documentation.

It is the authors' belief that instead of concentrating almost entirely on the mechanics of a language, a book on introductory programming should also provide a sufficient introduction to the concepts of programming. It has been their teaching experience that if students are pushed into the details of a language before being properly introduced to what computer programming is about, they become confused and attempt to parrot the instructor or the examples in the book without developing an understanding of programming itself. The language and its particular set of rules is incidental; what is important is that students develop a programming technique which includes good programming practice. They must be able to state their problems concisely and then translate them into a form that both the computer and other people will understand.

It is also the authors' contention that remembering an accumulation of rules and being able to utilize these rules in a variety of ways is very difficult unless one has an understanding of why the rules are the way they are and why their limitations are necessary. Because the rules reflect the constraints of the computer hardware and software used to create and run a program, it is necessary first to present the overall organization of computer hardware and the process by which programs are generated. Therefore, Chap. 0 gives a general introduction to computer systems and their uses, and Chap. 1 discusses computer hardware and how it affects programming, and examines the underlying programming concepts and the process by which programs are put into an executable form.

Chapter 2 is almost a book within a book. It presents all of the material needed to write FORTRAN programs, but concentrates on short, single-task programs that require very little planning. Its purpose is to introduce the elementary concepts of programming and show how they can be implemented using the basic statements of FORTRAN. Although numerous ideas are presented in this chapter, almost all of the examples and exercises are short and are designed to emphasize only one or two points. The chapter closes with a summary that includes a brief example which incorporates all of the major concepts given in the chapter.

Chapter 3 assumes that the reader has acquired an ability to write single-task programs and begins to explain the process of formulating more complicated problems, breaking them into tasks, and organizing them in a way that is compatible with high-level language programming. After completing Chap. 3 the reader should be ready to study the details of the FORTRAN language and the more sophisticated features that permit the use of FORTRAN in solving complex problems.

Chapter 4 discusses how FORTRAN is used to form the elementary program structures. It also presents some introductory material on testing, correcting, and documenting programs, although these topics are not covered in detail until Chaps. 9 and 10. Chapter 5 gives a detailed presentation of the ways in which data can be stored in memory, and Chap. 6 considers subprograms and how they are used to break lengthy programs down into tasks that can be easily fit together to solve complicated problems. Although the examples and exercises prior to Chap. 6 become progressively more complex, it is not until Chap. 6 that the concept of dividing a program into modules can be fully utilized. Upon completing this chapter the reader should be able to write programs that are broken into modules that are related according to several levels of subordination.

Even though Chaps. 0 through 6 provide the information needed to develop complex programs, they do so by using only a simple inflexible form of input and output. To permit nice-looking printed matter or input information that may be in a variety of forms, the programmer must be given the ability to tell the computer the form of the output or input. This is the subject of Chap. 7. Chapter 8 extends the ideas presented in Chap. 7 to transferring information to devices that hold large quantities of data. It also considers the ways in which data are stored on and retrieved from such devices. Upon the completion of Chap. 8, one should be able to formulate difficult problems and solve them using FORTRAN. These problems may involve several tasks, a variety of input and output formats, and large quantities of data that must be filed for future use.

At this point, with a complete description of FORTRAN having been given, Chap. 9 provides a more thorough discussion of program design and documentation than was possible in Chaps. 3 and 4. The final section in Chap. 9 is on numerical errors and how they relate to program design. It is the only section in the book that assumes at least some knowledge of calculus. Chapter 10 is on debugging and, as with Chap. 9, is able to cover this topic more thoroughly than was possible in Chap. 4.

This book contains two types of exercises. There are brief section-end exercises that are designed to force the reader to review the preceding section, and there are programming problems at the end of each chapter. Although a section-end exercise may request that a program be written, it is not intended that the program be run on the computer. On the other hand, the chapter-end programming problems should be solved and tested on a computer. The programming problems are practical problems that have been drawn from a variety of areas of engineering, science, mathematics, and business. They also vary in the degree of mathematical maturity needed in solving them, although few problems require more than an intuitive understanding of integration. Some of these problems are sequential in that they depend on having solved earlier problems, but most of them can be solved independently from the other problems. If the programming problems are assigned as homework in a course, the instructor should carefully choose from the problems according to the background of the students.

Many texts utilize a rather informal presentation of introductory programming material. Although the presentation given here is not written in a rigid style, it does define and use the terminology employed by professional programmers. It is assumed that those reading this book will be exposed to and expected to communicate with people who have made programming their business. Even though this material is a beginning treatise on programming, it is directed at the college-level student who needs to know all of the fundamental aspects of programming. Much of the terminology used here has never been rigorously defined and the definitions given are based on general usage.

The authors would like to express their appreciation to all the people who participated in the preparation of this book. In general, they would like to thank the Electrical Engineering Department at The University of Texas at El Paso for the support it has provided and to the several faculty members in the Colleges of Science and Engineering for helping develop the programming problems. In particular, they would like to thank Drs. John Starner and Darrell Schroder for commenting on several of the sections; Barry Nicholson for taking some of the photographs; Dr. Neal Wagner, who did a thorough and excellent job of reviewing the entire book; the other reviewers; and Mary Louise Gibson for typing the manuscript and proofreading the material at the various stages of production.

GLENN A. GIBSON
JAMES R. YOUNG

INTRODUCTION TO PROGRAMMING
USING FORTRAN 77

0

INTRODUCTION

In the time it takes a person to pick up a pencil, a large modern computer could add millions of nine-digit numbers. Such a computer could also retrieve and display any one of a billion pieces of information during that time. Speed and storage capacity —therein lies the tremendous potential of modern computers. Because of the computer's speed, scientists are now able to fully utilize theoretical formulas that have been known for more than a century, formulas whose practical application requires millions, or even billions, of precise calculations. Because of the computer's storage capacity, large banks and insurance companies can keep accurate records for millions of customers. The combination of speed and storage capacity permits medical scientists to use computers to correlate billions of medical facts while searching for the causes of diseases.

Despite its overwhelming power, a computer has its limitations and can do only what it is instructed to do. It can perform only certain elementary operations and attains its usefulness by performing combinations of these operations very rapidly. It is up to human beings to formulate a computer solution to a problem and decide the order in which the computer is to execute its operations. The process of "telling" a computer what to do is called *programming* and the vehicle of communication is called a *language*. The purpose of this book is to teach the reader how to formulate a solution to a problem and then program a computer solution using the FORTRAN 77 language.

0-1 COMPUTERS

Simple machines receive commands from their operators and respond with predefined actions, some of which affect the world outside the machine. As shown in Fig. 0-1(a), the commands can be interpreted as inputs and the actions that affect the external world can be interpreted as outputs. The machine itself determines the outputs based on the inputs. In an automobile the inputs are the ignition switch, gear shift, clutch,

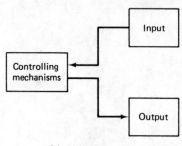

(a) A simple machine

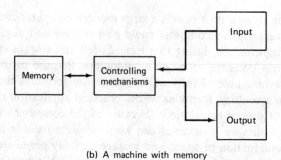

(b) A machine with memory

FIGURE 0-1 *Block diagrams of typical machines.*

brake, steering wheel, and accelerator. The automobile's outputs are its speed and direction, which depend on the positions of the steering wheel, accelerator, and so on. More complicated machines such as cruise missiles are depicted in Fig. 0-1(b). They include an additional very important ingredient, called a memory, which permits them to store information and base their outputs not only on the current inputs, but also on the history of inputs.

A computer is a machine with a memory that can rapidly input, process, store, and output information. Unlike most machines, its input–output relationships are not rigid and can easily be changed. Its internal processing and the relationships between its inputs and outputs are determined by a set of instructions, called a *program*, stored in its memory. By changing its program, a computer can be made to perform an entirely different function. The program dictates how information is to be input, processed, and output, and which information must be stored for future reference. Thus, a computer system consists of both tangible and intangible parts. The tangible, part that one can see and touch is called the *hardware*. The intangible part is the collection of instructions that is fed into the computer by human beings and stored in its memory. This part is referred to as *software*. Photographs of four typical computer systems are shown in Fig. 0-2. The system shown in Fig. 0-2(a) is a complete computer system that has been built into a carrying case (its weight is 40 lb) and is specifically

(a)

(b)

FIGURE 0-2 *Typical computer systems:* (a) *STC 3910 diagnostic computer* (Courtesy, *Storage Technology Corporation*); (b) *DEC PDP-IIV 23 computer* (Courtesy, *Digital Equipment Corporation*).

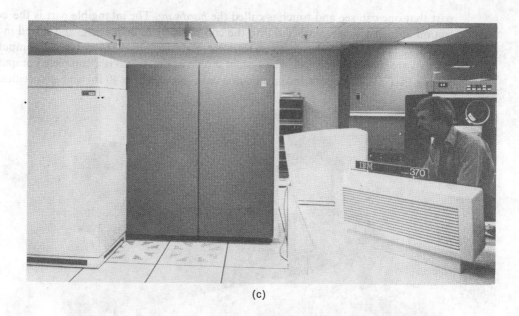

(c)

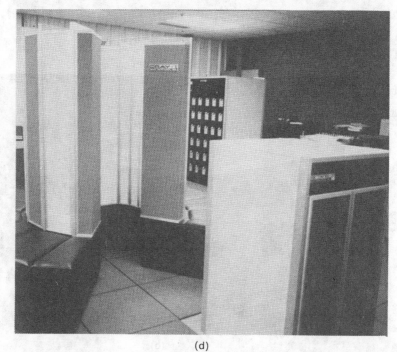

(d)

FIGURE 0-2 (*Cont.*)   (*c*) *IBM-370* (Courtesy, *Storage Technology Corporation*); (*d*) *Cray I* (Courtesy, *Cray Research, Inc.*).

designed to maintain other computer equipment. The overall design of this computer was led by co-author James Young. The picture in Fig. 0-2(b) shows a small minicomputer system designed for business applications, and Fig. 0-2(c) shows a medium sized business system. Figure 0-2(d) illustrates a Cray I, which is one of the fastest and most powerful computers in the world. The Cray I is so fast that its processor has been given a cylindrical shape so that the distances traveled by the electrical signals (which travel at the speed of light) are minimized.

The procedure for operating a computer is illustrated in Fig. 0-3. The procedure is to create a program that the computer understands, somehow put this program into the computer's memory, and then initiate the program's execution. The program will control the action of the computer until it is completed, then a different program may be brought in and executed.

Actually, the operation of a complex computer system is much more complicated than the simplistic picture painted above. Such a system would permanently contain programs that would help the users put their programs into the proper form, input their programs, aid in the input–output process, and generally control the flow of programs and information. Some systems permit several programs to reside in their memories simultaneously, and switch back and forth among these programs in such a way that the systems are more efficiently utilized. Others allow simultaneous execution of different programs or different parts of the same program. Although

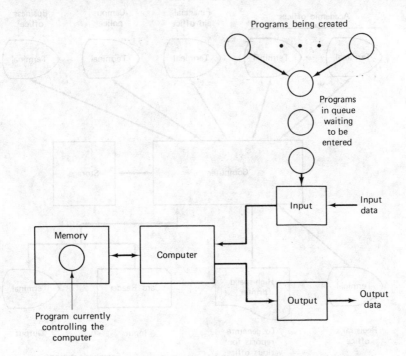

FIGURE 0-3 *The process of using a computer.*

these more complex situations are touched on in Chap. 1, for the most part they will be considered beyond the scope of this book. Because the material presented here is concerned primarily with the creation of a single program, little effort will be made to explain the many-faceted processes that take place inside a computer.

0-2 USES AND ABUSES

The uses of computers are extremely varied. There are minute computers, called micro-computers, in automobiles and household appliances, and very large computers used to control and monitor the entire defense apparatus of the United States. Computers are used in education, business, the military, medicine, police work, science, government, and the home.

One representative use is shown in Fig. 0-4. This figure illustrates a registration and student records system for a university. During the semester the registration personnel, campus police, the financial office, and the academic offices could enter or retrieve data such as grades, withdrawals, financial support, traffic violations, and other data that the university needs to maintain on individual students. At registration time it is assumed that the student gets a class card for each course he or she intends to take and submits these cards, together with an identification card, to a feetaker. The fee-

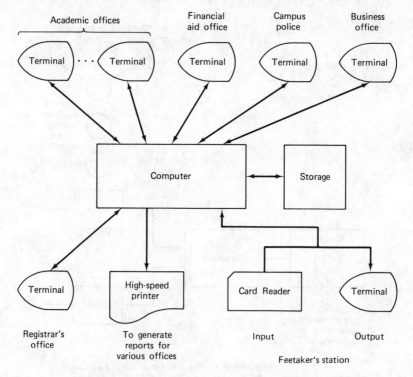

FIGURE 0-4 *Use of a computer for keeping student records.*

taker inputs the cards into the computer, and then the computer notes the enrollment on the appropriate class roles and outputs the fees to be charged. If the student has been suspended or has unpaid parking fees or other debts due the university, the computer will alert the feetaker so that appropriate action may be taken. Terminals could be placed in the college and departmental offices so that these offices could have ready access to their students' records, or at least selected portions of these records.

The hardware essentials of the system described above are:

1. The processing portion of the computer, which performs the necessary calculations and controls the activity within the system.
2. A large storage facility capable of storing thousands of student records.
3. A variety of terminals, some which have printing mechanisms and others which have only video screens.
4. A high-speed printer for outputting large quantities of information.
5. A card reader for inputting the student identification and class cards.

The software would need to include programs that can:

1. Search out a particular record or set of records.
2. Add and delete records as a whole.
3. Make additions to, corrections to, and deletions from the individual records.
4. Input and output the information required by the various devices connected to the system.
5. Permit those who manage the system to make changes in the software.
6. Control the processing of all the other programs.

In particular, note the last two items. No program that is used over an extended period of time will be used without change. New features will be needed and sometimes changes in the hardware will mandate changes in the software. Also, those who use the system will continually ask: "It would be nice if . . . , could you . . . ?" Therefore, all systems should be such that the software can be conveniently altered and new programs can be added. With regard to item 6, a computer system may include a wide spectrum of programs, but there must always be one program that controls all the rest. It determines when and under what circumstances the other programs will be run.

The software in this example is typical in that it consists of several interlocking programs under the control of a single program. Although this book will concentrate on how to create a single program, the reader should realize that, in practice, his or her program may be integrated with other programs written by other people. All but the most simple software systems are associated with a hierarchy of well-defined modules. This hierarchy usually extends down into individual programs. It is necessary to give the software a structure so that it can be created, corrected, documented, and changed in an organized manner. Therefore, it is not normally enough to know how to generate an isolated small program, and one should acquire a skill that is more generally applicable. From the outset, one should develop programming habits that will allow others to understand the programs that he or she writes. This will make it easy for others to use these programs in conjunction with their programs.

Unfortunately, computers can be used against our general betterment as well as for it. The speed and storage capacity that make them so useful also provide the basis for their misuse. Computers can be employed to invade privacy, embezzle money, or provide a means of misrepresenting facts, as well as to aid scientific research, identify criminals, and release us from mundane tasks. Personal files have existed for a long time, but never before have these files been so readily available and open to abuse. The student record system discussed above may sound efficient and convenient for everyone involved, but there is a price. The convenience the system offers both the student and the university administration also deprives the student of some privacy. It is too often relatively easy for unauthorized people to gain access to such records. Also, there are frequently too many authorized people and too much information made available to them. Not only does the computer provide a convenient means of obtaining information, but, by its very nature, it can quickly output this information in massive doses, thus increasing its capacity for misuse.

The modern computer is therefore a paradox. It can simultaneously free people from some of their cares and remove some of their freedoms. The wise use of computers is everyone's business, and in a free society it is everyone's responsibility to make certain that the negative aspects of computers are minimized while advantage is taken of the computer's tremendous capabilities.

1
INTRODUCTION TO COMPUTER SYSTEMS

The purpose of this chapter is to provide an overview of computer systems and programming that can be used as a background for the remaining chapters. Although numerous concepts are introduced here, it is not intended that they be fully understood until they are covered in detail later. What is presented here is a framework that the reader can use to organize his or her thoughts as the book progresses.

The *hardware* of a computer is its cabling, circuitry, cabinetry, and so on. It is generally broken down into components, each of which performs a specific function. A computer must have:

1. A memory for storing its instructions and the data to be operated on.
2. A component for performing arithmetic and other operations.
3. One or more components for storing large quantities of information.
4. A variety of devices that permit the computer to communicate with the external world.

The directions given a computer are called *instructions*. It should be made clear that the word "instruction" is a catchall term. There are high-level language instructions, assembler language instructions, and machine instructions. Ultimately, all instructions must be reduced to machine instructions. *Machine instructions* are instructions that can be directly understood by the computer (i.e., instructions that are presented to the computer in a form that its circuitry can decode). High-level language and assembler language instructions consist of strings of letters, numbers, and other characters, and are such that they are easy for people to understand. For example,

IF (X .GT. 0.0 .OR. Y .EQ. 1.0) GO TO 5

is an instruction in the high-level language FORTRAN that says:

> If the variable X is greater than 0 or the variable Y equals 1, get the next instruction from the point that is associated with the number 5.

Regardless of the programming level (high-level, assembler level, or machine level), a set of instructions that perform a specific task is called a *program*. A program that is presented to the computer in any level other than the machine level must be translated into the machine level. This is done by a separate program, called a *translator*. We will be concerned primarily with the FORTRAN language and its translator.

The *software* of a computer is a composite of all the programs executed by the computer. It can be divided into two major categories: system software and user software. *System software* consists of those programs, such as translators, whose purpose is to facilitate the creation and execution of other programs. *User software* consists of those programs written by the users to solve their specific problems. A typical university computer system might be used to compute payrolls, keep student records, keep library records, support research, provide computer-aided instruction, and teach programming. These applications would involve widely varying programs.

This chapter proceeds by first discussing the major hardware components of a computer, and then outlines how a computer executes instructions to perform its tasks. Next, the ways in which data are stored in the computer and the associated limitations are considered. Section 1-5 briefly discusses high-level languages in general and examines a representative high-level language program. The next three sections outline the commonly needed system software and the process used to create, prepare, and execute a high-level language program. The final section considers the underlying programming concepts and provides an introduction to the chapters that follow.

1-1 COMPUTER HARDWARE

Figure 1-1 illustrates the overall organization of a computer's hardware. The block in the center is the *central processing unit* (*CPU*). The CPU is broken into two major sections: the *control unit*, which decodes the instructions and controls the activity within the computer system, and the *arithmetic-logic unit* (*ALU*), which performs the arithmetic and other processing functions. The block on the left is the *memory*, which is used to store both the machine instructions and the data they operate on. The block on the lower right is labeled *mass storage* and is also a form of memory. Mass storage can be used to store both programs and data. However, the computer cannot execute the programs in mass storage directly; it must first transfer these programs to the memory. Similarly, the data in mass storage must be transferred to memory before they can be processed. The block on the upper right represents the *input–output* (*I–O*) *subsystem* which may consist of a number of devices, all of which allow the computer to communicate with the external world. The lines connecting the components of the computer together are called *buses* (or *channels*). The lines shown in the figure

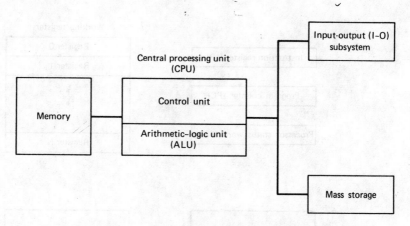

FIGURE 1-1 *Overall organization of a computer system.*

do not necessarily correspond to the connections made within any specific computer system. The bus configuration depends on the particular system. For example, there are usually paths that permit information to be transferred directly between mass storage and memory without passing through the CPU. The exact bus arrangement is not important to the high-level language programmer, and these arrangements will not be considered here.

1-1-1 The CPU

The *CPU* is the brain of the computer system. It decodes the instructions and initiates the actions called for by these instructions. Besides the circuitry needed to decode and carry out the actions of the machine instructions, it contains several electronic components, called *registers*, that are used to temporarily store data, instructions, and other critical information that is needed by the computer. Figure 1-2 summarizes the principal registers and components that must be present in all CPUs. The important registers are the:

Instruction Register (IR)—The *instruction register* holds the machine instructions while they are being decoded and executed by the computer's electronics.

Program Counter (PC)—The *program counter* points to the location in memory which contains the next machine instruction to be executed. It is updated after each instruction is brought in from memory.

Processor Status Word (PSW)—The *processor status word* contains a variety of information regarding the current state of the CPU and is updated after each instruction. Among other things, it reflects the results of arithmetic operations. It indicates whether the result of a just-concluded operation was negative, zero, or positive.

Working Registers—The *working registers* are used to aid in locating information in memory and in the processing of this information by the ALU. They are

11

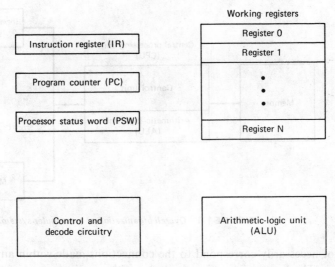

FIGURE 1-2 *Summary of the principal components of a CPU.*

frequently used to hold one or both of the operands during addition, subtraction, multiplication, or division. They function as a scratch pad, as opposed to memory, which can be viewed as a book, or mass storage, which can be viewed as a library. A computer can operate on data stored in the working registers much faster than on data stored in memory just as (and for more or less the same reasons) a person can operate on data on a scratch pad faster than on data in a book. One does not have to look up the data on a scratch pad or transfer it to a separate sheet of paper to make a calculation.

1-1-2 The Memory

A computer's *memory* is segmented into parts called *locations* (or *cells*). Each location has a unique number associated with it called its *address*. When the CPU needs a piece of information from memory, it sends to the memory the address of the location that contains the information, and the memory retrieves the information and relays it back to the CPU. The process of determining a location in memory is called *addressing*. The size of the memory locations determines the basic unit of information that the computer manipulates, although the computer is normally capable of working with several basic units at the same time. It may take several basic units (i.e., several locations) to store a single number or machine instruction.

1-1-3 Mass Storage

Mass storage devices are used to store both programs and data and are usually magnetic tape units or disk units, although alternatives of limited size are being produced using new technologies. A picture of a two-unit magnetic tape subsystem is shown in Fig. 1-3(a) and a picture of a two-unit disk subsystem is shown in Fig. 1-3(b).

12

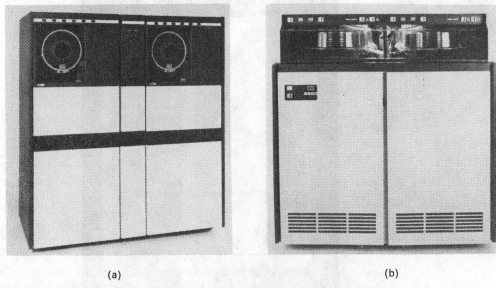

(a)   (b)

FIGURE 1-3 *Representative mass storage systems* (Courtesy, *Storage Technology Corporation*): (*a*) *STC 4500 tape subsystem;* (*b*) *STC 8650 disk subsystem.*

Magnetic tapes and disks are capable of storing hundreds of millions of pieces of information. A typical magnetic tape is 2400 ft long and can store 6250 pieces of information per inch. Therefore, it is capable of storing

$$12 \times 2400 \times 6250 = 180 \text{ million pieces of information}$$

(This is a maximum and does not account for wasted space.) In addition to the large capacity of a mass storage device, several mass storage devices can be connected to the same computer, and usually the medium that the information is stored on (the tape or disk) is portable. The fact that tapes and disks can be mounted or dismounted easily provides a computer with unlimited storage and a means of transporting programs and data from one computer system to another. A picture of a magnetic tape mounted in a tape unit is shown in Fig. 1-4(a) and a picture of a mounted disk pack is shown in Fig. 1-4(b). Figure 1-4(c) shows a bank of disk units.

Unlike memory, for which a single number, the address, gives the exact location of a piece of information, the mass storage system must be given several quantities before it can retrieve a given piece of information. One of these quantities would need to specify which mass storage device is being referenced. Then, assuming that the required tape or disk has been mounted, other identifying quantities would be needed to find the information. Typically, a tape or disk is divided into files which are subdivided into records, each record containing a set of information. Therefore, to designate a set of information one would need to specify the device, the file, and the record. If a given piece of information is required, one would need to search the record for the desired number or string of characters.

(a)

(b)

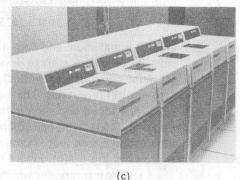

(c)

FIGURE 1-4 *Mass storage media and equipment: (a) Mounted tape* (Courtesy, *Pertec Computer Corporation*); *(b) Mounted disk; (c) Bank of disk drives.*

As mentioned in the introduction to this chapter, information that is stored on a mass storage device must first be transferred to memory before it can be operated on by the computer. This is usually done in blocks, and the process of getting information from a mass storage device consists of specifying the device, file, and record and transferring one or more blocks into memory where they can be searched directly. This procedure is explained in detail in Chap. 8.

1-1-4   The Input–Output Subsystem

The *I–O subsystem* is the array of devices that enable the computer to input programs and input and output data. There is a multiplicity of *I–O devices*, but some of the most important are:

Card Reader—For inputting information that has been punched into or marked on cards.

Line Printer—For outputting printed information. It is capable of printing one or more lines at a time.

Plotter—Enables the computer to output graphs, thus saving the user the task of putting numerical data into graphical form. It can also draw in the letters needed in the titles. A plotter is shown in Fig. 1-5(a).

Terminal—Normally used for inputting and/or outputting alphanumeric characters (letters, numbers, punctuation marks, etc.), although there are graphics terminals that can display computer-generated pictures. There are both printing and nonprinting terminals. The nonprinting terminals are called *cathode-ray tube (CRT) terminals* and display the characters on a screen that is similar to a television screen. A CRT terminal is shown in Fig. 1-5(b).

A computer system usually has one terminal, called the *console terminal*, that is special. It is in close proximity to the computer and is used by the operator to input commands to and receive commands from the system software.

(a)   (b)

FIGURE 1-5 *Typical peripheral equipment; (a) HP 7221C and HP 7221T plotters (Courtesy, Hewlett-Packard, Inc.); (b) DEC VT-100 CRT terminal (Courtesy, Digital Equipment Corporation).*

1-2 PROGRAM EXECUTION

Let us assume that a program has been translated into machine instructions and put into memory. A diagram showing the successive actions taken in executing the instructions is given in Fig. 1-6. The computer goes to the address specified by the PC, brings in the instruction located at this address, and puts it in the IR. It then decodes the instruction and takes the designated action. At the same time the computer examines the PSW, determines the address of the next instruction, and puts this address in the

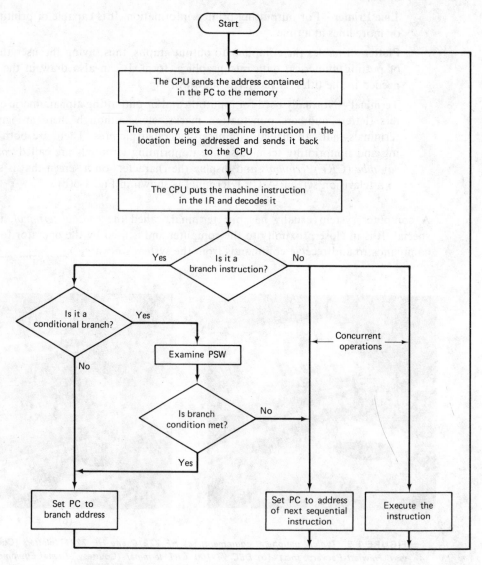

FIGURE 1-6 *Flow of actions taken during execution of an instruction.*

PC. Normally, the instructions are in consecutive memory locations and the address put in the PC is the next address in sequence. However, some instructions are *branch instructions* which can cause the instructions to be executed out of sequence (i.e., can cause the computer to jump around within memory). Branch instructions are extremely important in that they allow the computer to make decisions and to execute sets of instructions repeatedly (e.g., they allow it to execute one add instruction 1000 times instead of executing 1000 add instructions). There are both unconditional and conditional branch instructions. An *unconditional branch* causes a branch regardless of the state of the computer. A *conditional branch* uses the PSW to determine whether or not a branch should be taken. This gives the computer its decision–making capability. Recall that the PSW reflects the results of just–completed operations. A typical statement for performing a conditional branch in FORTRAN is

IF (A + B .GT. 0.0) GO TO 60

This statement is translated into machine instructions which cause A and B to be added and, if the PSW indicates that the sum is positive, to branch to the location associated with the number 60. (This number is not the memory address, but simply a label that represents an address.) If the sum is nonpositive, the next machine instruction will be taken in sequence.

As an illustration of how instructions can be put together to solve a problem, consider the following job of printing weekly payroll checks:

> A company has a given number of employees, each earning an individual hourly rate and having an individual amount of miscellaneous deductions. To determine the amount of each check, the hourly rate must be multiplied by the number of hours worked that week, 20% must be deducted for taxes, and then the miscellaneous deductions must be subtracted.

Figure 1-7 gives the layout of the computer system needed. The locations of the program and payroll data are shown in the memory block. The instructions are shown to start at address 1000, the pay rate data at address 2000, the hours worked data at address 2400, the deductions data at address 2800, and the employees' names at address 3200. The number of employees is stored at address 1500. It is assumed that all the employee data have already been brought into memory and are arranged so that the hourly pay rate, hours worked, deductions, and names are stored sequentially. The instructions needed to solve the problem are:

1. Read in the number of employees from the card reader and put it in the memory location whose address is 1500.
2. Put the contents of location 1500 in register 0.
3. Put the address 2000 in register 1.
4. Put address 2400 in register 2.
5. Put address 2800 in register 3.
6. Put address 3200 in register 4.

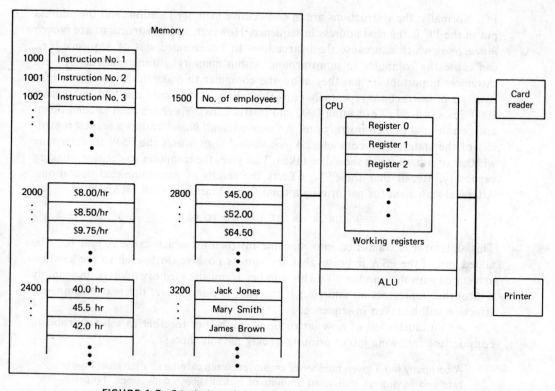

FIGURE 1-7 *Principal attributes of the computer system needed to solve the payroll problem.*

7. Put 0.8 in register 5.

8. Take the contents of the address given in register 4 (the name) and send them to the printer.

9. Put the contents of the address given in register 1 (the hourly rate) into register 6.

10. Put the contents of the address given in register 2 (the hours worked) into register 7.

11. Multiply the contents of register 6 by the contents of register 7 and put the result (the gross pay) in register 7. It is important to note that because register 7 can hold only one quantity at a time, the previous contents of register 7 (the hours worked) are lost; they have been replaced by the gross pay.

12. Multiply the contents of register 5 times the contents of register 7 and put the result (the after-taxes pay) in register 7.

13. Subtract the contents of the address given in register 3 (the deductions) from the contents of register 7 and put the result (the net pay) in register 7.

14. Send the contents of register 7 to the printer.

15. Cause the printer to space forward to the next blank check.
16. Increment the contents of register 1.
17. Increment the contents of register 2.
18. Increment the contents of register 3.
19. Increment the contents of register 4.
20. Decrement the count in register 0.
21. If the count in register 0 is positive, go back to instruction 8; otherwise, proceed to the next step.
22. Stop the program.

It should be noted that for reasons of simplicity certain liberties have been taken. Normally, instructions occupy more than one memory location and each piece of information in an employee's record may fill several locations. The name alone may fill 20 or 30 locations. Also, the instructions given here may represent more than one machine instruction.

The purpose of this simplified problem and the previous explanation of how instructions are executed is to give the reader some understanding of how a computer operates. The discussion above is designed to provide some insight as to why programs are structured the way they are and an intuitive feeling for the limitations of a computer. When programming in a high-level language, one does not need to be concerned with many of the details included in the example above. High-level language programmers need not be concerned with the movement of information between registers, or even that the registers exist. However, the number and size of these registers do have a bearing on the speed with which a program will be executed and the accuracy of the results it produces. Also, even though high-level language programmers do not need to be concerned directly with the details described above, these details are interrelated with the design of the high-level language and, to some degree, dictate the structure of high-level language programs. These statements will become clearer as the book progresses.

EXERCISES

1. Describe the step-by-step process of executing a machine instruction.
2. Assume that the coefficients a_3, a_2, a_1, and a_0 are stored in consecutive memory locations and that x is read in from a terminal. In a manner similar to that used in Sec. 1-2 and using a figure similar to Fig. 1-7, outline the solution to the following problem:

Input the variable x from a terminal, evaluate the polynomial
$$a_3x^3 + a_2x^2 + a_1x + a_0 = ((a_3x + a_2)x + a_1)x + a_0$$
and return the result to the terminal.
Give a verbal statement of the required instructions.

1-3 BITS, BYTES, WORDS, AND DOUBLE WORDS

Electronic circuitry can be made much more reliable if quantities within the circuitry can take on only two states, a 0 state and a 1 state. This is because the quantities, such as voltage, within the circuitry tend to drift with age. For example, the 0 state may be assigned to the voltage range 2 V or less, and the 1 state may be assigned the range 3 V or more. Thus the voltages could vary considerably and still the 0 and 1 states could be identified. For this reason, computers are binary in nature and everything in them must be stored in terms of 0s and 1s. All numbers, letters, punctuation marks, instructions, addresses, and so on must be stored as combinations of 0s and 1s. Each 0 or 1 in such a combination is called a *bit*.

Clearly, very little information can be stored in a single bit. If instructions consisted of only one bit, there could be only two instructions, one corresponding to the 0 state and one to the 1 state. Therefore, memory is divided into groups of bits. Most often, the basic unit of information, or location, consists of 8 bits and is called a *byte*. A byte is what has previously been referred to as a "piece of information". The number of possible 0–1 combinations that can be expressed with 8 bits is $2^8 = 256$. (Each additional bit doubles the number of combinations.) The combinations are:

$$
\begin{array}{l}
00000000 \\
00000001 \\
00000010 \\
00000011 \\
00000100 \\
\vdots \\
11111101 \\
11111110 \\
11111111
\end{array}
$$

Obviously, even bytes are severely limited in the amount of information they can hold and, consequently, bytes are grouped into words and double words. Typically, a *word* consists of 4 bytes and a *double word* consists of two words or 8 bytes. If this is the case, a word could store any one of $2^{32} \approx 4$ billion 0–1 combinations, and a double word could store any one of $2^{64} \approx 16 \times 10^{18}$ combinations.

A representative computer might have 16 million bytes in its memory, each byte having its own address. Instruction lengths vary and can be several bytes long. Numbers would be either one or two words long, depending on their type. Alphabetic and numeric characters, punctuation marks, and other symbols would be stored in single bytes. This means that up to 256 distinct characters could be used.

Machine instructions also consist of 0–1 combinations. An IBM 370 machine instruction that loads a register with the contents of a memory location is

$$
01011000 \qquad 00111000 \qquad 10010000 \qquad 00011000
$$

The first byte identifies the instruction as a load instruction, the next 4 bits designate the register that is to be filled, and the remaining bits determine the memory address from which the data are to be taken.

1. Find a general formula that gives the number of bits needed for an address as a function of the number of memory locations that have addresses.
2. If a memory has a 16 million-byte capacity, how many bits are needed to store an address provided that each byte has its own unique address? (*Hint:* One million is approximately 2^{20}.)

1-4 DATA TYPES AND PRECISION

Data are stored in a computer in three fundamental ways, each of which is a format for 0-1 combinations. The most easily understood of these three ways is to store the data as strings of characters, each character being 1 byte long. Each character would have assigned to it a unique 8-bit 0–1 combination. The correspondence between the characters and their 0–1 combinations is called an *alphanumeric code*. For the *American Standard Code for Information Interchange* (*ASCII*) a few of the assignments are:

00001101	Carriage return
00100000	Space
00101110	. (period)
00110000	0
00111001	9
01000001	A
01011010	Z
01100001	a

(A complete listing of the ASCII assignments is given in Fig. 5-4.) The character string

```
JOE GREEN
315 OAK ST.
SPRING, TEXAS  79925
```

would be represented by the string of 0–1 combinations which represent J, O, E, space, G, R, E, E, N, carriage return, line feed, 3, 1, 5, space, O, A, K, space, S, T, period, carriage return, line feed, and so on.

Although an alphanumeric code is a good format for inputting and outputting information, including numbers, it so happens that it is difficult for a computer to carry out arithmetic operations on numbers that are stored in this form. For this reason, additional formats are needed for storing numbers. There are two fundamental number formats, the integer format and the real (or floating-point) format.

In the *integer format* only integers can be specified, and they are represented using the binary number system. (The binary number system is a method for storing integers as 0–1 combinations which has rules similar to those of the decimal number system. It will not be discussed here but is summarized in Appendix A. There are numerous books that explain the binary number system, some of which are listed in the Bibliography. Knowledge of the binary system is not needed for most high-level language applications.) Integers are generally limited to one word, and if a word contains 32 bits, then only about 4 billion integers can be represented, usually negative 2 billion to positive 2 billion. This may seem like a lot of integers, but, in fact, this limitation is one of the basic limitations of computers. No matter how many bits are used to store a number, the number of numbers that can be represented is finite. As a result, computers are called *finite-state machines*. If an arithmetic operation such as multiplication is performed and the result is not in the available range, an *integer overflow* is said to occur.

The other strictly numeric format, the *real format*, is patterned after scientific notation and permits fractions as well as integers. In scientific notation a number is written as a fraction times a power of 10; for example, 0.321×10^{-2} is the number 0.00321 in scientific notation. In the real format, two numbers are stored, the *fraction* (or *mantissa*) and the *exponent* (or *characteristic*). Both may be stored using the binary number system, but that is not important to high-level language programmers. Once again, what is important is that the numbers must be represented using a finite number of bits. Typically, a real number is stored in one or two words, with the first byte being occupied by the exponent. If one 32-bit word is used, this leaves 24 bits for the fraction, and 24 bits permit $2^{24} \approx 16$ million distinct quantities to be represented. Since the fraction is between -1 and 1, 24 bits permit approximately 8 million divisions between -1 and 0 and 8 million between 0 and 1. This implies that a real format with 24 bits reserved for the fraction has roughly the same accuracy as is associated with seven significant figures. How finely the interval 0 to 1 can be subdivided by a given format is called the *resolution* of that format.

Although seven significant figures are adequate for many calculations, they are not enough for some. A computer's value lies in its ability to solve complex problems rapidly, and many of these problems require many more than seven significant figures. For example, seven significant figures are usually enough to solve up to 10 simultaneous equations, but become inadequate as the number of equations approaches 15. Computers are sometimes used to solve 100 or more such equations. The way to improve the resolution is to increase the number of bits reserved for the fraction. This can be done by storing the number in a double word and using all of the added bits for the fraction. In our example, 56 bits would be occupied by the fraction, and this implies a resolution of roughly 17 significant figures. If one word is used to store a real number, it is called a *single-precision* number; if a double word is used, it is called a *double-precision* number. The exact meaning of single and double precision in terms of significant figures clearly depends on the exact format and the number of bits in a word and therefore, on the computer. The example discussed here is similar to (but not the same as) the IBM 370 single-and double-precision real formats.

The exponent must also be stored in a finite number of bits. This restricts the sizes of the largest and smallest positive numbers the computer can store. If the exponent is stored in one byte, it can range from approximately 2^{-7} to 2^7. Internally, the computer does not use multipliers that are powers of 10; it normally uses powers of 2, 4, 8, or 16. Consequently, it is not obvious how the number of bits in the exponent is related to the largest and smallest positive numbers the computer can utilize. Suffice it to say that these limits may vary drastically from one computer to the next, but regardless of the computer, these basic limits are there. The largest possible number that can be stored on an IBM 370 is about 10^{76} and the smallest positive number is about 10^{-76}. The table in Fig. 1-8 summarizes some of the numeric properties of a few of the more popular computers. For each computer it indicates the largest pos-

Computer	Integer Size (digits)	No. of Significant Figs.—Precision		Max. Real Number	Min. Pos. Real No.
		Single	Double		
IBM 360/370	9	7	16	10^{76}	10^{-76}
Univac 1108	11	9	21	10^{38}	10^{-38}
CDC 6000/7000	14	15	29	10^{300}	10^{-300}
Burroughs 1700	10	7	20	10^{76}	10^{-76}
DEC PDP – 10	11	8	17	10^{38}	10^{-38}
DEC PDP – 11/34	5*	7	17	10^{38}	10^{-38}

*Could be 9, depending on software used

FIGURE 1-8 *Numeric limitations of various computers.*

sible integer for the integer format, and the resolution (in significant figures), largest possible real number, and smallest possible positive real number for the real format.

Just as an arithmetic operation on integers may produce a number that is too large for the integer format, an operation on real numbers may produce an exponent that is too large for the real format. When this happens an *exponent overflow* is said to occur. Also, an operation can result in a positive number that is smaller than is allowed. In this case an *exponent underflow* is said to occur. For example, 3.2×10^{-40} times 6.5×10^{-48} equals 2.08×10^{-88}, which is too small to be stored in an IBM 370.

The other basic arithmetic error is the *divide-by-zero error*, which is due to the fact that division by zero is not mathematically defined. It can occur when either the integer or the real format is being employed. All but the divide-by-zero error are due to the finiteness of the computer. These errors will be discussed further as the need arises.

EXERCISES

1. Give the ASCII code 0–1 representation of 9.09 using the sample code assignments given at the beginning of this section.
2. How many alphanumeric characters can be represented with a 6-bit code? A 7-bit code? An 8-bit code?
3. If there are 24 bits in a word, how many integers can be represented using a single-word integer format? A double-word integer format?
4. If 48 bits are used to represent the fraction in a real format, what is the approximate resolution in significant figures?
5. Summarize the various types of arithmetic errors that may occur while using a digital computer.
6. Show that if n bits are used to represent the magnitude of the fraction in a real format, the number of significant figures is approximately $n \log_{10} 2$.

1-5 HIGH-LEVEL LANGUAGE PROGRAMS

A high-level language instruction is usually referred to as a *statement* and is an abbreviated, precisely constructed English language sentence. There are several high-level languages, some of the more popular being FORTRAN, BASIC, COBOL, PL/I, C, PASCAL, and ALGOL. A language is defined by the set of rules used to construct its statements. A given language consists of a few statement types, and all statements in a given type must be constructed according to a set of rigidly defined rules. Therefore, even when "talking" to a computer in a high-level language, one is much more limited than when talking to a person. The composite set of rules for all statement types is called the *syntax* of the language. If a statement is not constructed according to its syntax, it is said to contain a syntax error and the translating process cannot be completed.

In designing a high-level language, the basic structure of computers in general determines the elementary statement types that should be included in the language. Also, the language must be designed so that internal references, such as memory addresses, register designations, and I–O device designations, can be made implicitly or through names or labels that are meaningful to and assigned by the programmer. With regard to memory addresses, the previous statement applies to both data references and instruction references that are required in branch instructions. I–O device references are made by assigning names and/or numbers to the devices and files.

The less the programmer needs to know about a computer and still be able to use it efficiently, the better.

When the computer communicates with the external world, if the format in which data are to appear at the input or are to be printed at the output is to be under the programmer's control, then special statements for performing this task must be available. These statements are called *format statements*.

Although the FORTRAN language is not introduced until Chap. 2, many of the FORTRAN statements can be explained intuitively and a preliminary example will provide the reader with an overview of things to come. The important aspects of a FORTRAN program are representative of those of high-level languages in general. A FORTRAN program for solving the payroll problem discussed in Sec. 1-2 is:

```
        INTEGER NOEMP
        REAL PAY, PAYRAT(400), HRSWKD(400), DEDUCT(400)
        CHARACTER*32 NAMES(400)
        READ (5,100) NOEMP
        CALL INPUT (NAMES, PAYRAT, HRSWKD, DEDUCT, NOEMP)
        DO 10 J=1, NOEMP
            WRITE (6,101) NAMES(J)
            PAY = 0.8*PAYRAT(J)*HRSWKD(J) − DEDUCT(J)
            WRITE (6,102) PAY
   10   CONTINUE
  100   FORMAT (I5)
  101   FORMAT (/TR20, A32)
  102   FORMAT (TR40, F7.2)
        END
```

The first statement designates only that the memory location associated with the name NOEMP (number of employees) is to be in the integer format. Similarly, the second statement designates PAY, PAYRAT, HRSWKD, and DEDUCT as being in the real format. In addition, the second statement reserves 400 words for each of the payroll items, and assigns the names PAYRAT (payrate), HRSWKD (hours worked), and DEDUCT (deductions) to these items. The space reserved for PAYRAT, HRS-WKD, and DEDUCT is sufficient to store the payroll data for up to 400 employees, with the first location corresponding to the first employee, the second location to the second employee, and so on. The third statement indicates that NAMES is to be used to store up to 400 strings of characters (the employees' names) with up to 32 characters in each string.

None of the first three statements requires action by the computer while the program is being run. They are instructions to the translating program which inform it how much space it is to reserve and which formats are to be used in storing the data.

The fourth statement reads in the number of employees and puts it in the location associated with the name NOEMP. Because of the limited space reserved for PAYRAT, HRSWKD, DEDUCT, and NAMES, this number cannot exceed 400. This READ statement is used in conjunction with the FORMAT statement labeled

100, which tells the computer the format of the data being input. Also indicated in this statement is the number of the device from which the input is to come (e.g., the number 5 may represent the card reader). The fourth statement is the first statement that is actually translated into machine instructions and executed by the computer.

The portion of the program for inputting the employee data into memory has not been included, but is to be in a separate set of statements which is initiated by the fifth statement. Such a set of statements is called a subprogram and, in this example, the CALL statement calls upon the subprogram INPUT to perform the task of transferring the necessary payroll data into memory.

The statement

DO 10 J=1,NOEMP

causes the statements between it and the CONTINUE statement associated with the label 10 to be repeatedly executed as J is incremented from 1 to NOEMP. Each time the statements are executed, J will point to different entries in PAYRAT, HRSWKD, DEDUCT, and NAMES (i.e., to the data for a different employee).

The first statement after the DO statement writes the employee's name on the check. Once again, the second number inside the parentheses, 101, designates the format to be used, and the first number, 6, designates the output device, which in this case is the printer. The next statement computes the net pay and the following statement outputs the net pay to the printer using the format statement labeled 102. The CONTINUE statement causes no action; it simply provides a means of labeling the end of the instructions that are repetitively executed as J is incremented.

The END statement notifies the translating program that there are no more instructions to be translated, and later, when the program is executing, the END statement causes the program to stop.

1-6 SYSTEM SOFTWARE

As discussed previously, there are usually several system programs that are designed to help users prepare and run their programs. A certain subset of these programs is called the *operating system* and the program that is the heart of the operating system is called the *resident monitor*. The word "resident" refers to the fact that it is in the computer at all times. The resident monitor acts as a traffic cop for the system. It receives the commands from the users, assigns priorities, and controls the operating system while it prepares and executes all other programs. If a program is input through a card reader, the set of cards being submitted is called a *deck*. Some of the cards in the deck which precede and follow the program are called *job control cards*, and serve only to give commands to the resident monitor, which, in turn, accesses the various programs in the operating system needed to carry out these commands. If a program is being initiated from a terminal, these commands must be typed in by the user.

Quite often, one program will be used in conjunction with another program. When a program references (i.e., branches to) a second program and causes it to be executed, the first program is said to *call* the second program. Frequently, the resident monitor or a user program will need to call a system program to perform a specific task.

In addition to the resident monitor, the operating system normally includes a number of commonly used programs that can be attached to, or called by, user programs. For example, it is not necessary to include a program segment to take the sine of an angle. Such program segments are called *system subprograms*. They are permanently stored in the computer system and can be attached, or "linked," to a user program by another program called a *linker* (or *linkage editor*). Also, high-level programs permit I–O to be initiated by single statements, even though the I–O may require a large program to be executed. What happens is that the user program causes the resident monitor to bring in and execute an I–O program called an *I–O driver*. Finally, the operating system must include a translating program for each high-level language. These programs are called *compilers*, *interpreters*, or *translators*, and the term "translator" is used in this book. Normally, the system subprograms, linker, I–O drivers, translators, and other parts of the operating system are stored on a special mass storage device, called the *system device*, and are called into memory only when they are needed. (It should be pointed out that "operating system" is an umbrella term and just what should be included under this term is somewhat nebulous. Some may argue that translators are system programs, but are not part of the operating system.)

Some operating systems are such that user programs are submitted sequentially, most often through a card reader. Such systems are referred to as *batch systems* and their use is referred to as *batch processing*. Other operating systems are capable of randomly receiving commands from terminals to execute programs. They are called *interactive systems*, and their use is referred to as *interactive processing*. Some operating systems accommodate both batch and interactive processing. Both types of systems are considered in this text.

1-7 PROGRAM CREATION

Given a problem to be solved using a computer, one must:

1. State the problem in precise terms.
2. Decide on the method for solving the problem.
3. Determine how this method is to be put into a high-level language and construct the resulting program structure using programming aids.
4. Write the high-level language program.
5. Put the program into a medium the computer can read.
6. Test the program for correctness and remove the errors.

The first step tends to be independent of the computer system or language being used. It is a very important step and emphasis should be given to the word "precise." Computers are machines that follow the instructions given them using fixed rules built into their circuitry. They must be "told" exactly what to do; they cannot make subjective decisions, only quantitative decisions. Therefore, if the user cannot state the problem precisely, he or she has no hope of deriving a solution that can be "explained" to the computer.

With regard to the second step the computer system and its limitations should be taken into account. For the third step, the properties of the language to be used need to be considered. If the third step is done properly, the fourth step consists only of the mechanical translation of the chosen method as outlined in step 3 into statements that obey the syntax of the language.

The fifth step depends on the medium. If the program is to be presented to the computer through a card reader, step 5 consists of simply punching the program into cards, adding the necessary control cards, and feeding the resulting deck through the card reader. If corrections are needed, it is simply a matter of changing the incorrect cards. If an interactive system is being utilized, a system program referred to as a *text editor* must be called using the appropriate system command. The text editor will receive the user's program as it is typed into the terminal and will store it as a file on a mass storage device. Text editors include features for adding, deleting, or changing the program, either while it is being created or later if mistakes are discovered. The end result is a file on a mass storage device that can be called using system commands. Figure 1-9 depicts the process involved in using a text editor. The

FIGURE 1-9 *Process of using a text editor.*

reverse arrows indicate that a file can be recalled and corrected. Whether the final form is a deck of cards or a file on a tape or disk, at this stage the program is called a *source module*.

The last step, that of testing and correcting the program, can be the most difficult and time consuming, particularly if the first five steps are not done carefully. Tests should be designed so that the segments within the program are checked as thoroughly as possible. Because of branching, the segments exercised by one set of data may differ from those exercised by another set of data; therefore, several tests may be needed to completely test a program. The process of correcting a program is called *debugging*. Because it is often impractical to verify all possible paths through a program, errors are frequently found even after a program is put into service. The process of correcting, updating, and modifying a program after it has been put into use is called *software maintenance*. Modern programming techniques are designed to minimize the number of errors and thereby reduce debugging and software maintenance.

1-8 PROGRAM TRANSLATION AND EXECUTION

Figure 1-10 illustrates the process a source module must go through before it becomes an executable program. Either by a command from a control card or from the user's terminal the operating system will identify which translator is to be used and will initiate its execution. The translator will bring in the source module and carry out the translation process. The output of the translator is the required machine instructions interspersed with other information that will be needed by the linker. The output is called an *object module*. Among other things, the object module contains a list of the other object modules, such as system subprogram object modules, that must be attached to it. The object module is normally stored as a file on a mass storage device.

Next, the operating system calls in the linker. This may be done automatically or may require a command from a control card or the user's terminal. In a batch system it is usually done automatically, and in an interactive system it usually requires a command. The linker joins the object module with the necessary system subprograms and other object modules that have been previously created. The output of the linker is called a *load module*. With one exception, the load module is a self-sufficient set of machine instructions, a machine language program. The exception is that it does not contain the I-O drivers, it contains only references to them that will cause the operating system to initiate their execution as they are needed. The load module is normally stored as a file in mass storage.

Finally, the operating system brings in and begins the execution of the load module. As with the linker, this may require a command or may be done automati-

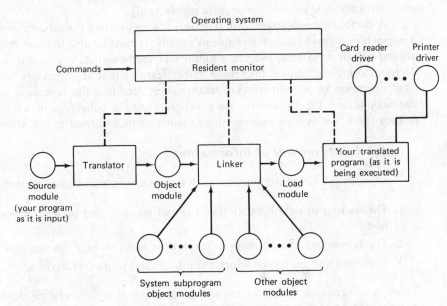

FIGURE 1-10 *Preparation and execution of a high-level language program.*

cally. As before, it is normally done automatically in a batch system and requires a command in an interactive system.

What has been presented in this section is a simplistic overview designed to give the reader an introduction to the most important steps in the preparation of a program for execution. Exactly how these steps are carried out varies considerably from one system to the next. It is not expected that this section be completely understood at this point. The purpose of this material is to provide a background for the discussions given in later chapters.

1-9 ESSENTIALS OF COMPUTER PROGRAMMING

The purpose of this section is to solidify some of the ideas presented previously and to introduce the material to be covered in detail in the next few chapters. This is done by discussing briefly the following five principal programming capabilities:

1. Movement of information
2. Mathematical operations
3. Branching and decision making
4. Repetitive execution
5. Program subdivision

These are the capabilities that any programming language and supporting system must accommodate in order to operate satisfactorily.

A computer needs to perform relatively few elementary operations, even though it is capable of solving complex problems rapidly. It must be able to move information around within its system, execute a number of mathematical operations, and make decisions using conditional branching. Other features that are necessary for the efficient operation of a computer are features that facilitate the repetition of sets of instructions and the subdivision of a program into a collection of smaller, well-defined tasks. Let us now examine these requirements and their ramifications.

1-9-1 Movement of Information

Obviously, a computer must be such that the programmer can control:

1. The transfer of data between its CPU and memory and between memory locations
2. The movement of information between its mass storage devices and memory
3. The input and output of information from and to its I–O devices

To move information within a computer is to transport it from one part of the computer to another. Except for certain output media, such as paper, the previous information in the part being transferred to is lost. Printed output is retained because new paper is continuously fed into the printer, but a working register, a memory location, or a specific area on a disk can hold only one piece of information at a time. Therefore, when new information is transferred to such a place, the old information is erased. This is an *extremely important point.*

Only the transfer of data between memory locations will be considered here. Transfers between the CPU and memory are done automatically by the high-level language instructions and are not directly controlled by the high-level language programmer. The transfers mentioned in items 2 and 3 above will be discussed in later chapters. The simple movement of a single piece of information from one memory location to another is normally initiated by a high-level language statement of the form

$$A = B$$

where B is the symbol representing the location the information is taken from and A is the symbol representing the location in which the information is to be placed. The information is transferred from B to A and the previous contents of A are lost. Statements of this type are referred to as *assignment* or *replacement statements* (A is being assigned or replaced by the contents of B) and the symbols A and B are referred to as *variables.* The form of assignment statements may vary from one language to the next, but most all language will accept the form given above.

A slightly different type of assignment statement is

$$X = 3.2$$

This statement causes the quantity 3.2 to be taken from a memory location (which is determined when the program is translated) and placed in the location associated with the variable X. The quantity 3.2 is referred to as a *constant.*

1-9-2   The Mathematical Operations

The arithmetic operations a computer can execute using its ALU are normally the unary operation negation and the four binary operations addition, subtraction, multiplication, and division. The four arithmetic operations are denoted by $+$, $-$, $*$, and $/$. Typical assignment statements that involve the execution of one or more arithmetic operations are

$$X = Y + Z$$
$$A = B*C + D/B$$

The first statement causes the contents of X to be replaced by the sum of the contents of Y and Z. The second replaces the contents of A with the sum of the product of B and C and the quotient D divided by B. In these more complicated assignment statements the notations to the right of the equal signs are called *expressions.* In general, an assignment statement consists of a variable followed by a special symbol, which is, in turn, followed by an expression. The special symbol represents the phrase "is replaced by." Just what the special symbol is depends on the language, and in FOR-TRAN it is the equal sign.

It is *very important* to note that the equal sign (or other special symbol) is not equality in the algebraic sense. The statements in the examples above cause the expressions to be evaluated and the contents of the variables on the left to be replaced by the results. The algebraic equation

$$x = x + y$$

implies that $y = 0$. The assignment statement

$$X = X+Y$$

implies no such thing— it merely sums X and Y and puts the result in the location represented by X.

An important computation that consists of repeated multiplication, and perhaps a division, is that of raising a quantity to an integral power. (A division is needed if the integer is negative.) This is usually accomplished through the special notation

$$X**N$$

which means X raised to the Nth power. Both X and N may be either variables or constants. For example, the statement

$$A = Y**(-3)+2**M$$

results in A being replaced by $Y^{-3} + 2^M$.

Except for very special cases the computer hardware is capable of performing only the arithmetic operations negation, addition, subtraction, multiplication, and division. Operations such as taking the sine of an angle can only be approximated using several machine instructions which perform only the elementary arithmetic operations. For example, it is known that for x between 0 and $\pi/2$ radians,

$$\sin x \approx x - \frac{x^3}{6} + \frac{x^5}{120} - \frac{x^7}{5040} + \frac{x^9}{362,880}$$

Therefore, because the expression on the right involves only the elementary operations, the computer can approximate the sine operation using a sequence of machine instructions. Almost all systems that include high-level language translators include system subprograms for performing the common algebraic and trigonometric operations (exponentiation, sine, cosine, tangent, etc.). As a result, these operations can be executed using familiar notation. The statement

$$A = SIN(X) + 5.6*EXP(Y)$$

causes the sum of the sine of X and 5.6 times the number e raised to the Y power (i.e., $\sin X + 5.6e^Y$) to be put into A.

As mentioned in Sec. 1-5, the rules for formatting a statement are called its syntax. The syntax used in the examples above is not standard to all languages but is valid for most languages (e.g., in some languages "↑" is used to take a power instead of "∗∗"). In particular, these examples have obeyed the syntax of FORTRAN.

1-9-3 Branching and Decision Making

Usually, the statements in a program are executed in sequence (just as the machine instructions they are translated into are executed in sequence). However, there are several ways in which a program can branch out of its normal sequence and continue its execution in a different part of the program.

The simplest type of branch is the unconditional branch. An unconditional branch must include a notation which indicates where to branch to, and this notation is called a *label* (or *statement number*). If the FORTRAN program segment

```
                    .
                    .
                    .
              A = B+3.0
              GO TO 500
      200     X = 0.0
                    .
                    .
                    .
      500     X = −1.5
              A = A+X
                    .
                    .
                    .
```

is executed, B + 3.0 will be put into A and the GO TO statement will cause execution to continue at the statement whose label is 500. Therefore, the next actions will be to put −1.5 into X and replace the current contents of A with the sum of A and X. The statement X = 0.0 will be performed only if a branch statement somewhere else in the program (one that is not shown) calls for a branch to the label 200.

Conditional branching must be used in decision-making situations and is such that if a condition is met, one action is taken, and if it is not met, another action is taken. With regard to a high-level language, a *condition* is a declaration that is either true or false depending on previous results within the program. A condition is said to have a *truth value* "true" if it is true and "false" if it is not true. The truth value is indicated by the PSW after the necessary calculations have been carried out. An example of a FORTRAN decision-making statement is

```
              IF (X. EQ. Y) GO TO 350
```

The condition is "X .EQ. Y". If X − Y = 0, the PSW will indicate that the condition is true and the program will continue at the statement labeled 350; otherwise, it will continue with the next statement in sequence. It should be emphasized that, although the condition "X .EQ. Y" is normally associated with the English phrase "X is equal to Y," its meaning is that the contents of the memory location corresponding to the symbol X are the same as the contents of the memory location corresponding to the symbol Y.

Just as declarations in the English language would be very limited if only simple statements could be formed, conditions would be inconveniently restricted if they could make only single comparisons. Two of the more prominent ways of extending the English language to include complex structures is to permit the use of modifying phrases and the use of conjunctions. For conditions, the logical operations NOT, OR, and AND are used. The operation NOT is equivalent to the modifying phrase "it is not true that." The operations OR and AND are equivalent to the conjunctions "and/or" and "and." The condition

.NOT. (A .EQ. B)

is true if A is not equal to B and is false if A is equal to B. The condition

(A .EQ. B) .OR. (J .EQ. 0)

is true if either A is equal to B is true or J is equal to 0 is true, *or if both are true*. It is false if and only if both parts are false. The condition

(A .EQ. B+3.0) .AND. (C .NE. 5.2)

is true if and only if both A is equal to B + 3.0 and C is not equal to 5.2.

Logical operations are formally defined by tabulating the truth value of the overall condition for all possible combinations of the truth values of its parts. These tabulations are called *truth tables*. The truth tables for NOT, OR, and AND are given in Fig. 1-11(a) through (c). In these tables "T" means "true," "F" means "false," U and V represent arbitrary simple conditions (such as "A .EQ. B"), and the columns on the right give the truth values of the overall conditions. For example, it is seen in the truth table for the OR operation that U .OR. V is false if and only if both of the parts U and V are false. Also given in Fig. 1-11 are the truth tables of two other less frequently used logical operations that are included in FORTRAN 77. They are the equivalence (EQV) and nonequivalence (NEQV) operations. (The NEQV operation is sometimes called the exclusive-OR operation.) A condition consisting of two parts connected by an EQV is true if and only if both parts are true or both parts are false, and NEQV is the logical negation of EQV. The EQV and NEQV operators are mentioned here only to make the reader aware of their existence and they are not considered further in this book.

In the preceding examples the conditions contained only the relational operators .EQ. , indicating equality, and .NE. , indicating inequality. Most languages also permit the use of the relational operators "greater than," "greater than or equal to," "less than," and "less than or equal to." The condition

(X .GT. 7.77) .AND. (Y .LE. A*B)

is true only if X is greater than 7.77 and Y is less than or equal to A*B.

U	.NOT.U
F	T
T	F

(a) The NOT operation

U	V	U .OR. V
F	F	F
F	T	T
T	F	T
T	T	T

(b) The OR operation

U	V	U .AND V
F	F	F
F	T	F
T	F	F
T	T	T

(c) The AND operation

U	V	U .EQV. V
F	F	T
F	T	F
T	F	F
T	T	T

(d) The EQV operation

U	V	U.NEQV. V
F	F	F
F	T	T
T	F	T
T	T	F

(e) The NEQV operation

FIGURE 1-11 *Defining truth tables for the elementary logical operations.*

The syntax for writing a condition varies from language to language. The standard FORTRAN syntax, which is treated in detail in subsequent chapters, was used in the preceding examples.

A language may include conditional branch statements that do not involve the true–false conditions discussed above. For example, FORTRAN permits a multipath branch, depending on the value of an integer variable. The FORTRAN statement

GO TO (40, 52, 85), I

causes a branch to the statement labeled 40, 52, or 85 if I contains 1, 2, or 3, respectively. This and the other branch statements that are available in FORTRAN are studied in Chap. 4.

The translations of high-level language conditional branch statements include one or more conditional branch machine instructions. The machine instruction sequences generated by a single high-level language statement can be quite long if the statement is complex. A discussion of the translation of such statements is clearly beyond the level of this book. Fortunately, the high-level language programmer does not need to have knowledge of this translation process or of the machine instruction sequences it produces.

1-9-4 Repetition

It frequently occurs that it is desirable to execute a set of statements over and over with only minor modifications being made between successive executions. Such a procedure is called *looping*. A simple example of looping is the FORTRAN program segment

```
        .
        .
        .
        SUM = 0.0
        DO 60 I=1,10
            SUM = SUM + X(I)
    60  CONTINUE
        .
        .
        .
```

which causes the sum of the 10 numbers in the set of numbers associated with the symbol X to be put into SUM. The segment accomplishes the task by first setting SUM to zero and then successively adding to SUM the numbers in the set corresponding to X.

The ease with which looping can be performed is an important attribute of any language. Looping not only saves the programmer a considerable amount of tedious work, but also permits shorter, more understandable programs which require less memory. How looping is performed when using FORTRAN is introduced in Chap. 2 and discussed in detail in Chap. 4.

1-9-5 Subdivision

For several reasons, all but the smallest programs are broken into tasks and at least some of these tasks are performed through the use of subprograms. By dividing a program into tasks it is easier to:

1. Comprehend and discuss the overall problem without worrying about the details.
2. Allow more than one person to work on the problem.
3. Use portions of one program in other programs that involve some of the same tasks. As mentioned in Sec. 1-6, subprograms for performing frequently encountered tasks, such as taking the sine of an angle, could be stored on mass storage devices.
4. Document the program in an understandable manner.

A *subprogram* is simply a program that is attached to another program in such a way that the two programs can share at least some data. Figure 1-12 shows the relationships among a program and two subprograms that are attached to it. The figure

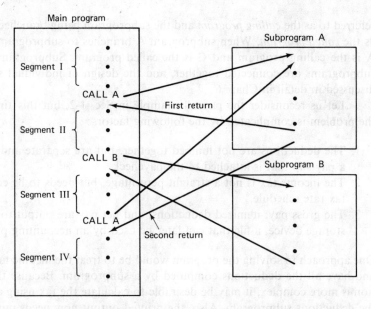

FIGURE 1-12 *Relationships among a program and its subprograms.*

indicates that segment I executes first and then the program branches to, or *calls*, subprogram A. After subprogram A is completed it branches back, or *returns*, to the original program and segment II is executed. Then subprogram B is called and executed, and once again a return is made to the original program. Next, segment III is performed and then a second call is made to subprogram A. Finally, the original program is returned to and segment IV is executed.

Figure 1-13 shows a hierarchical program structure. In such a structure the program to which all other programs are subordinate is called the *main program*. At any level within the hierarchy, the program that is branching to a subprogram is

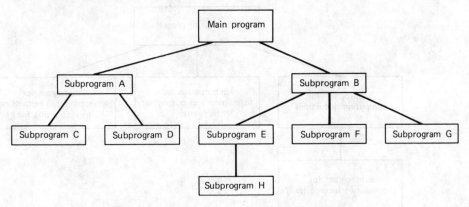

FIGURE 1-13 *Typical hierarchical subprogram structure.*

referred to as the *calling program* and the subprogram being branched to is referred to as the *called program*. When subprogram A branches to subprogram C, subprogram A is the calling program and C is the called program. Subprogram structures, how subprograms are connected together, and the design of individual subprograms are discussed in detail in Chap. 6.

Let us reconsider the payroll example in Sec. 1-2, but this time suppose that the problem is complicated by the following factors:

1. The deductions are not lumped together, but are separate and are itemized on a pay slip that is attached to the paycheck.
2. The income tax is not a straight percentage, but needs to be computed using a tax rate schedule.
3. The gross pay, itemized deductions, and net pay are output to a file on a mass storage device, a file that can later be used by an accounting program.

One approach to solving the program would be to treat the income tax as a deduction and have all the deductions computed by a subprogram. Because the tax computation is more complex, it may be desirable to calculate the tax using a subprogram to the deductions subprogram. Also, the printed output now needs more lines of print and may require greater formatting flexibility. Therefore, it may be better to perform this task through a subprogram. Finally, a subprogram could be used to output the pay and deductions data to the accounting program in a format that is compatible with an accounting program. The resulting structure is depicted in Fig. 1-14.

Even with the proposed extensions the payroll program is too simple to require more than one programmer to develop it. However, if each deduction requires a complex calculation and other features are needed, the program may justify an extensive planning and development stage that would require several people. If this were the case, breaking the program into tasks that could be individually discussed, developed, and documented would certainly be advantageous.

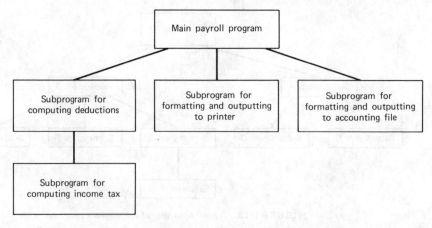

FIGURE 1-14 *Subprogram structure for the payroll example.*

EXERCISES

1. Outline the essential programming features discussed in this section.
2. What purposes do assignment statements serve?
3. What are the two main types of branch statements, and what purposes do they serve?
4. What is the relationship between conditional branches and logical expressions?
5. Why is it important to be able to subdivide a program?

2

BASIC FORTRAN

The purpose of this chapter is to introduce the elementary FORTRAN statements and show how simple FORTRAN programs are constructed. Although most of the principal concepts of programming are introduced, all the examples and exercises concern short programs that do not include subprograms. The programming problems will increase in complexity as the book progresses and as the reader becomes better equipped to master problems involving several tasks.

As noted previously, there are several versions of the FORTRAN language. Because FORTRAN was the first popular high-level language, the earlier versions were designed before programming was fully understood and complex supporting software was available. As a result, the first versions of FORTRAN were quite limited. As computers became more sophisticated, the pressure to develop more flexible high-level languages began to build. This caused new features to be added to FORTRAN and in 1966 the American National Standards Institute (ANSI) set forth a collection of standard rules for the FORTRAN language that included the more important features that were available at the time. The versions of FORTRAN based on this standard adopted the name FORTRAN IV. As one would expect, the development of FORTRAN continued and by 1977 ANSI announced a new standard called FORTRAN 77. Since 1977, FORTRAN has expanded even more and, most certainly, refinements will be made in the future.

This book is based on FORTRAN 77 and some of its recent extensions. The first section of this chapter describes the composition of a source module and the commands needed to create and execute it. The remaining sections, except for Sec. 2-5, which introduces flowcharts, discuss the FORTRAN implementation of the basic programming features considered in Sec. 1-9. They give the syntax and basic rules that govern the execution of the FORTRAN statements that perform computations, assignments, limited I-O, conditional and unconditional branching, and looping. Sections 2-10 and 2-11 introduce methods for working with related sets of data called arrays, and the final section provides a summary of the chapter.

2-1 CREATION AND EXECUTION OF A SOURCE MODULE

As explained in Secs. 1-7 and 1-8, the product of a programming effort is a source module. The source module is input to a translator which uses it to produce an object module. The object module is, in turn, input to a linker that appends to it any other object modules that are needed, and outputs a load module which may be loaded and executed. During this process, commands must be given to the resident monitor indicating the action to be taken next. These commands constitute a language of their own, which is often referred to as the *job control language (JCL)*. The *JCL is not a programming language*, but serves only to give commands to the operating system. The JCL may, however, be quite powerful and effective when used to perform certain system-related tasks.

2-1-1 Batch Processing

If a batch-processing system is being used and the source module is punched into cards, the commands are given to the resident monitor by including control cards in the deck of cards. These control cards are often referred to as *JCL cards*. The format of the control cards and the points at which they are inserted in a deck vary radically from one computer system to the next. For this reason a programmer must determine the JCL and deck structure required by the particular system being used.

A typical deck structure is shown in Fig. 2-1. In this example, the first card is called the accounting card; it identifies the user and gives the system the number of the account to which the work is to be charged. The second card indicates the actions to be taken. In this case, the FORTRAN translator is to be used to translate the source module that follows. The CLG suffix informs the system that the program is to be translated (or compiled), linked, and executed. The next section of the deck is the source module, which for this example is a FORTRAN program. If the program requires data that are to be input from cards, the source module is followed by a card that informs the system that the next group of cards contain data, and the data cards are placed immediately after this card. The last card indicates the end of the programming task.

The processing task determined by a deck beginning with an accounting card and ending with a termination card, which for this example is the "//" card, is called a *job* and the termination card is called an *end-of-job card*. Normally, jobs are submitted to a computer system by stacking them one after the other on a card reader. The jobs are then processed in turn, or perhaps according to some predetermined priority.

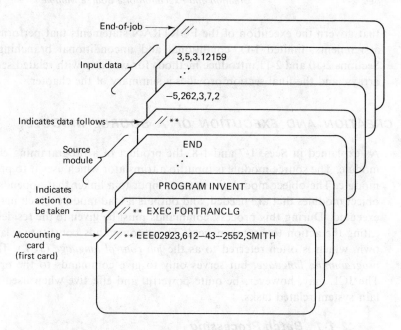

```
                                    ╱╱
End-of-job ─────────────────────╱╱
                              ╱╱
                  ╱╱      3,5,3.12159
Input data ─────╱╱          ⋮
               ╱          ⋮
              ╱       −5,262,3,7,2
Indicates data follows ────────►  ╱╱ **
                              ╱╱
            Source          ╱╱      END
            module ────────╱╱        ⋮
                          ╱        ⋮
                         ╱     PROGRAM INVENT
Indicates
action to
be taken ──────────────►  ╱╱ ** EXEC FORTRANCLG
Accounting ──────────►  ╱╱ ** EEE02923,612−43−2552,SMITH
card
(first card)
```

FIGURE 2-1 *Representative deck structure for a FORTRAN program.*

JCL commands, program statements, and input data are recorded on the cards by punching holes in the cards using a keypunch machine such as the one shown in Fig. 2-2. The description of the operation of keypunch machines is not considered here, but is left to the appropriate manuals.

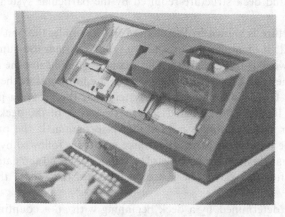

FIGURE 2-2 *Keypunch machine.*

2-1-2 *Interactive Processing*

If an interactive system is being used, the procedure is first to create the source module using a text editor and then to store it as a file on a mass storage device. The necessary commands and the FORTRAN statements of the source module are com-

FIGURE 2-3 *DEC LA-34, LA-38, and LA-120 printing terminals*
(Courtesy, *Digital Equipment Corporation*).

municated to the system through either a CRT terminal, such as the one shown in Fig. 1-5(b), or a printing terminal, such as those shown in Fig. 2-3. Just as the control card commands vary from system to system, so do the interactive commands needed to create and execute an interactive program. When generating and running a program on an interactive system, not only must one know the commands to be given to the resident monitor, but one must also know the commands to be given to the text editor while a program is being created. Although it would be wasteful to present a detailed example assuming a specific system, it is worthwhile to briefly outline the procedure assuming a somewhat limited fictitious system.

Figure 2-4 shows a typical dialogue that might occur between a system and a user while a program is being created and run. The computer responses are underlined and the user commands are not underlined. It is assumed that when the user approaches the terminal it has "Login:" written on it. This is the usual prompting message that invites the user to identify himself or herself. The user types his or her identification and the system returns a prompting character, the "%," indicating that it is ready to accept a command. Because the text of a source module is to be created, the user types "Run EDIT," which initiates the execution of the text editor. The text editor (i.e., the program named EDIT) is now running and returns its prompting character, the "∗," indicating that it is ready to accept a command. At this point, the user gives a variety of commands interspersed with the text of the FORTRAN program until the source module is created. Then the program EDIT is given the write command which consists of "w" followed by the filename (for this example the

```
Login : GIB425
% Run EDIT
*            .
             .
             .
    Commands and FORTRAN text
             .
             .
             .
* w INVENT. SRC
* exit
% Run FORTRAN      INVENT.SRC INVENT.OBJ
             .
             .
             .
    Source module listing
             .
             .
             .
% Run LINK    INVENT.OBJ INVENT. LDM
% Run INVENT
? -5.262, 3, 7.2
             .
             .
             .
    The distance is:  -3.659
             .
             .
             .
    Other work
             .
             .
             .
% Bye
Login:
```

FIGURE 2-4 *Representative dialogue on an interactive system.*

filename is INVENT.SRC). This causes the source module to be stored on a mass storage device under the name INVENT.SRC. The last command directed to the text editor is the exit command, which causes the program EDIT to terminate and control to be returned to the system's resident monitor. The resident monitor then prints "%," indicating that it is ready to accept another system command.

With the source module in the file INVENT.SRC, the user is ready to translate, link, and execute a program. First, the FORTRAN translator is run to produce, from the source module INVENT.SRC, the object module INVENT.OBJ. Next, the linker is executed to produce the load module INVENT.LDM from the object module INVENT.OBJ. Finally, the resident monitor is given the command to execute the user's program. If while the user's program is executing, it requires data to be input from the user's terminal, it prints a prompting character, the "?," on the terminal. Whenever a "?" appears, the user must respond by typing the proper input data. Output is provided according to the print statements in the program. When the program is through, control is returned to the resident monitor and a "%" is printed.

The user may then create and/or run other programs, or may terminate a programming session by logging off the system. In the present example, this is done by typing "Bye," to which the system responds "Login:", and the cycle is complete.

2-1-3 Structure of a FORTRAN Statement

The source module is the composite of the FORTRAN statements that make up the program. After inputting a source module, either from cards or a file, the user will frequently want the statements in the source module to be printed. Such a printout is called a *listing*. Program listings are important during the creation and correction stages of a program because they provide the programmer with an uncluttered printing of the program exactly as the translator sees it. Whether or not a listing is produced is determined by the JCL, but they are normally output each time a program is translated.

A single FORTRAN statement may consist of several lines. (If cards are being used, a line is the information on a card.) A line of FORTRAN code is broken down into the four fields indicated below. For standard 80-column cards, these fields are assigned to columns as shown in Fig. 2-5.

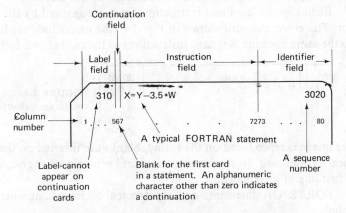

FIGURE 2-5 *Format of a FORTRAN statement card.*

Label Field (Columns 1–5)—This field is either blank or contains a statement label. A label is a number consisting of up to five digits and may appear anywhere in the first five columns. Except for only two types of statements (the END statement that cannot have a label and the FORMAT statement that must have one), labels are optional and are normally used only when the statement is referred by other statements in the program. Only the first line of a statement may have a label.

Continuation Field (Column 6)—When there is not enough space on one line and a statement must be continued on succeeding lines, a character is placed in the continuation fields of all but the first line. This indicates that the latter lines are continuations of the first line and together the lines form a single statement. (Most translators permit up to 20 lines—19 continuations—per statement.) Although any alphanumeric character other than a zero or blank can be used to indicate a continuation, usually colons, plus signs, or numbers in sequence are placed in column 6.

Instruction Field (Columns 7–72)—This field contains the FORTRAN instruction.

Identifier (or **Comments**) **Field** (Columns 73–80)—This field is not examined by the translator, but is printed on the listing. If cards are being used, this field normally contains card or program identification information (e.g., the cards could be numbered in sequence so that if they were dropped they could easily be put back in their proper order). This field could be used for comments which describe the program, but comments are more frequently inserted using the comment cards described in Chap. 4.

Although the column assignments for cards are standardized, for interactive systems the column assignments for these fields may vary and the user must check the appropriate manuals. Because the card column assignments also apply to most interactive systems, they are assumed throughout this book.

Blanks in the label and instruction fields are ignored by the FORTRAN translator. Therefore, the card shown in Fig. 2-6 (the carets indicate blanks) is translated into the same machine language instructions as the card shown in Fig. 2-5. Because an

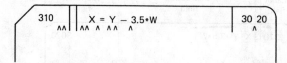

FIGURE 2-6 *Card with inserted blanks that is equivalent to the card shown in Fig. 2-5.*

exact image is reproduced on the listing, blanks are inserted on the listing just as they appear on the card. In the continuation field a blank, of course, indicates the line is the first line of a statement.

FORTRAN statements are constructed of letters, numbers, and the special symbols

$$= + - * / ( ) , . \ ' \ \$ \ :$$

using the syntax of the FORTRAN language. (Other symbols may appear, but may occur only in situations in which they are not reflected in the machine instructions determined by the statement; therefore, they are not viewed as FORTRAN symbols.)

2-1-4 Structure of a Source Module

Normally, the first statement in a program is a PROGRAM statement which has the form

PROGRAM Name

where *Name* consists of from one to six alphanumeric (i.e., alphabetic or numeric) characters, the first of which must be alphabetic. The PROGRAM statement serves only to give the program a name. The statement

PROGRAM FIT3

gives the program that follows the name FIT3. A PROGRAM statement is optional and if one is not present, most translators give the program the name MAIN by default. If a PROGRAM statement is present, it must be the first statement in the program.

The last statement in a program must be a statement of the form

END

The END statement serves two purposes: (1) at translation time it indicates the end of the source module, and (2) at execution time it causes the program to terminate and a return to be made to the resident monitor. The END statement may *not* have a label.

A third important statement that serves no computational function is the one that causes a program to cease its execution at intermediate points within the program. It has the form

STOP

and is translated into a machine instruction that directs the computer to branch to the resident monitor. There may be several STOP statements in a program. Because there are branch statements, programs are not always executed in sequence; therefore, it is possible that more than one point in a program may be a program termination point. The structure of a source module with two intermediate termination points is shown in Fig. 2-7.

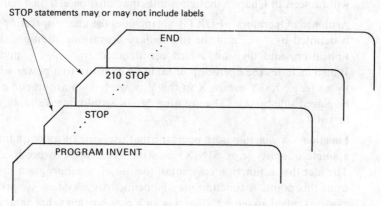

FIGURE 2-7 *Source module with two intermediate termination points.*

EXERCISES

1. Describe the structure of a batch job.
2. Describe the dialogue that is necessary to create and execute a program on an interactive system.

3. Give the purpose of:
   (a) The label field
   (b) The continuation field
   (c) The instruction field
   (d) The identifier field

4. Discuss the difference between the STOP and END statements.

2-2 ASSIGNMENT STATEMENTS

We are now prepared to introduce the FORTRAN statements that cause computational, decision-making, I–O, and other actions. Because all but the simplest FORTRAN programs include some computations, the assignment statement will be studied first. The purpose of an assignment statement is to use the rules of algebra to produce a single quantity from several quantities and then store the result in a specified location. The principal parts of an assignment statement are:

Variable—A *variable* is a symbol (or name) for a memory location whose value may change as the program progresses. A variable consists of one to six alphanumeric characters, the first of which must be alphabetic.

Constant—A *constant* is a quantity whose value remains unchanged throughout the execution of a program. They normally appear as numbers; however, it will be seen in Chap. 5 that constants may also be assigned names.

Arithmetic Operators—FORTRAN includes the unary operation negation, which is denoted by "$-$," and the four binary operations addition, subtraction, multiplication, and division, which are denoted by $+$, $-$, $*$, and $/$, respectively. It also includes the operation of taking a quantity to a power which is indicated by $**$ (e. g., X$**$Y means X to the Y power). Two arithmetic operators cannot be placed side by side. The notation $2*-K$ would be invalid, but $2*(-K)$ would be valid.

Function—A *function* is an operator that uses one or more quantities to produce a single quantity [e.g., SIN(X) uses the value of X to produce the sine of X]. The fact that a function may entail the use of a subprogram need not concern us at this point. A function may be defined by a system subprogram, in which case it is called an *intrinsic function*, or a user-written subprogram. Prior to Chap. 6 we will be concerned only with intrinsic functions; Chap. 6 will describe how user functions are written.

Grouping Symbols—*Grouping symbols* are used as they are in ordinary algebra, to indicate the order in which quantities are to be evaluated. The only grouping symbols recognized by FORTRAN are parentheses. For example,

$$A*(B+C)$$

means that B and C are to be added and the sum is to be multiplied by A.

Expression—An *expression* is a concatenation of variables, constants, arithmetic operators, functions, and grouping symbols according to the rules of algebra. For example, several FORTRAN expressions and their algebraic equivalents are:

FORTRAN	Algebraic
`A*X**2+B*X+C`	$AX^2 + BX + C$
`A+B*C**2/4.1`	$A + \dfrac{BC^2}{4.1}$
`X+Y*(2.5+SIN(X-0.5))**2`	$X + Y(2.5 + \sin(X - 0.5))^2$
`(X/Y)**2+A*EXP(2.0*X)`	$\left(\dfrac{X}{Y}\right)^2 + Ae^{2.0X}$

Assignment Operator—The *assignment operator* is used to assign to a variable the quantity obtained by evaluating an expression. In FORTRAN the assignment operator is "=."

The form of an assignment statement is

Variable = Expression

The assignment statement causes the expression to be evaluated and the result to be put in the location associated with the variable, and *the old contents of this location are lost*. The statement

`X = 2.0*Y+3.5*SIN(W+1.0)`

causes the sum of 2.0 times Y and 3.5 times the sine of the expression W + 1.0 to replace the current contents of X.

An example of a complete but simple program is

```
PROGRAM SUM
X = 5.0
Y = -7.21
W = X+5.0*(Y+3.2)
END
```

Although this program is useless because it gives no output, it does provide our first example of a program. I-O is introduced in Sec. 2-3 and more practical examples are provided there.

2-2-1 Variable and Constant Data Types

The *type* of a variable or constant determines how its value is stored in memory. Variables and constants may be of several types, but the only types considered in this chapter are the integer and real types. Other types are discussed in Chap. 5.

A variable name that begins with an I, J, K, L, M, or N is of the integer type (i.e., its value will be stored in its memory location in the integer format), and one that begins with any other letter is of the real type (i.e., its value will be stored in the real format). Assigning variable types according to this rule is called *implicit typing*.

Variables may be typed explicitly by using special statements, thus providing a means of getting around this rule. These special statements will be considered in Chap. 5. A few valid and invalid variable names are given in Fig. 2-8.

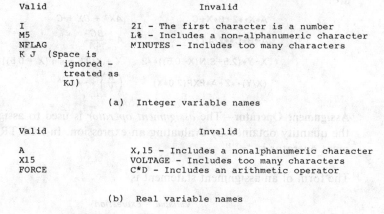

```
Valid                                Invalid

I                          2I - The first character is a number
M5                         L% - Includes a non-alphanumeric character
NFLAG                      MINUTES - Includes too many characters
K J (Space is
     ignored -
     treated as
     KJ)

              (a)  Integer variable names

Valid                                Invalid

A                          X,15 - Includes a nonalphanumeric character
X15                        VOLTAGE - Includes too many characters
FORCE                      C*D - Includes an arithmetic operator

              (b)  Real variable names
```

FIGURE 2-8 *Examples of valid and invalid variable names.*

The type of a constant is determined by whether or not the number includes a decimal point. If a decimal point does not appear, the constant is stored using the integer format; if one does appear, the constant is stored in the real format. Examples of integer constants are

$$-1 \qquad 5 \qquad 0 \qquad 512 \qquad 10126$$

and examples of real constants are

$$7.2 \qquad 2. \qquad -2.516 \qquad 1025.22$$

There are two ways to write a real constant. One is to simply write the number using a decimal point, as shown in the preceding examples. The second is to write the constant using scientific notation. Because FORTRAN statements cannot handle superscripts, a number usually written in the form

$$Number \times 10^{Exponent}$$

is written

$$Number \ \text{E} \ Exponent$$

Such a format is called an *E-format*. For example, the number 32.51×10^{-1} may be written in an E-format as 32.51E-1. Clearly,

$$32.51\text{E}-1 = 3.251\text{E}0 = 0.3251\text{E}1 = 3.251$$

2-2-2 Mixed Mode

If a binary operator is applied to two quantities of the same type, the result is of the same type as the operands. In the case of integer division the remainder is ignored and the result is the quotient (7/2 produces 3 and $-5/4$ produces -1).

A fundamental question that may have already occurred to the reader is:

Is it possible for integer constants or variables to appear in the same assignment statement with real constants or variables, even though they are stored using very different formats?

The answer is yes. To examine the question further, note that an assignment statement causes two distinct actions:

1. Evaluation of the expression on the right
2. Assignment of the result to the variable on the left

An expression that contains both types of constants or variables is called a *mixed-mode expression*. An assignment statement that assigns an integer or real result to a variable of opposite type is called a *mixed-mode assignment*.

The result of a mixed-mode expression is dependent upon what happens when an arithmetic operation operates on quantities of different types. The FORTRAN rule is that the contents of the integer location are converted to the real format and then combined with the contents of the real location to produce a real result. The expression

$$I+SUM$$

causes the contents of I to be changed to the real format and then added to SUM, thus producing a real result. It should be noted that the original contents of the memory locations I and SUM are left unchanged; if I and SUM were originally −2 and 5.6, respectively, they would remain −2 and 5.6. The converted contents of I, −2.0, and the sum 3.6 would be stored in temporary locations that the FORTRAN programmer need not worry about.

With regard to a mixed-mode assignment, if the expression on the right results in an integer quantity and the variable on the left is real, the integer quantity is converted to the real format and then assigned to the variable (e.g., X = 3 causes 3.0 to be put into X). If the expression results in a real quantity and an integer variable is being assigned the quantity, the fractional part of the quantity is dropped and the whole part is put into the integer format before it is assigned to the variable (e. g., I = 5.2 stores 5 in I and J = −0.52 stores 0 in J).

The statement

$$ICODE = X+(7/3)$$

first performs the integer division 7/3, producing the integer quotient 2, which is then converted to 2.0 and added to the real quantity X. If X contains 1.6, the result is 3.6. The 3.6 is truncated and the integer 3 is put in ICODE.

Although it is acceptable to use mixed-mode statements, they should be avoided. Because the integer and real formats are somewhat different, it may take the computer a significant amount of time to perform the conversions between these formats. A single conversion takes very little time, but in complex programs the total conversion time may be appreciable. Also, it is less confusing if all the operands in an expression are of the same type, because the programmer does not need to be concerned with the mixed-mode rules.

2-2-3   Taking a Power

The actions performed when raising a quantity, called the *base*, to a power differ depending on the type of the exponent. If the power is an integer, the operation can be carried out using successive multiplications and, in the case of a negative integer, a division. The expression

$$X**(-2)$$

is the same as 1.0/(X*X). This is true regardless of the type of the base and the result will always have the same type as the base. Note that, because of the truncation involved in the division, 2**(−3), which is equal to 1/8, produces a 0.

If the exponent is real, a system subprogram is used to compute the result, which is always real. The value of X**2 is computed by taking the product X*X, and the value of X**2.0 is computed using a system subprogram. Although the use of the system subprogram is not necessarily apparent to the FORTRAN programmer, the programmer should be aware of the subprogram's existence. Because fractional powers of negative numbers are not always defined, the base must be nonnegative. The evaluation of Y**X will cause an error if Y is negative; this is true even if X is a whole number such as 2.0. On the other hand, Y**I can be computed for any nonzero value of Y even if I is negative. Because the subprogram procedure is more complicated, more time is required to raise a number to a real power than to an integer power.

2-2-4   Intrinsic Functions

The format of a function is

Function Name (Expression, . . . , Expression)

where the *Function Name* consists of up to six alphanumeric characters, the first of which must be alphabetic. The *Expressions* are called *arguments* and a function may have one argument or several arguments.

Some of the intrinsic functions that are available under FORTRAN 77 are given in Fig. 2-9. (The reader should refer to the appropriate manual to determine the exact functions included in the version of FORTRAN being used.) Functions may be categorized according to function type and argument type. A function that produces a real result is called a *real function* and one that produces an integer result is called an *integer function*. A real function may require either real or integer arguments and, similarly, an integer function may require either real or integer arguments. The function type and the types of its arguments must be known before a function can be used. If the note "Same as argument" appears in the "Function Type" column of Fig. 2-9, then the result is real if the argument is real and is integer if the argument is integer.

Funct. Name	Funct. Type	Argument Type	No. of Arguments	Results
ABS	Same as argument	Real or Integer	1	Absolute value of the argument
SQRT	Real	Real	1	Square root of the argument
EXP	Real	Real	1	Value of e^x, where x is the argument
LOG	Real	Real	1	Natural logarithm of the argument
LOG10	Real	Real	1	Common logarithm of the argument
SIN	Real	Real	1	Sine of the argument in radians
COS	Real	Real	1	Cosine of the argument in radians
TAN	Real	Real	1	Tangent of the argument in radians
ASIN	Real	Real	1[1]	Arcsin in radians between $-\frac{\pi}{2}$ and $\frac{\pi}{2}$
ACOS	Real	Real	1[1]	Arccos in radians between 0 and π
ATAN	Real	Real	1[1]	Arctan in radians between $-\frac{\pi}{2}$ and $\frac{\pi}{2}$
SINH	Real	Real	1	Hyperbolic sine of the argument
COSH	Real	Real	1	Hyperbolic cosine of the argument
TANH	Real	Real	1	Hyperbolic tangent of the argument
INT	Integer	Real or Integer	1	Obtained by truncating the argument [e.g. ,INT (−2.7) results in −2]
AINT	Real	Real		
NINT	Integer	Real	1	Obtained by rounding to the nearest whole number [e.g. , NINT (−2.7) results in −3]
ANINT	Real	Real		
FLOAT	Real	Integer	1	Real equivalent of argument
REAL	Real	Real or Integer	1	Real equivalent of argument
SIGN	Same as arguments	Real or Integer[2]	2	Sign of second argument and magnitude of first argument
DIM	Same as arguments	Real or Integer[2]	2	First argument minus the second argument if first argument is greater than second argument; otherwise, zero
MAX	Same as arguments	Real or Integer[2]	>1	Largest of the arguments
MIN	Same as arguments	Real or Integer[2]	>1	Least of the arguments
MOD	Same as arguments	Real or Integer[2]	2	Remainder obtained by dividing the whole part of the first argument by the whole part of the second argument. Second argument cannot be 0

[1] Some FORTRAN translators permit these functions to also have two arguments, in which case the first argument is divided by the second argument and the result of the function is assigned an angle between $-\pi$ and $+\pi$, depending on the signs of the two arguments.

[2] All arguments must be of the same type.

FIGURE 2-9 *Summary of the commonly available intrinsic functions.*

In the statement

$$\text{LARGE} = \text{MAX(X,Y+1.0,−2.1)}$$

the function MAX would return the real number that is the largest of the three quantities X, Y + 1.0, and −2.1. This real number would then be truncated and put into the integer location LARGE. If X and Y contain 3.1 and −0.5, respectively, the integer put into LARGE would be 3.

Because an argument may be any valid expression it is possible for a function to appear in an argument expression. The statement

$$\text{DISP} = \text{SIN(ABS(X−Y))}$$

would cause the sine of the absolute value of X−Y to be put into DISP.

2-2-5 *Precedence*

If one were to write

$$\frac{9.0}{2.0 \times 3.0}$$

it would be clear that the intended result is 1.5. However, if one were to write 9.0/2.0∗3.0, the intended result would not be obvious. Would it be

$$(9.0/2.0)*3.0 = 13.5 \quad \text{or} \quad 9.0/(2.0*3.0) = 1.5?$$

The *rules of precedence* determine the exact order in which operations are to be carried out. Although these rules for FORTRAN are essentially the same as for algebra, there are added details that are important when using a computer. The associative law of algebra states that

$$(X + Y) + Z = X + (Y + Z)$$

for all values of *X*, *Y*, and *Z*, thus permitting one to simply write $X + Y + Z$. Because the memory locations and internal registers of a computer are finite and cannot store numbers precisely, a computer may give slightly different answers depending on the order in which the additions are done. If a computer's internal registers can hold only six significant figures and X = 5, Y = 5, and Z = 1000000, then (X + Y) + Z would yield 1000010, which is correct, but X + (Y + Z) would produce 1000000 because only the six most significant figures of the sum Y + Z could be retained. For these and other subtle reasons it is important that high-level language programmers know the exact rules of precedence of the translators they are using.

The rules of precedence for FORTRAN are summarized in Fig. 2-10. The topmost operation in the figure has the highest precedence and bottommost operation has the lowest precedence. Function evaluations are performed before taking a power, taking a power is performed before multiplication and division, and multiplication and division are performed before addition and subtraction. Within a given level of precedence the operations are executed from left to right, except for successive ∗∗ operators, which are executed from right to left (e.g., 2∗∗3∗∗2 = 512, not 64). These

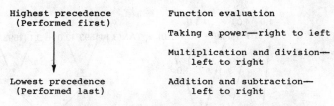

Highest precedence (Performed first)	Function evaluation
	Taking a power—right to left
	Multiplication and division— left to right
Lowest precedence (Performed last)	Addition and subtraction— left to right

Parentheses overrule the order of precedence. An expression inside a pair of parentheses must be evaluated before it can be operated on by an operator outside the parentheses.

FIGURE 2-10 *FORTRAN rules of precedence for algebraic expressions.*

rules may, of course, be overridden by parentheses. An expression inside a set of parentheses must be evaluated before it is operated on by an operator outside the parentheses. If pairs of parentheses are nested, the expression in the innermost pair must be evaluated first, and so on.

From these rules it is seen that for the example given at the beginning of this section, the result would be

$$9.0/2.0*3.0 = 13.5$$

because the division is to the left of the multiplication and is therefore done first. If the multiplication were to be performed first, the expression would need to be written

$$9.0/(3.0*2.0)$$

in which case the parentheses would force the expression 3.0*2.0 to be computed before the division takes place.

Figure 2-11 indicates the order in which the expression

$$X+Y*(3.0*(X+2.0)+TAN(3.141593/12.0+3.141593/6.0))$$

is evaluated. It is assumed that $X = -1.0$ and $Y = 4.0$. It is seen from the figure that the quantities 3.141593/12.0 and 3.141593/6.0 are computed before they are added, $X + 2.0$ is determined before it is multiplied by 3.0, the product 3.0*(X + 2.0) and the tangent are evaluated before they are added, and the entire expression in the outer parentheses is multiplied by Y before it is added to X.

Figure 2-12 shows the order in which the expression

$$I+4*J/2+3*(4/(I+K))$$

is computed. It is assumed that $I = 1$, $J = -2$, and $K = 4$. Note the truncation that results from the division $4/(I + K)$.

As a final example consider the mixed-mode assignment statement

$$NIT = 5.0*X+2*Y**2-2.0*MAX(5,I+1)$$

Figure 2-13 assumes that $X = 2.0$, $Y = -3.0$, and $I = 3$ and indicates the order of evaluation.

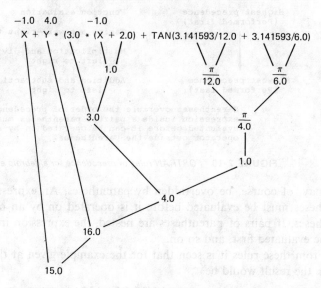

$$
\begin{array}{ccc}
-1.0 & 4.0 & -1.0 \\
\end{array}
$$

X + Y * (3.0 * (X + 2.0) + TAN(3.141593/12.0 + 3.141593/6.0)

$\frac{\pi}{12.0}$ $\frac{\pi}{6.0}$

1.0

$\frac{\pi}{4.0}$

3.0

1.0

4.0

16.0

15.0

FIGURE 2-11 *Example demonstrating the rules of precedence for a real expression.*

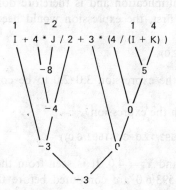

$$
\begin{array}{cccc}
1 & -2 & 1 & 4 \\
\end{array}
$$

I + 4 * J / 2 + 3 * (4 / (I + K))

−8   5

−4   0

−3   0

−3

FIGURE 2-12 *Example demonstrating the rules of precedence for an integer expression.*

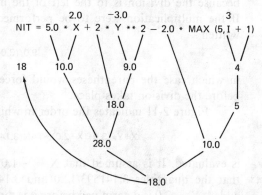

$$
\begin{array}{ccc}
2.0 & -3.0 & 3 \\
\end{array}
$$

NIT = 5.0 * X + 2 * Y ** 2 − 2.0 * MAX (5, I + 1)

18   10.0   9.0   4

18.0   5

28.0   10.0

18.0

FIGURE 2-13 *Example demonstrating the rules of precedence for a mixed mode expression and an assignment.*

EXERCISES

1. Give the algebraic expressions that are equivalent to each of the following FORTRAN expressions.
(a) A**2+B**2+C**2
(b) SQRT(X**2+25.0)
(c) (A+B*X − C*X**2)/(D+E*X)
(d) 2.0*X+SIN(X−2.5)**(−1)−2.6/Y

2. Determine which of the following variable names are invalid and give the reason why they are invalid.

AN 5	DISTANCE	X592	5×2
WI	IW	INK12	J:25
J%	ITEMNOS		

3. Give the types of the following constants.

$$2 \quad 52.691 \quad 5291 \quad 6.611E-3 \quad 723.$$

4. Describe, in detail, the actions that take place when each of the following assignment statements is executed.
   (a) X=X+2.0∗Y
   (b) X=I+J/2
   (c) I=X+3∗J
   (d) Y=EXP(ABS(X−2.1))
   (e) I=2∗∗J
   (f) X=Y∗∗2.0
   (g) W=Y∗∗2

5. Assume that

$$A = 1.0, \quad B = 2.0, \quad C = -1.0, \quad E = e, \quad I = 1, \quad J = 2$$

and use a diagram similar to the one shown in Fig. 2-13 to indicate the order in which each of the following expressions and assignment statements are executed.
   (a) B∗∗2+A−C∗LOG(E)
   (b) I+J/3
   (c) I+J/3.0
   (d) A∗B/EXP(A+C)
   (e) (I+J)∗∗(3/2)
   (f) X=A∗COS(A−1)+3.0∗∗J
   (g) L=(A+1)∗C+J/2
   (h) A∗∗2∗∗J

2-3 LIST-DIRECTED INPUT–OUTPUT

At this point we are capable of programming a computer to do computational processing, but processing of what? The next logical step is to provide ourselves with instructions that will allow us to use the computer as an input–process–output machine. This section discusses a limited form of input–output (I–O) for which the format of the information being input or output is determined by the FORTRAN translator, not by the programmer. That is, the FORTRAN translator will use fixed patterns built into the translator and selected according to the types of variables involved in the I–O, and the programmer will have little control over the way the quantities being input or output appear. The sequence of quantities being input or output is called the *list*, and the I–O statements being considered here are called *list-directed I–O statements.* I–O statements that give the programmer formatting control are discussed in Chap. 7.

2-3-1 The PRINT * Statement

List-directed output is accomplished by using the PRINT * statement, whose form is

PRINT *, *Output List*

where the *Output List* is the list of items, separated by commas, whose values are to be output. List items may be expressions or string constants (string constants are defined below). The * indicates that the PRINT statement is list-directed. The list items are output in the order in which they appear, and the number of columns (i.e., horizontal spaces) allotted to each quantity resulting from an expression evaluation is determined by the type of the result. As mentioned above, these allotments depend on the translator being used. For the examples presented in this book, it is assumed that eight columns are allotted for integer quantities and 13 for real quantities. For reasons that are discussed in Chap. 7, an extra blank is printed at the beginning of each line. As an example, the statement

PRINT *, I,X+5.1,J8

would cause a blank to be printed in the first column, the value of I to be printed in the next eight columns, the value of X + 5.1 to be printed in the next 13 columns, and the value of J8 to be printed in the next eight columns.

The group of columns allotted to an item in the output list of a PRINT * statement is called a *field* and a line of print can be viewed as a collection of fields. The next question is: How is the value of an item printed within the item's field? Integer items are right-justified (i.e., they are printed in the rightmost columns in the field). Items of the real type are left-justified with a fixed number of leading blanks.

For real items there is also a question regarding how they are printed. Just as constants may be expressed using an E-format (e.g., 3.28E-19), real items may be output using an E-format. The exact format of the numbers printed, and when an E-format is used instead of the normal format, depend on the FORTRAN translator. The examples in this book will follow the rule:

All numbers are rounded to six significant figures. If the absolute value of the number being printed is greater than or equal to 1 but less than 10^6, it will be printed left-justified with a leading blank, a blank (for plus) or a minus sign, six digits and a properly placed decimal point, and four trailing blanks. Otherwise, the number will be printed with a leading blank followed by the format

SX.XXXXXE$\pm$XX

where S represents a blank (for plus) or a minus sign and X represents a digit. If the exponent is in the range −9 through 9, a zero will be printed for the first digit in the exponent.

Value of Variable	Format of Output Field
−2.156	∧−2.15600∧∧∧∧
15672.87	∧∧15672.9∧∧∧∧
725988.4	∧∧725988.∧∧∧∧
−760.0	∧−760.000∧∧∧∧
0.456	∧∧4.56000E−01
−2157695.2	∧−2.15770E+06
0.0052	∧∧5.20000E−03
756.2E+15	∧∧7.56200E+17
0.2159782E−10	∧∧2.15978E−11

FIGURE 2-14 *Examples of the format in which real variables are output.*

Several examples showing the value of an item, and how it is printed in its field, are given in Fig. 2-14.

As an example, suppose that $X = 2.1E6$, $Y = −0.0126$, $Z = 12.5$, and $J = 1252$ and

    PRINT *, X,Y,Z,J

is executed. The output would be as follows:

The reader should verify both the formats of the printed numbers and the placement of the numbers in their fields.

Although we now have a means of outputting numerical results, it would be difficult to read these results if the numbers were printed without headings or labels. It is possible for a list item to be a character string enclosed in single quotes. For example,

    PRINT *, 'PAY RATE'

will cause the line

to be printed. Single quotes used in this way are called *delimiters* and the character string is called a *string constant*. For a more complicated example, suppose that INUM = 41 and WGT = 10.95. The statement

    PRINT *, 'ITEM NO.',INUM,'   UNIT WEIGHT',WGT

would cause the following line to be printed:

> ITEM NO.   41   UNIT WEIGHT 10.9500

Finally, it is possible for a PRINT * statement not to have an output list. The statement

> PRINT *

will cause a blank line to be inserted in the output text.

To demonstrate the use of a PRINT * statement in a program, let us examine the program CIRCLE given in Fig. 2-15(a). This program computes the diameter

```
PROGRAM CIRCLE
PI = 3.14159
R = 10.0
DIAM = 2.0*R
CIRC = PI*DIAM
A = PI*R**2
PRINT *, 'RADIUS =',R,'DIAMETER =',DIAM
PRINT *
PRINT *, 'CIRCUMFERENCE =',CIRC,'AREA =',A
END
```

         (a) Program

```
RADIUS =  10.0000   DIAMETER =  20.0000

CIRCUMFERENCE =  62.8318   AREA =  314.159
```

         (b) The output

FIGURE 2-15 *Program that uses PRINT * statements.*

DIAM, circumference CIRC, and area A of the circle whose radius is R = 10.0, and prints the results as shown in Fig. 2-15(b).

The output due to a PRINT * statement is the same regardless of the output device, be it a line printer or, in the case of an interactive system, a terminal. The line lengths may be different, and the effect of line length is discussed in Sec. 2-3-3.

The overall output of a program is called a *report*. A program's report includes all titles, headings, data, and messages output by the program while it is executing.

2-3-2   The READ * Statement

The form of the list-directed input statement is

> READ *, *Input List*

where the *Input List* consists of the names of the variables being input, separated by commas. The READ * causes quantities to be read from an input device, with the first quantity being put in the memory location associated with the first variable in the input list, and so on. The input quantities must be separated by a blank or a comma and may be separated by several blanks or several blanks with an embedded comma.

The quantities being read *cannot* include embedded blanks. Integer quantities must consist of successive digits with no decimal point. If an input quantity contains a decimal point and the corresponding list variable is of integer type, an error will occur. Real quantities may be expressed in either the normal format or an E-format. If the normal format is used, a decimal point is not required, but if one is not present, it will, by default, be assumed to be to the right of all the digits in the quantity (e.g., 329 would be interpreted as 329.0).

It is possible to have two separators side by side. This occurs when two commas appear side by side or with only blanks between them. Two consecutive separators cause the next input variable in the list to be skipped. If the input for the statement

$$\text{READ} *, \text{I,J,X}$$

were

$$3,,-7.43E1$$

then 3 would be put into I, J would be left unchanged, and −74.3 would be put into X.

If a variable appears in the input list more than once, it will be read into more than once and the last value input to the variable will, of course, be the value of the variable. For example, if

$$\text{READ} *, \text{X,I,X,Y}$$

were used to read

$$-3.14, 5, 2.05, 0.01$$

then the value of X would be 2.05.

Consider the program CYLVOL given in Fig. 2-16(a) and the typical card input given in Fig. 2-16(b). The program inputs a radius to R and a height to H, computes the volume of a cylinder having these dimensions, and outputs the result. The output for the given input values is shown in Fig. 2-16(c). This program is a considerable improvement over the program CIRCLE given in Fig. 2-15, which would calculate only the diameter, circumference, and area of a particular circle, one of radius 10.0. This program can find the volume of any cylinder whose dimensions are input by the user.

The format of the input is the same whether the input device is a card reader or a terminal. However, if a batch system is being used, the necessary cards will be read automatically when a READ * statement is encountered, but with an interactive system the user must type the input into his or her terminal. For a batch system the user must put the cards in their proper order in the data section of the deck. For an

```
PROGRAM CYLVOL
READ *, R,H
V = 3.14159*H*R**2
PRINT *, 'THE VOLUME IS:', V
END
```

(a) Program

```
10.0  20.0
```

(b) Input

```
THE VOLUME IS:  6283.18
```

(c) Output

FIGURE 2-16 *Program that demonstrates the READ * statement.*

interactive system, the user must know both what is to be input next and when to
input it. Therefore, it is required that some type of prompt be written on the user's
terminal whenever an input is needed. Most interactive systems automatically print a
prompting character at the beginning of the input line and the programmer does not
need to be concerned with inserting a PRINT * for this purpose. For the examples
in this book it will be assumed the prompting character "?" is automatically printed
in the first column of the input line.

With an interactive system the programmer has the option of using a PRINT *
statement to print a prompting message just prior to an input request. This message
would be in addition to the prompting character and would not only enable the program to inform the user that input is needed, but would also indicate what input is
needed. This would release the user from the burdensome task of remembering the
order of the inputs. Figure 2-17(a) shows the program CYLVOL discussed above as it
might be modified for an interactive system. Figure 2-17(b) gives a typical dialogue
with this program. Note the absence of the extra blank at the beginning of the output

```
PROGRAM CYLVOL
PRINT *, 'INPUT RADIUS AND HEIGHT'
READ *, R,H
V = 3.14159*H*R**2
PRINT *
PRINT *, 'THE VOLUME IS:',V
END
```

(a) Program

```
INPUT RADIUS AND HEIGHT
?10.0,20.0

THE VOLUME IS:  6283.18
```

(b) Dialogue

FIGURE 2-17 *Program CYLVOL as
modified for an interactive system.*

62

lines. Most interactive systems suppress this blank when outputting to the user's terminal, even though they output it when communicating with a line printer.

2-3-3 Records

Until now the possibility of input or output requiring more than one line has not been discussed. Before examining this possibility, let us consider how I–O is handled in general. I–O is done by sets of information called *records*. For a line printer a record is one line of print, which usually consists of either 120 characters or 132 characters, depending on the printer. For a card reader a record is the information on one card and is the number of columns on the card. Card readers are almost always designed to accept the standard 80-column card. For terminals a record is the information on a line and is typically either 72 or 80 characters long. For the examples in this book, 132-column line printers, 80-column card readers, and 80-column terminals are assumed.

Every PRINT * statement will begin a new record even if the last record was not completely filled by a previous PRINT * statement. If the quantities being printed cannot be written on a single record, the output will be continued on one or more succeeding records. This is done in such a way that a number field is never divided in the middle. If $N1 = 10$, $N2 = 20, \ldots, N9 = 90$, the statement

```
PRINT *, 'PART NOS.',N1,N2,N3,N4,N5,N6,N7,N8,N9
```

will cause a terminal to print

```
PART NOS.   10   20   .      .      .   80
             90
```

Every READ * statement will read beginning with a new record. If a terminal is being used, the input to a record is terminated when the RETURN key is depressed. If the number of items in a record is less than the number of variables in the input list, the program will request (via the prompting character if the system is interactive) input from succeeding records. If more information is present in a record than is required by the input list, the extra quantities, which appear last, are ignored. If the cards

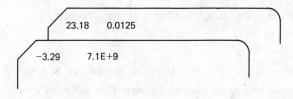

are read by the statement

```
READ *, W,X,Y,Z
```

then −3.29, 7.1E + 9, 23.18, and 0.0125 will be input to W, X, Y, and Z, respectively. If the card

5, 13, 4

is read by the statement

READ *, I,J

then 5 and 13 will be input to I and J, respectively, and the 4 will be ignored.

EXERCISES

1. Show how the following constants would be printed within their fields if they are output using PRINT * statements.

(a) 51   (b) 51.   (c) −0.7521
(d) −735   (e) 6.3E6   (f) 73.59687
(g) 0.05271   (h) 6.5928E−1   (i) 7.9875502E1

2. Given that
$$X = 5.251 \quad Y = 73.2E-1 \quad V = 0.01256782 \quad I = 95$$
determine the exact line printer output caused by each of the following statements.

(a) PRINT *, X,Y,I
(b) PRINT *, X,I,Y
(c) PRINT *
(d) PRINT *, 'VOLTAGE=', V, '   AT POINT', I
(e) PRINT *, I,I,I
(f) PRINT *, '   ', I,V, '   ', Y

3. Write a program that will compute the distance between the points whose Cartesian coordinates are (1, 2) and (5, −2) and then print out

DISTANCE=(*Value of distance*)

Also show exactly how the output would be printed.

4. Give a card that will, when input by the statement

READ *, X,I,W5

cause −5.21, −62, and 62.1E−6 to be read into X, I, and W5, respectively.

5. Write an interactive program segment that will print

INPUT THE TEMPERATURE AND PRESSURE

. and then input values into T and P from the user's terminal.

6. Write a program for a batch system that will read values into PAY and DEDUCT, compute PAYNET according to the formula

$$PAYNET = 0.8*PAY-DEDUCT$$

and print out

GROSS PAY = (*Value of PAY*)
LESS   (*Value of 0.2*PAY+DEDUCT*)
NET PAY   = (*Value of PAYNET*)

Modify the program so that it will execute on an interactive system by causing the prompting message

TYPE IN THE GROSS PAY AND DEDUCTIONS

to be printed just prior to the input.

7. Write a batch program that will input five integers, determine the largest and smallest of these integers, and print

THE MAXIMUM IS: (*Value of the largest integer*)
THE MINIMUM IS: (*Value of the smallest integer*)

8. If the statement

READ *, X,Y,Z

is used to input the cards

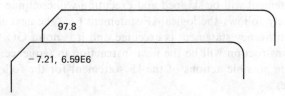

find the values put into X, Y, and Z.

9. If the statement

READ *, X,I,J,I

is used to input the card

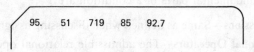

what values are put into X, I, and J, and what happens to the 92.7?

2-4 BRANCHING: GO TO AND IF STATEMENTS

As indicated in Chap. 1, branching capability adds considerably to the flexibility of the computer. The FORTRAN unconditional branch statement is of the form

GO TO *Label*

where *Label* is the label of the statement to which the branch is being made. The sequence

$$GO\ TO\ 50$$
.
.
.

$$50\quad X=Y+1.0$$
.
.
.

will cause the statement $X = Y + 1.0$ to be executed immediately after the GO TO 50 statement and the intervening statements will be skipped.

Conditional branch statements in FORTRAN have taken several different forms. The original basic form is the IF (or *logical* IF) statement and it is this statement that is discussed at this point. The extensions of the IF statement, the IF block statements, that are incorporated into FORTRAN 77 are introduced in Chap. 4.

The IF statement has the form

IF *(Condition)* Contingency Statement

where the *Condition* is a logical expression and the *Contingency Statement* can be an assignment, I–O, GO TO, or STOP statement. The logical IF statement will cause the contingency statement to be executed if the condition is true; otherwise, the contingency statement will be skipped and execution will continue with the instruction that immediately follows the logical IF statement (i.e., the next instruction in sequence). If the contingency statement is executed and it is not a GO TO or STOP statement, the next instruction will be the next instruction in sequence. Figure 2-18 graphically depicts the possible actions of the IF statement for the following contingency statement cases:

1. Neither a GO TO nor a STOP statement
2. A GO TO statement
3. A STOP statement

The fundamental parts of a condition are:

Expressions—Same as defined when discussing assignment statements.

Relational Operators—The admissible relational operators in FORTRAN are:

.EQ.	equal to	.NE.	not equal to
.GT.	greater than	.LE.	less than or equal to
.LT.	less than	.GE.	greater than or equal to

Note that each entry in the right column has the opposite truth value from the corresponding entry in the left column, when one is true the other is false, and vice versa.

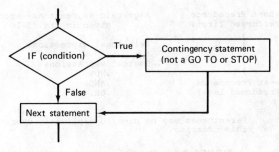

(a) Not a GO TO or STOP

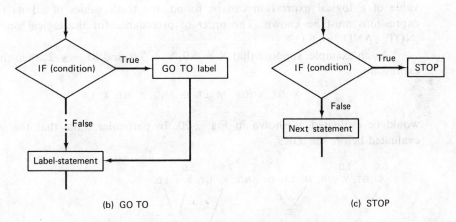

(b) GO TO   (c) STOP

FIGURE 2-18 *Possible paths taken by a logical IF statement.*

Relational Expression—An expression of the form

Expression   Relational Operator   Expression

Logical Operator—The admissible logical operators in FORTRAN 77 are:

.NOT.   logical negation
.AND.   logical AND
.OR.   logical OR

Logical Expression—A joining of relational expressions and logical operators. For example,

(X.EQ.(Y+1.0)).OR.(I.NE.0)

Just as with the algebraic expressions in assignment statements, in the absence of parentheses, rules of precedence must be used to evaluate the truth value of a logical expression. The rules of precedence for FORTRAN are summarized in Fig. 2-19. Clearly, before the truth value of a relational expression can be found, the algebraic expression it operates on must be evaluated. For algebraic expressions the rules of precedence given in Fig. 2-10 apply. It should be equally obvious that before the truth

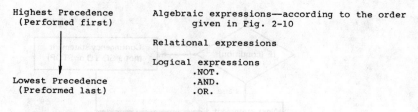

Highest Precedence   Algebraic expressions—according to the order
(Performed first)   given in Fig. 2-10

                          Relational expressions

                          Logical expressions
                              .NOT.
Lowest Precedence   .AND.
(Preformed last)   .OR.

        Parentheses may be used to explicitly overrule
        this ordering.

FIGURE 2-19 *Rules of precedence for logical expressions.*

value of a logical expression can be found, the truth values of all its relational expressions must be known. The order of precedence for the logical operators is .NOT., .AND., and .OR. .

As an example, suppose that X = 5.0, Y = 7.0, and M = −2; then the logical expression

$$X\ .GT.\ Y\ .OR.\ M\ .LT.\ 0\ .AND.\ Y\ .GT.\ X{+}1.0$$

would be evaluated as shown in Fig. 2-20. In particular, note that the .AND. is evaluated before the .OR. .

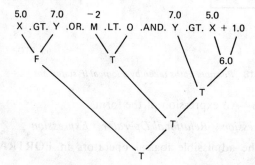

FIGURE 2-20 *Order of evaluation of a logical expression.*

Three examples that demonstrate the use of the logical IF statement are given below. In the first example the contingency statements are assignment statements, and in the second and third examples the contingency statements are GO TOs. The second example indicates how special processing that requires more than one statement can be handled using a logical IF, and the third example gives a procedure for performing exactly one of two distinct actions based on a single decision.

Example 1

Figure 2-21(a) shows a program ORDER that reads in a part number NP, computes the quantity NUM of that part number that needs to be ordered, and prints both the part number and the quantity to be ordered. If the part number is 2, the quantity to be ordered is 150; if it is 6, the quantity to be ordered is 175; and if it is any other number,

```
PROGRAM ORDER
READ *, NP
NUM=100
IF (NP .EQ. 2) NUM = 150
IF (NP .EQ. 6) NUM = 175
PRINT *, 'ORDER',NUM,'  OF PART NO.',NP
END
```

(a) Program

(b) Input

ORDER   150 OF PART NO.   2

(c) Output

FIGURE 2-21 *Program for the ordering example.*

100 parts are to be ordered. Figure 2-21(b) and (c) show representative card input and line printer output.

Example 2

Suppose that the total price of several items of a specified type is to be computed and that each type has an item number associated with it. All items are to cost $30 apiece. Because of a shortage the quantity for an order for item number 1 is automatically reduced by 10%. A program COST for solving this problem is given in Fig. 2-22. The program brings in an item number ITEM and a quantity IQUAN, computes the total cost and adjusted quantity, and prints the result. Because the special processing requires more than one statement, it cannot be done with a contingency statement. Therefore, the condition

ITEM .NE. 1

is used to branch around the special processing when the item number is other than 1.

Example 3

Assume that a space probe is approaching a planet and at 100 km from the center of the planet the thrusters are turned on to slow its descent. The total force on the probe is the gravitational force less the thruster force. A program for computing the force F on the probe as a function of its distance D from the center of the planet is given in Fig. 2-23(a). Typical interactive dialogue for the program is given in Fig. 2-23(b). It is assumed that the free flight force is 5000.0/D**2 and that the force of the thrusters, once they are turned on, is 8. The problem requires that two distinct actions be taken,

```
      PROGRAM COST
      READ *, ITEM,IQUAN
      IF(ITEM .NE. 1) GO TO 5
      IQUAN = IQUAN - INT(0.1*REAL(IQUAN))
      PRINT *, 'DUE TO SHORTAGE THE QUANTITY IS REDUCED'
    5 AMT = 30.0*REAL(IQUAN)
      PRINT *, 'ITEM NO.',ITEM,'    QUANTITY-',IQUAN
      PRINT *
      PRINT *, 'COST-',AMT
      END
```

(a) Program

1, 150

(b) Input

DUE TO SHORTAGE THE QUANTITY IS REDUCED

ITEM NO.   1   QUANTITY   135

COST- 4050.00

(c) Output

FIGURE 2-22 *Program for the cost-computation example.*

```
      PROGRAM FORCE
      PRINT *, 'INPUT DISTANCE TO PLANET'
      READ *, D
      IF (D .LE. 100.0) GO TO 10
      F = 5000.0/D**2
      PRINT *, 'FREE FLIGHT'
      GO TO 20
   10 F = 5000.0/D**2-8.0
      PRINT *, 'THRUSTERS ON'
   20 PRINT *, 'FORCE =',F
      END
```

(a) Program

```
      INPUT DISTANCE TO PLANET
      ?60.0
      THRUSTERS ON
      FORCE =   -6.61111
```

FIGURE 2-23 *Program for the space-probe example.*

(b) Dialogue

depending on the truth value of the condition

D .LE. 100.0

One of the actions immediately follows the logical IF and the contingency GO TO statement directs the program to the other action. At the end of the first action, an unconditional GO TO is used to branch around the second action. As will be seen later, this is a cumbersome procedure that is avoided in FORTRAN 77 by using IF blocks.

EXERCISES

1. Assume that

$$X = 3.0 \quad Y = -1.0 \quad Z = 2.0 \quad I = -2 \quad J = 0$$

and use a diagram similar to the one given in Fig. 2-20 to show the procedure for evaluating:

(a) X .EQ. Y+Z .OR. I+2 .EQ. J
(b) X .NE. Z .AND. J .LE. 0 .OR. X .LT. 0.0
(c) X .NE. Z .AND. (J .LE. 0 .OR. X .LT. 0.0)
(d) .NOT. X .GT. Z .OR. I+Z .EQ. 0

2. For

$$A = 3.0 \quad B = 6.0 \quad I = 2$$

describe the action taken by each of the following statements.
(a) IF(A .EQ. B+3) GO TO 10
(b) IF(A .LT. 0.0 .OR. A .GT. 5.5) PRINT *, A
(c) IF(I .GE. 2) STOP
Repeat for

$$A = -2.0 \quad B = -5.0 \quad I = 0$$

3. Write a program that will input two numbers into the variables A and B, use IF statements to put the smaller number in X and the larger number in Y, and print out

SMALLER NO. = *(Value of X)*
LARGER NO. = *(Value of Y)*

4. Write a program that will input a number into PAY, compute TAX using the following table:

Pay	Tax
≤$10,000	0
>$10,000 but ≤$20,000	20% of pay over $10,000
>$20,000 but ≤$30,000	Tax on $20,000 plus 30% of pay over $20,000
>$30,000	Tax on $30,000 plus 40% of pay over $30,000

and print

PAY = *(Value of PAY)*   TAX = *(Value of TAX)*

5. Write a program that will use determinants to solve the system of equations

$$AX + BY = E$$

$$CX + DY = F$$

The program is to first input A, B, C, and D and compute the determinant of coefficients.

If the determinant is 0, the program is to print

DETERMINANT IS ZERO

and STOP. Otherwise, it is to input E and F, find X and Y, and print

X = (Value of X)   Y = (Value of Y)

2-5 FLOWCHARTS

Until now, only very simple programs have been considered and simple explanations were adequate to describe their actions. As programs become more complex, verbal descriptions become insufficient and graphic means are needed to help design, discuss, and document a program. There are several graphic and other aids that are used to facilitate programming, and one of the most widely used and easily understood such aids is the *flowchart* (or *flow diagram*). A flowchart consists of blocks that contain descriptive notations and are connected by arrows. Each block represents an action, and the way in which the blocks are connected by the arrows indicates the order in which the actions are executed and the paths the program may take. The shape of a block as well as the notation contained in the block indicates the action being represented. The more important flowcharting symbols and their names are summarized in Fig. 2-24. Their meanings are:

Terminal Symbol—A *terminal symbol* represents the beginning or end of a program or subprogram. If it contains the word START or the name of the program, it indicates the beginning of the main program; if it contains the title of a subprogram, it indicates the beginning of that subprogram. A terminal symbol containing STOP is used to represent any point in the program (either the main program or a subprogram) at which execution of the entire program is to cease, Terminal symbols containing RETURN are used in subprograms to indicate returns to their calling programs.

Processing—A *processing symbol* represents any computational action. The notation within the symbol indicates the action to be taken. This symbol most often represents one or more assignment statements.

Decision—A *decision symbol* represents a conditional branch. Although only one path leads to a decision symbol, several paths may emanate from such a symbol. The notation inside the symbol is either a condition or a set of criteria. If it is a condition (as with an IF statement), two paths will leave the symbol; one path will be labeled "T" (for true) and the other "F" (for false). A set of criteria may result in more than two paths, and each path is accompanied by a symbol or notation indicating which possibilities would cause it to be taken.

Preparation—The standard use of this symbol is to indicate a step that is needed solely to set up a processing sequence. In this book, as in many others, the normal *processing block* is used for this purpose and this symbol is associated with the beginning of a DO loop (see Sec. 2-9).

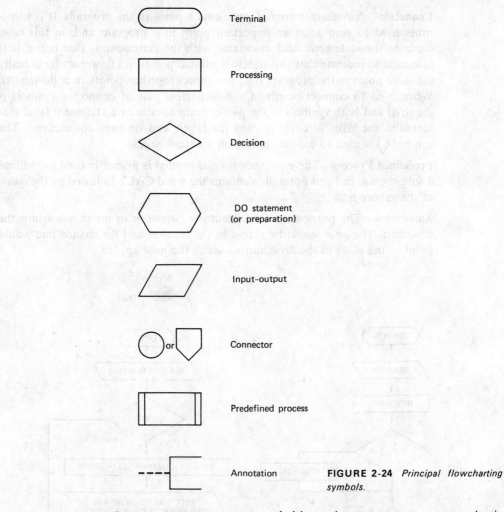

Terminal

Processing

Decision

DO statement
(or preparation)

Input-output

or Connector

Predefined process

- - - - Annotation

FIGURE 2-24 *Principal flowcharting symbols.*

Input–Output—An *input–output symbol* is used to represent a communication with the external world. The symbol shown in Fig. 2-24 is a general symbol; sometimes special symbols are used to indicate a particular type of I-O transfer. For example,

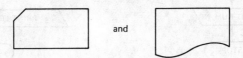

and

are often used to represent card reader input and printer output, respectively. Notations inside the I-O symbol are used to indicate the quantities to be input or output.

Connector—A *connector symbol* represents a point in the program. It is sometimes used to emphasize an important point in a program and, in this case, contains the statement label associated with the statement at that point. It is also used to indicate that two widely separated points in a flowchart are actually the same point in the program (i.e., to connect together points in a flowchart). When used to connect points in a flowchart, a pair of connector symbols is required and both symbols in the pair contain a letter or a statement label that identifies the pair. A circle is used for labels and on-page connections. The symbol ▽ is used to connect points on different pages.

Predefined Process—The *predefined process symbol* is primarily used to indicate a subprogram call and normally contains the word CALL followed by the name of the subprogram.

Annotation—The purpose of the *annotation symbol* is to insert notes into the flowchart. The note would be placed in the bracket and the dashed line would point to the place in the flowchart to which the note applies.

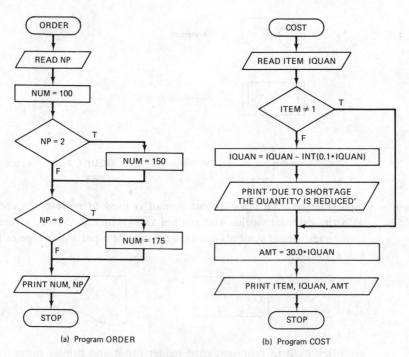

(a) Program ORDER   (b) Program COST

FIGURE 2-25 *Flowcharts of the programs given in Figs. 2-21, 2-22, and 2-23.*

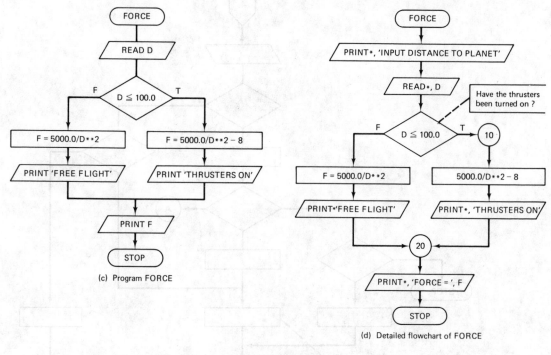

FIGURE 2-25 (*Cont.*)

(c) Program FORCE

(d) Detailed flowchart of FORCE

Flowcharts of the programs ORDER, COST, and FORCE which were discussed in the preceding section are given in Fig. 2-25(a) through (c). Just how much notation a programmer puts inside the flowchart symbols depends on how much emphasis is to be placed on the various aspects of the program. Figure 2-25(d) is a flowchart of the program FORCE in which the labels 10 and 20 and the identifying string constant 'FORCE=' have been assigned enough importance that they have been included. Also, the prompting message 'INPUT DISTANCE TO PLANET' is included and the asterisks show that list-directed I–O is being used. The annotation provides additional information about the decision DIST .LE. 100.0. The flowchart in Fig. 2-25(c) assumes these details to be incidental or to be explained adequately elsewhere.

Figure 2-26 is a flowchart that illustrates the use of connectors. The connector containing the 4 is an entry point from another page and is to be connected to the exit point 4 on the other page. Similarly, the connector containing the 5 is an exit point that is to be connected to the entry point 5 on another page. The connector symbols 4 and 5 could be page numbers. The connectors containing A are to be treated as if a flowline were drawn between them.

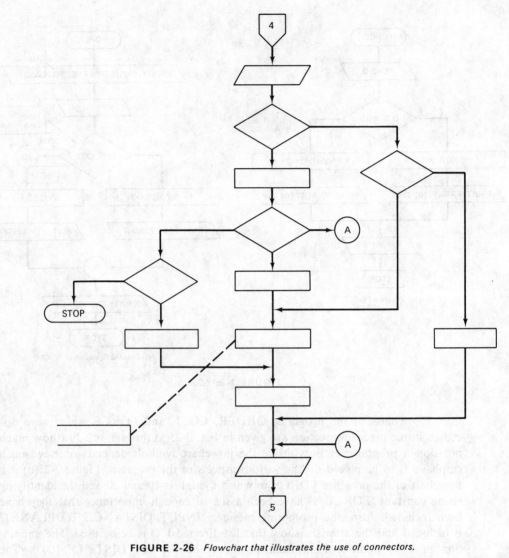

FIGURE 2-26 *Flowchart that illustrates the use of connectors.*

EXERCISES

1. Sketch a flowchart for the program requested in:
   (a) Exercise 3 at the end of Sec. 2-4.
   (b) Exercise 4 at the end of Sec. 2-4.
   (c) Exercise 5 at the end of Sec. 2-4.

2. Flowchart a program that will input any real number, find its cube root, and print

THE CUBE ROOT = (Value of cube root)

(Remember, you must first determine whether the number is positive or negative.) Use the flowchart to write the needed program.

2-6 LOOPING

The programs considered in the preceding sections are somewhat limited in that they only input data, process them, and then output the results. Although the computations made by such programs could be quite complex, they cannot, in a single run, repetitively perform the same computations on different sets of data. If the program ORDER in Fig. 2-21 were needed to process several orders, it would have to be run over and over. However, by structuring the program as shown in Fig. 2-27, this prob-

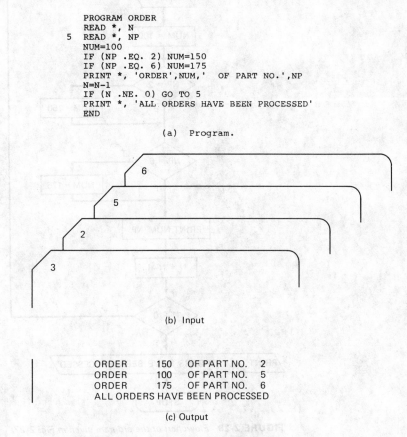

```
    PROGRAM ORDER
    READ *, N
5   READ *, NP
    NUM=100
    IF (NP .EQ. 2) NUM=150
    IF (NP .EQ. 6) NUM=175
    PRINT *, 'ORDER',NUM,'  OF PART NO.',NP
    N=N-1
    IF (N .NE. 0) GO TO 5
    PRINT *, 'ALL ORDERS HAVE BEEN PROCESSED'
    END
```

(a) Program.

(b) Input

```
ORDER      150    OF PART NO.   2
ORDER      100    OF PART NO.   5
ORDER      175    OF PART NO.   6
ALL ORDERS HAVE BEEN PROCESSED
```

(c) Output

FIGURE 2-27 Program that includes looping.

lem is overcome. The new program first reads the number of types of parts to be ordered into N. It then reads in the first part number, computes the quantity to be ordered, prints the result, reads in the second part number, computes the quantity, prints the result, and so on. Each time a part is processed, the variable N is decremented by 1 and an IF statement is used to compare N to zero. When N becomes 0 there are no more parts to be processed and the program stops. The message printed

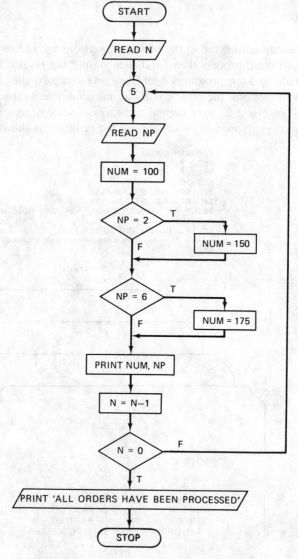

FIGURE 2-28 *Flowchart of the program given in Fig. 2-27.*

by the last print statement makes it clear to anyone reading the printout that the program has terminated properly. A flowchart of the program is given in Fig. 2-28.

A potential problem with the program in Fig. 2-27 is that it does not take into account the case when N is initially zero. The statements in the loop, called the *range of the loop*, must be executed at least once regardless of the initial value of N. Because it is presumed that the program would not be run if no orders were to be processed, this problem could be ignored for this program, but for other programs it may need to be considered.

There are basically two types of loops, post-testing loops and pretesting loops, and they are illustrated in Fig. 2-29. Both types include the steps initialization, pro-

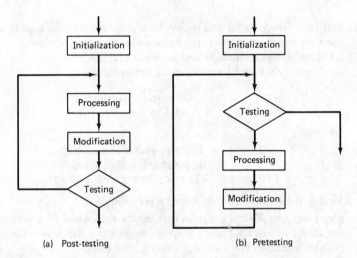

FIGURE 2-29 *Basic types of looping.*

cessing, modification, and testing. Initialization includes the actions that set up the loop (in Fig. 2-27 the first READ * statement is the initialization step); processing consists of the actions in the loop that do the desired work (the second READ * statement, the assignment statement, the first two IF statements, and the PRINT * statement); modification makes the changes that are necessary before the loop is reexecuted (the N = N − 1 statement); and testing determines whether or not the loop is to be reexecuted (the third IF statement). The difference in the two types is the order in which these steps are performed. The loop shown in Fig. 2-29(a) is called a *post-testing loop* and determines whether additional repetitions are to be made at the end of the loop. *Pretesting*, shown in Fig. 2-29(b), performs the testing at the beginning of the loop and, therefore, may cause the loop to be skipped altogether. The program ORDER as shown in Fig. 2-27 uses a post-testing loop. By reordering the steps as shown in Fig. 2-30 the program is made to use a pretesting loop.

```
      PROGRAM ORDER
      READ *, N
    9 IF (N .EQ. 0) GO TO 7
      READ *, NP
      NUM=100
      IF (NP .EQ. 2) NUM=150
      IF (NP .EQ. 6) NUM=175
      PRINT *, 'ORDER',NUM,'  OF PART NO.',NP
      N=N-1
      GO TO 9
    7 PRINT *, 'ALL ORDERS HAVE BEEN PROCESSED'
      END
```

FIGURE 2-30 *Program ORDER using pretesting.*

EXERCISES

1. Prepare a flowchart for and then write a program that will read in a number M and then use a post-testing loop to perform the following steps M times.
   (a) Read in a magnitude D and an angle THETA.
   (b) Compute forces F1 and F2 using the formulas

   $$F1 = (D+5.0)*COS(THETA)$$
   $$F2 = (D+5.0)*SIN(THETA)$$

   (c) Print

   READING (*Value of loop index*)
   HORIZONTAL FORCE (*Value of F1*)
   VERTICAL FORCE (*Value of F2*)

   Modify the solution so that it uses a pretesting loop.

2. Flowchart and write a program that inputs a principal P, a number of years N, and an annual interest rate R; uses a loop to compute the principal at the end of each of the first N years assuming annual compounding; and prints

   THE PRINCIPAL AT END OF YEAR (*No. of years*) IS (*Value of P*)

3. Write a program that uses a loop and the following tax table to calculate the taxes of N employees.

≤$10,000	No tax
>$10,000 but ≤$20,000	20% of pay over $10,000
>$20,000 but ≤$30,000	Tax on $20,000 plus 30% of pay over $20,000
>$30,000	Tax on $30,000 plus 40% of pay over $30,000

2-7 ACCUMULATION, COUNTING, AND FLAGS

There are three mechanisms that occur over and over in computer programming and deserve special attention at the outset of any study of programming. They are accumulation, counting, and flags, and are used for summing, flow control, limit control, and repetition control. The first two are demonstrated in the solution of the following grading problem:

> Read in an integer N and then read in N grades one at a time. Count the number of grades which are greater than or equal to 70 and put the result in ICOUNT. Compute the mean (i.e., average) grade and put the result in AVE. Finally, write out the values of ICOUNT and AVE.

A program for solving this problem and the corresponding flowchart are given in Figs. 2-31 and 2-32. First the number of grades is read into N and then the loop is

```
      PROGRAM GRADE
      READ *, N
      ICOUNT = 0
      SUM=0.0
      I = 1
   8  READ *, GRADE
      IF (GRADE .GE. 70.0) ICOUNT = ICOUNT+1
      SUM = SUM+GRADE
      I = I+1
      IF (I .LE. N) GO TO 8
      AVE = SUM/REAL(N)
      PRINT *, 'NO. OF PASSING GRADES:',ICOUNT
      PRINT *, 'AVERAGE GRADE:',AVE
      END
```

FIGURE 2-31 *Program that demonstrates counting and accumulation.*

executed N times. The loop is used to read in the grades, keep a running total of the grades, and count the grades that are greater than or equal to 70. After executing the loop the proper number of times, the mean is calculated and the required quantities are output.

To compute the mean, the grades must be totaled, and this is done with the variable SUM. A variable that is used to keep a running total is called an *accumulator*. As in the solution given here, the accumulator is normally set to 0 before entering the loop in which the accumulation is to take place. Then, each time the loop is traversed, a new number is added to the accumulator. In the problem at hand, SUM is initially set to 0 and inside the loop the grades are successively added to SUM.

The solution to the grading problem involves two counting processes. The variable ICOUNT is used to count the grades greater than or equal to 70 and the variable I is used to keep track of the number of times the loop has been executed. A variable used for counting is, reasonably enough, called a *counter*. Before entering the loop the counters ICOUNT and I are initialized to 0 and 1, respectively. Inside the loop, 1 is added to ICOUNT each time a grade of 70 or above is encountered, and 1 is added to I each time the loop is traversed. When I exceeds N the loop will have been executed N times and the number of grades greater than or equal to 70 will be in ICOUNT.

Sometimes variables are set or input to at one point in a program for the sole purpose of determining the path to be taken at another point in the program; such variables are called *flags* (or *switches*). If a flag is read in at execution time it is sometimes called a *code*. Codes give the user the opportunity to direct the program flow while a program is being run. For example, consider the flowchart given in Fig. 2-33.

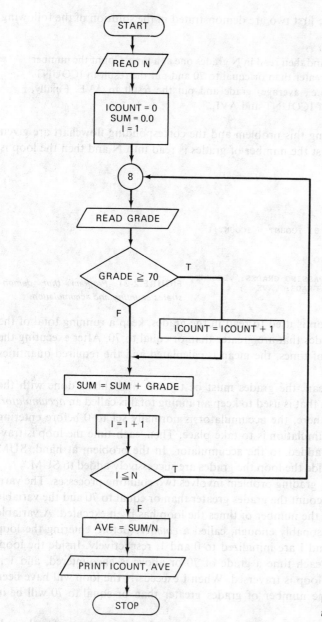

FIGURE 2-32 *Flowchart of a solution to the grading problem.*

ICODE is read just prior to the decision and the value of ICODE dictates which path is taken. Thus, the user can determine whether the indicated table is to be printed in form 1 or form 2 while the program is executing. ICODE may be entered through a card reader if batch processing is being used, or a terminal if interactive processing is being used.

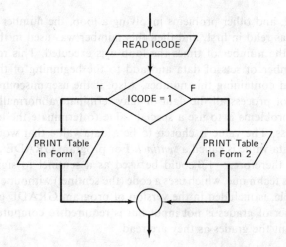

FIGURE 2-33 *Use of a code to provide control at execution time.*

Alternatively, a flag may be computed within a program. For example, it often occurs that an abnormal condition detected while a program is in progress will require special actions at various points later in the program. Figure 2-34 depicts a situation in which the variable D is normally used as a divisor, but if D is found to be 0, then IFLAG is set to 1 so that special processing will be performed later.

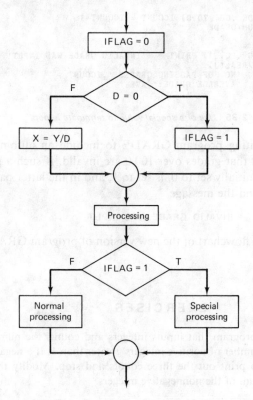

FIGURE 2-34 *Use of a flag to identify an abnormal condition.*

In program GRADE and other problems involving a loop, the number of sets of data to be processed was read in first, and then this number was used in the loop testing step to determine the number of times the loop was executed. This required the user to count the number of sets of data and add to the beginning of the data portion of the deck a card containing this number. Also, if the user miscounted the data, the program may not process all the data or may terminate abnormally. One way to get around these problems is to use a special value to terminate the loop instead of a counting process. The value is chosen to be a data value that would not normally occur. Such a data value is called a *sentinel*. For program GRADE a negative grade cannot occur; therefore, -1.0 could be used as a sentinel to signal the end of the input data. This technique, which uses a code (the sentinel) without employing a separate code variable, is included in the version of program GRADE given in Fig. 2-35. Since the number of grades is not input but is required to compute AVE, a counter J is used to count the grades as they are read.

```
      PROGRAM GRADE
      NFLG=0
      ICOUNT=0
      SUM=0.0
      J=0
   8  READ *, GRADE
      IF (GRADE .LT. 0.0) GO TO 15
      IF (GRADE .LE. 100.0) GO TO 12
      NFLG=1
      GO TO 8
   12 IF (GRADE .GE. 70.0) ICOUNT = ICOUNT+1
      SUM = SUM+GRADE
      J=J+1
      GO TO 8
   15 IF (NFLG .EQ. 1) PRINT *, 'INVALID GRADE WAS INPUT'
      AVE=SUM/REAL(J)
      PRINT *, 'NO. OF PASSING GRADES:',ICOUNT
      PRINT *, 'AVERAGE GRADE:',AVE
      END
```

FIGURE 2-35 *Use of a special value to terminate a loop.*

In addition, in rewriting program GRADE to include an automatic termination code, it was assumed that grades over 100.0 are invalid. If such a grade is read, the flag NFLG, which is initially set to 0, is set to 1, and in the latter part of the program NFLG is checked and the message

INVALID GRADE WAS INPUT

is printed if NFLG is 1. A flowchart of the new version of program GRADE is shown in Fig. 2-36.

EXERCISES

1. Flowchart and write a program that inputs integers and counts the number of 0s, the number of 1s, and the number of positive integers greater than 1. If a negative number is input, the program is to print out the three counts and stop. Modify the program to compute and print the sum of the nonnegative integers.

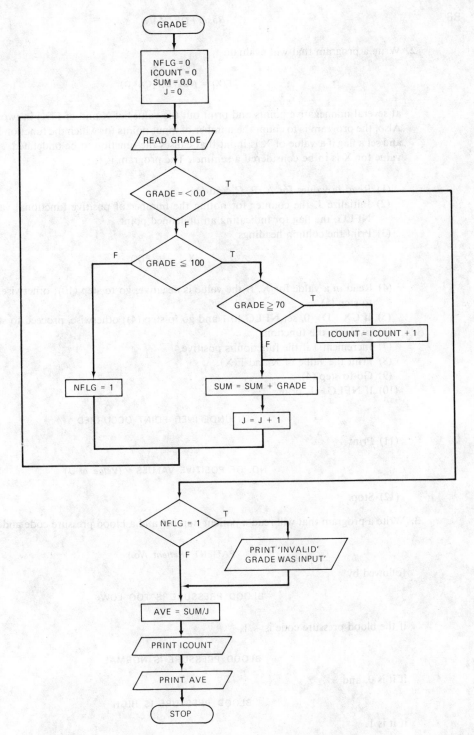

FIGURE 2-36 *Flowchart of the program in Fig. 2-35.*

2. Write a program that will evaluate

$$F(X) = (AX+B)/(CX+D)$$

at several nonnegative points and print out the values of X and of F(X) in two columns. Also, the program is to count the number of input points for which the function is positive and set a flag if a value of X is input that causes the function to be undefined. A negative value for X is to be considered a sentinel. The program is to:

(1) Read in values for A, B, C, and D.
(2) Initialize J, the counter for noting the number of positive functional values, and NFLG, the flag for indicating an undefined point.
(3) Print the column headings

X   F(X)

(4) Read in a value for X. If the value is negative, go to step (10); otherwise, proceed to step (5).
(5) If $CX+D=0$, set NFLG to 1 and go to step (4); otherwise, proceed to step (6).
(6) Evaluate the function.
(7) Increment J if the function is positive.
(8) Print the value of X and F(X).
(9) Go to step (4).
(10) If $NFLG=1$, print

AN UNDEFINED POINT OCCURRED

(11) Print

NO. OF POSITIVE VALUES = (*Value of J*)

(12) Stop.

3. Write a program that will read a patient number and a blood pressure code and print

PATIENT (*Patient No.*)

followed by

BLOOD PRESSURE IS TOO LOW

if the blood pressure code is -1,

BLOOD PRESSURE IS NORMAL

if it is 0, and

BLOOD PRESSURE IS HIGH

if it is 1.

2-8 THE CONTINUE STATEMENT

The CONTINUE statement has the form

CONTINUE

It causes no action, but may have a label associated with it. The CONTINUE statement serves two principal purposes:

1. It is used to mark the end of a distinct program segment.
2. It can be used for labeling a point that is branched to from other points in the program. By inserting a labeled CONTINUE at the beginning of the actions to be taken at a "branched to" point, these actions can easily be changed without altering the "branched to" statement.

The value in the first of these purposes is that, by tending to segment the program, the CONTINUE statement makes the program more readable. Consider the segment

```
      READ *, N
      M = N
      SUM = 0.0
    2 IF (M .EQ. 0) GO TO 3 ⎫
      READ *, X                ⎪
      SUM = SUM + X            ⎬ Loop
      M = M - 1                ⎪
      GO TO 2                  ⎭
    3 CONTINUE
      AVE = SUM/N
          .
          .
```

Here the CONTINUE statement marks the end of a loop. Also, if a programmer makes a habit of using a CONTINUE statement at points being branched to, these points could be more easily identified.

The other reason for making statement 3 a CONTINUE statement is much stronger. If

```
    3 AVE = SUM/N
          .
          .
```

had been used in place of

```
    3 CONTINUE
      AVE = SUM/N
          .
          .
```

and it were decided to print SUM (or do some other additional processing) before computing AVE, statement 3 would have to be changed in addition to inserting the PRINT $*$ (or other statement(s)). By using the CONTINUE statement, the programmer could simply insert the new statement(s). This may seem like a small point, but most programs are not simply created, they are the result of a tedious process of testing and refinement, and the changes made during this process are a primary source of errors. The number of errors made by adding statements is much less than the number caused by changing statements.

An even more serious mistake would be to replace

3   AVE = SUM/N

with

3   PRINT *, SUM
AVE=SUM/N

only while the program is being tested, and then restore the statement

3   AVE = SUM/N

after the testing process is complete. Making changes after the testing is finished is a very poor practice.

It would be difficult to advise one on exactly when CONTINUE statements should be used. The point here is that they are quite useful in certain situations and it would be a mistake to avoid them.

EXERCISE

1. Rewrite Exercise 2 at the end of Sec. 2-7 using CONTINUE statements at all points being branched to.

2-9 THE DO STATEMENT

As seen from Fig. 2-29, looping involves initializing, processing, modifying, and testing. Three of the four steps are concerned with the control of the loop itself; only one is concerned with the needed processing. Although, as in the examples in Sec. 2-6, assignment statements may be used for initializing and incrementing a counter and an IF statement for testing and branching, it would be much better if a single statement were available to perform these functions. In FORTRAN, the DO statement fulfills this need.

A loop that is constructed using a DO statement is called a *DO loop*. The structure of a DO loop is shown in Fig. 2-37(a) and a typical DO loop is given in Fig. 2-37(b). The DO statement is of the form

DO *Label, Index = Initial Value, Limit, Increment*

DO *Label*   *Index = Initial Value, Limit, Increment*

⟩ Range of the DO loop

Label Foot of the DO loop

(a) Structure

```
DO 15 I = 1, 6, 2
     READ *, X
     SUM = SUM+X
15 CONTINUE
```

(b) Example

FIGURE 2-37 *Structure of a DO loop.*

where

Label is the label associated with the last statement in the loop. The comma after *Label* is optional and does not change the meaning of the statement.

Index is a real or integer variable.

Initial value, Limit, and *Increment* are real or integer expressions. Increment is optional and if it is not present its default value is 1; if it is present it must be nonzero. The values of these expressions are converted to the same type as the index before they are used. These conversions are done according to the mixed-mode replacement rules given in Sec. 2-2-2.

The last statement in a loop is called the *foot of the loop* and all the statements starting with the first statement *after the DO statement and ending with* the foot of the loop is called the *range of the loop.*

When a DO statement with a positive increment is encountered, the *Index* is set equal to the *Initial value* and is compared to the *Limit.* If the *Index* is greater than the *Limit,* the loop is exited (i. e., the program continues beginning with the statement immediately following the foot of the loop). Otherwise, the range of the loop is executed with the *Index* equal to the *Initial value.* After the foot is executed, the *Increment* is added to the *Index* and the result is put in the *Index.* Once again the *Index* is compared to the *Limit.* If the *Index* is greater than the *Limit,* the loop is exited; otherwise, the range of the loop is repeated with the index equal to its new value. The looping process continues until the *Index* becomes greater than the *Limit* or until a branch statement within the loop causes a branch to a statement outside the loop. For the example shown in Fig. 2-37(b), I = 1 during the first execution of the range of the loop, I = 3 during the second execution, I = 5 during the third execution, and then I is set to 7. Because 7 > 6 the loop is exited before the range is executed a fourth time.

For the negative-increment case the procedure is similar except that the loop is executed until the *Index* becomes less than the *Limit,* and if the *Initial Value* is less than the *Limit,* the loop is not executed at all. The statement

DO 75 J=2,0,−1

would cause the range to be executed three times, once with J = 2, once with J = 1, and once with J = 0.

The flowchart symbol for the beginning of a loop varies from one book or manual to another. The one used in this text is shown in Fig. 2-38(a) as part of a flowchart for a general DO loop. Figure 2-38(b) illustrates an equivalent flowchart that employs the previously given flowchart symbols.

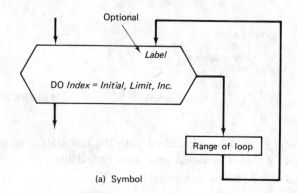

DO Index = Initial, Limit, Inc.

(a) Symbol

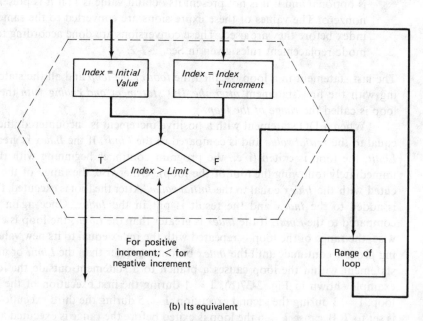

(b) Its equivalent

FIGURE 2-38 *DO statement flowcharting symbol and its equivalent.*

Figure 2-39(a) is a rewrite of the program GRADE given in Fig. 2-31, and Fig. 2-39(b) shows the corresponding flowchart. Note that for readability the range of the loop has been offset so that it can be easily identified.

```
      PROGRAM GRADE
      READ *, N
      ICOUNT = 0
      SUM = 0.0
      DO 9 I = 1,N
          READ *, GRADE
          IF (GRADE .GE. 70.0) ICOUNT = ICOUNT + 1
          SUM = SUM + GRADE
 9    CONTINUE
      AVE = SUM/REAL(N)
      PRINT *, 'NO. OF PASSING GRADES:',ICOUNT
      PRINT *, 'AVERAGE GRADE',AVE
      END
```

(a) Program

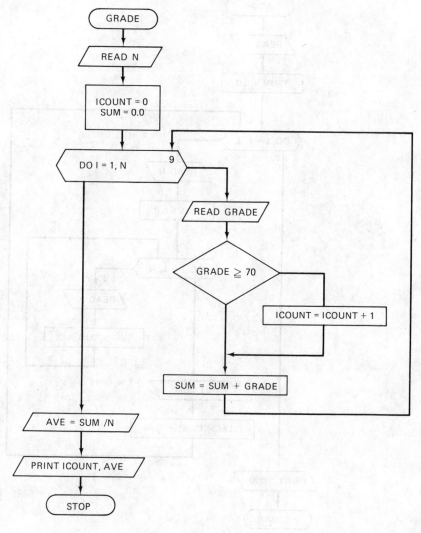

(b) Flowchart

FIGURE 2-39 *Program GRADE rewritten with a DO loop.*

```
PROGRAM ADD
READ *, L
TSUM = 0.0
DO 20 J=1,L
    READ *, N
    SUM = 0.0
    DO 10 I=1,N
        READ *, X
        SUM = SUM + X
10      CONTINUE
    PRINT *, 'SUM =',SUM, '       FOR COLUMN',J
    TSUM = TSUM + SUM
20  CONTINUE
    PRINT *, 'GRAND TOTAL =',TSUM
    END
```

(a) Program

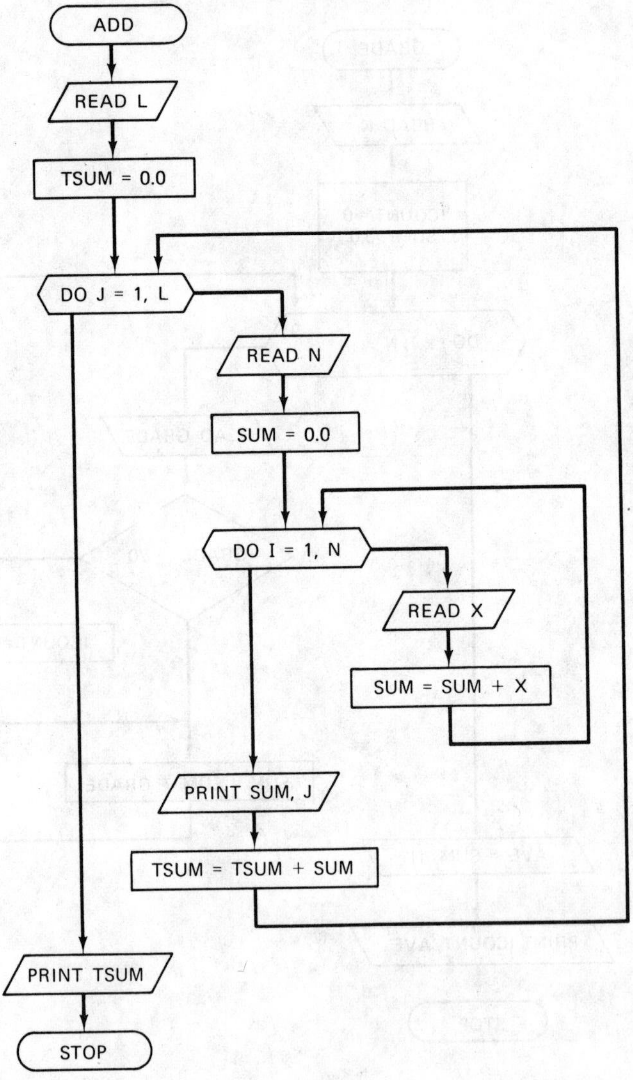

(b) Flowchart

FIGURE 2-40 *Program with nested loops.*

Although CONTINUE statements are used to terminate the loops in the examples above, the foot of a loop can be an assignment or I–O statement. For the reasons given in the preceding section, however, it is recommended that the CONTINUE statement be used. This provides more freedom in moving and changing the foot of the loop and makes it more clearly identifiable. FORTRAN also allows certain types of IF statements to be used, but in order to maintain a readable program structure (see Chap. 3) a good programmer would never put a branch statement at the foot of a loop.

Placing one loop inside another is called *nesting*. The loop that is part of the other loop is called the *inner loop* and the other loop is called the *outer loop*. Several loops may be nested. If a nest consists of one loop inside another, then there is said to be *one level of nesting;* if a nest consists of a loop inside a loop which, in turn, is inside a loop, there are said to be *two levels of nesting;* and so on. A program ADD, which adds L columns of numbers and prints the overall total TSUM as well as the column sums is given in Fig. 2-40. To make the ranges of the loops easy to identify, they have been indented with the range of the inner loop being indented more than the range of the outer loop.

The rules regarding the structure of DO loops are summarized in Fig. 2-41. This figure consists of two columns; the left column contains the rules and the right column contains comments about the rules. The reader should study these rules and the corresponding comments carefully and refer to them as the need arises.

To illustrate the last three rules given in Fig. 2-41, several valid DO loop struc-

Rule	Comments
The index, initial value, limit, or increment should not be changed within the range of the loop.	These quantities are for controlling the loop and should not be part of the processing within the loop.
An inner loop cannot use the same index variable as an outer loop in the same nest. However, loops not in the same nest may use the same index variable.	Because the inner loop increments its index, if the outer loop has the same index then the rule above would be violated.
The range of a loop may not be branched into from a statement outside the loop, but branches may be made within a loop or from within the loop to a statement outside the loop.	One of the steps performed by the DO statement is the initialization step. If a loop were branched into without performing this step, the index would not be set to its initial value [see Fig. 2-38(b)].
Nested loops may share the same foot, however the shared foot is in the range of the inner loop.	Although two or more loops may share a foot, this is not recommended. Programs are more readable and more flexible if a separate CONTINUE statement is used to terminate each loop.
The foot of one loop cannot be in the range of another loop unless the loops are nested (i.e., loops cannot be overlapped unless they are nested).	If one loop overlaps another, then the latter loop would be successively reentered without being completed and this is not permissible.

FIGURE 2-41 *Rules governing the structure of DO loops.*

tures are shown in Fig. 2-42(a) and several invalid structures are shown in Fig. 2-42(b). In the diagrams in these figures the line on the left represents the program sequence, the solid backward flowlines represent the backward branch at the end of the loop, and the dashed flowlines represent branches due to GO TO or IF statements. The bottom of a solid flowline represents the foot of a loop, and if the bottoms of two or more solid flowlines are superimposed [as in the bottommost diagram in Fig. 2-42 (a)], a shared foot is to be assumed. In particular, note the last valid and last invalid structures. Because the foot is in the range of the loop, a branch may be made to a shared foot from within the inner loop but not from outside the inner loop, even if the branch is from within the outer loop. This is a moot point for those who follow the suggested practice of never using a shared foot.

Although the value of the *Index* is not usually important after a loop is exited, it is available for use by the subsequent statements. If the exit is due to a branch statement within the range of the loop the value of the index variable after the branch is made is clearly the same as its value just prior to the branch. If the loop exits normally (i. e., due to the incrementing and testing steps), the index variable will be equal to its value during the last execution of the range of the loop *plus the* value of the *Increment*. This is because the incrementing step is performed before the testing step. Although the index is available after a loop is exited, it is considered poor programming practice to use it at that point.

The examples above used integer variables and constants for the *Index*, *Initial Value*, *Limit*, and *Increment*, and this is normally the case. However, the rules permit real quantities and a programmer may wish to take advantage of this flexibility, but before doing so the programmer should be aware of an important pitfall. Most translators do not actually determine the number of times a loop is executed by successively adding the increment to the index and comparing the result to the limit, but determine this number by adding 1 to the truncation of the quantity

$$(Limit - Initial\ Value)/Increment$$

This fact is not important if integer quantities are used, but is important if real quantities are employed. Recall that, because of the finiteness of the computer, real numbers are not always stored precisely and, just as the decimal fraction 0.3333333 is slightly less than $\frac{1}{3}$, the 0–1 combination in the computer which represents 0.9 may be slightly smaller than 0.9. Because of such inaccuracies the sequence

```
        DO 10  X=0.1,1.0,0.1
        PRINT *, SQRT(X)
    10  CONTINUE
```

may not print 10 values; it may print only 9. For this reason a programmer should study the situation carefully before using real quantities in a DO statement.

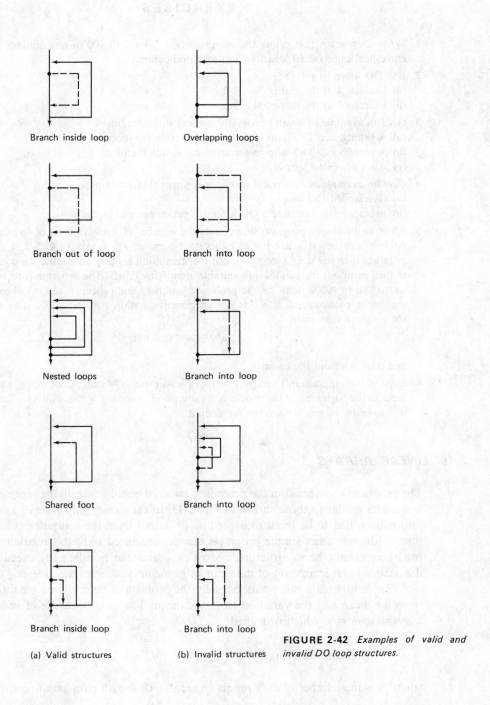

Branch inside loop

Overlapping loops

Branch out of loop

Branch into loop

Nested loops

Branch into loop

Shared foot

Branch into loop

Branch inside loop

Branch into loop

(a) Valid structures

(b) Invalid structures

FIGURE 2-42 *Examples of valid and invalid DO loop structures.*

EXERCISES

1. Write a program that prints the even numbers from 2 to 100 in one column and their corresponding base 10 logarithms in a second column.
2. Use DO loops to solve:
   (a) Exercise 1 at the end of Sec. 2-6.
   (b) Exercise 2 at the end of Sec. 2-6.
3. Give an example of a valid program segment that contains:
   (a) A branch in a DO loop to a statement within the loop.
   (b) A branch in a DO loop to a statement outside the loop.
   (c) A set of nested loops.
4. Give an example of an invalid program segment that contains:
   (a) Overlapped DO loops.
   (b) A branch from outside a DO loop to a statement within the loop.
5. Write an inventory program that counts the number of items in each of five categories. An item's category is determined by its item number, which may be 1, 2, 3, 4, or 5. The program is to use a DO loop to input the item numbers and determine the counts. It is to then print out the counts with suitable identifying labels. The program is to be written so that up to 10000 items can be processed and the input process is to stop when a 0 item number is encountered. If a 0 is not encountered within the first 10000 item numbers, the program is to print

   CAPACITY EXCEEDED

   and then print out the counts.
6. Expand the program in Exercise 5 so that it can process M batches of items, where M is input at the beginning of the program. In addition to outputting the counts for each batch, it is to print the grand total for each count.

2-10 LINEAR ARRAYS

The programs considered in the preceding material could generally be represented by flowcharts similar to those shown in Fig. 2-43. In each case only a small amount of information had to be input to, stored in, or output from the computer at any given time. Although many simple programs can be structured to fit this restriction, most programs cannot be so structured. Most programs can be efficiently executed only if a relatively large amount of data can be in memory at one time.

To demonstrate this point, consider the problem of determining passing grades from the mean and the variation from the mean. The usual measure of variation is *standard deviation*, which is defined:

$$\text{standard deviation} = \sqrt{\frac{1}{N}\sum_{i=1}^{N}(G_i - M)^2} = \sqrt{\frac{1}{N}\sum_{i=1}^{N}G_i^2 - M^2}$$

where N is the number of data points (students), G_i the ith data point (grade for the

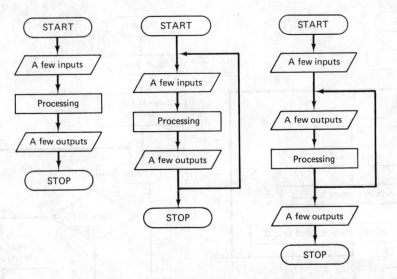

FIGURE 2-43 *General flowcharts for the preceding examples.*

*i*th student), and *M* the mean of the data points (grades). If it is decided that a grade that is less than the mean minus 1 standard deviation is failing, then two actions are needed to determine which students are failing. First the mean minus 1 standard deviation must be computed, and then all grades must be compared with the result. The problem is that both actions require access to the entire set of data. One solution would be to base the program on the flowchart in Fig. 2-44(a), but this would require that the data be input twice.

A solution that avoids bringing in the data twice is indicated by the flowchart in Fig. 2-44(b), but this procedure would require that the entire set of grades be kept in memory until the failing grades are found. Until now, we have considered variable names that are associated with only one quantity and one memory location. If only a few grades are involved, say 5, they could be assigned the names G1, G2, G3, G4, and G5 and there would be no problem, but a difficulty arises if there are 1000 grades. How could one input, process, and output 1000 distinct values? This difficulty can be circumvented by allowing variables to be subscripted and permitting the subscripts to be varied by the program.

An *array* is a set of data which is designated by a name and whose elements are indicated by subscripts. In this section only arrays with single subscripts will be introduced—such arrays are called *linear* (or *one-dimensional*) *arrays*. In FORTRAN an *array name* is a variable name (i.e., it has up to six alphanumeric characters, the first being alphabetic), and an *element* of a linear array is written in the form

$$Name(Subscript)$$

where *Name* is the array name and *Subscript* is an integer expression. An element of an array is also called a *subscripted variable*. The type of an array is determined in

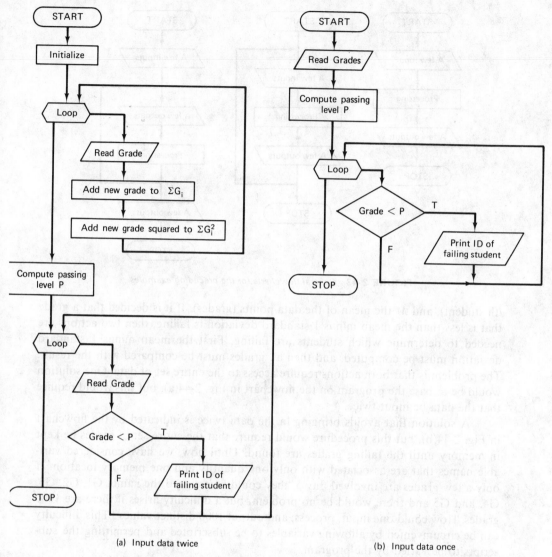

(a) Input data twice　　　　　　　　　　　　(b) Input data once

FIGURE 2-44 *Two methods for solving the grading problem.*

the same way that the type of a variable is determined. The notation

$$COST(7)$$

indicates the element, or subscripted variable, in the real array COST which is associated with the subscript 7. The notation

$$M(3*I+2)$$

indicates the element in the integer array M which is associated with the value of the expression $3 * I + 2$.

When arrays are used in a program, the translating process must be informed in advance which symbols represent arrays and the sizes of the arrays so that it can identify the arrays and reserve, or *allocate*, the proper amount of memory space. Informing the translator of the size of an array is called *dimensioning the array*. In FORTRAN the DIMENSION statement is used to dimension arrays and its format is

DIMENSION   *Name(Limit Notation)*, . . . , *Name(Limit Notation)*

where the *Names* are the names of the arrays for which memory space is to be allocated, and the *Limit Notation* gives the smallest and largest permissible subscripts. For linear arrays the *Limit Notation* consists of a single integer constant or two integer constants separated by a colon. If it consists of only one constant, the constant is the largest permissible value the subscript may attain and 1 is the smallest permissible value. If there are two constants in the *Limit Notation*, they indicate the subscript range, with the lower limit of the range being given on the left. The dimension statement

DIMENSION A(100), B(−10:10)

allocates 100 memory locations for array A and 21 for array B. The elements of A are written A(1), A(2), . . , A(100) and the elements of B are denoted B(−10), B(−9), . . ., B(10). Figure 2-45 depicts the areas in memory that are assigned to the arrays A and B. As seen from the figure, the elements of an array are associated with consecutive memory locations. The element A(1) is assigned to the first location, A(2) to the second, and so on.

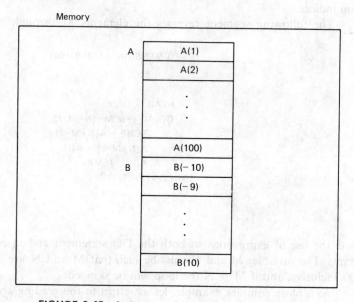

FIGURE 2-45 *Assignment of elements to memory locations.*

Several DIMENSION statements may be used to specify the arrays in a program. Because the purpose of DIMENSION statements is to identify arrays and allocate memory space, and because the array assignments must be known to the translator at the beginning of the translating process, all DIMENSION statements must be placed at the beginning of a program and no array can be dimensioned more than once (i.e., no array can appear more than once in the collection of all DIMENSION statements).

The following sequence demonstrates how an array might be used in conjunction with looping:

```
                 PROGRAM SUM
                 DIMENSION A(1000)
                       .
                       .
                       .
                 SUM=0.0
                 DO 10 I=1,1000
                       SUM=SUM+A(I)
            10   CONTINUE
                       .
                       .
                       .
```

The DIMENSION statement must appear at the beginning of the program. The loop adds the elements in the array A by adding A(1) to SUM during the first execution of the loop, A(2) during the second execution, and so on. As in this brief program segment, array subscripts are normally equal to or, at least, dependent on one or more loop indices.

The following segment reverses the elements M through N in the array A:

```
                 DIMENSION A(-100:100)
                       .
                       .
                       .
                 READ *, M,N
                 DO 10 I=M,M+(N-M)/2
                       TEMP = A(N+M-I)
                       A(N+M-I) = A(I)
                       A(I) = TEMP
            10   CONTINUE
                       .
                       .
                       .
```

Note the use of expressions in both the DO statement and in computing the subscripts. The variables M and N must be such that M and N are between -100 and 100, inclusive, and if M $>$ N the loop will be skipped.

As a more complex example, let us return to the grading problem described in the introduction to this section. Figure 2-46 gives a solution to the problem. After

```
            PROGRAM GRADES
            DIMENSION G(1000)
            READ *, N
            DO 10 I=1,N
                READ *, G(I)
     10     CONTINUE
            S1 = 0.0
            S2 = 0.0
            DO 20 I=1,N
                S1 = S1 + G(I)
                S2 = S2 + G(I)**2
     20     CONTINUE
            AVE = S1/REAL(N)
            SD = SQRT(S2/REAL(N) - AVE**2)
            PLEVEL = AVE - SD
            DO 30 I = 1,N
                IF (G(I) .LT. PLEVEL)
            :       PRINT *, 'THE',I,'TH STUDENT IS FAILING'
     30     CONTINUE
            END
           └─Note continuation
```

FIGURE 2-46 *Program for solving the grading problem.*

the number of students is input to N, the grades are input to a linear array G, then the mean and standard deviation are computed, and lastly, the IDs of the students with failing grades are printed.

An expanded solution to the problem is given in Fig. 2-47. In this solution the input is terminated by the sentinel −999999 and student IDs are read in as well as the grades. Each input record is to contain the student's ID followed by his or her

```
            PROGRAM GRADES
            DIMENSION ID(1001), G(1001)
            N = 0
            DO 10 I=1,1001
                READ *, ID(I), G(I)
                IF (G(I) .LT. 0.0 .OR. G(I) .GT. 100.0) G(I) = -1.0
                IF (ID(I) .EQ. -999999) GO TO 20
                N = N+1
     10     CONTINUE
            N = 1000
            PRINT *, 'NO. OF GRADES EXCEEDS 1000 - ONLY 1000 PROCESSED'
     20     CONTINUE
            S1 = 0.0
            S2 = 0.0
            M = 0
            DO 40 I=1,N
                IF (G(I) .EQ. -1.0) GO TO 30
                S1 = S1 + G(I)
                S2 = S2 + G(I)**2
                M = M + 1
     30         CONTINUE
     40     CONTINUE
            IF (M .EQ. 0) GO TO 45
            PRINT *, 'NO VALID GRADES'
            GO TO 80
     45     AVE = S1/REAL(M)
            SD = SQRT(S2/REAL(M) - AVE**2)
            PLEVEL = AVE - SD
            DO 70 I=1,N
                IF (G(I) .GE. PLEVEL) GO TO 60
                IF (G(I) .EQ. -1.0) GO TO 50
                    PRINT *, 'STUDENT', ID(I), ' IS FAILING'
                    GO TO 60
     50             PRINT *, 'INVALID GRADE FOR STUDENT', ID(I)
     60         CONTINUE
     70     CONTINUE
     80     CONTINUE
            END
```

FIGURE 2-47 *Expanded version of program GRADES.*

grade. Because the array G cannot hold more than 1000 grades, if the sentinel is not encountered during the input of the first 1001 records the message

NO. OF GRADES EXCEEDS 1000 – ONLY 1000 PROCESSED

is printed and the program proceeds to process the first 1000 grades. If a grade outside the range 0 through 100 is detected, the program changes the grade to a -1.0. Later, when computing the mean and standard deviation, the -1.0 grades are not included, and when the failing grades are printed, a -1.0 grade causes

INVALID GRADE FOR STUDENT (*Value of student's ID*)

to be printed instead of the usual "failing" message.

EXERCISES

1. Consider the DIMENSION statements given below. If a statement is valid, show how the elements of its arrays are assigned memory locations (see Fig. 2-45); if a statement is invalid, give the reason it is invalid.
   (a) DIMENSION A(20)
   (b) DIMENSION I(20 – 30)
   (c) DIMENSION CHARGE(-2:6)
   (d) DIMENSION A(0:5), ITEM(3)
   (e) DIMENSION (X(10),Y(10))

2. Rewrite the solution to Exercise 5 at the end of Sec. 2-9 so that all items are brought into an array ITEM before they are counted, and the counts are put into an array ICOUNT.

3. Write a program for computing the profit statistics on 100 types of items. The program is to read in an item number, cost, and retail price from each of up to 2000 cards. From these data it is to produce a report that includes a table with the column headings

ITEM NO.	QUANTITY	TOTAL COST	TOTAL INCOME	TOTAL PROFIT

The program is also to print out the average profit for each type of item and the corresponding standard deviation.

2-11 IMPLIED DO LOOPS

In program GRADES in Fig. 2-46 the loop

```
            DO 10 I=1,N
              READ *, G(I)
         10 CONTINUE
```

was used to input the grades. This permits all N grades to be brought in with a small number of statements, but it has one major weakness. The READ * statement is encountered N times and each time it is executed it must read from a new input record. If the input medium is cards, each grade must be punched into a separate card; and if the input is through an interactive terminal, each grade must be typed on a separate line. It would be much better if only a few input records were required. Similar statements could be made regarding output. What is needed is a way of inputting or outputting arrays, or portions of arrays, using a specially constructed list item that would permit READ * (or PRINT *) statements of the form

READ *, List item, ..., Special list item, ..., List item

where the *Special list item* could cause several elements in an array to be input (or output). This would allow several elements of an array to be input or output by a single execution of an I–O statement.

    The programming feature for circumventing the problem noted above is called an implied DO loop. An *implied DO loop* is a list item of the form

(Variable, ..., Variable, Index = Initial Value, Limit, Increment)

where *Index*, *Initial Value*, *Limit*, and *Increment* are defined just as they were in the discussion of the DO statement. A *Variable* may be a subscripted variable, and if one of the variables is subscripted with the *Index* being the subscript, which is almost always the case, the *Index* must be an integer variable. When an implied DO loop is encountered, the variables in the loop (i.e., the variables inside the parentheses) are repeatedly input to or output from as the *Index* increments from the *Initial Value* to the *Limit*. The statement

READ *, (T(I),I=1,3)

has exactly the same effect as

READ *, T(1),T(2),T(3).

    Several other statements and their equivalents are given in Fig. 2-48. In the third example note that both implied DO loops use the same index. This is permissible because the execution of the first loop is completed before the execution of the second loop begins. The two implied DO loops could also have different index variables. On the other hand, the sequence

DO 10 I=1,3
READ *, N(I),(X(I), I=1,2)
10 CONTINUE

is not allowed, because if the index of the implied DO loop is the same as the index of the DO loop, the index of the DO loop would be changed within its range. This is the same as having nested loops with the same index.

Statement with Implied DO Loop	Equivalent
PRINT *, (A(N), N=1,6,2)	PRINT *, A(1),A(3),A(5)
READ *, X,(Y(J), J=1,2), Z	READ *, X,Y(1),Y(2),Z
READ *, (N(I),I=1,2),(X(I),I=1,2)	READ *, N(1),N(2),X(1),X(2)
READ *, (N(I),X(I),I=1,2)	READ *, N(1),X(1),N(2),X(2)
PRINT *, (A,B(J), J=1,2)	PRINT *, A, B(1), A, B(2)
PRINT *, (B(I), I=N,N+4,M)	PRINT *, B(3),B(5),B(7)
	where it is assumed that N=3
	and M=2

FIGURE 2-48 *Examples of implied DO loops.*

Particular attention should be given to the last example in Fig. 2-48. In this example it was necessary to know the values of N and M before constructing the equivalent PRINT * statement. The ability of the implied DO loop to use a variable *Initial Value*, *Limit*, or *Increment* extends its application considerably. If variables could not be used, these quantities would have to be known at the time the program is written; as it is, they may be input at execution time.

Another useful possibility for inputting to an array is demonstrated by the statement

READ *, N,(X(I). I=1,N)

The *Limit* N can be input by the same statement provided that it is read first. The statement

READ *, (X(I), I=1,N), N

may not execute properly because N may be unknown at the time the X array is being filled. The following statement shows that the *Initial Value* and *Increment* can similarly be read into using the same statement as is used for the array:

READ *, L,M,N,(W(J), J=N,L,M)

Figure 2-49(a) shows a program for inputting L values into each of the arrays N and M, computing the sum and difference of the corresponding elements of N and M, and putting the results in arrays ISUM and IDIFF, respectively. The program then prints N(I), M(I), ISUM(I), and IDIFF(I), I = 1, . . . , L, in columns. The statement that causes N and M to be read into is such that N(1) and M(1) are input first, then N(2) and M(2) are input, and so on. The output is done through an ordinary DO loop, so that the successive sets of four values will appear in columns. Typical card input and printer output for L = 3 are shown in Fig. 2-49(b) and (c). The two READ * statements could be replaced with the single statement

READ *, L, (N(I), M(I), I=1,L)

```
PROGRAM SUMDIF
DIMENSION N(100),M(100)
READ *, L
READ *, (N(I),M(I),I=1,L)
DO 10 I=1,L
    ISUM(I) = N(I) + M(I)
    IDIFF(I) = N(I) - M(I)
10  CONTINUE
PRINT *, ' 1ST NO. 2ND NO.    SUM  DIFFERENCE'
DO 20 I=1,L
    PRINT *, N(I),M(I),ISUM(I),IDIFF(I)
20  CONTINUE
END
```

(a) Program

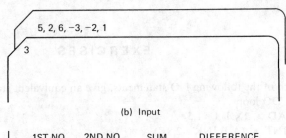

(b) Input

1ST NO.	2ND NO.	SUM	DIFFERENCE
5	2	7	3
6	-3	3	9
-2	1	-1	-3

(c) Output

FIGURE 2-49 *Program that demonstrates both implied DO loop and ordinary DO loop I–O.*

If this is done, the input record would need to appear as follows:

```
3,    5, 2, 6,  -3, -2, 1
```

If an entire array is to be input or output, a helpful shortcut is permitted that allows one to give only the array name in the I–O *List*. The READ * or PRINT * statement will perform the I–O just as if an implied DO loop, whose *Initial Value* and *Limit* are the lower and upper subscript limits, had been used. If A is dimensioned with 1 as the lower subscript limit and 10 as the upper subscript limit and X is an unsubscripted variable, then the statement

PRINT *, (A(I), I=1,10),X

has the same effect as the statement

PRINT *, A,X

It is particularly useful to insert I–O statements with this abbreviated form while a program is being corrected (see Chap. 4).

In accordance with the rules of list-directed I–O, if all of the information to be input cannot be put in a single record, then successive records will be read until the *Input List* is satisfied. If there are 10 numbers in each input record, the statement

READ *, (A(I), I=1,200)

would read 20 records. Also, if L has 47 elements and there are 5 numbers per record, the statement

READ *, L

would read 10 records with only the 46th and 47th elements being filled from the last record. Similarly, a PRINT * statement will print on successive lines until the *Output List* is satisfied.

EXERCISES

1. For each of the following I–O statements, give an equivalent statement that **does not use** implied DO loops.
   (a) READ *, (X(I),I=1,5)
   (b) PRINT *, (A,B,INK=2,8,3)
   (c) READ *, (X(I), I=1,2,2),(Y(J), J=5,50,5),Z
   (d) PRINT *, (X(I),Y(I),I, I=1,5)
   (e) PRINT *, (A(J), J=N,M+2,L) for N=−1, M=6, L=4

2. For each I–O statement in Exercise 1, assume that all of the unknown numbers being input or output are 5.02 and show how the output would appear:
   (a) On an 80-column terminal.   (b) On a 132-column line printer.

3. For each of the following I–O statements, find an equivalent I–O statement that uses implied DO loops wherever possible.
   (a) READ *, A(1),A(2),A(3),B(1),B(2)
   (b) READ *, X(−1),Y(−1),X(1),Y(1),X(3),Y(3)
   (c) PRINT *, A,A,C(1),A,C(2),A,C(3),B
   (d) PRINT *, 3,A(0),5,A(2),7,A(4)
   (e) PRINT *, W(1),W(1),W(2),W(3),W(1)

4. Write a program that reads in an integer N, uses an implied DO loop to read N values into an array X, computes values for Y(1), ..., Y(N) from the respective values of X(1), ..., X(N) by assuming the function

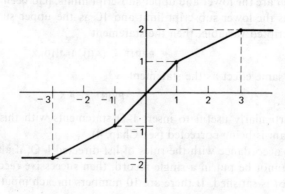

and then uses an implied DO loop to print out the N values of Y.

5. Write a solution to Exercise 2 of Sec. 2-10 that uses implied DO loops where possible for performing the I–O.

6. Write a program that reads in integers N and M, uses implied DO loops to read N + 1 values into an array A and M values into an array X, computes values for an array Y according to the formula

$$Y(I) = A(N)*X(I)**N + A(N-1)*X(I)**(N-1) + \ldots + A(0)$$

and outputs the array Y using an implied DO loop. The program is to print appropriate messages for the cases N = 0, M = 0, or A(N) = 0. Use *Horner's Rule*, which states that for any polynomial

$$a_n x^n + a_{n-1} x^{n-1} + \ldots + a_1 x + a_0 = (\ldots ((a_n x + a_{n-1})x + a_{n-2})x + \ldots)x + a_0$$

For example,

$$3x^3 + 2x^2 + x - 1 = ((3x + 2)x + 1)x - 1$$

2-12 SUMMARY

This chapter has introduced the basic FORTRAN statements needed to perform the principal computer tasks of inputting, processing, and outputting information. Although extensions of the statements presented in this chapter are considered in later chapters together with other statements that provide additional flexibility, the statements discussed here are sufficient to write programs for solving a variety of problems. This chapter has also discussed the ways in which the fundamental data types, integer and real, are identified in FORTRAN and how large quantities of data can be handled using subscripted variables. The topics that have been covered are outlined in Fig. 2-50.

It has been seen that interactive processing requires prompting messages to indicate the time and order in which data are to be input and, for output, headings and messages must be organized together with the data to produce a readable report.

```
Input
        Prompting
        Unsubscripted variables
        Arrays--implied DO loops
        Codes
        Sentinels
Output
        Headings and error messages
        Unsubscripted variables
        Arrays--implied DO loops
Processing
        Assignment
        Branching - decision making
            Unconditional
            Conditional
            Flags and codes
        Looping - accumulation and counting
Data Types
        Integer
        Real
        Arrays
```

FIGURE 2-50 *Summary of the programming concepts presented in Chap. 2.*

Sentinels have been introduced as a way of terminating the input data. It has been noted that I–O statements may include in their lists simple variables for storing relatively few, but perhaps unrelated, quantities and implied DO loops for working with large sets of related quantities. Also mentioned was the possibility of using codes to permit the input to determine the format of the output.

The FORTRAN means of accomplishing the primary processing tasks of assignment, branching, and looping were studied. In the discussion of branching both unconditional and conditional branches were considered. Conditional branches were related to decision making and the application of codes and flags. Looping, a means of performing repetitious actions, was examined, with particular attention being given to the processing of related information contained in arrays. The concepts of accumulation and counting which are often used in conjunction with looping were also considered.

The purpose of this chapter has been to provide enough of the FORTRAN language and general programming concepts to allow the reader to write reasonable programs and build a foundation for more detailed study. As an effort to solidify the ideas and rules presented thus far, let us consider an example that incorporates all the ideas listed in Fig. 2-50 into a single program.

A heartbeat is known to have the shape depicted in Fig. 2-51. Heartbeats are

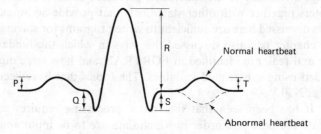

FIGURE 2-51 *Typical heartbeat.*

often compared by examining the ratios P/R, Q/R, S/R, and T/R. It is possible for the height T to be nonpositive, but this is known to be a characteristic of a seriously failing heart. Suppose that a scientist wants to examine the ratio Q/R for a certain population and to compare those heartbeats with nonpositive values of T to the normal heartbeats with positive values of T. The study is to compare the ratios Q/R for the abnormal heartbeats to the quantities:

Mean of Q/R + various multiples of the standard deviation of Q/R

where the mean and standard deviation are computed using only normal heartbeats. The results are to indicate the number of abnormal heartbeats for which Q/R is outside the ranges of the mean ± 0.5, ± 1.0, ± 1.5, and ± 2.0 standard deviations.

Figure 2-52 gives an interactive program HBEAT for performing the statistical analysis of the heartbeats and producing the needed report. The program first

```
      PROGRAM HBEAT
      DIMENSION QR(1000), T(1000), ICNTQ(4)
      DO 10 I=1,4
          ICNTQ(I) = 0
   10 CONTINUE
      SUMM = 0.0
      SUMSD = 0.0
      N = 0
      M = 0
      DO 20 I=1,1000
          PRINT *, 'INPUT HEIGHT PARAMETERS'
          READ *, Q, R, T(I))
          IF (R .LT. 0.0) GO TO 30
          N = N+1
          IF (T(I) .LE. 0.0) GO TO 15
              M = M+1
              QR(I) = Q/R
              SUMM = SUMM + QR(I)
              SUMSD = SUMSD + QR(I)**2
   15     CONTINUE
   20 CONTINUE
      PRINT *, 'MAXIMUM NO. OF 1000 SAMPLE HEARTBEATS HAS BEEN REACHED'
   30 CONTINUE
      IF (M .EQ. 0) STOP
      QRM = SUMM/REAL(M)
      QRSD = SQRT(SUMSD/REAL(M) - QRM**2)
      DO 50 I=1,N
          IF (T(I) .GT. 0.0) GO TO 45
              DO 40 J=1,4
                  IF (ABS(QR(I)-QRM) .GT. 0.5*REAL(J)*QRSD)
     :                  ICNTQ(J) = ICNTQ(J) + 1
   40         CONTINUE
   45     CONTINUE
   50 CONTINUE
      PRINT *, 'INPUT THE OUTPUT FORMAT CODE'
      READ *, ICODE
      IF (ICODE .NE. 1) GO TO 70
          PRINT *, 'SAMPLE NO.    Q/R RATIO'
          DO 60 I=1,N
              IF (T(I) .LE. 0.0) PRINT *, I, '          ', QR(I)
   60     CONTINUE
   70 CONTINUE
      PRINT *
      PRINT *, 'NO. OF BAD HEARTBEAT SAMPLES', N-M
      PRINT *, 'NO. OF STANDARD DEVIATIONS FROM MEAN',
     :              (0.5*J, J=1,4)
      PRINT *, 'NO. OF BAD HEARTBEAT SAMPLES          ',
     :              (ICNTQ(J), '      ', J=1,4)
      END
```

FIGURE 2-52 *Program for solving the heartbeat example.*

dimensions the arrays QR, T, and ICNTQ, which are for storing the Q/R ratios, the heights T, and the numbers of bad heartbeats that are more than 0.5J, J=1,...,4, standard deviations away from the Q/R mean for normal heartbeats. The elements of ICNTQ are then zeroed along with the accumulators SUMM and SUMSD and the counters N and M. The accumulators SUMM and SUMSD are used to total the Q/R ratios and the squares of these ratios, respectively. The variable N is for counting all heartbeat samples and M is for counting the good samples. A DO-loop is used to input the Q, R, and T values and to compute N, M, SUMM, SUMSD, and the elements of QR. A negative value of R is used as a sentinel to indicate that the input, and the associated loop, is to be terminated. Next, the mean and standard deviation of Q/R are found for the good heartbeats and are put into QRM and QRSD. Then another DO-loop is entered and the elements of ICNTQ are determined. Finally, the report is printed in one of two possible forms by inputting a code value to ICODE. If a 1 is put into ICODE, the sample number and the Q/R ratio are printed for each of the bad heartbeats; otherwise, this detailed information is not printed. In either case the counts in ICNTQ are printed under the numbers of standard deviations used in arriving at the values in ICNTQ.

PROGRAMMING PROBLEMS

If the Programming Problems in this chapter and the following chapters are to be interactive, they should include the necessary input prompting messages.

1. Write a program for demonstrating precedence and mixed-mode computations. The program is to input values to I, J, X, and Y, assign K and Z values using the assignment statements

$$K = X$$
$$Z = I$$

and compute and output the values of L and W determined by the following equations:

L = I+J/K	W = I+J/K
L = X+J/K	W = X+J/K
L = X+Y/K	W = X+Y/K
L = X+Y/Z	W = X+Y/Z
L = (I+J)/K	W = (I+J)/K
L = (X+Y)/Z	W = (X+Y)/Z
L = J/I*K	W = Y/X*Z
L = J/(I*K)	W = Y/(X*Z)
L = I**K**J	W = X**Z**Y
L = I**K*J	W = X**Z*Y
L = I*J−X	W = I*J−X
L = I*(J−X)	W = I*(J−X)

Run the program using the data

$$I = 2 \qquad J = 3 \qquad X = 4.5 \qquad Y = 2.5$$

2. Comets are known to travel around stars in elliptical orbits. Suppose that a comet follows the elliptic path around a star as indicated below:

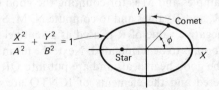

$$\frac{X^2}{A^2} + \frac{Y^2}{B^2} = 1$$

Using analytic geometry, it can be shown that X and Y can be expressed as functions of the angle ϕ by the equations

$$X = A \cos \phi \qquad Y = B \sin \phi$$

Write a program that will approximate the total distance traveled by the comet in one revolution by using straight-line segments between N successive points that are evenly spaced relative to the angle ϕ. The program is to input values for A, B, and N, compute the total distance DIST, and print

THE LENGTH OF ONE ORBIT = *(Value of DIST)*

Test the program using $A = 3 \times 10^{11}$, $B = 4 \times 10^{11}$, and $N = 36$, and retest it with the same values of A and B but with $N = 360$.

3. Consider the problem of surveying for altitude along a straight line. This can be done by measuring the distance and angular rise between successive points.

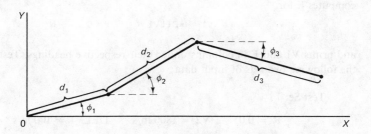

Write a program that will print the headings

LINEAR SURVEY INFORMATION
DISTANCE FROM   ALTITUDE ABOVE
STARTING POINT   STARTING POINT

and then read distance–angle pairs (one pair per input record) into the variables DIST and ANGLE. Each time a pair is read, the corresponding X and Y pair is to be computed and printed under the appropriate headings. The process is to terminate when a distance of 0 is encountered. Test the program by inputting the following set of test data:

Distances	Angles (deg)
50.0	0.0
25.0	20.0
50.0	30.0
75.0	10.0
75.0	20.0
100.0	10.0
0.0	0.0

4. The mechanical efficiency of a jet engine is given by the equation

$$E = \{1 + (1 + R)[(V_2/V_1) - 1]^2/2[(1 + R)(V_2/V_1) - 1]\}^{-1}$$

where R is the ratio of fuel mass to air mass in the combustion chamber, V_2 the velocity of the gases being discharged, and V_1 the air speed of the airplane.

Write a program that inputs values into R, V2, DELV1, and N, prints

INVALID AIR SPEED (*Value of DELV1*N*)

and stops if DELV1*N≥V2, and otherwise prints the headings

JET ENGINE EFFICIENCY
COMBUSTION RATIO = (*Value of R*)
EXHAUST VELOCITY = (*Value of V2*)
AIR SPEED   EFFICIENCY

computes E for

V1 = I*DELV1   I = 0, . . . , N

and prints V1 and E in columns under their respective headings. Test the program with the following two sets of input data:

Test Set 1:

R = 0.05   V2 = 1800 m/s   DELV1 = 100 m/s   N = 17

Test Set 2: Same as Test Set 1 except let N = 18.

5. Suppose that a farm equipment dealership refills its inventory of tractors once every 5 days and has kept records on how many tractors have been sold for the last 200 days (assume that for these days enough tractors were on hand to fill all orders). Using these records a study is to be made which is to tell the dealership the probability of depleting its inventory before the end of a 5-day period if it begins the period with N tractors, where N may equal 0, 1, . . . , 10. (The probability of an event is the ratio of the number of occurrences of the event to the number of experiments; e.g., the probability of a coin landing "heads" is 0.5.)

Write a program that reads in the daily data and, for each 5-day period, determines the number of tractors sold during that period. The results are to be put in a linear array MSALES. If M is the number of tractors sold during a 5-day period, the probability density function for this problem is a function that indicates, for each value of M,

$$P(M) = \frac{\text{no. of 5-day periods in which } M \text{ tractors were sold}}{\text{total no. 5-day periods}}$$

The probability distribution function indicates, for each M,

$$F(M) = \frac{\text{no. of periods for which} \leq M \text{ tractors were sold}}{\text{total no. of periods}}$$

The program is to assume that no more than 10 tractors are ever sold during a 5-day period. It is to compute the probability density and distribution functions, put the results in the linear arrays **PDEN** and **PDIST**, and print the functions under the headings

TRACTOR SALES

NO. OF TRACTORS SOLD	DENSITY FUNCTION	DISTRIBUTION FUNCTION

Test the program using the following 200-day sales data.

```
1 0 2 1 0 1 0 0 3 0 1 1 2 2 1 0 0 0 1 0
4 1 0 2 1 0 2 0 1 5 1 6 3 0 0 3 1 2 1 2
5 2 1 1 0 0 1 3 4 2 3 0 3 2 1 0 1 1 1 1
2 1 5 1 1 2 0 1 0 0 0 1 0 1 0 1 2 1 0 1
3 2 1 0 1 0 0 0 0 0 0 2 3 4 1 0 1 2 2 0
0 1 0 1 1 0 1 2 0 0 2 0 3 0 1 1 0 1 0 0
0 3 4 0 1 0 0 2 7 0 0 2 4 1 0 2 0 1 1 0
0 3 1 1 0 2 1 5 1 1 0 1 0 0 0 0 0 1 2 0
1 2 5 0 0 0 2 1 3 1 0 1 0 2 1 0 4 1 4 0
1 1 1 1 2 1 2 0 1 1 0 1 1 0 3 1 3 0 1 2
```

6. Consider the following helium turbine system for generating electric power:

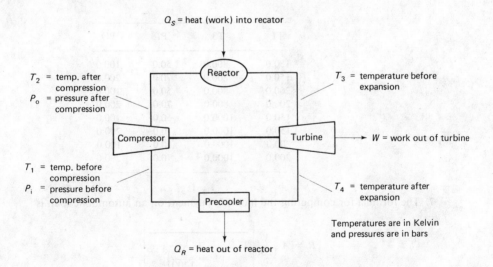

The equations for computing T_2, T_4, Q_S, Q_R, W, and the system's thermal efficiency

$$E = \frac{\text{net work out of turbine}}{\text{heat energy into reactor}}$$

from the quantities T_1, T_3, P_i, and P_o are

$$T_2 = T_1\left(\frac{P_o}{P_i}\right)^{0.4} \qquad T_4 = T_3\left(\frac{P_i}{P_o}\right)^{0.4}$$

$$Q_S = 5.1926(T_3 - T_2) \qquad Q_R = 5.1926(T_4 - T_1)$$

$$W = Q_S - Q_R \qquad E = W/Q_S$$

Write a program that reads values into the linear arrays T1, T3, PI, and PO and computes corresponding values in the linear arrays T2, T4, QS, QR, W, and E using the equations above. The input process is to stop when a 0 is read into PI. The program is to then determine which of the input combinations produces the highest thermal efficiency, put this value in EMAX and the associated index in M, and produce a report of the following form:

TURBINE EFFICIENCY REPORT

T1	T3	PI	PO	T2	T4	QS	QR	W	E
.	.	.	.	.	.	.	.	.	.
.	.	.	.	.	.	.	.	.	.
.	.	.	.	.	.	.	.	.	.

(Columns of data)

MAXIMUM EFFICIENCY IS *(Value of EMAX)* AND OCCURS WHEN:

T1 = *(Value of T1(M))*
T3 = *(Value of T3(M))*
PI = *(Value of PI(M))*
PO = *(Value of PO(M))*

Test the program using the following data:

T1	T3	PI	PO
150.0	800.0	50.0	100.0
150.0	800.0	70.0	200.0
200.0	800.0	50.0	100.0
200.0	800.0	70.0	200.0
150.0	1000.0	50.0	100.0
150.0	1000.0	70.0	200.0
200.0	1000.0	50.0	100.0
200.0	1000.0	70.0	200.0

7. The formula for computing the monthly payment on an automobile loan is

$$R = A \frac{X}{1200} \left[\frac{1}{1 - \dfrac{1}{\left(1 + \dfrac{X}{1200}\right)^{12N}}} \right]$$

where A is the total amount of the loan, X the annual percentage interest, and N the number of years over which the loan is to be paid. Note that if P is the principal at the beginning of a month, the payment at the end of the month will be divided as follows:

$$\text{interest} = B = P\frac{X}{1200} \qquad \text{toward principal} = C = R - B$$

and the principal for the succeeding month will be the old principal minus C. Because the last payment must account for small errors that accrue due to the subtractions, it may be slightly different from the other payments.

Write a program that will input A, X, and N; print

```
         PAYMENT BREAKDOWN
   INTEREST      TO PRIN.      BALANCE
```

compute monthly values for B, C, and P and print them under their proper headings; compute R, the total amount of interest paid (TI), and the total amount paid (TP); and print:

```
INTEREST = (Value of X) %
ORIGINAL LOAN = $(Value of A)
NUMBER OF YEARS = (Value of N)
MONTHLY PAYMENT = $(Value of R)
TOTAL INTEREST = $(Value of TI)
TOTAL AMOUNT PAID = $(Value of TP)
```

Test the program using the data:

$$X = 12 \qquad A = 10000 \qquad N = 3$$

8. If a person puts P dollars a month in a savings account and the money draws X percent annual interest compounded monthly, the balance B at the end of N months will be

$$B = P\left[\frac{(1 + A)^N - 1}{A}\right]$$

where

$$A = \frac{X}{1200}$$

Write a program that will input values for P, L, X1, X2, and M $\leq$ 5; compute the balance at the end of each year for L years for each of the interest rates

$$X = X1 + I*(X2 - X1)/M \qquad I = 0, \ldots, M$$

and print a report of the following form:

	SAVINGS ACCUMULATION	
NO. OF YEARS	INTEREST RATES	
	(Lowest Interest rate) · · ·	*(Highest interest rate)*
(Column indicating years)	*(Column of balances for lowest rate)* · · ·	*(Column of balances for highest rate)*

Test the program using

$$P = 100.0 \qquad L = 40 \qquad X1 = 5.0 \qquad X2 = 15.0 \qquad M = 5$$

9. The slope-intercept form of a straight line is

$$Y = PX + Q$$

It frequently occurs in business, engineering, and science that straight lines are used to approximate experimental data. In such situations, a set of experimental data points

(X_i, Y_i), $i = 1, \ldots, N$, are known and what is desired are the slope P and intercept Q of the line that best fits the data. It can be shown that the slope and intercept of the line that minimizes the sum of the squares of the vertical distances between the data points and the line can be found by solving the equations

$$AP + BQ = E$$
$$CP + DQ = F$$

where

$$A = \sum_{i=1}^{N} X_i^2 \qquad B = \sum_{i=1}^{N} X_i$$

$$C = \sum_{i=1}^{N} X_i \qquad D = N$$

$$E = \sum_{i=1}^{N} X_i Y_i \qquad F = \sum_{i=1}^{N} Y_i$$

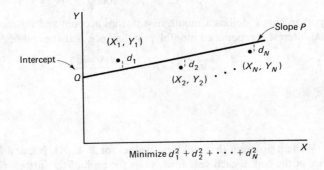

Minimize $d_1^2 + d_2^2 + \cdots + d_N^2$

Suppose that an ion is known to be traveling at a constant velocity along a straight line and that its velocity and starting point are to be approximated from N data points. Write a program that will read a value into N and print

INSUFFICIENT DATA

if $N < 2$. Otherwise, N time–distance pairs are to be read (one pair per record) into arrays X (time) and Y (distance), the optimal P and Q are to be computed using the equations above, and the following report is to be printed:

INPUT DATA

TIMES	DISTANCES
(Column of values	(Column of values
from X array)	from Y array)
.	.
.	.
.	.

VELOCITY = (Value of P)
STARTING POINT = (Value of Q)

Test the program using the data:

X	Y
1.0	0.10
1.2	0.25
1.4	0.41
1.6	0.53
1.8	0.69
2.0	0.86

3

USING THE COMPUTER
TO SOLVE PROBLEMS

The purpose of a computer is to solve problems. These problems may be scientific, business-related, or they may involve using the computer to perform a repetitive task. The programmer's function is to state the problem precisely, analyze it, decide on a method to solve it, and finally put the solution into a form that the computer can understand. When attacking a problem, the programmer must be concerned with what programming tools are present and how these programming tools should be used to solve the problem at hand.

The purpose of this chapter is to introduce the general approach to solving problems using a computer. The four major steps in readying a program for use are:

1. Analyzing the problem and deciding on how it is to be solved.
2. Writing the program.
3. Testing and debugging the program.
4. Documenting the program.

This chapter is concerned with steps 1 and 2, step 3 is discussed in Sec. 4-4 and Chap. 10, and step 4 is considered in Sec. 4-5 and Chap. 9. It should be noted that step 4 is not entirely a distinct step because some documenting is done while carrying out steps 1 and 2.

The programs considered in Chap. 2 were short and required little planning. Most programs, however, are much more complex and must be subdivided into manageable tasks and subtasks before they can be fully comprehended and solved. Each task or subtask may be a distinct program unit, such as a subprogram, or may be a program segment within a program unit, but in either case the subprogram or program segment is called a *program module*, or simply a *module*. The primary steps in analyzing and writing any program are to first break the problem into tasks and then to write the module for solving each task. Because modules are normally subprograms, the subdivision of a program cannot be discussed in detail until Chap. 6, but in order to provide an overall picture of how programs are designed a brief introduction to modularizing programs is given here.

This chapter consists of two sections. The first section discusses the procedure for analyzing a problem and putting its solution into a form that can be easily programmed. Included in this discussion is the introduction of two important programming aids, hierarchical diagrams and pseudocode. The second section considers the permissible ways of organizing the structure of a module so that it is relatively error free and understandable. This section examines the elementary control structures that have been widely accepted as the fundamental building blocks for constructing computer programs. How these elementary structures are put into FORTRAN statements is considered in the first three sections of Chap. 4.

3-1 PROBLEM FORMULATION

In Chap. 2 all the examples and exercises were short, usually involving only one simple task. Most practical problems are much more complex and may require tens of thousands of statements to program. Fortunately, large programs are composites of several small tasks that, once defined, can be programmed individually without worrying about the problem as a whole. It is this modularity of computer programs that reduces them to a manageable level, a level that permits the human mind to concentrate on blocks of fewer than 100 statements at a time.

The purpose of this section is to indicate an overall procedure for preparing a problem for computer solution. At this point the reader should not be at all concerned with how the problem is going to be put into a computer language, but concentrate on how to identify the important facts concerning the problem, dissect it into its major components, and then formulate its solution.

The principal steps needed to prepare a problem for computer solution are:

1. State the problem precisely.
2. Outline the overall solution, break it into tasks, and decide on the data formats and names of the principal variables.
3. Decide on a method for solving each task.
4. Give an informal step-by-step procedure for solving each task.
5. Write a program segment or subprogram for solving each task using abbreviated English-language statements that are compatible with the high-level language features discussed in Sec. 1-9.

It seems obvious that one must be able to state a problem precisely before attempting to solve it, yet all too often a programmer will proceed to write a program without really understanding the problem the program is to solve. A good problem statement should include a description of the necessities, inputs, outputs, and result specifications (e.g., accuracy), as well as a clear statement of the basic processing that must be accomplished.

After the problem has been stated as clearly as possible, it should be divided into tasks and subtasks. This process normally results in a hierarchical structure with one task controlling the principal subtasks and each of these subtasks controlling sub-subtasks, and so on. In order to visualize the structure decided upon, the programmer should illustrate it using a block-oriented figure, called a *hierarchical diagram*, which is constructed as shown in Fig. 3-1. Hierarchical diagrams summarize

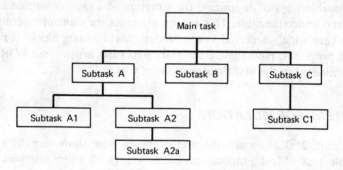

FIGURE 3-1 *Typical hierarchical diagram.*

the relationships between tasks and subtasks so that they can easily be studied and modified by the programmer and others involved in a project. They look very much like and serve the same purpose as organizational charts for corporations. The main task would correspond to the president of the corporation, the principal subtasks to the vice-presidents, and so on. A hierarchical diagram shows the chain of subordination that exists among the tasks and subtasks just as an organizational chart indicates the chain of command within a corporation.

As one becomes experienced in programming it will become apparent that in subdividing a problem into tasks, the inputting and outputting of information within a task and the passing of information between tasks are primary considerations. Usually, it is best to assign separate tasks for inputting and outputting each major block of information. The reason for this is that detailed descriptions of the information and how it is formatted are required, and both the documentation and the program are easier to understand if these descriptions and the corresponding program segments are in readily identifiable sections.

With regard to passing information between tasks, it is good to define the tasks so that the information being communicated is limited to well-defined and related groups. The amount of information that must be sent from one task to another is referred to as the *data coupling* between the two tasks. In deciding whether or not a task should be broken into two tasks, the data coupling between the resulting tasks should be studied carefully. Generally, a problem should be broken into tasks in such a way that the data coupling is minimized. Modularization and coupling are discussed further in Chaps. 6 and 9.

Once the tasks have been determined, a method for solving each task can be decided upon. A procedure for solving a specific task is called an *algorithm*. If the task is mainly for inputting or outputting data, both the external and internal formats of the data must be resolved. (The external format is the placement of the data on the I-O medium—cards, paper, and so on—and the internal format is how it is stored in memory—integer, real, and so on.) If the task is primarily computational, the numerical technique, or algorithm, to be used must be determined. In either case, decisions must be made regarding how the task is to receive and/or pass on the data it shares with the other tasks with which it must communicate.

After the decisions concerning the tasks have been made, the programmer is ready to solve each task. This may be done in two steps, the first consisting of an informal step-by-step description of the algorithm. The second step is to reduce the informal description to abbreviated statements that are compatible with the features of high-level languages. Such statements constitute what is called *pseudocode*. Pseudocode statements may look similar to the statements of the high-level language being employed, but are not constructed using the syntax of any particular language. The similarity between the pseudocode and the language being used makes the translation from the pseudocode to the language almost mechanical.

The development of these two steps may be aided by a flowchart which graphically depicts the algorithm being formulated. The flowchart may reflect every detail, so that there is more or less a one-to-one correspondence between the flowchart symbols and the high-level language statements in the final program, or may include blocks that describe more complicated actions. The flowcharting detail used at this stage is left to the judgment of the programmer.

An experienced programmer may write the pseudocode directly and not bother with the intermediate step-by-step informal description. Informal descriptions are solely for the programmer's benefit and are to help construct the algorithms for the various tasks. Normally, no one else will read these descriptions and the programmer may write them in his or her personal style, a style that is most comfortable to the programmer. In any event, for all but the simplest problems the pseudocode should be written before attempting to write the high-level language program. The value of pseudocode is twofold:

1. It permits the programmer to write a solution in a computer-related language without worrying about the precise syntax of a particular high-level language.
2. It forces a programmer to organize his or her thoughts in a computer-oriented way.

As an example of a complete, albeit simple program, let us study the problem:

A program INTPOL is needed to compute functional values according to the graph given in Fig. 3-2. The program is to first print the headings

X-VALUES   Y-VALUES

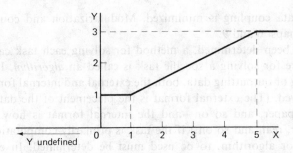

FIGURE 3-2 *Value of Y as a function of X for the linear interpolation example.*

It is then to read a value into X and, if the value is less than zero, the program is to print

PROCESSING IS COMPLETE

and stop. Otherwise, the program is to compute a value for Y, print the values of X and Y, and read another value into X. The process is to continue until a negative value for X is input.

After stating the problem, the next step is to break it into tasks. Although the problem at hand is too simple to require a hierarchical diagram, one is given in Fig. 3-3 for illustrative purposes. The diagram shows that the main task prints the headings, prints the termination message

PROCESSING IS COMPLETE

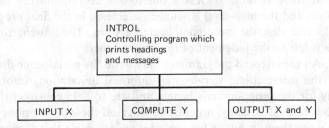

FIGURE 3-3 *Hierarchical diagram for the linear interpolation problem.*

and contains the subtasks for inputting the values of X, computing the values of Y, and outputting the values of X and Y. In particular, note that the loop that is implied by the statement of the problem is not indicated by the hierarchical diagram. Hierarchical diagrams show only the organizational aspects of a program; the control aspects are left to flowcharts.

An informal description of a solution to the problem being considered is:

1. Print the headings

X-VALUES   Y-VALUES

2. Read a value into X.

3. If $X < 0$, go to step 9; otherwise, continue.
4. If $X < 1$, set $Y = 1$ and go to step 7; otherwise, continue.
5. If $X < 5$, set $Y = 1 + (1/2)(X - 1)$, and go to step 7; otherwise, continue.
6. Set $Y = 3$.
7. Print X and Y.
8. Return to step 2.
9. Print 'PROCESSING IS COMPLETE'.
10. Stop.

As indicated above, there are no rules for writing these informal verbal descriptions because their value lies in the ease with which they can be written. Their purpose is to allow the programmer to formulate a solution without being burdened with rules.

Pseudocode for solving this problem is:

```
                START INTPOL
                Print 'X-VALUES     Y-VALUES'
             2  Read X
                IF  (X < 0.0)  GO TO 9
                   IF  (X < 1.0)  THEN
                              Y = 1.0 (and go to second ENDIF)
                      ELSE
                         IF  (X < 5.0)  THEN
                                    Y = 1.0 + 0.5*(X - 1.0)
                                        (and go to first ENDIF)
                            ELSE
                                 Y = 3.0
                         ENDIF
                   ENDIF
                Print X and Y
                GO TO 2
             9  Print 'PROCESSING IS COMPLETE'
                STOP
```

A flowchart corresponding to this pseudocode is given in Fig. 3-4. The connector labels 2 and 9 are optional. A programmer may insert at least some labels if the flowchart is related to a given set of pseudocode and the pseudcode includes corresponding labels. Just which labels should be included and which could be left out depends on their importance to understanding the program. Usually, not all of the labels would be included because they tend to clutter up the flowchart and obscure the more important points.

The parenthetical comments "go to ENDIF" are not normally included in the pseudocode, but are understood. They indicate that the process should continue at the ENDIF corresponding to the IF currently being considered. In the problem at hand this has the effect of continuing the process at the second print statement.

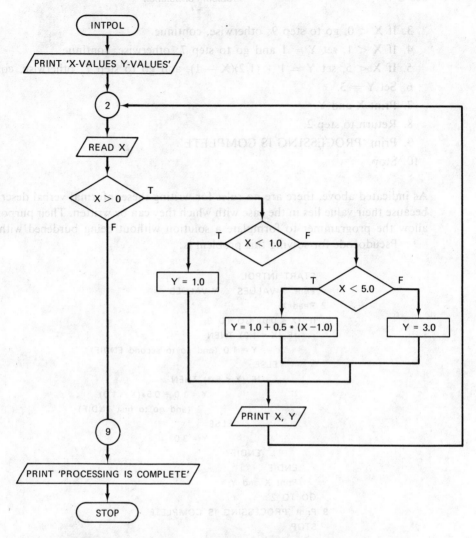

FIGURE 3-4 *Flowchart of the solution of the linear interpolation problem.*

Once the pseudocode is finished, the program analysis and development phase is complete and all that remains is the translation of the pseudocode into the high-level language. For well-designed languages this is a straightforward process, but for others, such as the older versions of FORTRAN, it is more awkward. The problem with this awkwardness is not that it consumes more time, but that it increases the chance for errors.

For a more complex example, let us suppose that a projectile follows a parabolic arc and that its firing point and landing point are to be found by measuring the projectile's position at three points on the arc. If the arc is described by the equation

$$Ax^2 + Bx + C = y$$

where x and y are the horizontal and vertical positions, respectively, and (x_1, y_1), (x_2, y_2), (x_3, y_3) are the three measured points on the arc, then A, B, and C can be found by solving the simultaneous equations

$$Ax_1^2 + Bx_1 + C = y_1$$
$$Ax_2^2 + Bx_2 + C = y_2$$
$$Ax_3^2 + Bx_3 + C = y_3$$

After A, B, and C have been determined, the firing and landing points can be found by using the quadratic formula to solve the equation

$$Ax^2 + Bx + C = 0$$

A more precise statement of the problem is:

> The program is to compute the firing and landing points of a projectile assuming that the trajectory is described by the quadratic equation
>
> $$Ax^2 + Bx + C = y$$
>
> and that three points on the arc, (x_1, y_1), (x_2, y_2), and (x_3, y_3), are known. It is to read in the three points, use these points to determine the coefficients A, B, and C, compute the x-coordinates XF and XL of the firing (left root) and landing (right root) points, and print out the results in the form
>
> THE FIRING POINT IS (*Value of XF*)
> THE LANDING POINT IS (*Value of XL*)
>
> If, while solving for A, B, and C, the equations are found to be dependent, the program is to print out the message
>
> INCOMPATIBLE INPUT COORDINATES
>
> and stop.

Figure 3-5 gives a logical way of dividing the program into tasks. The program has been given the name TRAJCT and has been broken into four tasks, with one of these tasks having a subtask. The tasks are:

> INPUT—for inputting the three known points.
>
> SIMEQ—for solving the simultaneous equations to determine A, B, and C. It uses the subtask DEVAL to evaluate the necessary determinants. The task SIMEQ is to be a subprogram of TRAJCT and its subtask DEVAL is to be a subprogram of SIMEQ.
>
> QUAD—for solving the quadratic equation to determine XF and XL.
> OUTPUT—for outputting the results.

The next step is to decide on a method for solving each task. Except for SIMEQ, the needed algorithms are obvious and there is little to decide. There are

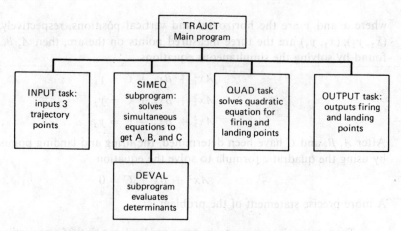

FIGURE 3-5 *Division of the trajectory problem into tasks.*

several ways of solving simultaneous equations, however. The most straightforward method is to use determinants and that is the algorithm assumed here. (Another well-known algorithm, which the reader is probably familiar with and which happens to be much better for larger numbers of equations, is Gaussian elimination—see Programming Problem 4 at the end of Chap. 6.)

An example of an informal step-by-step statement of a procedure for solving a task is demonstrated by considering the subprogram SIMEQ:

1. Form the array

$$D = \begin{bmatrix} x_1^2 & x_1 & 1 \\ x_2^2 & x_2 & 1 \\ x_3^2 & x_3 & 1 \end{bmatrix}$$

2. Use DEVAL to evaluate the determinant of the array given in step 1 and put the result in DET.

3. If DET = 0, print

INCOMPATIBLE INPUT COORDINATES

and go to step 13.

4. Otherwise, form an array D1 by replacing the first column of array D with the array

$$Y = \begin{bmatrix} y_1 \\ y_2 \\ y_3 \end{bmatrix}$$

5. Use DEVAL to put the determinant of D1 into DET1.

6. Set A = DET1/DET.

7. Form an array D2 by replacing the second column of D with Y.

8. Use DEVAL to put the determinant of D2 into DET2.

9. Set B = DET2/DET.

10. Form an array D3 by replacing the third column of D with Y.

11. Use DEVAL to put the determinant of D3 into DET3.

12. Set C = DET3/DET.

13. Return to the main program TRAJCT.

Presumably, the main program would also test DET and branch to the end of the program if DET = 0.

The pseudocode for SIMEQ is

```
START SIMEQ
Form array D
CALL DEVAL to evaluate the determinant DET of array D
IF (DET = 0) THEN
        Print "INCOMPATIBLE INPUT COORDINATES"
    ELSE
        Form array D1
        CALL DEVAL to evaluate the determinant DET1 of D1
        Set A = DET1/DET
        Form array D2
        CALL DEVAL to evaluate the determinant DET2 of D2
        Set B = DET2/DET
        Form array D3
        CALL DEVAL to evaluate the determinant DET3 of D3
        Set C = DET3/DET
ENDIF
RETURN to the main program TRAJCT
```

A flowchart of the subprogram SIMEQ is shown in Fig. 3-6. Note especially the use of the terminal symbols at the beginning and end of the subprogram, and the predefined process symbol to indicate a call to the subprogram DEVAL. The terminal symbol at the beginning of the subprogram contains the name of the subprogram and a list of the variables that must be input to or output from the subprogram. From the predefined process symbols which indicate DEVAL subprogram calls, it is seen that such calls must also include a list of the variables to be communicated. Communication between programs and subprograms is discussed in detail in Chap. 6.

The examples above were chosen because their simplicity permitted us to emphasize the major software design steps without becoming immersed in explanations of detail. Computers, however, are normally used to attack much more complicated problems and we will now consider how steps 1 and 2 of the design procedure are applied to such problems.

Suppose that a wholesaling company has a computer system which includes a file named INVNT that contains a record for each item in the company's inventory. The record corresponding to each item includes an identifying number, the quantity

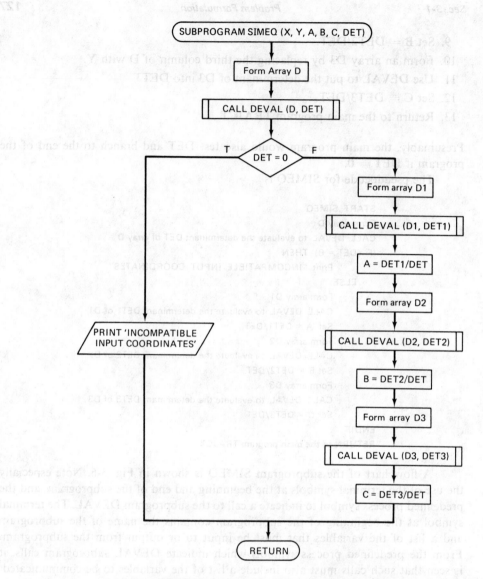

FIGURE 3-6 *Flowchart of the subprogram SIMEQ.*

presently in stock, the cost, the price to be charged, and other important information about the item. The company wishes to add to its system an automatic updating, invoicing, and ordering program. The program is to be used by the manager of the warehouse, who is to communicate with the system through a CRT terminal and a printer. A preliminary statement of the problem might be:

The program must be capable of receiving an item number typed at the manager's CRT terminal, searching the file INVNT for the corresponding record, and displaying the contents of the record on the terminal. If the item is not found, an error message is to be sent to the terminal; otherwise, after the requested record is found, it is to be displayed on the terminal. The program then waits for a command which indicates whether a shipment is being received or sent and the quantity to be added to or subtracted from the inventory, respectively. If the shipment is outgoing, the program is automatically to check the quantity presently available and output a message to the user if the number in stock is insufficient. In this case the inventory quantity is to be left unchanged and the program is to wait for a new command. If the quantity is sufficient but is below a predetermined level (which is also stored in the record) and no order is pending, the program is to ask the user to put an order form in the printer and then type the quantity to be ordered on the terminal. Upon getting a response from the user, the program is to print the order form and note the pending order in the record. If the quantity to be shipped is on hand, the program is to ask the user to put an invoice in the printer and then type READY on the terminal. The program is then to print the invoice.

Accompanying this statement should be detailed descriptions of the formats of the file INVNT and its records, the order form, and the invoice form. Also, any restrictions on the lengths or formats of the messages to be output to the user or commands to be received from the user should be noted. As a project develops, questions usually arise which necessitate a clarification or restatement of some aspects of a problem; however, this does not excuse the programmer from carefully summarizing the problem before proceeding to solve it.

Figure 3-7 gives a logical way of dividing the program into tasks. The main

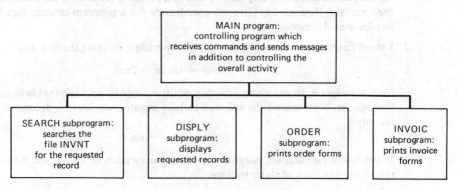

FIGURE 3-7 *Division of the inventory program into tasks.*

program would be responsible for receiving commands and dispensing messages, and for calling the subprograms as they are needed. The main program would be accompanied by four major subprograms:

SEARCH—for searching for requested records.

DISPLY—for formatting and displaying a record on the CRT terminal.

ORDER—for formatting and printing an order form.

INVOIC—for formatting and printing an invoice form.

The main program would communicate with the subprograms by giving them the information they need to perform their tasks and, in the case of the search subprogram, by receiving the record information from it. Once it is understood exactly what information must be passed and what form it is to be in, different programmers could simultaneously work on the different tasks. For a program of this size, the hierarchical diagram may be broken down even more by associating sub-subtasks with the major subtasks (e.g., SEARCH would probably have a separate subprogram to perform its input).

EXERCISES

1. It is known that for x in the interval 0 through $\pi/2$ radians,

$$\sin x \approx x - \frac{x^3}{6} + \frac{x^5}{120} - \frac{x^7}{5040} + \frac{x^9}{362,880} - \frac{x^{11}}{39,916,800}$$

to within seven significant figures, and that

$$\sin x = \begin{cases} \sin (\pi - x) & \frac{\pi}{2} < x \leq \pi \\ -\sin (x - \pi) & \pi < x \leq 2\pi \end{cases}$$

Give an informal step-by-step description of a program for finding the sine of any angle in the interval 0 through 2π. Give the pseudocode for a program module that follows this step-by-step description.

2. Extend Exercise 1 to accommodate any positive angle by using the fact that

$$\sin x = \sin (x - 2\pi n)$$

for any integer n, to reduce an arbitrary positive angle to an angle that is in the interval 0 through 2π. Now extend the solution to take negative angles into account by using the identity

$$\sin (-x) = -\sin x$$

3. In the following diagram, point $P = (x, y)$ is the location of a ship, and points $(0, 0)$ and $(10, 0)$ are locations of shore stations.

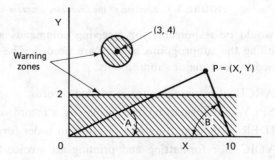

Suppose that the shore stations are able to measure the angles A and B and use a computer to determine the coordinates x and y. The computer is to output the coordinates and, if $y < 2$ or P is within 1 of the point $(3, 4)$, it is to print

SEND WARNING TO SHIP

From the law of sines it can be shown that

$$x = \frac{10 \cos A \sin B}{\sin (\pi - A - B)} \qquad y = x \tan A$$

Restate the problem in your own words, precisely indicating the inputs, outputs, and necessary processing. Break the problem solution into tasks and give an informal step-by-step description of the algorithm for solving each task. (One sentence is adequate to describe the input and output tasks.) Give the pseudocode for solving each task and then put all the pseudocode together to form an overall solution.

4. Give a more precise statement of the following problem:

> Write a program that will update the principal amounts of all the savings accounts in a bank. The savings account records are in a file SAVACC on a mass storage device and are referenced by savings account number. Interest for all accounts is 5.25% annually, compounded daily.

Make logical assumptions about withdrawals, deposits, error messages, and error correction. Assume that additions of new accounts and deletions of old accounts are made by a separate program and are not your concern. Outline the solution and break it into tasks, and draw a hierarchical diagram.

3-2　THE ELEMENTARY CONTROL STRUCTURES

When solving a problem of any type one must develop a structure for the solution. This is true for a student who is answering a question on a mathematics test as well as for a government that is designing a space project or a tax collection system. If the problem is to be solved with a computer, the characteristics of the computer must be taken into account, particularly those characteristics related to branching and the sequential nature of computer programs. If a structure emphasizes the possible paths that exist within a solution, it is called a *control structure* or *construct*. Experience and the constraints of computers have shown that computer solutions have structures that can be built from a small set of elementary control structures. To standardize the documentation of computer programs and to facilitate the correction and maintenance of computer software in general, the set of elementary control structures used in computer work to indicate the flow of the solution has been reduced to those whose flowcharts are shown in Fig. 3-8. Note that all five of these structures have only one entry point and one departure point. This is the attribute that allows them to be pieced together to form complex programs without producing a hard-to-read overall structure.

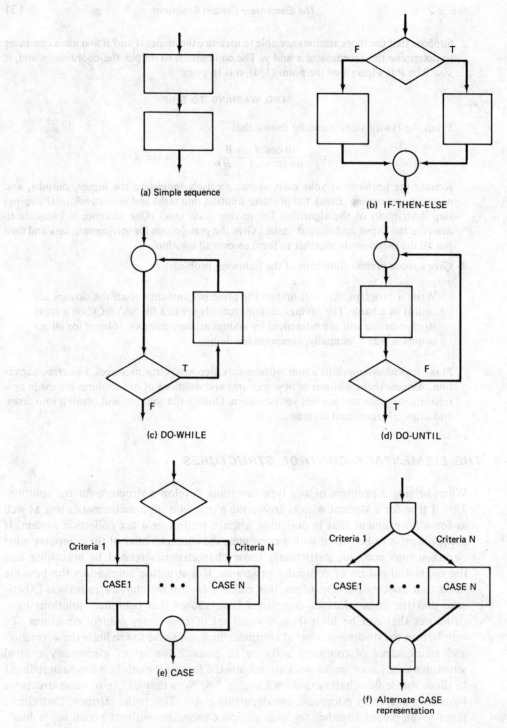

(a) Simple sequence

(b) IF-THEN-ELSE

(c) DO-WHILE

(d) DO-UNTIL

Criteria 1   Criteria N

CASE1   ...   CASE N

(e) CASE

Criteria 1   Criteria N

CASE1   ...   CASE N

(f) Alternate CASE
representation

FIGURE 3-8 *Elementary control structures.*

Some of the control structures shown in Fig. 3-8 have already been used in the examples given in the preceding material. Although they may seem unimportant at this point, they have proved to be a valuable tool in computer programming and will appear throughout the remainder of the book. Their definitions are:

Simple Sequence—A *simple sequence* is the successive performance of two or more processing steps. The state of the solution after the first step is completed is the state just prior to the execution of the second step, and so on.

IF-THEN-ELSE—The *IF-THEN-ELSE* structure is one in which a condition is given; if the condition is true one set of actions is taken, and if it is false a different set of actions is taken. Both paths return to a common point in the solution after the selected actions are completed. The connector symbol at the common point is optional.

DO-WHILE—A *DO-WHILE* structure is a pretesting loop in which a given condition is tested; if it is true, specified actions are taken and the condition is tested again. The given actions are repeated over and over as long as the condition is true. When the condition becomes false, the loop is exited. Clearly, the action in the loop must modify at least one of the variables in the condition; otherwise, the loop would be repeated ad infinitum.

DO-UNTIL—A *DO-UNTIL* structure is similar to a DO-WHILE structure except that it is a post-testing loop in which the actions are executed before the condition is tested; therefore, they are always executed at least once. Also, the loop is repeated until the condition is true (instead of false), at which time the loop is exited. Once again, at least one of the variables in the condition must be changed within the loop if exiting is to be possible.

CASE—The *CASE* structure includes a decision that may have more than two outcomes. Normally, a symbol or notation identifying the decision is given inside the diamond and the circumstances that cause a particular path to be taken are noted beside the line representing the path. All paths return to a common point. An alternative representation of the CASE structure which uses special decision and connector symbols is shown in Fig. 3-8(f). Although this representation is common, the one shown in Fig. 3-8(e) is used in this book.

It should be understood that the process blocks represented by the rectangles in Fig. 3-8 may themselves involve one or more of the elementary control structures. For example, Fig. 3-9 shows a DO-UNTIL structure that includes an IF-THEN-ELSE structure and is itself part of a simple sequence.

As an example, consider the control structure of the solution of the quadratic equation

$$Ax^2 + Bx + C = 0$$

given in Fig. 3-10. From the figure it is seen that the overall control structure is of the IF-THEN-ELSE type. The ELSE path contains a CASE structure and the THEN path contains a second IF-THEN-ELSE structure. It often occurs that the THEN

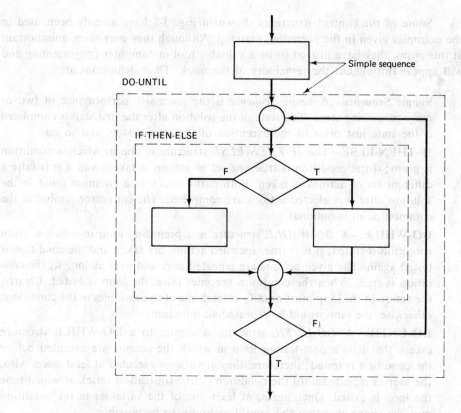

FIGURE 3-9 *Example showing elementary control structures within elementary control structures.*

or ELSE path will include an IF-THEN-ELSE structure. When this happens the result is called a *nested IF-THEN-ELSE structure*.

Certainly, control structures that are not composites of the elementary structures can be derived and used. One such control structure is shown in Fig. 3-11. Conversely, it has been shown that computer solutions could always be found if the programmer were restricted to the control structures given in Fig. 3-8(a) through (c). After an accumulation of thousands of person-years of experience, however, it has been determined that all five of the elementary control structures shown in Fig. 3-8 should be permitted when developing computer solutions, and other control structures should be used only after careful consideration of the alternatives. The five elementary control structures are simple and make the resulting computer programs easy to understand. They also lead to a modularity that is amenable to change.

The flowcharts of the elementary control structures do not need to be drawn exactly as shown in Fig. 3-8. For example, the IF-THEN-ELSE configuration may be put into the form shown in Fig. 3-12(a), or if the ELSE path requires no action, into the form given in Fig. 3-12(b). Also, as shown for the CASE structure given in Fig. 3-12(c), the flowcharts are often drawn horizontally instead of vertically.

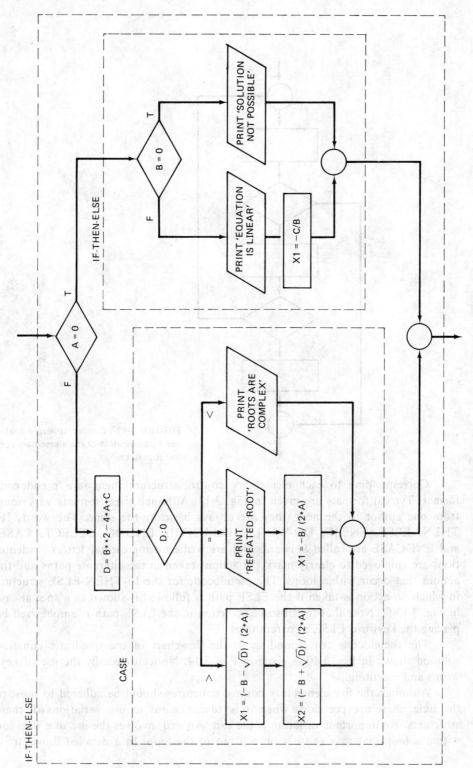

FIGURE 3-10 Flowchart of a solution to the quadratic equation problem.

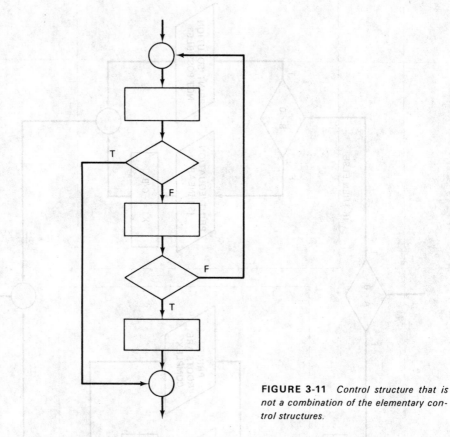

FIGURE 3-11 *Control structure that is not a combination of the elementary control structures.*

Corresponding to each elementary control structure there is a pseudocode format. Typical formats are given in Fig. 3-13. Although these formats vary some from one author to the next, they are always basically the same. The words IF, THEN, ELSE, ENDIF, DO-WHILE, DO-UNTIL, ENDDO, SELECT, CASE, and ENDCASE are called *keywords* and are written using capital letters. Indentations are employed to clearly mark the actions taken in the alternate paths and the actions that occur within loops. The pseudocode for the IF-THEN-ELSE structure in which no action is taken if the ELSE path is followed is shown as a special case in Fig. 3-13(f). Note that the absence of action in the ELSE path is emphasized by placing the keyword ELSE in parentheses.

The pseudocode corresponding to the flowchart of the quadratic equation solution shown in Fig. 3-10 is given in Fig. 3-14. Notice especially the use of keywords and indenting.

Although the five elementary control structures should be adhered to most of the time, there are occasions when it is advantageous to use variations of these structures. An important variation is the exit. An *exit* involves the use of a decision within a loop that may cause a branch out of the loop. In a detailed flowchart it

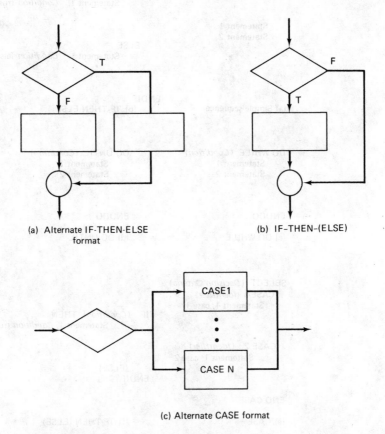

(a) Alternate IF-THEN-ELSE
format

(b) IF-THEN-(ELSE)

(c) Alternate CASE format

FIGURE 3-12 *Alternative flowcharts of the elementary control structures.*

would be indicated by the usual decision symbol (a diamond), but in a not-so-detailed flowchart it may be represented graphically as shown in Fig. 3-15(a).

The accepted definition of an exit requires that the branched to point be either the point at the beginning of the loop, as shown in Fig. 3-15(b), or the point immediately following the loop, as shown in Fig. 3-15(c). In the first case the resulting structure is called a *cycle structure* and in the second it is called an *escape structure*. An exit may be made from a path in either an IF-THEN-ELSE or CASE structure. Even though the definition of an escape does not permit any statements between the end of the loop and the "branched to" statement, most programmers do sometimes place a few statements between these two points. Therefore, in this book the definition of an exit is extended to include the structure shown in Fig. 3-15(d). However, *no more than two or three statements* should be placed between the end of the loop and the "branched to" point because a larger number of statements would make it difficult to identify the overall exit structure and its component processing segments.

Most programming experts admit the importance of allowing exits but agree

```
                                        IF  (Condition)  THEN
                                            Statement 1,  Condition true
                                                    .
        Statement 1                                 .
        Statement 2                                 .
                .                       ELSE
                .                           Statement 1,  Condition false
                .                                   .
                                                    .
                                                    .
        (a) Simple sequence             ENDIF       (b) IF-THEN-ELSE


        DO-WHILE  (Condition)           DO-UNTIL  (Condition)
            Statement 1                     Statement 1
            Statement 2                     Statement 2
                .                               .
                .                               .
                .                               .
        ENDDO                           ENDDO

        (c) DO-WHILE                    (d) DO-UNTIL


        SELECT  (Decision Criteria)
            CASE 1 (Identifier)
                Statement 1, case 1
                    .                   IF  (Condition)  THEN
                    .                       Statement 1, Condition true
                    .                               .
            CASE 2  (Identifier)                    .
                Statement 1, case 2                 .
                    .                       (ELSE)
                    .                   ENDIF
                    .
        END CASE

        (e) CASE                        (f)  IF-THEN-(ELSE)
```

FIGURE 3-13 *Pseudocode formats for the elementary control structures.*

```
IF   (A = 0)   THEN
        IF   (B = 0)   THEN
                Write "SOLUTION NOT POSSIBLE"
        ELSE
                Write "EQUATION IS LINEAR"
                X1 = -C/B
        ENDIF
ELSE
        D = B**2 - 4*A*C
        SELECT (Compare D with 0)
                CASE (D > 0)
                        X1 = (-B -√(D))/(2 * A)
                        X2 = (-B +√(D))/(2 * A)
                CASE  (D = 0)
                        Write "REPEATED ROOT"
                        X1 = -B/ (2*A)
                CASE  (D < 0)
                        Write  "IMAGINARY ROOTS"
        ENDCASE
ENDIF
```

FIGURE 3-14 *Pseudocode corresponding to the flowchart of the quadratic equation solution shown in Fig. 3-10.*

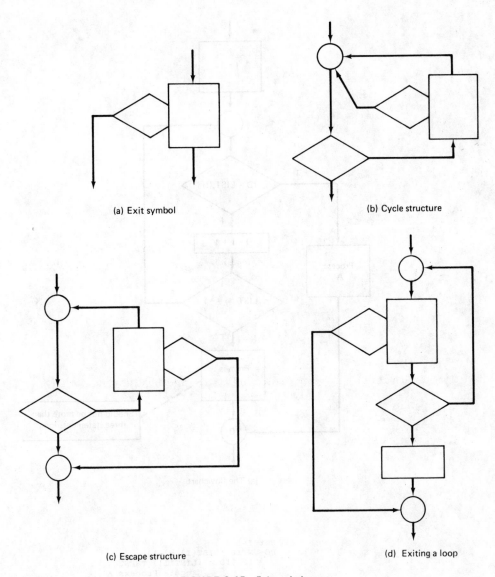

(a) Exit symbol

(b) Cycle structure

(c) Escape structure

(d) Exiting a loop

FIGURE 3-15 *Exit variations.*

that they should be used sparingly, and some argue that they should be used only in limited ways. The extension of the exit submitted here is generally shunned, but is sometimes used even by those who dislike it. In certain situations the alternative to this extension is to use a flag. It is the authors' contention that when the processing following the loop is short, the flag is an unnecessary complication.

As an application of the exit, consider the problem of consecutively searching the entries in an array LIST until an entry is found that matches the contents of ID.

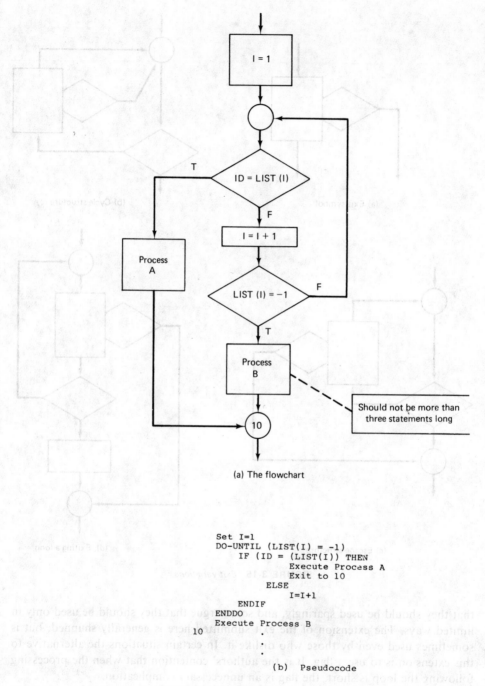

(a) The flowchart

```
Set I=1
DO-UNTIL (LIST(I) = -1)
    IF (ID = (LIST(I)) THEN
            Execute Process A
            Exit to 10
        ELSE
            I=I+1
    ENDIF
ENDDO
Execute Process B
10 .
   .
   .
```

(b) Pseudocode

FIGURE 3-16 *Solution to the sequential search problem.*

Such a procedure is called a *sequential search*. Suppose that the last entry in LIST is known to be the only one equal to -1, and action A is to be executed if a match is found. If a match is not found, action B, which should not be more than two or three statements long, is to be executed. Both the flowchart and pseudocode for the needed program segment are given in Fig. 3-16.

EXERCISES

1. Give pseudocode and flowcharts for solving each of the problems:
   (a) Put the smaller of the two numbers contained in A and B into X and the larger of the two numbers into Y.
   (b) Put the smallest of the three numbers contained in A, B, and C into X, the next larger number into Y, and the largest number into Z.

2. Give a flowchart and the corresponding pseudocode for solutions to each problem given below. In each flowchart clearly indicate the control structures.
   (a) Reverse the order of the numbers in an array L.
   (b) Suppose that P contains a pressure and T contains a temperature. If $3.1*P - T$ is less than 10.0, the message

   INCREASE PRESSURE

   is to be written. Otherwise, the temperature is to be compared with 0.0 and

   INCREASE TEMPERATURE

   is to be written if T is less than 0.0, and

   OPERATION SATISFACTORY

   is to be written if T is greater than or equal to 0.0.
   (c) Read in N and write the multiples of 10 from 10 to $10*N$.
   (d) Sequentially search A(1) through A(10) for the number in X. Print "X FOUND" if X is found; otherwise, print "X NOT FOUND". Use only the elementary control structures with no exits. (*Hint:* Initially set a variable IFLAG to 0 and then set it to 1 if there is a match. At the bottom of the loop test IFLAG as well as the loop index.)
   (e) Read in 100 numbers one at a time, and keep a running total of the positive numbers in PSUM and of the negative numbers in NSUM; then write out PSUM and NSUM. If the sum of PSUM and NSUM is negative, also write

   DEFICIT

3. Give the pseudocode and a flowchart of a program that reads N grades into an array G, puts the number of grades less than 60 in ICNTF, puts the number of grades less than 70 but greater than or equal to 60 in ICNTD, puts the number of grades less than 80 but

greater than or equal to 70 in ICNTC, puts the number of grades less than 90 but greater than or equal to 80 in ICNTB, puts the number of grades greater than or equal to 90 in ICNTA, and then prints the counts beside appropriate descriptive phrases.

4. Suppose that for each employee, his or her name, pay rate, number of hours worked, and deductions are read in, the gross pay is computed according to the rules

> Less than 40 hours worked—straight time
> Between 40 and 50 hours worked—time and a half
> More than 50 hours worked—double time

and the taxes are computed according to the rules

> 10% tax for all income less than or equal to $400
> 20% tax for all income in excess of $400

A program is needed that will read in the name and pay data of each employee, compute the gross pay, compute the net pay, write out an itemized statement, and print the employee's check. The program is to process one employee at a time until a pay rate of 0 is detected, at which time it is to stop. Give a flowchart and the corresponding pseudocode of a solution to this problem.

5. Suppose that a company must fill out one of four different types of forms on each of its employees, depending on the classification of the employee. Some of the information, referred to as data set S, is to be in the same form for all employees, but data sets A, B, C, and D are to have forms that correspond to the employee's classification. Give the flowchart and pseudocode for a program that will read in the number of employees to be processed, read in data set S, and then, for each employee:
(1) Write the standard portion of the form.
(2) Read in the classification code (1 for A, 2 for B, etc.).
(3) Read in the remainder of the employee information (data set A, B, C, or D).
(4) Write out the remainder of the form.

PROGRAMMING PROBLEMS

1. Euclid's algorithm of finding the greatest common divisor of two integers M and N proceeds as follows:

$$K_1 = \text{remainder of } M/N$$
$$K_2 = \text{remainder of } N/K_1$$
$$K_3 = \text{remainder of } K_2/K_1$$

.
.
.

until a remainder of $K_n = 0$ is obtained, at which time K_{n-1} will be the greatest common divisor of M and N.

Give a preliminary informal description, a flowchart, and a set of pseudocode for a program which inputs two integers into M and N, computes the greatest common divisor of M and N and puts it in L, and prints

THE GREATEST COMMON DIVISOR OF *(Value of M)*
AND *(Value of N)* IS *(Value of L)*

Implement the program using FORTRAN 77. Test the program with the following pairs of integers:

$$M = 40, \quad N = 24; \quad M = 10, \quad N = 1; \quad M = 5, \quad N = 11$$

2. The rate of heat flow through a layered wall is

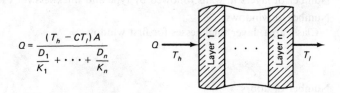

$$Q = \frac{(T_h - CT_l)A}{\dfrac{D_1}{K_1} + \cdots + \dfrac{D_n}{K_n}}$$

where:
$\quad Q$ = rate of heat flow (W)
$\quad T_l$ = lower temperature (K)
$\quad C$ = wind-chill factor
$\quad T_h$ = higher temperature (K)
$\quad D_i$ = thickness of ith layer (m)
$\quad K_i$ = thermal conductivity of ith layer (W/m·K)
$\quad A$ = area of wall (m²)

If a heated building is constructed of several walls of different compositions, the total rate at which heat would escape (and therefore the amount of heat needed to keep the building at a constant temperature) is

$$Q_T = Q_1 + \cdots + Q_n$$

where Q_j, $j = 1, 2, \ldots, n$, is the rate of heat loss through the jth type of surface.

Write a program that will compute the heat flow rate for a rectangular building. Assume that the roof is of a single type of construction, the walls are of a single type of construction except that they may include windows and doors, the windows may be either Class 1 (thermal—glass, air, glass layers) or Class 2 (nonthermal—glass layer only), the doors are all made of wood, and there is no heat loss through the floor. The permissible building materials are to be concrete, brick, wood, glass, dead air space, wallboard, insulation, and asphalt roofing, and their thermal conductivities are to be assigned within the program as follows:

$$K(1) = 0.80 \qquad \text{(concrete)}$$
$$K(2) = 0.60 \qquad \text{(brick)}$$
$$K(3) = 0.08 \qquad \text{(wood)}$$
$$K(4) = 0.80 \qquad \text{(glass)}$$
$$K(5) = 0.025 \qquad \text{(dead air)}$$
$$K(6) = 0.04 \qquad \text{(wallboard)}$$
$$K(7) = 0.01 \qquad \text{(insulation)}$$
$$K(8) = 0.04 \qquad \text{(asphalt roofing)}$$

The input is to be of the form

Height, length, and width of building
Number of layers in roof followed by type and thickness for each layer
Number of layers in walls followed by type and thickness for each layer
Number of windows
    Class, area, layer thicknesses for first window
       .
       .
       .
Number of doors
    Area and thickness for first door
       .
       .
       .
Values of T_h, T_l, and C

and the output is to be

$$\text{RATE OF HEAT FLOW} = (\textit{Value of } Q_T)$$

Before writing the program, draw a hierarchical diagram of the solution and generate the pseudocode for each module. Test the program with the following data:

4.0		30.0	20.0						
4	8	0.003	3	0.01	7	0.1	6	0.01	
3	2	0.1	5	0.1	6	0.01			
3									
1		2.0	0.002	0.01	0.002				
2		1.0	0.005						
1		3.0	0.002	0.01	0.002				
2									
		2.0	0.03						
		1.8	0.04						
300.0		275.0	0.98						

3. Assume that a person has a choice between two retirement plans. One is a tax-sheltered plan (plan 1) that is offered by an insurance company and the other is a personal investment plan (plan 2) that is not tax-sheltered. In both plans P_i before-tax dollars are invested at the end of the ith year for N consecutive years and then is withdrawn at the end of M consecutive years (starting with year $N + 1$) at the rate of X after-tax dollars per year. If the amount accumulated at the end of N years is A, then for plan 1 A and X are given by the equations

$$A_1 = (1 - D) \sum_{i=1}^{N} (1 + B)^{N-i} P_i \qquad X_1 + R = \frac{B}{1 - (1 + B)^{-M}} A_1$$

and for plan 2 they are given by the equations

$$A_2 = (1 - E) \left\{ \left[\sum_{i=1}^{N-1} (1 - T_i) P_i \prod_{j=i+1}^{N} [1 + (1 - T_j)C] \right] + (1 - T_N)P_N \right\}$$

$$X_2 = \frac{C}{1 - (1 + C)^{-M}} A_2$$

where: T_i = income tax rate on P_i and investment income for nonsheltered plan
R = income tax on retirement income for sheltered plan
B = annual interest on sheltered income
C = annual interest on nonsheltered income
D = investment fee for sheltered income
E = investment fee for nonsheltered income

Suppose that it is necessary to produce a report that will inform a group of people having various lengths of time before retirement which plan would be better for them. Write a program that will input K, M, B, C, D, and E and T(I) and P(I) for I = 1, ..., K. It is then to compute values for A and X for both plan 1 and plan 2 for N = 1, ..., K and put the results in the linear arrays A1, X1, A2, and X2. For plan 1 the income tax R must be computed according to the following tax table:

Before-tax income $(X_1 + R)$	Tax
≦$10,000	0.0
>$10,000 and ≦$20,000	10% of income over $10,000
>$20,000	$1,000 plus 20% of income over $20,000

The output report is to appear as follows:

```
        NO. OF RETIREMENT YEARS = (Value of M)
                PLAN 1 - SHELTERED
        INVESTMENT FEE = (Value of D)
        ANNUAL INTEREST = (Value of B)
                PLAN 2 - NONSHELTERED
        INVESTMENT FEE = (Value of E)
        ANNUAL INTEREST = (Value of C)
```

PLAN	NO. OF INVESTMENT YEARS	AMOUNT AT RETIREMENT	ANNUAL RETIREMENT INCOME
(*Plan giving highest return*)	(*Value of N for* $N = 1, \ldots, K$)	(*Amount for plan given in 1st col.*)	(*Income for plan given in 1st col.*)
.	.	.	.
.	.	.	.
.	.	.	.

Before writing the program, draw a hierarchical diagram and write pseudocode for each module. Test the program with the data

$$K = 40 \quad M = 10 \quad B = 0.10 \quad C = 0.14 \quad D = 0.04 \quad E = 0.02$$

and

$$P(I) = \$100 + 50I \qquad T(I) = \begin{cases} 0.30 & I \leq 20 \\ 0.40 & I > 20 \end{cases} \qquad I = 1, \ldots, K$$

4

EXTENSIONS OF BASIC FORTRAN

This chapter discusses several extensions to the basic FORTRAN statements given in Chap. 2. These extensions are designed to make the FORTRAN language more flexible and easier to use, and to facilitate the implementation of the elementary control structures introduced in Chap. 3. Although some of the extensions examined here are due to the FORTRAN 77 standard, some were part of the very earliest versions of FORTRAN, and others are even extensions of FORTRAN 77. Also contained in the chapter is some preliminary material on testing, correcting, and documenting programs.

Unfortunately, not all high-level languages were created with the elementary control structures in mind. FORTRAN came into being in the 1950s and the elementary control structures were only beginning to be identified as important programming tools in the 1960s. Therefore, not all languages, particularly not the earlier versions of the various languages, include instructions especially designed to implement the elementary control structures. This does not mean that the elementary structures cannot or should not be used, it just means that their implementation may be more cumbersome than they would be if the language had been designed more carefully. FORTRAN 77 was specifically designed to eliminate some of the previous structural shortcomings of FORTRAN.

This chapter discusses those extensions that allow many of the elementary control structures that appear in pseudocode to be translated directly into FORTRAN. Section 4-1 considers IF blocks, which are blocks of FORTRAN statements that are related to the IF-THEN-ELSE control structure; Sec. 4-2 discusses the use of IF and DO statements in developing the DO-WHILE and DO-UNTIL structures and considers DO-WHILE and DO-UNTIL statements that are available in some enhanced versions of FORTRAN 77; and Sec. 4-3 discusses CASE structure implementations. In FORTRAN 77, general CASE structures are normally built around the IF block statements. There are, however, two other limited CASE-related statements, the computed GO TO and arithmetic IF statements, which have been part of FORTRAN almost from its inception. Although they can be used in special situations, the use of the computed GO TO is discouraged, and the arithmetic IF should be avoided altogether. These two statements are discussed in this book only for the sake of completeness and because the reader may encounter older programs that include them.

The last two sections provide an outline for testing and correcting programs, a topic that is discussed in detail in Chap. 10, and describe how comments should be interspersed with the program statements so that the program can be readily understood. Inserting comments in a program is an important part of the documentation process that takes place while a program is being written.

4-1 IF BLOCKS

An *IF block* is a section of FORTRAN code that begins with an IF-THEN statement whose form is

IF(Condition) THEN

and ends with an ENDIF statement whose form is

ENDIF

The group of statements between the IF-THEN and ENDIF statements is called the *range of the IF block* and is executed if the *Condition* is true; otherwise, these statements are skipped and execution resumes immediately following the ENDIF statement. The ENDIF causes no action; it only marks the end of the IF block. An IF block is depicted in Fig. 4-1(a) and has a major advantage over the simple IF statement introduced in Chap. 2 in that its range can include several statements, while the IF statement can contain only one contingency statement.

By permitting the ELSE statement whose form is

ELSE

to be included in the range of the IF block as shown in Fig. 4-1(b), FORTRAN acquires a direct implementation of the IF-THEN-ELSE control structure. If an ELSE statement is contained in the range of an IF block, the block is divided into a THEN subblock and an ELSE subblock with the THEN subblock being executed if the *Condition* is true and the ELSE subblock being executed if the *Condition* is false. In either case, after the subblock selected by the truth value of the *Condition* has been executed, the program continues with the first statement after the ENDIF. It is possible for these subblocks to contain no statements. An ELSE statement

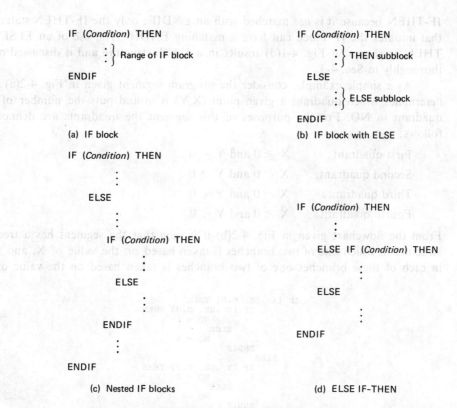

FIGURE 4-1 *Typical IF block structures.*

cannot appear outside an IF block; its sole purpose is to introduce an ELSE sub-block. Neither subblock can be branched into from outside the subblock.

IF blocks may be nested; however, each IF-THEN statement must be matched with an ENDIF statement in such a way that the outermost IF-THEN statement is matched with the outermost ENDIF statement, and so on. The FORTRAN translator automatically matches IF-THEN and ENDIF statements in the same way that it matches left and right parentheses when evaluating an expression. Consequently, IF blocks cannot be overlapped. A two-level nest of IF blocks is shown in Fig. 4-1(c). At most one ELSE statement can appear within each level of nesting for, otherwise, an IF block would be ambiguous.

The most frequent form of nesting is to follow an ELSE statement with an IF-THEN statement. FORTRAN permits such a sequence to be combined into a single ELSE IF-THEN statement of the form

ELSE IF(*Condition*) THEN

A representative usage of an ELSE IF-THEN statement is given in Fig. 4-1(d). An ELSE IF-THEN statement is not entirely equivalent to an ELSE followed by an

IF-THEN because it is *not* matched with an ENDIF; only the IF-THEN statement that initiates the IF block can have a matching ENDIF. The use of an ELSE IF-THEN as shown in Fig. 4-1(d) results in a CASE structure and is discussed more thoroughly in Sec. 4-3.

As a simple example, consider the program segment given in Fig. 4-2(a) that determines which quadrant a given point (X,Y) is in and puts the number of the quadrant in NQ. For the purposes of this segment the quadrants are defined as follows:

First quadrant: $X \geqq 0$ and $Y \geqq 0$

Second quadrant: $X < 0$ and $Y \geqq 0$

Third quadrant: $X < 0$ and $Y < 0$

Fourth quadrant: $X \geqq 0$ and $Y < 0$

From the flowchart given in Fig. 4-2(b) it is seen that the segment has a treelike structure in which one of two branches is taken based on the value of X, and then in each of these branches one of two branches is taken based on the value of Y.

```
IF (X .GE. 0.0) THEN
        IF (Y .GE. 0.0) THEN
                NQ = 1
        ELSE
                NQ = 4
        ENDIF
ELSE
        IF (Y .GE. 0.0) THEN
                NQ = 2
        ELSE
                NQ =3
        ENDIF
ENDIF
```

(a) Program segment

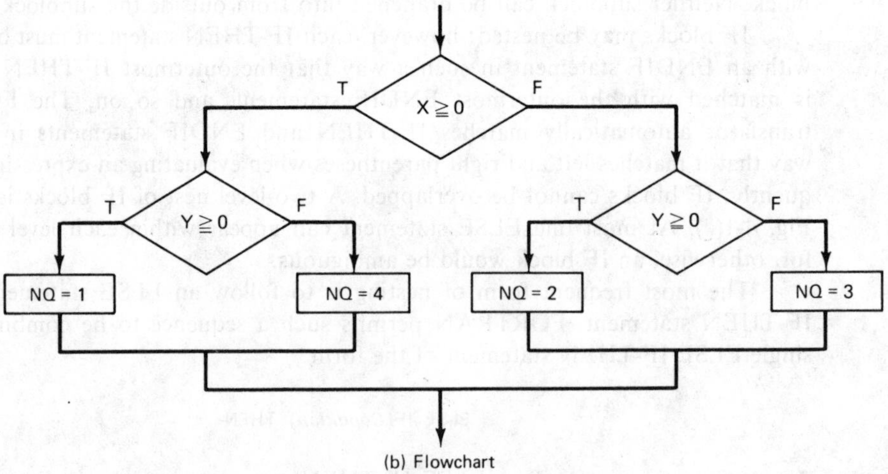

(b) Flowchart

FIGURE 4-2 *Program segment for assigning quadrant numbers.*

```
IF (X .GE. 0.0 AND Y .GE. 0.0) THEN
      NQ = 1
   ELSE IF (X .LT. 0.0 .AND. Y .GE. 0.0) THEN
      NQ = 2
   ELSE IF (X .LT. 0.0 .AND. Y .LT. 0.0) THEN
      NQ = 3
   ELSE
      NQ = 4
ENDIF
```

(a) Program segment

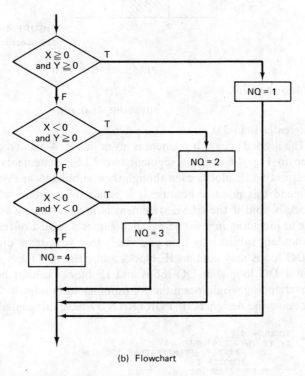

(b) Flowchart

FIGURE 4-3 *Alternative program segment for assigning quad-rant numbers.*

Figure 4-3 shows an alternative program segment and flowchart for accomplishing the same task. The alternate segment uses ELSE-IF-THEN statements to produce a CASE structure.

A similar but more complicated problem consists of assigning code values to points according to the areas given in Fig. 4-4. Assume that the temperature T and pressure P have already been input to a program and the problem is to add a program segment that sets ICODE to the area number indicated in the figure and prints

TEMPERATURE TOO LOW

if T is less than 2.0,

TEMPERATURE TOO HIGH

if T is greater than 4.0,

151

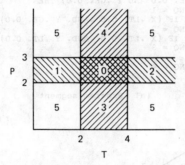

FIGURE 4-4 *Diagram for the temperature-pressure example.*

PRESSURE TOO LOW

if *P* is less than 2.0, and

PRESSURE TOO HIGH

if *P* is greater than 3.0.

The needed program segment is given in Fig. 4-5 and a corresponding flowchart is given in Fig. 4-6. In this segment two ELSE statements have been included in their respective IF blocks even though their subblocks are void. Many programmers recommend this practice because it is easier to ascertain whether or not an ELSE subblock is void if the ELSE statement is present than it is if it is absent. (This is similar to including in a list of baseball games a sublist of teams that did not play—the redundant sublist may help you verify that your team did not play.)

DO loops may contain IF blocks and either a THEN or ELSE subblock may contain a DO loop, but DO loops and IF blocks cannot be overlapped. Allowing such overlapping would permit a programmer to indulge in very poor programming practices, so the designers of FORTRAN 77 have eliminated the spaghetti-like pro-

```
      ICODE = 0
      IF (T .LT. 2.0) THEN
            PRINT *, 'TEMPERATURE TOO LOW'
            ICODE = 1
        ELSE IF (T .GT. 4.0) THEN
            PRINT *, 'TEMPERATURE TOO HIGH'
            ICODE = 2
        ELSE
      ENDIF
      IF (P .LT. 2.0) THEN
            PRINT *, 'PRESSURE TOO LOW'
            IF (ICODE .EQ. 0) THEN
                  ICODE = 3
              ELSE
                  ICODE = 5
            ENDIF
        ELSE IF (P .GT. 3.0) THEN
            PRINT *, 'PRESSURE TOO HIGH'
            IF (ICODE .EQ. 0) THEN
                  ICODE = 4
              ELSE
                  ICODE = 5
            ENDIF
        ELSE
      ENDIF
             .
             .
             .
```

FIGURE 4-5 *Program segment for the temperature-pressure example.*

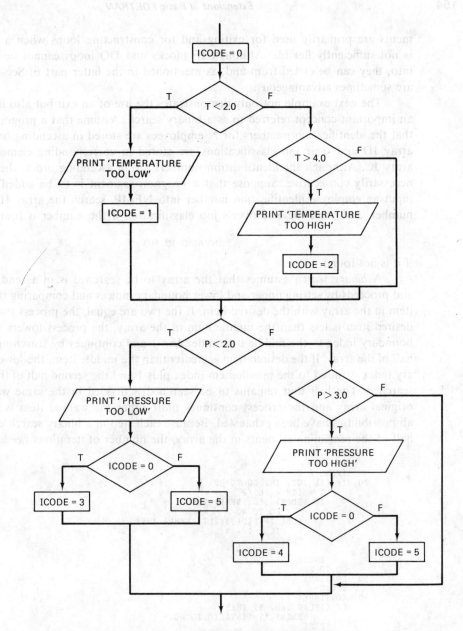

FIGURE 4-6 *Flowchart for the temperature-pressure example.*

gram structures that might have resulted from such practices. Recall that the elementary control structures each have only one incoming path and one outgoing path.

The simple IF statements discussed in Chap. 2 may be included in IF blocks. Some programmers may prefer the consistency of using only complete IF blocks, but others prefer to use IF statements whenever they result in shorter code. IF statements are primarily used for exiting and for constructing loops when a DO loop is not sufficiently flexible. Although IF blocks and DO loops cannot be branched into, they can be exited from and, as mentioned in the latter part of Sec. 3-2, exits are sometimes advantageous.

The next example not only demonstrates the use of an exit but also introduces an important concept referred to as a binary search. Assume that a program is such that the identification numbers for N employees are stored in ascending order in an array ID and their job classifications are stored in corresponding elements in an array JC. Although the identification numbers are in ascending order, they are not necessarily consecutive. Suppose that a program segment is to be added that will input an employee identification number into NEMP, search the array ID for this number, and print the employee's job classification if the number is found and

INVALID ID NO.

if it is not found.

A *binary search* assumes that the array to be searched is in ascending order and proceeds by setting upper and lower boundary indices and comparing the middle item in the array with the desired item. If the two are equal, the process stops. If the desired item is less than the middle item in the array, the process lowers the upper boundary index to the middle item index less 1 and continues by searching the first half of the array. If the desired item is greater than the middle item, the lower boundary index is raised to the middle item index plus 1 and the second half of the array is searched. The half that remains to be searched is divided in the same way as the original array and the process continues until either the wanted item is found or all possibilities have been exhausted. Because each step in a binary search eliminates half of the remaining elements in the array, the number of iterations needed to find

```
        IL = 1
        IH = N
        IFLAG = 0
    20  IF (IL .GT. IH) GO TO 30
        I = (IH + IL)/2
        IF (ID(I) .EQ. NEMP) THEN
                    GO TO 40
            ELSE IF (ID(I) .LT. NEMP) THEN
                    IL = I + 1
            ELSE
                    IH = I - 1
        ENDIF
        GO TO 20
    30  CONTINUE
        IFLAG = 1
    40  CONTINUE
        IF (IFLAG .EQ. 1) THEN
                PRINT *, 'INVALID ID NO.'
            ELSE
                PRINT *, 'EMPLOYEE',ID(I),'   HAS CLASSIFICATION',JC(I)
                            .
                            .
                            .

        ENDIF
            .
            .
            .
```

FIGURE 4-7 *Solution to the binary search example.*

an element in an array having N elements is less than or equal to M, where M is the smallest integer such that $N < 2^M$ [i.e., $M = 1 + $ truncation of $\log_2 (N)$].

A program segment for searching the employee identification array is given in Fig. 4-7 and a corresponding flowchart is shown in Fig. 4-8. The segment consists of a loop followed by an IF-THEN-ELSE structure. The loop includes an IF-THEN-ELSE structure for exiting the loop when the identification NEMP is found and for updating the upper and lower boundary indices IH and IL, respectively. Before entering the loop, IFLAG is set to 0. If the loop is terminated because IL > IH

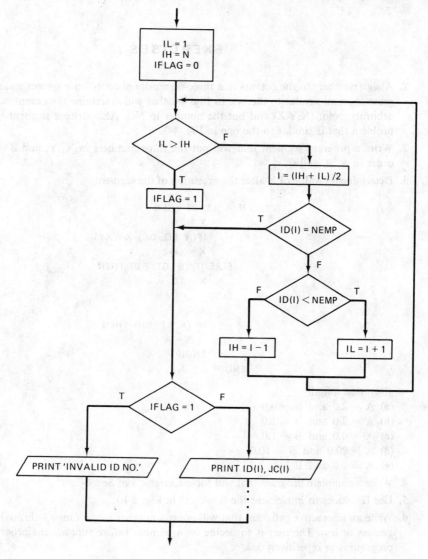

FIGURE 4-8 *Flowchart of the solution to the binary search example.*

occurs, IFLAG is set to 1, but if the loop is exited because ID(I) = NEMP, IFLAG remains at 0. The IF-THEN-ELSE structure following the loop will then print

INVALID ID NO.

and perform the "not found" processing if IFLAG = 1; otherwise, the employee identification and job classification is printed and the "found" processing is performed.

EXERCISES

1. Assign numbers to the octants in a three-dimensional coordinate system and write a program segment similar to the one in Fig. 4-2 that will determine the octant number of an arbitrary point (X,Y,Z) and put the number in NQ. Also write a segment to solve this problem that is similar to the one in Fig. 4-3.

2. Write a program segment that will put the three numbers in X, Y, and Z in ascending order in A, B, and C.

3. Determine the value of X after the execution of the segment

```
          IF(A .LT. B) THEN
              X = 2.0
              IF(A .EQ. 0.0) X = X+1
              X = X**2
          ELSE IF (B .GT. 5.0) THEN
              X = 3.0
          ELSE
              A = B
              IF (A .LT. 0.0) THEN
                 X = A
              ENDIF
          ENDIF
```

given that initially
(a) A = 2.0 and B = 4.0
(b) A = 2.0 and B = 1.0
(c) A = 0.0 and B = 1.0
(d) A = 20.0 and B = 10.0
(e) A = 0.0 and B = −2.0

4. Write a complete program that will solve Exercise 3 of Sec. 3-2.

5. Use IF blocks to implement the flowchart in Fig. 3-10.

6. Write an interactive program that will guess a number in the range 1 through 1000 in 10 guesses or less. The user is to decide on a number before running the program and the program is to repetitively ask

IS IT (Value of guess)

If the guess is correct the user is to respond with 0, if the number is greater than the guess the user is to respond with a 1, and if the number is less than the guess the user is to answer with a −1. When the number is found the program is to print

SEE HOW SMART I AM

and stop. If a number is not found in 10 guesses, the program is to print

YOU HAVE SELECTED AN INVALID NUMBER, CHOOSE ANOTHER ONE

and return to its beginning.

4-2 DO-WHILE AND DO-UNTIL IMPLEMENTATIONS

A FORTRAN 77 implementation of a DO-WHILE structure is given in Fig. 4-9. It utilizes an IF statement to form the loop and can use a complicated logical expression as the condition for determining whether or not the range of the loop is to be executed. Presumably, some of the variables in the logical expression are changed within the loop so that sooner or later the truth value of the logical expression can switch, thus causing the loop to be exited.

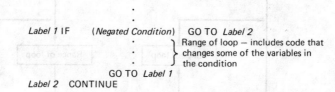

FIGURE 4-9   *FORTRAN implementation of a DO-WHILE loop.*

Two FORTRAN implementations of the DO-UNTIL construct are shown in Fig. 4-10, one using an IF statement and one using a DO statement. The former has the flexibility of a logical condition, whereas the latter is restricted to testing an

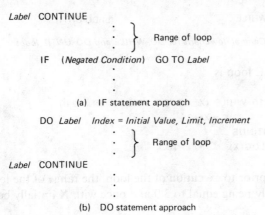

FIGURE 4-10   *FORTRAN implementations of the DO-UNTIL control structure.*

index. On the other hand, the IF statement construction includes an undesirable backward pointing GO TO, and if the condition can be stated in terms of an index, the latter approach can take advantage of the incrementing and testing capabilities of the DO statement. Although the DO statement is DO-UNTIL in nature in that the index is incremented *until* the limit is exceeded, it will cause the loop to be skipped if the initial value is larger than the limit (or smaller than the limit if the increment is negative).

Some FORTRAN dialects include statements that correspond exactly to the DO-WHILE and DO-UNTIL control structure pseudocode. The DO-WHILE statement is of the form

DO *Label* WHILE (*Condition*)

The *range of the DO-WHILE* extends from the first statement after the DO-WHILE statement to the statement whose label is *Label*, which is referred to as the *foot of the loop*. The range of the DO-WHILE is repetitively executed as long as the *Condition* is true. When the *Condition* is found to be false, execution resumes with the first statement following the foot of the DO-WHILE. A general flowchart of a DO-WHILE loop is given in Fig. 4-11(a).

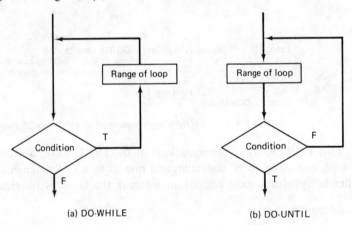

(a) DO-WHILE   (b) DO-UNTIL

FIGURE 4-11   *General flowcharts for DO-WHILE and DO-UNTIL loops.*

A typical DO-WHILE loop is

<pre>
        DO 10 WHILE (X .GT. 2.0 .AND. X .LT. 12.0)
              X = X**2
    10 CONTINUE
        Y = LOG(X)
</pre>

If X were equal to 3.0 just prior to execution of the loop, the range of the loop would execute once with X initially being equal to 3.0 and once with X initially being equal to 9.0. At the end of the second execution of the range, X would equal 81.0 and the loop would be exited. If X were 20.0 at the time the DO-WHILE statement is first encountered, the range would be skipped. Whether the loop is exited or skipped, execution would continue with the statement

$$Y = LOG(X)$$

Another form of the DO-WHILE structure is the one found in the WATFIV-S version of FORTRAN. In this form the loop appears as follows:

WHILE (*Condition*)
  ·⎫
  ·⎬ Range of loop
  ·⎭
ENDWHILE

The loop is executed as long as the *Condition* is true; when the *Condition* becomes false, the first statement after the ENDWHILE statement is executed.

The form of the DO-UNTIL statement is

DO *Label* UNTIL (*Condition*)

Statements similar to those made about the DO-WHILE loop also hold for DO-UNTIL loops, except that the loop is repeated until the *Condition* is true and it must be executed at least once. A general flowchart for a DO-UNTIL loop is given in Fig. 4-11(b).

For the same reasons that CONTINUE statements are normally used to terminate simple DO loops, they are normally used to terminate DO-WHILE and DO-UNTIL loops. That is, by making the foot of a loop a CONTINUE statement, it marks the end of the loop and changes involving the foot of the loop can be made more easily. The definitions above are typical, but the exact syntax depends on the version of FORTRAN being used and the reader should check the appropriate manual for his or her system. The DO-WHILE and DO-UNTIL statements are not part of the FORTRAN 77 standard but may be included in enhanced translators.

As with simple DO loops, branches into DO-WHILE and DO-UNTIL loops are not permitted. However, all three types may be nested within each other as long as they are not overlapped. The sequence given in Fig. 4-12(a) is valid, but the one given in Fig. 4-12(b) is invalid for two reasons. (It is left to the reader to determine the reasons.) Unlike the simple DO loops for which the index cannot be changed within its range, at least some of the variables in the *Condition* of a DO-WHILE or DO-UNTIL statement must be changed within the range of the loop; otherwise, the loop would repeat indefinitely. Because erroneous *Conditions* could result in errors that are very difficult to find, the *Conditions* should be chosen carefully, particularly if loops are being nested. In nesting situations the *Conditions* for the various

```
        DO 30 I=2,N,2
              .
              .
            DO 20 WHILE (X .GT. 0.0)
                  .
                  .
                DO 10 UNTIL (J .EQ. 5)
                      .
                      .
10                      CONTINUE
                      .
                      .
20              CONTINUE
                  .
                  .
30  CONTINUE
```

(a) Valid nest

```
        DO 50 UNTIL (Y .LT. X)
              .
              .
            IF (X + 1.0 .NE. 2.0) GO TO 40
              .
              .
            DO 75 WHILE (Y .GT. 0.0)
                  .
                  .
40                X = X - 2.0
                  .
                  .
50      CONTINUE
                  .
                  .
75  CONTINUE
```

(b) Invalid nest

FIGURE 4-12 *Examples of valid and invalid nests.*

levels must be compared to make certain that they are coordinated in a logical manner. For example, the segment

```
        DO 25 WHILE (X .GT. Y .OR. Y .LT. 0.0)
            DO 20 WHILE (X .LT. Y .AND. Y .EQ. 1.0)
                  .
                  .
20              CONTINUE
                  .
                  .
25  CONTINUE
```

would be nonsensical in that the inner loop would never be executed.

160

Let us demonstrate the application of a DO-UNTIL loop by considering the normal way of finding the square root of an arbitrary real number C using only the four basic arithmetic operations. The procedure is to let

$$X_0 = C$$

$$X_1 = 0.5(X_0 + C/X_0)$$

$$X_2 = 0.5(X_1 + C/X_1)$$

$$\vdots$$

and to continue finding values of the X_i's until $X_n^2 - C$ is smaller than some pre-selected value. An interactive program that is based on this algorithm for determining the square root of a number is given in Fig. 4-13. The program reads a number into

```
       PROGRAM SQROOT
       PRINT *, 'INPUT A NUMBER'
       READ *, C
       IF (C .EQ. 0.0) THEN
             X = 0.0
          ELSE
             D = ABS(C)
             X = D
             DO 10 UNTIL (ABS(X**2 - D) .LT. (0.5E-7)*D)
                X = (X + D/X)/2.0
    10       CONTINUE
       ENDIF
       IF (C .GE. 0.0) THEN
             PRINT *, 'SQUARE ROOT OF',C,' IS',X
          ELSE
             PRINT *, 'SQUARE ROOT OF',C,' IS',X,'I'
       ENDIF
       END
```

FIGURE 4-13 *Program for taking the square root of a number.*

C, computes the square root of C to seven significant figures, and puts the result in X. If C = 0, X is set to 0; if C > 0, the algorithm is applied directly; and if C < 0, the absolute value of C is taken before the algorithm is applied. After the square root of C is found and put in X, the program prints

SQUARE ROOT OF (*Value of C*) IS (*Value of X*)

if C is nonnegative and

SQUARE ROOT OF (*Value of C*) IS (*Value of X*)I

if C is negative. A flowchart of the program is given in Fig. 4-14.

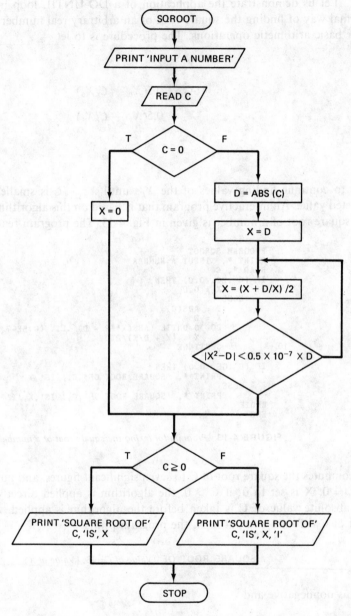

FIGURE 4-14 *Flowchart of the program for taking the square root of a number.*

EXERCISES

1. Rewrite the binary search segment given in Fig. 4-7 using a DO-WHILE statement.
2. For X = 1.0 and Y = 5.0 describe the action taken while executing each of the following loops and give the value of X after they have terminated:

   (a)   DO 20 WHILE (X .LT. 5.0)
                X = X+1.0
      20   CONTINUE

   (b)   DO 20 UNTIL (X .GT. 5.0)
                X = X+1.0
      20   CONTINUE

   (c)   DO 30 WHILE (X .LT. Y .OR. Y .LE. 20.0)
                Y = X+10.0
                X = X**2 + 1.0
      30   CONTINUE

3. Given that the real cube root of a real number C can be found as accurately as desired by successively computing

$$X_0 = C$$

$$X_1 = \frac{1}{3}\left(2X_0 + \frac{C}{X_0^2}\right)$$

$$X_2 = \frac{1}{3}\left(2X_1 + \frac{C}{X_1^2}\right)$$

$$\vdots$$

write a program that uses only the IF statement for looping and computes the cube root of all real whole numbers between A and B, where A and B are read in from cards. Modify the solution so that it uses only DO-UNTIL statements for looping.

4-3 CASE STRUCTURES IN FORTRAN

Although FORTRAN does not include statements with the keywords SELECT or ENDCASE, CASE structures can easily be implemented using ELSE IF-THEN statements within an IF block. This is accomplished by using the form given in Fig. 4-15. As seen from the figure, the IF-THEN and ELSE IF-THEN are executed until a true condition is found. At this point the true subblock is executed and then the program continues immediately following the ENDIF that matches the IF-THEN statement. If none of the conditions are true, the ELSE subblock is executed.

CASEs are mutually exclusive sets of possibilities and are normally defined so that they are totally inclusive. Mutually exclusive means that the defining rules for any two CASEs cannot be satisfied simultaneously (i.e., the CASEs cannot overlap). Totally inclusive means that the composite of all CASEs includes all possibilities. Totally inclusive CASEs are usually defined so that the conditions for all but one

```
        IF (Condition – CASE 1)  THEN
              ·
              ·      CASE 1 code
              ·
        ELSE IF  (Condition – CASE 2)  THEN
              ·
              ·      CASE 2 code
              ·
              ·      CASE 3 through N–2
              ·
        ELSE IF  (Condition – CASE N–1)  THEN
              ·
              ·      CASE N–1 code
              ·
        ELSE
              ·
              ·      CASE N code  (Catchall CASE)
              ·
        ENDIF
```

FIGURE 4-15 *Using an IF block to form a CASE structure.*

CASE are stated and the remaining CASE is the catchall CASE which consists of all other possibilities. For example, CASE 1 might be the real numbers from 0 to 1 inclusive, CASE 2 the real numbers greater than 1 and less than 2, and CASE 3 the set of all other real numbers. In this instance, no real number is in more than one CASE, any given real number is in at least one CASE, and CASE 3 is the catchall case.

Two commonly occurring CASE relationships are depicted in Fig. 4-16. In

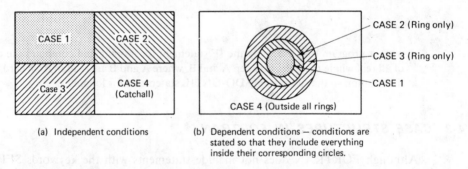

(a) Independent conditions

(b) Dependent conditions — conditions are stated so that they include everything inside their corresponding circles.

FIGURE 4-16 *Two principal categories of CASE relationships when developing CASE structures.*

Fig. 4-16(a) it is assumed that the defining conditions for each CASE must be stated in such a way that they do not rely on the conditions of the other CASES. For this situation the *Condition* for any one of the IF-THEN or ELSE IF-THEN statements does not depend on the *Conditions* in the remaining statements. Figure 4-17 gives a collection of CASEs and a corresponding FORTRAN language CASE structure for such a CASE relationship.

At the other extreme is the situation illustrated in Fig. 4-16(b), in which each CASE is defined as all events that meet certain conditions, but do not meet the conditions of any of the previous CASEs. Figure 4-18 gives a collection of CASEs

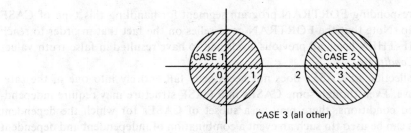

CASE 3 (all other)

(a) Case definitions

```
IF (SQRT(X**2 + Y**2) .LT. 1.0) THEN
    .
    .        CASE 1
    .
ELSE IF (SQRT((X - 3.0)**2 + Y**2) .LT. 1.0) THEN
    .
    .        CASE 2
    .
ELSE
    .
    .        CASE 3 — catchall
    .
ENDIF
```

(b) FORTRAN code

FIGURE 4-17 *Independent CASE conditions.*

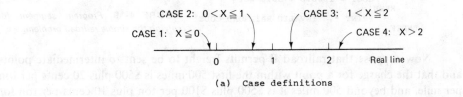

(a) Case definitions

```
IF (X .LE. 0.0) THEN
    .
    .        CASE 1
    .
ELSE IF (X .LE. 1.0) THEN
    .
    .        CASE 2
    .
ELSE IF (X .LE. 2.0) THEN
    .
    .        CASE 3
    .
ELSE
    .
    .        CASE 4 — catchall
    .
ENDIF
```

(b) FORTRAN code

FIGURE 4-18 *Dependent CASE conditions.*

and a corresponding FORTRAN program segment for handling this type of CASE relationship. Note that the FORTRAN code relies on the fact that in order to reach an ELSE IF-THEN level, all previous levels had to have resulted in false truth values for their *Conditions*.

A collection of CASEs does not necessarily fall entirely into one of the categories above. Even though some CASEs in a CASE structure may require independently stated conditions, there may be a subset of CASEs for which the dependent conditions can be used. In such an event a combination of independent and dependent *Conditions* could be used in the IF-THEN and ELSE IF-THEN statements.

Suppose that there are railroads A and B from Denver to Chicago and that railroad A charges $500 plus $100 per ton and railroad B charges $1000 plus $50 per ton. A program segment for computing the shipping charge COST, which assumes that the weight is in WGT and the railroad designation—1 for railroad A and 2 for railroad B—is in ICODE, is given in Fig. 4-19. If ICODE is not equal to 1 or 2, the message

INVALID RAILROAD CODE

is printed. CASE 1 corresponds to ICODE=1, CASE 2 to ICODE=2, and CASE 3, the catchall case, to all other values of ICODE.

```
IF (ICODE .EQ. 1) THEN
        COST = 500.0 + 100.0*WGT
    ELSE IF (ICODE .EQ. 2) THEN
        COST = 1000.0 + 50.0*WGT
    ELSE
        PRINT *, 'INVALID RAILROAD CODE'
ENDIF
```

FIGURE 4-19 *Program segment for solving the simple railroad problem.*

Now suppose that railroad B permits freight to be sent to intermediate points and that the charge for a point within the first 500 miles is $500 plus 20 cents per ton per mile, and beyond 500 miles it is $500 plus $100 per ton plus 10 cents per ton for each mile over 500 miles. The per ton charge is shown in Fig. 4-20(a) and a program segment for solving the problem is given in Fig. 4-20(b). This solution assumes that DIST contains the distance and that

NEGATIVE DISTANCE

is printed if DIST<0 and

DISTANCE TOO LONG

is printed if DIST>1000, where 1000 is the distance between Denver and Chicago.

Although the discussion above assumes the availability of IF blocks, two limited CASE-oriented FORTRAN statements, the computed GO TO and the arithmetic IF statements, are included in all versions of FORTRAN. Structurally, these statements are not as appealing because they are awkward to use and involve GO TO

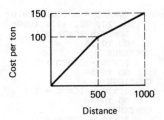

(a) Cost per ton as a function of distance.

```
IF (ICODE .EQ. 1) THEN
        COST = 500.0 + 100.0*WGT
    ELSE IF (ICODE .EQ. 2) THEN
        IF (DIST .LT. 0.0) THEN
                PRINT *, 'NEGATIVE DISTANCE'
            ELSE IF (DIST .LE. 500.0) THEN
                COST = 500.0 + 0.2*WGT*DIST
            ELSE IF (DIST .LE. 1000.0) THEN
                COST = 500.0 + (100.0 + 0.1*DIST)*WGT
            ELSE
                PRINT *, 'DISTANCE TOO LONG'
        ENDIF
    ELSE
        PRINT *, 'INVALID CODE'
ENDIF
```

(b) Program segment

FIGURE 4-20 *Solution to the modified railroad problem.*

statements. The computed GO TO has the form

GO TO (*Label 1, Label 2, . . . , Label N*), *Integer Variable*

and causes a branch to *Label 1* if the *Integer Variable* is 1, *Label 2* if the *Integer Variable* is 2, and so on. If the *Integer Variable* is not in the range 1 through N, no branch is taken and execution continues in sequence. Figure 4-21 shows how the simple railroad example given in Fig. 4-19 could be rewritten using a computed GO TO statement.

```
      GO TO (10,20), ICODE
            PRINT *, 'INVALID RAILROAD CODE'
            GO TO 30
10      CONTINUE
            COST = 500.0 + 100.0*WGT
            GO TO 30
20      CONTINUE
            COST = 1000.0 + 50.0*WGT
30    CONTINUE
```

FIGURE 4-21 *Solution of the railroad example that uses a computed GO TO statement.*

Computed GO TO statements seem to be very limited because they must depend on an integer variable to direct the branching. However, by applying a little ingenuity and using an assignment statement in conjunction with a computed GO TO, a reasonable degree of flexibility can be attained. Figure 4-22 gives a program segment for incrementing ICNTD if GRADE is less than or equal to 70 but greater

```
        ICODE = (GRADE - 50.001)/10.0
        GO TO (10, 20, 30, 40), ICODE
            ICNTF = ICNTF + 1
            GO TO 50
   10       CONTINUE
            ICNTD = ICNTD + 1
            GO TO 50
   20       CONTINUE
            ICNTC = ICNTC + 1
            GO TO 50
   30       CONTINUE
            ICNTB = ICNTB + 1
            GO TO 50
   40       CONTINUE
            ICNTA = ICNTA + 1
   50   CONTINUE
```

FIGURE 4-22 *Solution to the grading problem that uses a computed GO TO statement.*

than 60, ICNTC if GRADE is less than or equal to 80 but greater than 70, **ICNTB** if GRADE is less than or equal to 90 but greater than 80, ICNTA if **GRADE is** less than or equal to 100 but greater than 90, and ICNTF if GRADE is any **other** value. It is assumed that grades are specified to no more than two decimal **places,** so that a grade over 60 must be at least 60.01, a grade over 70 must be at least 70.01, and so on. Note that other statements would be needed to build in protection against invalid grades less than 0 or greater than 100.

Arithmetic IF statements are of the form

IF *(Expression) Label 1, Label 2, Label 3*

where *Expression* is an algebraic expression and causes a branch to *Label 1* if the value of the *Expression* is negative, to *Label 2* if it is zero, and *Label 3* if it is positive. For example,

IF (B**2 − 4.0*A*C) 10,20,30

would cause a branch to 10, 20, or 30 if B**2 − 4.0*A*C were negative, zero, or positive, respectively.

Although the arithmetic IF may seem convenient for some special situations, its use is not recommended. The arithmetic IF implies the use of GO TO statements at the ends of the cases, and these GO TO statements are not needed in IF blocks. Also, programs are more readable and error-free if the programmer adheres to employing as few ways of doing things as possible, and avoids structures that apply only to special cases. The arithmetic IF is presented here because such statements are found in programs written in the older versions of FORTRAN, programs the reader may encounter and need to understand.

Another statement that is sometimes used to develop CASE structures is the ASSIGN statement, which associates a variable with a label and has the form

ASSIGN *Label* TO *Integer Variable*

Because it tends to lead to unstructured programming, it is of dubious value and is not considered further in this book. As with the arithmetic IF statement, it is mentioned only to make the reader aware of its availability.

EXERCISES

1. Suppose that an item may come in two lengths and three weights, and is priced according to the following table:

Length category	Weight category 1	2	3
1	1.20	1.40	1.60
2	1.50	1.80	2.00

Write a program segment which assumes that the length and weight category numbers are in NLEN and NWGT, respectively, and uses an IF block to put the price in PRICE. If an invalid category number is found in NLEN or NWGT, the segment is to print

INVALID CAT. NO.

2. Write a program that uses an IF block with independent conditions [as shown in Fig. 4-16(a)] to evaluate a function whose graph is

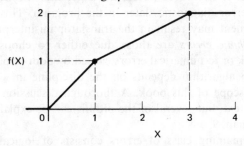

The program is to read in a value, evaluate the function, and print the result. Resolve the problem using an IF block with dependent conditions [as shown in Fig. 4-16(b)].

3. What is the principal limitation of the computed GO TO statement, and what are its disadvantages?

4. Modify the program segment in Fig. 4-22 to guard against data less than 0 and greater than 100.

5. Write a program segment that uses a computed GO TO statement to evaluate the function whose graph is

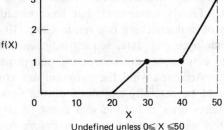

Undefined unless $0 \leqslant X \leqslant 50$

Resolve the problem using an IF block.

Debugging a program can be the most time-consuming part of a programming effort, and the longer the program, the larger the proportionate share of the debugging phase. Although modern programming techniques tend to minimize the number of errors, lengthy and complex programs are never completely error-free. The errors in a program fall into the three main categories:

1. Syntax errors
2. Logical errors
3. Algorithmic errors

of which syntax errors are the easiest to correct. All translators have built into them the ability to detect syntax errors and print out messages, called *diagnostics*, that alert the programmer to the errors. The degree of sophistication of the diagnostics included in translators varies from simple one-letter codes to detailed explanatory messages, with some translators providing pointers that indicate the exact location of the errors. It should be noted, however, that a syntax error in a program may cause false error diagnostics later in the program. This is because the error in the earlier statement may result in the translator misinterpreting later statements.

Algorithmic errors are those due either to choosing the wrong method for solving a task or to numerical errors caused by poor implementation of an algorithm. Choosing an algorithm depends on the discipline in which one is working and is beyond the scope of this book. A thorough discussion of numerical errors is also beyond this text, but several of the pitfalls can be explained intuitively and are considered in Chap. 9.

The remaining class of errors consists of logical errors. *Logical errors* are caused by mistakes made in translating the task algorithms into program modules and in fitting the modules together to form a complete program. Separating logical errors from algorithmic errors is often very difficult, but even assuming that the algorithms have been properly selected, finding the logical errors can be a very difficult job.

Debugging can be separated into the two categories indicated by the major titles in Fig. 4-23. The first category is desk checking and consists of thoroughly examining the program before it is run. Figure 4-23 contains only those items concerning the FORTRAN statements that have already been introduced; a more extensive listing of desk checking is given in Chap. 10. Figure 4-24 gives a program for inputting employee pay data, sequentially searching for and printing the pay rates of selected employees, and computing and printing the average pay rate for these employees. Accompanying the program are comments noting some of the points that should be carefully examined during desk checking. Although careful desk checking takes time, it is time well spent. Wasted computer runs that result from inadequately examining the program before running it consume both programmer time and computer time.

      1. Spelling of variables and headings
      2. Variable types
      3. Loop initialization
      4. DO statement and implied DO loop
         parameters and indices
      5. Conditions in IF and other statements
      6. Flags and codes
      7. Limits in DIMENSION and DO statements
      8. Input data
      9. I-O statement variable lists

II. Testing

      1. Test data selection
      2. Echo printing
      3. Milepost PRINTs
      4. Printing of intermediate values

FIGURE 4-23 *Debugging summary.*

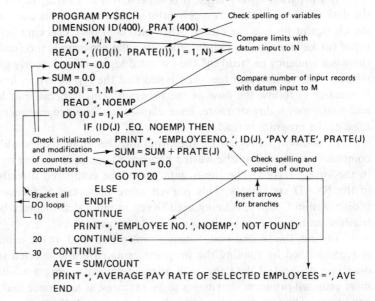

FIGURE 4-24 *Items that should be examined during desk checking.*

Some of the most obvious errors, but sometimes the most difficult to find, are spelling errors. A spelling error occurs when a variable or printed message, such as a heading or error message, is incorrectly written. Since FORTRAN does not detect an error if a variable is spelled wrong (it simply assumes that a new variable has been declared), these bugs often persist until some other error causes the programmer to check the area of code that contains the misspelling. On the other hand, although the misspelling of words in error messages, column headings, and other identifying information on the printout does not cause the program to execute incorrectly, it is quite noticeable to the user. Even though this type of spelling error does not cause incorrect results, it does reduce the effectiveness of the printout.

There are several points in programs that contain errors often enough that special attention should be given to them during desk checking. The initialization statements just prior to loops and the statements used to implement the loops are prime examples of points at which errors frequently occur. The parameters in the DO statements and the *Conditions* in the IF statements should be verified, and DO loop indices should be reexamined, particularly if nesting is involved. The limits in both the DO statements and DIMENSION statements should be reviewed and, if they are related, they should be compared. If loops are nested, they should be double-checked to ensure that the rules for nesting have not been violated. This comment also applies to implied DO loops. A recommended method for verifying that nesting and branching rules have been obeyed and that the labels in DO and GO TO statements are correct is to draw a bracket connecting the beginning and end of each DO loop and an arrow showing each branch (see Fig. 4-24).

If a program is very large, it is suggested that a listing of it be obtained before the desk checking is done. A nicely printed copy reduces the confusion and increases the chance of finding the errors. Also, although desk checking before a program is typed (or keypunched) is helpful, too often the program is too fresh at this time and there is a tendency to "read in" the intended logic and not clearly see what is actually written. After a program has been typed and the typing errors have been removed, it is easier to follow the flow of the program. This is because at least a few hours, and sometimes a day or more, have elapsed and the programmer must rethink the logic as the program is read.

In addition to reviewing the program, the input data should be checked. A computer run should not be wasted because a comma is missing or a datum appears in the wrong record. The input data should be compared directly with input lists in the READ statements. This is even more important if formatted input, which is discussed in Chap. 7, is being used. Keep in mind that incorrectly spaced or punctuated data may appear to the computer to be good data.

Testing, the second major item given in Fig. 4-23, is the debugging phase that is accomplished by running the program using carefully selected sets of data. How does one design test data that will adequately test a program? Basically, the data must cause all program statements to be executed at least once and under worst-case conditions. The test data should be designed to strain the program, to push it to its limits.

All loops should be made to perform to their limits at least once during the test. For example, if a loop is being used to perform a calculation on an array, the array should be full for at least one of the calculations. Every data value should be taken to the extreme at least once during the test. A program to calculate the sine of an angle should be tested at $0°$, $90°$, and some values in between. It should also be tested at values in each of the four quadrants, values greater than $360°$, and at some negative values.

All IF statements should be made to take all the possible branches during a test run or set of test runs. For example, if a variable is being tested for zero, data should be supplied to cause the variable to be zero and nonzero at different times during the testing. All error messages should be tested by forcing the occurrence of every error which the program is designed to detect. This not only ensures that the program will detect those errors, but it also causes the programmer to check the format and spelling of the error messages themselves. In addition, it shows whether or not the program can recover correctly after detecting the errors that caused the error messages. In general, a program should detect as many errors as possible during each run so that the number of runs is minimized.

As an example, a program segment for solving the quadratic equation

$$AX^2 + BX + C = 0$$

(such as the one flowcharted in Fig. 3-10) should be tested with at least five sets of coefficients. There should be two sets of coefficients with $A = 0$ (one with $B = 0$ and one with $B \neq 0$) and three sets with $A \neq 0$ (one with a negative discriminant, one with a zero discriminant, and one with a positive discriminant). If, as shown in Fig. 4-25, the segment were part of a program that uses a loop to compute the solution to N different quadratic equations, the program should be run using a variety of values of N. In particular, a nonpositive value would check the program's ability to print a warning message and request a new value of N, and a very large value of N could be used to test a program segment for printing an error message indicating that an array size has been exceeded.

Even though computers can compute very rapidly, testing every path in every possible order is not always possible because, for some programs, the possibilities are so numerous that the time needed to run a complete check would be longer than the life of the computer. To demonstrate this point, note that an IF-THEN-ELSE control structure has two paths, two such structures in a simple sequence have four paths, and ten such structures in a simple sequence have 1024 paths. A program with several thousand statements may combine IF-THEN-ELSE, CASE, and loop structures in such a way that the number of paths is essentially infinite. Choosing test data for all but the simplest problems is both an art and a science. For problems for which checking all possible paths is impractical, it is obvious that certain paths must be checked, but a combination of experience, common sense, and a few heuristic rules is required to determine the marginally necessary test paths. Considerable research has been done in the area of testing large programs and programs that must be highly reliable, such as programs for controlling nuclear power plants. An extensive study of test data selection is clearly beyond an introductory book such as this one, but some of the common rules for testing more complex programs are considered in Chap. 10.

The second step in preparing for test runs is to modify the program so as to maximize the information obtained from a test run. Because the only results that a programmer can see are the ones that are printed, this step consists primarily of inserting **PRINT** statements at strategic points within the program. Normally, these statements would be removed once debugging is complete, but at least one additional test run should be made after this removal to guarantee that no errors have been created by their deletion. Just how many temporary **PRINT** statements

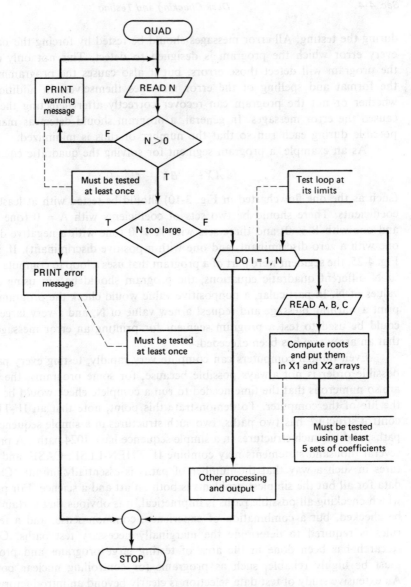

FIGURE 4-25 *Example showing the paths that must be tested.*

should be put in a program before its first test run depends on the length and complexity of the program and is left to the judgment of the programmer. If mistakes are found after the first run, the programmer may insert additional PRINT statements in order to pinpoint the problem.

The three most important concepts associated with outputting test results are echo printing, milepost printing, and printing intermediate results. *Echo printing* is immediately printing the input data in a form that is the same as or similar to the form of the input records. By printing the input data before they are involved in computations, the programmer can be sure that no mistakes were made in typing or inputting the data and that it is the intended data that are actually being processed. In some cases, the normal program output may be used to verify the input, but if problems arise that seem to be related to the input, echo print statements should be placed immediately following the appropriate input statements.

Milepost PRINTs are statements that are inserted solely to inform the programmer which paths were followed while the program was executing. They are also useful when a program abnormally ends (ABENDs) due to an irrecoverable error detected during execution (e.g., an exponent overflow or invalid input format). Ordinarily, milepost PRINTS are not used until a- problem arises and additional information concerning the control flow within the program is needed to solve the problem.

To demonstrate the use of echo printing and milepost PRINTs, let us consider the simple program given in Fig. 4-26, which converts temperatures in degrees Fahrenheit to degrees Celsius, or vice versa. The program is supposed to input a

```
      PROGRAM TEMP
10    READ *, TEMP, ICODE
      IF (TEMP .EQ. -99999.0) GO TO 20
         IF (ICODE .EQ. 0) THEN
               CDEG = (5.0/0.0)*(TEMP-32.0)
               PRINT *, TEMP,'FAHRENHEIT =',CDEG,'CELSIUS'
            ELSE
               FDEG = (9.0/5.0)*TEMP+32.0
               PRINT *, TEMP,'CELSIUS =',FDEG,'FAHRENHEIT'
         ENDIF
         GO TO 10
20    CONTINUE
      PRINT *, 'END OF PROGRAM'
      END
```

FIGURE 4-26 *Incorrect temperature-conversion program.*

temperature and a code which indicates the type of conversion (zero for Fahrenheit to Celsius conversion and nonzero for Celsius to Fahrenheit conversion), compute the temperature in the specified units, and print the converted temperature beside the proper label. The program is to continue processing temperatures until a temperature of −99999 is detected, at which time it is to print

END OF PROGRAM

and stop. If the test data are

32.0,   0

98.6,   0

212.0,   0

0.0,   1

37.0,   1

100.0,   1

the only output will be an ABEND message indicating an arithmetic error. At this point there is some question as to whether the input data were improperly formatted or there is a mistake in a processing statement. Also, there may be no indication as to which branch in the IF block had been taken prior to the ABEND.

Figure 4-27 shows the same program with echo print and milepost print state-

```
      PROGRAM TEMP
   10 READ *, TEMP, ICODE
      PRINT *, 'TEMPERATURE:',TEMP,'CODE:',ICODE
      IF (TEMP .EQ. -99999.0) GO TO 20
         IF (ICODE .EQ. 0) THEN
            PRINT *, 'FAHRENHEIT TO CELSIUS CONVERSION'
            CDEG = (5.0/0.0)*(TEMP-32.0)
            PRINT *, TEMP,'FAHRENHEIT =',CDEG,'CELSIUS'
         ELSE
            PRINT *, 'CELSIUS TO FAHRENHEIT CONVERSION'
            FDEG = (9.0/5.0)*TEMP+32.0
            PRINT *, TEMP,'CELSIUS =',FDEG,'FAHRENHEIT'
         ENDIF
         GO TO 10
   20 CONTINUE
      PRINT *, 'END OF PROGRAM'
      END
```

FIGURE 4-27 *Temperature-conversion program with echo print and milepost print statements added.*

ments added. When the program is run again using the same data, the output is

```
        TEMPERATURE: 32.0000    CODE:        0
        FAHRENHEIT TO CELSIUS CONVERSION
```

followed by the same ABEND message. It is now apparent that the input data were correct and the THEN branch was taken before the error occurred. The error is now easily found to be that a 0 was typed instead of a 9 in the statement

$$\text{CDEG} = (5.0/\underset{\underset{\displaystyle 9}{\uparrow}}{0.0}) \cdot (\text{TEMP}-32.0)$$

The third principal application of PRINT statements in debugging a program is to use them to print intermediate values. The purpose of such statements is to determine exactly where within a series of computations an erroneous computation has occurred. These statements can be used to find algorithmic errors as well as logical errors.

To find errors in lengthy assignment statements it is sometimes necessary to break them into parts and then intersperse them with PRINT * statements. To demonstrate this point, let us reconsider the program in Fig. 4-26, except that this time let us suppose that the statement for converting from degrees Fahrenheit to degrees Celsius is erroneously written

$$CDEG = 5/9*(TEMP-32.0)$$

If the input indicated above were used, the output would be

32.0000	FAHRENHEIT	=	0.00000	CELSIUS
98.6000	FAHRENHEIT	=	0.00000	CELSIUS
212.000	FAHRENHEIT	=	0.00000	CELSIUS
0.00000	CELSIUS	=	32.0000	FAHRENHEIT
37.0000	CELSIUS	=	98.6000	FAHRENHEIT
100.000	CELSIUS	=	212.000	FAHRENHEIT

END OF PROGRAM

It is seen from the output that the Celsius to Fahrenheit conversion is correct, but there is an error in Fahrenheit to Celsius conversion. Therefore, one may choose to break the assignment statement for performing the incorrect conversion into parts and print out the result of each part as follows:

```
T1 = 5/9
T2 = (TEMP-32.0)
CDEG = T1*T2
PRINT *, 'T1 =', T1, 'T2 =', T2, 'CDEG =', CDEG
```

After replacing the suspected problem statement with this combination, the output is

T1 = 0.00000	T2 = 0.00000	CDEG = 0.00000
32.0000	FAHRENHEIT = 0.00000	CELSIUS
T1 = 0.00000	T2 = 66.6000	CDEG = 0.00000
98.6000	FAHRENHEIT = 0.00000	CELSIUS
T1 = 0.00000	T2 = 180.000	CDEG = 0.00000
212.000	FAHRENHEIT = 0.00000	CELSIUS

Now it is apparent that the problem is caused by the integer division 5/9, which gives a quotient of 0. (Incidentally, this is a type of error that is commonly made by inexperienced programmers, and it is because of such errors that mixed-mode arithmetic is discouraged.)

Note that in all of the examples above the program could be returned to its original state by simply removing the PRINT * statements. It is important that any program changes that are made for the sole purpose of debugging a program be such that they can easily be reversed. This is true because the reversal process may introduce new errors. Therefore, it is better to insert additional **PRINT** statements than to modify **PRINT** statements that are part of the program, statements that would need to be remodified once debugging is complete.

EXERCISES

1. Suppose that a program consists of a simple sequence of an IF-THEN-ELSE structure, having a CASE structure with 10 cases in the THEN path and a CASE structure with five cases in the ELSE path, followed by a CASE structure with 10 cases. What is the number of possible paths through the program?

2. Give sets of test data for thoroughly checking the binary search segment given in Fig. 4-7.

3. Give sets of test data for thoroughly checking the program requested in Exercise 2 at the end of Sec. 4 3.

4-5 COMMENTING A PROGRAM

The development of a program may involve several people, and documentation of a software project must be generated as the project progresses so that these people can maintain a common ground. After the initial work on a project has been completed, the documentation must be put into a form that can be understood by others who have not participated in the original development. As the work proceeds toward completion, and for some time after completion in some cases, there is a continual process of debugging. Even after a program is put into use, errors can occur as a result of defective storage or transmission of the program, or because of very subtle errors that went undetected during the debugging phase. The process of monitoring and correcting the errors in a program or complete software package, and of updating software to take into account system changes, is called *software maintenance*. Because the final debugging stage and the maintenance stage of a program may involve people other than those who wrote the program, it is extremely important that a program be well documented.

Software documentation as a whole is studied in Sec. 9-2, but one important aspect of documenting a program, called *commenting a program*, needs to be discussed at this point. Commenting a program is the insertion of remarks in the program so that it can be readily understood from its listing. Although high-level languages are much closer to the English language than the more primitive forms of giving instructions to a computer, they are not designed to give descriptive information, and this must be provided by supplemental comments.

In FORTRAN, comment lines may be added at any point within a program. These lines are identified by placing an asterisk or the letter "C" in the first column of the line. Upon recognizing the asterisk or "C" in the first column, the FORTRAN translator does not treat the remainder of the line as a FORTRAN statement, but simply passes it through to the listing. This means that comment lines may contain any symbols, whether they are legal FORTRAN symbols or not. As a special case, lines that are completely blank are treated as comment lines even though they do not have an asterisk or "C" in the first column. Blank lines permit visual segmentation of a program.

A program should begin with a series of comment lines that include an overall explanation of the program and a description of each variable that is used throughout the program. Also, each task and subtask would normally be preceded by a brief explanation and a description of the variables that it uses but are not used in the remainder of the program (i.e., are not described at the beginning of the program). A variable description includes a statement of the quantity it represents and, perhaps, indicates its type. Auxiliary variables that exist solely to expedite the shuffling of information are not normally individually described but may be noted as a group and labeled as being auxiliary. An index is individually noted in the comments only if it is important or is used consistently for a specific purpose.

The comments in a program should be such that they would, by themselves, provide an outline of the program. The explanations of the tasks and subtasks should be as brief as possible, with the other material in a documentation package providing the details. However, they should be complete enough that anyone familiar with the project would rarely need to refer back and forth between the listing and the other supporting material. The explanations may be only one sentence and indicate only the name of a computational algorithm or the form in which data are to be put for input or are to be printed. Because comments that are too long detract from the program, they can be worse than comments that are too short.

To demonstrate a fully commented program, let us consider the following program for ordering employees according to their hourly rates.

Write a program SORT that will input employee identification numbers into an array ID and their hourly rates into respective elements in an array RATE, rearrange both arrays so that the employees' identifications and hourly rates are such that the hourly rates are in ascending order, and print the reordered arrays in two columns under the headings

ID NO.   HOURLY RATE

A solution of the problem based on insertion sorting is given in Fig. 4-28. An *insertion sort* consists of putting the first two elements in ascending order, then comparing the third element with the second element, and perhaps the first element, and inserting it in its proper position; then successively comparing the fourth element with the third, second, and first elements until it is properly inserted; and so on. The comments assume that either the user knows what an insertion sort is or that a detailed explanation is in the accompanying documentation.

```
**************************************************************
*                      PROGRAM SORT                          *
* PROGRAM SORT READS EMPLOYEE ID NOS. AND HOURLY WAGE         *
* RATES INTO TWO SEPARATE ARRAYS, USES AN INSERTION SORT TO   *
* REORDER BOTH ARRAYS SO THAT THE RATES ARE IN ASCENDING      *
* ORDER, AND PRINTS THE REORDERED ARRAYS                      *
*     N         - NO. OF EMPLOYEES                            *
*     ID(1000)   - INTEGER ARRAY OF EMPLOYEE ID NOS.          *
*     RATE(1000) - REAL ARRAY OF HOURLY RATES                 *
**************************************************************

      PROGRAM SORT

* STORAGE ALLOCATION

      DIMENSION ID(1000), RATE(1000)

* I.  INPUTS NO. OF EMPLOYEES AND THEN INPUTS ID NO. --
*     HOURLY RATE PAIRS, ONE PAIR PER CARD

      READ*, N
      DO 10 I=1,N
         READ*, ID(I),RATE(I)
   10 CONTINUE

* II. USES AN INSERTION SORT TO REORDER ARRAYS.
*     OUTER LOOP INCREMENTS THROUGH EMPLOYEES.
*     INNER LOOP DETERMINES POSITION FOR EACH EMPLOYEE.
*         TEMP1, TEMP2 - AUXILIARY VARIABLES

      DO 40 I=2,N
         TEMP1 = RATE(I)
         TEMP2 = ID(I)
         DO 20 K=I-1,1,-1
            IF (TEMP1 .GE. RATE(K)) GO TO 30
            RATE(K+1) = RATE(K)
            ID(K+1) = ID(K)
   20    CONTINUE
         K=0
   30    RATE(K+1) = TEMP1
         ID(K+1) = TEMP2
   40 CONTINUE

* III.OUTPUTS REORDERED ID AND RATE ARRAYS IN TWO COLUMNS

      PRINT*, '   ID NO.    ', ' HOURLY RATE'
      DO 50 I=1,N
         PRINT*, ID(I),RATE(I)
   50 CONTINUE
      END
```

FIGURE 4-28 *Commented solution to the sort problem.*

EXERCISES

1. Comment the program requested in Exercise 3 of Sec. 4-2.

2. Write a fully commented program that:

(a) Reads $N+1$ values into arrays X and Y beginning with X(0) and Y(0).

(b) Finds the area, from X(0) to X(N), under the function F formed by connecting the pairs of points by straight line segments, that is, evaluates

$$A = \sum_{I=1}^{N} 0.5(Y(I)+Y(I-1))(X(I)-X(I-1))$$

(c) Prints

$$AREA = (Value\ of\ A)$$

3. A second method for sorting is called a *bubble sort*. For an array that is to be put in ascending order, a bubble sort starts with the first entry in the array and successively interchanges it with the other entries until a larger entry is found. Then it is left at that point and the interchanging continues using the larger entry. The process continues until the last entry, the one in the last (Nth) element, is compared. After this comparison the largest entry will be in the Nth element. The entire process is repeated for only the first N−1 elements and the second largest entry is left in the N−1th element. Similar succeeding passes are used to sort the remaining N−2 elements. Modify the program SORT (and its comments) so that it uses a bubble sort. Which is more efficient, a bubble sort or an insertion sort? Why?

PROGRAMMING PROBLEMS

For each problem only a few sets of test data are suggested, not enough to really test the program. Therefore, propose other sets of data that would test the limits of the programs more thoroughly. Also, comment each program.

1. The flow Q (m³/s) through a pipe of length Z (m) is related to the diameter D (m) of the pipe by the equations

$$F = \frac{1.325}{\left\{\ln\left[\frac{V_e}{3.7D} + 4.62\left(\frac{VD}{Q}\right)^{0.9}\right]\right\}^2}$$

$$X = 0.102(Z + AD/F)/H$$

$$D = 0.66[V_e^{1.25}Q^{9.5}X^{4.75} + Q^{9.4}VX^{5.2}]^{0.04}$$

where: V_e = kinematic eddy viscosity (m²/s)
            V = kinematic viscosity (m²/s)
            A = minor loss coefficient
            H = pressure (meters of head)
            F = friction factor
            X = intermediate value of no physical significance

The method used for solving these equations to find the diameter that produces a desired flow is to assume a value for D, compute F, compute X, compute D, recompute F, recompute X, and so on until D changes by no more than a specified amount E.

    Write a program that inputs values to VE, V, A, H, Z, Q, and an initial value for D, assigns 0.001 to E, computes F and D, and prints

            KINEMATIC EDDY VISCOSITY = (*Value of VE*)
            KINEMATIC VISCOSITY = (*Value of V*)
            MINOR LOSS = (*Value of A*)
            HEAD = (*Value of H*)
            LENGTH OF PIPE = (*Value of Z*)
            DESIRED FLOW = (*Value of Q*)
            FRICTION FACTOR = (*Value of F*)
            DIAMETER = (*Value of D*)

Test the program with the data

$$VE = 46.0 \times 10^{-6} \qquad V = 1.308 \times 10^{-6} \qquad A = 10.0 \qquad H = 5.0$$
$$Z = 1000.0 \qquad Q = 0.5 \qquad \text{Initial } D = 1.0$$

2. An object that radiates the maximum possible amount of energy at any given temperature is called a blackbody, and many objects, such as the sun, may be considered to be blackbodies. Energy is radiated by frequencies and the Stefan–Boltzmann law states that the total energy (including all frequencies) radiated by a blackbody at a temperature $T(°K)$ is given by the equation

$$E = 5.67 \times 10^{-8}T^4 \qquad \text{W/m}^2$$

It is known that the fractional part of the total energy emitted by frequencies whose wavelengths are less than W is determined by the table

WT	E_f = fractional part of energy for all frequencies less than W
0.001	0.0003
0.002	0.0667
0.003	0.2733
0.004	0.4809
0.005	0.6338
0.006	0.7379
0.007	0.8082
0.008	0.8563
0.010	0.9143
0.015	0.9691
0.030	0.9954
0.100	1.0000

Suppose that linear interpolation is sufficiently accurate to estimate E_f for an arbitrary value of WT. The energy radiated by a blackbody at a temperature T for all frequencies in a band that extends from W_1 to W_2 can then be calculated from the table by determining the values of E_{f1} and E_{f2} corresponding to W_1T and W_2T, and then computing

$$\text{energy in band} = E_b = 5.67 \times 10^{-8}(E_{f2} - E_{f1})T^4$$

Write a program that will input W1, W2, and T; print

INVALID TEMPERATURE (*Value of T*)

and stop if T is negative; print

INVALID WAVELENGTH (*Values of W1 and W2*)

and stop if W1 or W2 is nonpositive or W1 > W2; and otherwise compute EB and print

TEMPERATURE = (*Value of T*)
LOWER WAVELENGTH = (*Value of W1*)
HIGHER WAVELENGTH = (*Value of W2*)
EMITTED ENERGY = (*Value of EB*)

Test the program using: W1 $= 8.0 \times 10^{-7}$ W2 $= 19.0 \times 10^{-7}$ T $= 2500\,°K$

3. Assuming the rate at which chemicals and so on enter a lake are held constant, the algae in the lake is known to grow according to the logistical growth curve given by the equation

$$Y = A \frac{1 + B}{1 + Be^{-CT}}$$

where: Y = amount of algae (g/m³)
           T = time (years)
           A = amount of algae at $T = 0$ (g/m³)
       B,C = experimentally determined positive constants

If the amount of algae is measured at $T = 0$, $T = T_1$, and $T = T_2$, the constants B and C must be such that

$$Y_i = A \frac{1 + B}{1 + Be^{-CT_i}} \quad i = 1, 2$$

where Y_1 and Y_2 are the amounts corresponding to T_1 and T_2. By solving the $i = 1$ case for B and substituting into the $i = 2$ case, the equation

$$W = \left(\frac{Y_2}{A} - 1\right)e^{-CT_1} + \left(\frac{Y_2}{Y_1} - \frac{Y_2}{A}\right)e^{-CT_2} - \left(\frac{Y_2}{Y_1} - 1\right) = 0$$

is obtained. A graph of this expression as a function of C is as follows:

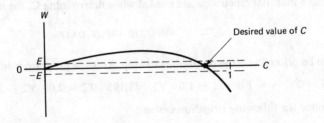

If E is a preselected constant and C is known to be less than 1, C can be found by the procedure

   1. Let $C_l = 0.0$, $C_h = 1.0$, and $C = 0.5$.
   2. Compute W.
   3. If $W > E$, let

$$\text{New } C_l = \text{Old } C$$
$$\text{New } C = 0.5(C_h + \text{New } C_l)$$

     If $W < -E$, let

$$\text{New } C_h = \text{Old } C$$
$$\text{New } C = 0.5(\text{New } C_h + C_l)$$

     If $-E \leq W \leq E$, exit the process.
   4. Return to step 2.

Such a procedure is called a *bisection* process.

Write a program that will input N (the number of years for which growth is to be projected), A, T1, Y1, T2, Y2, and a value for E; compute the constants B and C and the amounts of algae at T = 0, ..., N and at T = ∞; and print a report of the following form:

```
MEASURED DATA:
        INITIAL AMOUNT OF ALGAE = (Value of A)
            T1 = (Value of T1)          Y1 = (Value of Y1)
            T2 = (Value of T2)          Y2 = (Value of Y2)
    EXPERIMENTAL CONSTANTS:
            B = (Value of B)
            C = (Value of C)
    ALGAE GROWTH
            YEAR                    AMOUNT OF ALGAE
            0                       (Initial amount)
            1                       (Amount after 1 year)
            .                           .
            .                           .
            .                           .
            N                       (Amount after N years)
    LIMITING AMOUNT OF ALGAE = (Amount as T ⟶ ∞)
```

If more than 100 repetitions are needed while determining C, the message

INVALID INPUT DATA

is to be printed and the program is to stop. Test the program using the data

$$N = 20 \quad A = 1.0 \quad T1 = 1.0 \quad Y1 = 1.195 \quad T2 = 2.0 \quad Y2 = 1.422 \quad E = 0.00005$$

4. Assume the following irrigation system:

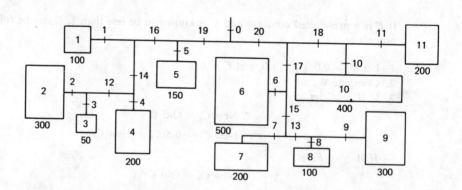

where the numbers in the squares are the field numbers, the numbers below the squares are the areas in hectares, (1 hectare = 10^4 m²), and the numbers beside the marks in the ditch segments are the gate numbers. The only constraint is that gate 0, the gate at the dam, can supply no more than 30 m³/s. The fields can be irrigated in minimum time by opening the dam to full capacity and then adjusting all the other gates so that all the fields to be irrigated will get their required amounts of water in the same length of time.

Write a program that reads in the number of fields to be irrigated and then reads in a record for each field that contains:

Field No.   Depth of water in centimeters

The input data are to be put in the linear arrays NF and DEPTH, and as the data are brought in they are to be checked for validity. If an invalid field number is found, the message

INVALID FIELD NO. – (*Field No.*)

is to be printed, and if a depth outside the range 0 to 20 cm is encountered, the message

INVALID DEPTH – (*Depth*) CM   FIELD – (*Field No.*)

is to be printed. If an input datum is invalid, the program is to stop; otherwise, it is to compute the time T the gates are to be open and the exact amount of water flow for each gate in m³/s. The flow for the Ith gate is to be put in the Ith element of the linear array FLOW. Zeros are to be put in FLOW for those gates that are to be left closed. The program is to then print the headings

IRRIGATION TIME: (*Value of T*)
GATE FLOWS
GATE NO.   FLOW RATE

followed by columns containing the gate numbers and flow rates for all the gates. In designing the program, use arrays in such a way that the flows can be computed by a simple loop and a single assignment statement. Run the program three times, once for each of the following sets of test data:

Test set 1		Test set 2		Test set 3	
1	10.0	1	10.0	2	7.0
3	5.0	3	5.0	5	10.0
5	25.0	9	7.0	3	20.0
9	2.0	0	5.0	6	12.0
10	10.0	5	10.0	4	14.0
				11	10.0

5

DATA ASSIGNMENT AND STORAGE

As we know, the smallest unit of storage in memory or a mass storage device is a bit, and bits are capable of storing only 0s and 1s. In order to store and access meaningful data, these bits have been grouped into larger storage units called bytes, words, and double words, which are typically 8, 32, and 64 bits in length, respectively. A byte is the smallest grouping that can be accessed in FORTRAN and is the size required to hold the alphanumeric coded 0–1 combination for a single character. Words are needed to store integer-type and real-type numbers, and double words are needed for double-precision numbers. Sequences of consecutive locations are used for arrays.

In a high-level language, the memory locations used by a program can be divided into those that do not change while the program is running (the ones associated with constants) and those that do change (the ones associated with variables), with the latter being associated with symbols called variable names. Because the different types of constants and variables (integer, real, double precision, etc.) have different 0–1 formats, a language must provide some means of allowing the programmer to tell the translator the type of each constant and variable. Only the integer and real types have been considered so far, and we have found that integer constants are those without decimal points and real constants are those with decimal points, and that variables are implicitly specified according to the first letters of their names. For programs more sophisticated than those heretofore studied, other types are needed and a flexible means of specifying the integer, real, and other types is desirable.

The primary purpose of this chapter is to introduce additional ways of specifying, assigning, and storing data. Section 5-1 discusses the variety of variable types that are available in FORTRAN and statements for explicitly specifying these types. Section 5-2 considers the means of assigning variables to constants without using assignment statements, and of assigning symbols to constants so that the constants can be easily identified and changed. The next section considers the ordering of statements within a program, and the following section introduces arrays with more than one dimension (e.g., two-dimensional tables) and nested implied DO loops for inputting to and outputting from such arrays. The last section shows how a location or area may be given more than one name and discusses why this is sometimes advantageous.

5-1 VARIABLE TYPES AND DATA DECLARATION STATEMENTS

Until now our FORTRAN discussions have included only integer and real variables and have assumed implicit specification in which a variable's type is determined by the first letter in its name. Although these limitations are not too restrictive to permit the solution of most problems, many applications require other variable types and a means of specifying these types. Also, the requirement that integer names can begin with only the letters I through N and real names can begin with only the remaining letters becomes more than a nuisance when writing a long program. As the number of variables in a program increases, it becomes necessary to give them descriptive names that can be easily remembered, and the restriction on assigning the first letter in the variable name becomes increasingly inconvenient.

To circumvent the problem with implicit data-type declarations, FORTRAN includes the INTEGER statement

INTEGER List

and the REAL statement

REAL List

where in both cases the *List* consists of variable and array names separated by commas. Any variable in the *List* of an INTEGER statement is of the integer type and any variable in the *List* of a REAL statement is of the real type. If a variable type is assigned by an INTEGER or REAL statement, it is said to be *explicitly typed. Explicit typing overrides implicit typing.*

Because INTEGER and REAL statements (and the other types of statements discussed below) instruct the FORTRAN translator how to store information, they must appear at the beginning of a program, although they may be placed before or after or interspersed with DIMENSION statements.

Examples of the INTEGER and REAL statements are

INTEGER A, ITEM, X
REAL I, POWER

where any of the items in the list could be array names. The INTEGER statement causes the data stored in the locations associated with A, ITEM, and X to be stored in the integer format, and the data stored in the locations associated with I and POWER to be stored in the real format. Note that variables such as ITEM and POWER can be explicitly typed to be of the same type as would result from implicit typing. It should be obvious, however, that a variable cannot be explicitly specified to be of two different types; for example, the sequence

REAL LIM

INTEGER LIM

would be invalid. (The variable type determines the format of the 0–1 bit combination in a memory location and, clearly, two different formats could not be used for the same location.)

In addition to specifying variable type, the INTEGER, REAL, and other type statements can be used to dimension arrays. The statements

INTEGER A, AMT(−5:5), FLAG

REAL MOMENT, X(100)

would assign A, AMT, and FLAG to integer locations and MOMENT and X to real locations, and allocate 11 locations to AMT and 100 locations to X. Because arrays can be dimensioned only once the sequence

INTEGER X(100)

DIMENSION X(100)

would be invalid even though both statements dimension X to the same size. On the other hand

INTEGER X

DIMENSION X(100)

would be valid because the first statement only specifies the type.

In lengthy programs it is best to explicitly specify all variables, except possibly indices, including those that would be correctly typed through implicit specification. This practice would provide a complete listing of the variables at the beginning of the program which would indicate their types. If someone reading the program wanted to verify the type of a variable, he or she could quickly check the specification statements. It would take longer to verify the absence of a variable, and therefore assume implicit specification, than it would to find a variable. This is because the *Lists* would have to be examined closely to make certain that the variable is not overlooked. If a program is used extensively by several people, it is worth taking the time to list the variables in alphabetical order, although this would be done late in a program's development. A typical program might begin as follows:

```
PROGRAM INCTAX
INTEGER CODE, DDNUM(0:5), IDNUM, SSN
REAL DEDUCT(100), GPAY, NPAY, TAX, TEMP
                      .
                      .
```

Note that DIMENSION statements are not needed if all arrays are allocated with type statements.

There are several other types of variables available to the FORTRAN programmer. The subsections below consider double precision, complex, character, and logical variable and array names. Some FORTRAN translators may accommodate other types of variables, such as octal and hexadecimal variables, but they are not widely needed and are not considered in this book.

5-1-1 Double-Precision Quantities

As mentioned in Sec. 1-4, numbers in the real format occupy only one word of memory, and this may not provide enough bits to give the accuracy needed for some applications. When this is so, two words of memory need to be assigned to each number that requires extra accuracy. Variables associated with numbers that reside in only one word are real or single-precision variables that are designated either by the REAL statement or by default using variable names that do not begin with I through N. Variables associated with numbers that occupy two words are double-precision variables and *must* be explicitly associated with two words in memory by a type statement of the form

DOUBLE PRECISION *List*

where *List* is a list of the variables and arrays (separated by commas) to be assigned two words.

The DOUBLE PRECISION statement may also be used to allocate space for arrays. The statement

DOUBLE PRECISION A, X(−5:5), I

causes the allocation of 11 double words for X and associates A, each element of X, and I with a double word. Because double-precision numbers are extensions of real numbers (i.e., they are *always* in the fraction-exponent format), the variable I will be in an extended form of the real format, *not* in an extended form of the integer format.

A double-precision constant can be designated as such by using the exponent form with the E replaced by a D. The statements

DOUBLE PRECISION MOMENT
MOMENT = −3.153D−3

causes the double-precision constant $-3.153D\text{-}3$ to be put in the double-precisison variable MOMENT.

Mixed-mode arithmetic and assignment are permitted. When an addition, subtraction, multiplication, or division is being carried out and one of the quantities is double precision and the other is integer or real, the integer or real quantity is converted to double precision, the operation is executed, and the result is in double precision. If a double-precision quantity is raised to a real power or a real or integer quantity is raised to a double-precision power, the real or integer quantity is converted to double precision and the result is in double precision. If a double-precision quantity is raised to an integer power, the operation is carried out by multiplication, and perhaps a division, and the result is in double precision. When an expression that evaluates to an integer or real quantity is assigned to a double-precision variable, a conversion is made to double precision. When an expression evaluates to a double-precision quantity and is assigned to an integer or real variable, a conversion is made to the integer or real format, respectively.

Conversions are made according to the following rules:

Double precision to real—Quantity is truncated to single precision.

Real to double precision—Second word is appended to the real quantity, but the number is unchanged.

Double precision to integer—Quantity is truncated just as it is in a real to integer conversion.

Integer to double precision—Quantity is converted to real and a second word is appended.

There is one possible exception to these rules: some FORTRAN translators use rounding when converting from double precision to real.

There are several intrinsic functions for working with double-precision quantities and they are summarized in Fig. 5-1. Some of the functions are designed specifi-

Function Name	Description
DBLE	Converts any integer, real, double precision, or real part of a complex argument to a double precision result
DPROD	Multiplies two real arguments and returns a double precision result
INT, NINT, REAL	Performs conversions on double precision arguments just as they do with real arguments (results are as indicated in Fig. 2-9)
AINT, ANINT, ABS, MOD, SIGN, DIM, MAX, MIN, SQRT, EXP, LOG, LOG10, SIN, COS, TAN, ASIN, ACOS, ATAN, ATAN2, SINH, COSH, TANH	Operates on double precision arguments just as they do real arguments. If the arguments are double precision, the results are double precision (see Fig. 2-9)

FIGURE 5-1 *Intrinsic double-precision functions.*

cally for double-precision usage, but most of the functions are the same as those given in Fig. 2-9. In the latter case, if the argument(s) is double precision, the result will be double precision.

List-directed input of double-precision values is the same as input of real values. The input data may appear in the usual decimal format or in an E-format with the quantities separated by blanks or commas. However, so that a user can identify those numbers that are to be input to double-precision variables, it is permissible to replace the E in the E-format with a D, in which case the number is said to be in a *D-format*. Thus if

$$5.2895672201D\ 2$$

appeared on a data card, it could easily be recognized as a number to be input to a double-precision list item.

List-directed output of double-precision numbers depends on the translator. The rule assumed here is that if the absolute value of a number is greater than or equal to 1 but less than 10^{16}, it will be printed to 16 significant figures, left-justified with a leading blank, in the normal decimal format in a field of 23 columns. Otherwise, it will be printed left justified with a leading blank in the form

$$SX.XXXXXXXXXXXXXXXD+XX$$

in a field of 23 columns. In other words, double-precision numbers will be printed just as real numbers are printed, except that 16 significant figures will be output instead of six and the number of columns used will be 23 instead of 13.

5-1-2 Complex Quantities

Many scientific and engineering computer applications require the manipulation of complex quantities. Although the operations on complex numbers could be programmed using the real operations, it would be much more convenient if they could be performed directly. Therefore, even some of the older forms of FORTRAN include complex arithmetic and at least some complex functions. FORTRAN 77 includes an extensive set of complex capabilities.

A complex number is stored in its rectangular form as a pair of real numbers, a real part and an imaginary part. Therefore, it takes two words of memory to hold a complex number and an array having N elements will occupy 2N consecutive words in memory. A complex constant is denoted by writing two real numbers (in any acceptable real constant format) separated by a comma and enclosed in parentheses. The first number is the real part and the second number is the imaginary part. If W and Z are complex variables, the statement

$$W = Z + (1.3,5.12E-1)$$

causes the real part of W to become the real part of Z plus 1.3, and the imaginary part of W to become the imaginary part of Z plus 0.512).

Complex variables must be explicitly designated with a statement of the form

COMPLEX *List*

where *List* is a list of the variables and arrays that are to be complex. The COMPLEX statement can also be used to dimension arrays. The statement

COMPLEX A, I, W(0:3)

would cause eight words to be allocated to W. A pair of words would be assigned to A, I, and each element of W.

Mixed-mode expressions and assignments are allowed with the integer and real types, but not with the double-precision type. A mixed-mode arithmetic operation is performed by converting the integer or real quantity to complex form, carrying out the operation using complex arithmetic, and leaving the result in complex form. Conversions are done according to the following rules:

Complex to real—Real part becomes real quantity, imaginary part is dropped.
Real to complex—Real quantity is put in the real part, 0 is put in the imaginary part.
Complex to integer—Real part is truncated and put in integer, imaginary part is dropped.
Integer to complex—Integer is converted to real and put in the real part, 0 is put in the imaginary part.

There are several intrinsic functions for working with complex quantities and they are summarized in Fig. 5-2. Some of them are new since they *must* involve com-

Function Name	Description
CMPLX	Can have one argument or two arguments of the same type. Converts integer, real, or double precision argument(s) to complex result with first argument being the real part and the second argument being the imaginary part. If there is only one argument it is the real part and 0 is the imaginary part.
AIMAG	Result is real and is the imaginary part of the complex argument.
CONJG	Result is the complex conjugate of the complex argument.
INT, REAL, DBLE	Performs conversions on real part of complex arguments. Results are integer, real, or double precision, respectively (see Fig. 2-9).
ABS	Result is the magnitude of the complex argument.
SQRT, EXP, LOG, SIN, COS	Result is complex if the argument is complex (see Fig. 2-9).

FIGURE 5-2 *Intrinsic complex functions.*

plex arguments or results, the others are extensions of the functions given in Fig. 2-9.

For list-directed input a datum corresponding to a complex list item must appear as a pair of real numbers (in any acceptable real format) separated by a comma and enclosed in parentheses. List-directed output causes a complex item to be printed as two real numbers (according to the rules for outputting real numbers) separated by a comma and enclosed in parentheses.

5-1-3 Character Strings

Character strings are stored, one character per byte, in consecutive bytes of memory using an alphanumeric code to store each character as a 0–1 bit combination. The most frequently encountered alphanumeric codes are the American Standard Code for Information Interchange (ASCII) and the IBM code known by the acronym EBCDIC. A sequence of memory locations for storing a character string can be assigned a variable name just as a location for storing a number can be given a variable name. There can also be character string arrays for manipulating sets of character strings. Character string variables and arrays must be explicitly specified using a statement of the form

CHARACTER*Length List

where *List* is a list of character string variable and array names and *Length* is the number of bytes reserved for each string (i.e., the maximum number of characters each string can contain). The statement

CHARACTER*7 J, CHARR(10)

assigns 7 bytes of memory to the variable J and each element in the array CHARR. The *Length* applies to all variables and all elements of the arrays appearing in *List*. If a *Length* is not given, it is 1 by default. Therefore,

CHARACTER*1 A,B,C

and

CHARACTER A,B,C

are equivalent. An alternative form of the CHARACTER statement is

CHARACTER Name1*Length1, . . . , NameN*LengthN

which permits the variables and arrays to be assigned lengths individually. The statement

CHARACTER ID*12, NAME(1000)*20

allocates 12 bytes of memory for ID and 20 bytes of memory for each of the 1000 elements of NAME.

String constants are character strings that cannot be changed during the execution of a program; they appear in a program enclosed in single quotes. The statements

```
CHARACTER*5 A
A = 'HELLO'
```

allocate 5 bytes of memory to A and put the alphanumeric code for H in the first byte, the code for E in the second byte, and so on. If a single quote must be included in a string, it may be inserted by typing two single quotes consecutively. If X is a string variable with 5 bytes, then

```
X = 'DON''T'
```

causes DON'T to be stored in X.

Blanks are alphanumeric characters and if CHAR is a string consisting of 11 bytes, the statement

```
CHAR = 'A GRAY CAT '
```

will cause the code for a blank to be put in the second, seventh, and eleventh bytes of CHAR.

Assignment statements involving character strings are somewhat limited. Character string expressions may include character string variables and constants, but it would make no sense to apply arithmetic operations to character strings, and mixed mode involving other types of variables is clearly invalid. The only character string operation is concatenation. *Concatenation* is performed by placing two slashes between the strings being operated on and causes the right string to be appended to the right end of the left string. For example, the statements

```
CHARACTER*4 P, Q
CHARACTER*12 R
P = 'SUE '
Q = 'ANN '
R = P//Q//'GREY'
```

would result in SUE ANN GREY being put into R. Note that blanks had to be included in P and Q in order for them to be put into R. When concatenating strings, it is invalid to include the variable to the left of the equal sign in the concatenation, e.g.,

```
X = X // Y
```

is invalid.

It is possible to refer to only a portion of a character string, or *substring*, by writing an expression of the form

Variable (Integer Exp 1 : Integer Exp 2)

where *Variable* is a string variable or string array element name, *Integer Exp* 1 is an integer expression whose value is the number of the beginning character in the substring, and *Integer Exp* 2 is an integer expression whose value is the number of the final character in the substring. Either *Integer Exp* 1 or *Integer Exp* 2 can be left out of the notation. The default value for *Integer Exp* 1 is 1 and the default value for *Integer Exp* 2 is the number of the last character in the string. As an example, the statements

```
CHARACTER*6 X, Y, Z(5)
X = 'ABCDEF'
Z(4) = '123'//X(3:5)
Y = X( :2)//Z(4)(3:4)//X(5: )
Z(5) = 'MATTER'
Z(5)(2:4) = 'OTH'
```

result in the fourth element of Z containing 123CDE, Y containing AB3CEF, and the fifth element of Z containing MOTHER.

The intrinsic functions involving character strings are given in Fig. 5-3. The function CHAR, which is the only function with a character result, is of primary interest at this point because it is the only one that can occur in a character string expression. The functions ICHAR (which is the inverse of CHAR), LEN (which returns the length of its character string argument), and INDEX (which is for searching strings) return integer results and may appear in algebraic expressions. The LGE, LGT, LLE, and LLT functions result in truth values. The functions INDEX, LGE, LGT, LLE, and LLT are discussed later in this section.

Function Name	Description
CHAR	Result is the character whose code is the binary equivalent of the integer argument.
ICHAR	Result is the integer that is the decimal equivalent of the code for the single character argument.
LEN	Result is integer and is the length (in characters) of the character string argument.
INDEX	This function has two character string arguments and produces an integer result. The first argument is searched from the left until an exact match with the second argument is found. The result is the position in the first argument of the first character in the substring of the first argument that is matched by the second argument.
LGE, LGT, LLE, LLT	These functions have two character string arguments. Each argument is converted to an ASCII equivalent string and then they are compared using the .GE., .GT., .LE., or .LT. relational operator, respectively. The result is the truth value of the comparison.

FIGURE 5-3 *Intrinsic character string functions.*

The function CHAR returns a one-character string that is determined by its integer argument. The resulting character is the character whose code (0–1 combination) is the binary equivalent of the integer argument. For example, the 0–1 combination for a 'B' in ASCII code is 01000010 = 66; therefore, for a system that uses the ASCII code, CHAR(66) returns the string 'B'. One of the principal applications of the CHAR function is in inserting the carriage return and line feed characters when communicating with a terminal. Again assuming the ASCII code, the statement

$$X = \text{'JOE'}//\text{CHAR}(13)//\text{CHAR}(10)//\text{'JONES'}$$

would cause a carriage return, whose ASCII code is 00001101, and a line feed, whose ASCII code is 00001010, to be inserted between JOE and JONES. Thus if X were output, JOE would appear on one line and JONES on the following line. (Both a carriage return and line feed are required because a carriage return only moves the carriage; the line feed provides the vertical spacing and prevents an overprint.)

If an assignment statement assigns a string expression to a string variable or array element whose length (in bytes) is different from the number of characters in the string resulting from the expression, the following rules are employed:

1. If the variable or array element is shorter, the expression result is truncated from the right (the rightmost characters are not assigned).
2. If the variable or array element is longer, the expression result is padded on the right side with blanks.

For example, the statements

```
CHARACTER*5 X, Y
X = 'GOODBYE'
Y = 'BYE'
```

cause the code for GOODB to be put in X, and the code for BYE(blank)(blank) to be put in Y.

Character string variables and arrays can be input to or output from using list-directed I-O in the usual way. An input datum is enclosed in quotes and all characters, including blanks, inside the quotes are part of the datum. If the length of an input datum is different from the length of the corresponding input list item, the same rules as those given for assignment statements apply. That is, if the list item is shorter, the datum is truncated from the right, and if the datum is shorter, it is padded on the right with blanks before being put in the list item. On output, the number of characters printed is determined by the length of the list item and they are printed without quotes. Consider the program segment

```
CHARACTER*4 A,B,C
READ *, J,A,C
B = A( :1)//' '//A( :1)
PRINT *, B,J,C,'26'
```

If the input line is

```
 15, 'X Y', 'SMITH'
```

the output will be

```
     B    J     C  26
   X∧X∧¦∧∧∧∧∧∧15¦SMIT¦26 . . .
```

If two consecutive single quotes appear in an input datum, they are not inter-preted as the end of the string but cause one single quote to be input as part of the string. A similar statement can be made regarding string constants that are being output. If the input record is

```
 'DON' 'T ', 'COME'
```

and the statements

```
                      CHARACTER*5 A(2)
                      READ *, (A(I),I=1,2)
                      DO 10 I=1,2
                         PRINT *, A(I)
                   10 CONTINUE
                      PRINT *, 'IT''S DANGEROUS'
```

are executed, the output would be

```
              DON'T
              COME
              IT'S DANGEROUS
```

(The examples above should be studied carefully.)

One very important application of computers is text editing or, more generally, word processing. Text editing is the process of inputting, changing, and outputting character strings, some of which may be pages long. This book was written with the aid of a text-editing program, or text editor, and, as mentioned in Chap. 1, interactive FORTRAN programs are usually written with a text editor. Although we do not have the space here to give even an abbreviated discussion of text editors, the INDEX function defined in Fig. 5-3 provides an important feature needed in the design of text editors and is worth our brief consideration. In changing text one must first search out the substring to be altered. The INDEX function has two string arguments and searches the first argument until a substring is found that exactly matches the second argument. It then returns the integer that indicates the position of the first letter of the matched substring within the string being searched. If no match is found or the second argument is longer than the first argument, the INDEX function returns a 0. The statements

```
X = 'THE SHEEZ JUMPED OVER THE FENCE'
Y = 'EEZ'
I = INDEX(X,Y)
X(I:I+2) = 'EEP'
```

would cause the integer 7 to be put into I, and the substring 'EEZ' to be changed to 'EEP'.

The final topic regarding character strings that deserves our immediate attention concerns their ordering. Because characters are related to 0–1 combinations through an alphanumeric code, the characters can be ordered according to the binary numbers that are equivalent to the 0–1 combinations. Such an ordering for a given code is called the *collating sequence* for that code. The complete collating sequence for the ASCII code is given in Fig. 5-4. The decimal equivalents of the binary numbers that represent the characters are given instead of the binary numbers because the CHAR function result and the ICHAR function argument are in decimal form. From the figure it is seen that ICHAR(', ') would result in 44 and CHAR(69) would yield 'E'.

Because for many applications alphabetic ordering is as important as numerical ordering, alphanumeric codes must be designed so that strings can be compared easily with respect to alphabetic ordering. Although a computer cannot make alphabetic comparisons, it can readily make numeric comparisons, which, in FORTRAN, are accomplished through the relational operators .LE., .GT., and so on. Therefore, alphabetic comparisons can easily be made if, as the letters increase alphabetically, the collating sequence increases (i.e., as the letters increase, the 0–1 combinations that represent them increase numerically). In the ASCII code the two strings 'ABE' and 'ACE' are represented by

```
01000001 01000010 01000101
01000001 01000011 01000101
```

respectively. The string 'ACE' is higher in the alphabet and the second 0–1 combination, when taken as a whole, is greater numerically.

In addition to letters, practical rules for ordering character strings must include rules for handling commas, blanks, digits, and other characters. FORTRAN includes a standard for collating sequences which states that in order for a code to be usable by FORTRAN, it must obey the following rules:

1. The uppercase letters are such that A is lower in the sequence than B, B is lower in the sequence than C, and so on.
2. The digit 0 is lower in the sequence than 1, 1 is lower in the sequence than 2, and so on through 9.
3. The collating subsequences for the digits and letters do not overlap.
4. The blank character is lower in the sequence than any letter or digit.

Decimal Value	ASCII Character	Usage	Decimal Value	ASCII Character	Usage	Decimal Value	ASCII Character	Usage
0	NUL	FILL character	43	+		86	V	
1	SOH		44	,		87	W	
2	STX		45	−		88	X	
3	ETX	CTRL/C	46	.		89	Y	
4	EOT		47	/		90	Z	
5	ENQ		48	0		91	[	
6	ACK		49	1		92	\	
7	BEL	BELL	50	2		93	]	
8	BS		51	3		94	^ or ↑	
9	HT	HORIZONTAL TAB	52	4		95	_ or ←	
10	LF	LINE FEED	53	5		96	` Grave accent	
11	VT	VERTICAL TAB	54	6		97	a	
12	FF	FORM FEED	55	7		98	b	
13	CR	CARRIAGE RETURN	56	8		99	c	
14	SO		57	9		100	d	
15	SI	CTRL/O	58	:		101	e	
16	DLE		59	;		102	f	
17	DC1		60	<		103	g	
18	DC2		61	=		104	h	
19	DC3		62	>		105	i	
20	DC4		63	?		106	j	
21	NAK	CTRL/U	64	@		107	k	
22	SYN		65	A		108	l	
23	ETB		66	B		109	m	
24	CAN		67	C		110	n	
25	EM		68	D		111	o	
26	SUB	CTRL/Z	69	E		112	p	
27	ESC	ESCAPE[1]	70	F		113	q	
28	FS		71	G		114	r	
29	GS		72	H		115	s	
30	RS		73	I		116	t	
31	US		74	J		117	u	
32	SP	SPACE	75	K		118	v	
33	!		76	L		119	w	
34	''		77	M		120	x	
35	≠		78	N		121	y	
36	$		79	O		122	z	
37	%		80	P		123	{	
38	&		81	Q		124	| Vertical Line	
39	'		82	R		125	}	
40	(		83	S		126	~ Tilde	
41	)		84	T		127	DEL RUBOUT	
42	*		85	U				

FIGURE 5-4 *ASCII collating sequence.*

Also, it is highly desirable for at least the comma, and perhaps other punctuation marks, to be before the digits and letters in the collating sequence. Having the blank lowest in the collating sequence and the comma lower than the letters would mean that the character strings

JONES, SAM

JONESS, MARY

would have the proper numerical ordering for normal alphabetic ordering.

The ordering of the digits, the letters, the important punctuation marks, and the blank are given in Fig. 5-5 for both the ASCII and EBCDIC codes. From this

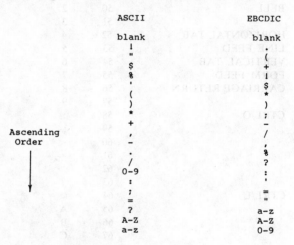

FIGURE 5-5 *Ordering of the principal characters in the ASCII and EBCDIC codes.*

figure it is seen that these codes satisfy the rules given above. For most applications it is better for the codes for the digits to be lower in the collating sequence than the codes for the letters; therefore, ASCII is preferred over EBCDIC.

For the ASCII, EBCDIC, and other well-designed codes, character-string alphabetic comparisons can be made with the relational operators .LT., .LE., and so on. When such comparisons are performed, if the character strings are not of the same length, the shorter one is padded from the right with blanks. For example, if A, B, and X are strings containing six characters, then X and the string constant 'TEXAS' could be placed in alphabetical order in A and B using the IF block

```
IF (X .LT. 'TEXAS') THEN
        A = X
        B = 'TEXAS'
ELSE
        A = 'TEXAS'
        B = X
ENDIF
```

The string 'TEXAS' is padded, so it becomes 'TEXAS ' before it is compared with the six-character variable X. As a more useful example, essentially the same insertion sort program given in Fig. 4-28 could be used to alphabetize a character string array (see Exercise 11).

For codes whose collating sequences are not properly designed, standard FORTRAN 77 includes the LGE, LGT, LLE, and LLT functions that convert their two string arguments to ASCII strings and then compare the two ASCII strings to produce a truth value. In the segment above that compares the string variable X with the string constant 'TEXAS', if the strings were not in a well-designed code, the IF-THEN statement could have utilized the LLT function as follows:

```
IF (LLT(X,'TEXAS')) THEN
```

Thereby, the ASCII collating sequence could be assumed even if the computer system being used relied on a code with a much different collating sequence. The LGE, LGT, LLE, and LLT functions would, however, have to be designed for the code of the particular computer system. If a system uses the ASCII code, these functions would have the same effect as the .GE., .GT., .LE., and .LT. relational operators.

FORTRAN 77 requires that only character-type variables and arrays be permitted to contain characters, but older versions of FORTRAN allow variables and arrays of all types to be used to store characters. In fact, the 1966 ANSI standard FORTRAN does not even include a CHARACTER statement, and in some FORTRAN dialects characters *have to* be stored in variables and arrays of the other types. If another type is used to store characters, the length of the variables or array elements (i.e., character strings) is determined by the number of bytes associated with that type. For example, suppose that integers and real numbers are stored in words containing 4 bytes and double-precision numbers are stored in double words containing 8 bytes. Then, if X, Y, and Z are used to store characters, the statements

```
INTEGER X
REAL Y
DOUBLE PRECISION Z
```

would have the same effect as

```
CHARACTER X*4, Y*4, Z*8
```

Once the length is established, all of the rules for inputting, outputting, and manipulating a character string can be applied.

5-1-4 Logical Variables

For some special applications and for added flexibility in working with the *Conditions* that appear in IF, IF-THEN, ELSE IF-THEN, DO-WHILE, and DO-UNTIL statements, FORTRAN permits constants and variables, called *logical constants* and *variables*, that can take on only the truth values true and false. The two truth values are, of course, stored as distinct 0–1 combinations, but just what these combinations are is not important to the FORTRAN programmer. Logical constants appear in a program as .TRUE. or .FALSE.. Logical variables must be specified as such by a statement of the form

LOGICAL List

where *List* is a list of the logical variable or array names separated by commas. An array whose elements are logical can also be dimensioned by a LOGICAL statement. The statement

LOGICAL A, J(10)

reserves 10 locations for the array J and causes A and the elements of J to be associated with memory locations that may hold only the 0–1 combination for .TRUE. or the 0–1 combination for .FALSE..

Logical assignment statements consist of logical variables being equated to logical expressions. It should be obvious that mixed mode with variables of other types would not make sense. The statements

```
LOGICAL COM1, COM2
X = 1.0
COM1 = .TRUE.
COM2 = X .GT. 2.0
```

would cause the truth value .TRUE. to be put in COM1 and the truth value .FALSE. to be put in COM2. The statements

```
LOGICAL LV
READ *, X
LV = X .GT. 0.0 .AND. X .LT. 1.0
IF (LV .AND. .TRUE.) PRINT *, 'TEST'
```

would cause TEST to be printed if the value input to X were positive and less than 1.0; otherwise, the program would continue in sequence without printing TEST. (The phrase .AND. .TRUE. is superfluous and is included for demonstrative purposes only.)

A datum corresponding to a logical list-directed input item must consist of an optional period followed by either a T, for true, or F, for false. The T or F may optionally be followed by other letters, but normally a simple T or F is used. Similarly, if a logical value is being output by a PRINT * statement, either a T or an F is printed. The exact form of the output may vary from one system to the next.

5-1-5 IMPLICIT Statements

It has been stated that, except for the implicit typing of integer and real variables according to the first letters of their names, all variables must be explicitly typed using the INTEGER, REAL, DOUBLE PRECISION, COMPLEX, CHARAC-

TER, and LOGICAL statements. This is not completely true because in most versions of FORTRAN, including FORTRAN 77, the keywords in these statements can be prefixed with the word IMPLICIT to form IMPLICIT statements which permit implicit specification of all types of variables. An implicit statement is of the form

IMPLICIT *Type (List of Letters)*

where *Type* is one of the keywords INTEGER, REAL, DOUBLE PRECISION, COMPLEX, CHARACTER, or LOGICAL and *List of Letters* is a list of single letters or designations of the form

Letter-Letter

separated by commas. An IMPLICIT statement causes all the variable and array names whose first letters are included in the *List of Letters* to be of the type indicated by *Type*. IMPLICIT statements may not be used for dimensioning.

For example, the statements

```
IMPLICIT INTEGER (A,R-T)
IMPLICIT REAL (I)
IMPLICIT CHARACTER*8 (L-N,U-W)
```

causes all variables and arrays that begin with A, R, S, and T to be of the integer type, all variables and arrays that begin with I to be of the real type, and all variables and arrays that begin with L, M, N, U, V, and W to be of the character type with length 8. By normal implicit type declaration, variables and arrays that begin with J and K will be integer variables and arrays. Similarly, those that begin with B through H, O, P, Q, and X through Z will be real variables.

The order of precedence for type declaration is:

Highest precedence	Explicit type declaration using INTEGER, REAL, etc., statements.
↓	Type declaration using IMPLICIT statements.
Lowest precedence	Implicit type declaration of real and integer variables and arrays.

Because IMPLICIT statements determine the typing process, they must appear at the very beginning of a program. The use of IMPLICIT statements is recommended only in special cases for which the variables and arrays can be naturally associated with their first letters. In almost all cases the following statement applies:

All variables and arrays, except possibly for indices, should be explicitly typed, thus providing a complete list of the variables and arrays that leaves no doubt as to their types.

EXERCISES

1. Give type statements that will cause:
   - (a) IN, N125, and JAX to be real variables, S to be an integer variable, and CODES to be an integer array having subscripts from -3 to 5.
   - (b) MIX to be a real array with subscripts from 3 to 18, NEW to be a real array with subscripts from 1 to 5, and X, XX, and X3 to be double-precision variables.
   - (c) V1 and V2 to be complex variables and DP to be a double-precision array with subscripts from 1 to 1000.
   - (d) CS1, CS2, and CS3 to be character strings of length 8 and STR to be a character string array with subscripts from 0 to 10 whose elements are 12 characters long.
   - (e) LV to be a logical variable, LARR to be a logical array with subscripts from -5 to 5, COMP to be a complex variable, and X to be a double-precision array with subscripts from 1 to 100.

2. Assuming 4 bytes to a word and two words to a double word, and that each character occupies a byte, an integer, real, or logical quantity occupies a word, and a double-precision or complex quantity occupies a double word, find the amount of memory in bytes needed to store the variables and arrays indicated in each part of Exercise 1.

3. Describe what each of the following statements does.
   - (a) INTEGER X1, IT, Y(-1:1)
   - (b) REAL X, Y, Z
   - (c) DOUBLE PRECISION A(100), AA(50)
   - (d) COMPLEX COMP1, COMP2, COMP3
   - (e) CHARACTER*10 SARRAY(5:15), CHAR
   - (f) LOGICAL A, B(25), C
   - (g) CHARACTER XLABEL*10, YLABEL*20, CS(10)*4
   - (h) CHARACTER DIGIT, LETTER

4. Determine whether or not the following statements contain syntax errors, and correct those statements that are invalid.
   - (a) REAL X, Y, Z(-1,1)
   - (b) INTEGER*8 A, I
   - (c) DOUBLE PRECISION DP, VOLTAGE
   - (d) COMPLEX (R,I)
   - (e) CHARACTER*32 A, CI5(32)
   - (f) LOGICAL A .EQ. 1.0

5. Given that X is real, I is integer, D is double precision, C is complex, S is a character string, and L is logical, describe the exact procedure by which each of the following mixed-mode assignment statements is executed. Indicate those statements that are invalid.
   - (a) X = 5.0 + X*I + C
   - (b) C = X**I + 2
   - (c) D = I + (1.0D-2)*SIN(D)
   - (d) S = S//'NEW YORK'//CHAR(10)//CHAR(13)//'NEW YORK'
   - (e) L = X .LT. X**2 $-$ 1.0 .OR. .TRUE.

    (f) L = X .LT. .TRUE.
    (g) I = D−X
    (h) S = I//S
    (i) I = C + (5.0,2.0)

6. Assume that a program begins with

```
INTEGER I, FLAG
REAL X, NPAY, A(3)
DOUBLE PRECISION P(−2:2)
COMPLEX U, V
CHARACTER*2 C1, C2
LOGICAL L, M
```

For each of the following statements, give a valid set of input or output data.
    (a) READ *, X, (P(K), K=−1,2),A(2)
    (b) READ *, L,M,U,V
    (c) READ *, C1,U,C2,V
    (d) PRINT *, (A(K), K=1,3,2),C1
    (e) PRINT *, I,'INVALID DATA',NPAY
    (f) PRINT *, 'THE FLAG IS',FLAG
    (g) PRINT *, L, '   ',U

7. Given that a program begins with

```
INTEGER X
CHARACTER*4 A, B
CHARACTER*6 Y
LOGICAL V
```

find the contents of X, A, B, Y, and V after the execution of each of the following sets of statements. (Note those quantities that cannot be determined from the given information and statements that are invalid.)
    (a) A = 'BYE'
        B = 'HOWDY'
        A = B//A
        Y = A//' '//B
    (b) A = '(1)'
        DO 10 I = 1,4
            Y = Y//A
        10   CONTINUE
    (c) X = 5.2
        IF (X .GT. 5) THEN
            A = '5.0'
        ELSE
            B = 'GO'
        ENDIF

(d) X = 5
   V = X .EQ. X*3
   IF (V .OR. X .LT. 7) THEN
           V = .TRUE.
       ELSE
           X = X+54
           PRINT *, A//B
   ENDIF

8. Given that the input data are

$$\text{'OLD', '123456', '123456', T}$$

and that S1 and S2 are character strings of length 5, S3 is a string of length 7, and LOGIC is a logical variable, find the contents of S1, S2, S3, and LOGIC after the execution of:
   (a) READ *, S1,S2,S3,LOGIC
   (b) READ *, S3,S1,S2,LOGIC
   (c) READ *, S3,S2,S1,LOGIC

9. Write a program that uses only double-precision variables and evaluates the polynomial

$$Y = 3X^2 + 2X - 1$$

The program is to read a title into a string variable, read a double-precision number into X, compute Y, and print the title followed by the value of Y.

10. Write a program that reads in an integer P, reads P triplets of real numbers into the arrays A, B, and C, finds the complex solutions to the quadratic equations

$$A(I)X^2 + B(I)X + C(I) = 0 \quad \text{for } I = 1, \ldots, P$$

puts the results into the complex arrays X1 and X2, and prints the results under the headings

FIRST ROOT   SECOND ROOT

11. Write a program that reads in N, reads N strings of length 12 into an array SARRAY, uses an insertion sort to put the strings in alphabetical order, and prints the strings under the heading

NAMES OF STATES

12. Give the statements necessary to cause all variables that begin with I and X through Z to be integers, that begin with A through D to be real, S and T to be double precision, L through M to be logical, and Q, V, and W to be character strings of length 20.

5-2 PARAMETER AND DATA STATEMENTS

The memory locations that hold the data to be used by a program may be filled with values either at the time the program is translated or at the time it is executed. Constants are assigned at translation time and remain the same throughout the execution of the program. Until now, constants have appeared only as numbers within the program. When the statement

$$A = 3.14159*R**2$$

is translated, the constants 3.14159 and 2 become part of the program and are put in memory locations using the real and integer formats, respectively, at the time the program is loaded for execution. These locations remain the same during the execution of the program, although their contents are used at the time the assignment statement above is encountered.

Frequently, it is more convenient for constants that occur several times within a program to be assigned a name and then be referred to by the name. This is particularly true if the value of the constant is likely to change during the life of the program, but does not change so often that it should be replaced with a variable that is read into at execution time. In such a situation only the constant that is assigned to the name must be changed when the program is updated and the references to the constant, which may be scattered throughout the program, may remain the same. For example, when solving a problem involving the design of a pipeline the coefficient of expansion for the type of steel used may appear several times. If the program is later used to design another pipeline that uses a different type of steel, it would be necessary to replace the coefficient of expansion everywhere it appears. However, if the coefficient of expansion had been assigned the name COE and the name had been used in place of the numerical value for the coefficient, only the number assigned to COE would need to be changed.

It should be noted that assigning a name to a constant would not change the fact that constants cannot change values while a program is running (for this would defy their definition). Assigning a name would simply mean that the constant could be referred to by its descriptive name.

FORTRAN 77 permits the assignment of names to constants through statements of the form

PARAMETER (*Name 1 = Exp 1, . . . , Name N = Exp N*)

where *Name 1* through *Name N* are the names given to the constants whose values are determined by the expressions *Exp 1* through *Exp N*, respectively. The expressions are limited to including only numbers or names of constants that are assigned by previous PARAMETER statements, but can be mixed mode, in which case the mixed-mode rules for ordinary assignment statements apply.

Constants that are given names using PARAMETER statements are called *named constants*. Named constants are typed according to the same rules that regulate the typing of variables. Within a given program, the name of a constant cannot appear more than once in the collection of all PARAMETER statements. This is true because, once given a value, a constant cannot change its value. The statement

PARAMETER (COE=12.1E-6, FACTOR=7.19, IL=213)

causes the translator to treat the names COE, FACTOR, and IL just as if they were the numbers 12.1E-6, 7.19, and 213.

Not only can PARAMETER statements be used to give names to numbers that we normally view as constants, those that appear in assignment statements, they can also assign names to such things as *Limits* in dimensioning arrays and *Lengths* in character statements. As a general example, consider the statements

```
INTEGER X
DOUBLE PRECISION I,P
CHARACTER*4 T
PARAMETER (J=5, X=2, I=6.1D-3, Y=-9.651)
PARAMETER (L=X*J+9, T='NAME')
```

This program segment causes J, X, I, Y, L, and T to have the same effect in the program as the constants 5, 2, 6.1D-3, −9.651, 19, and 'NAME', respectively. If these statements were followed by

```
CHARACTER*X STRING
DIMENSION A(J)
W = Y + 1.5
Q = I
```

it would be the same as being followed by

```
CHARACTER*2 STRING
DIMENSION A(5)
W = -9.651 + 1.5
Q = 6.1D-3
```

A peculiarity that is permitted in conjunction with PARAMETER statements is the indefinite length assignment of a string constant. The statements

```
CHARACTER*(*) DD
PARAMETER (DD='MERRY CHRISTMAS')
```

causes the length of DD to automatically be adjusted to 15, the length of the string 'MERRY CHRISTMAS'.

As opposed to constants, variables can change values during the course of a program. This does not preclude the possibility that they can be given their *initial* values during translation, however. If a variable is given a value at translation time, it is said to be *preassigned*. Preassignment of variables is accomplished through statements of the form

DATA Variable List/Constant List/

where *Variable List* can be essentially any list that can be used with a READ * statement, and *Constant List* is a corresponding list of constants. The rules that govern the relationships between the *Variable List* and the *Constant List* are almost the same as those that apply to variables being input to by a READ * statement and the data being input. The exceptions are:

1. Only very restricted type conversions can be made by a READ ∗ statement, whereas the rules for mixed-mode assignments apply to DATA statements.
2. Implied DO loops in DATA statements must have integer constants for the *Initial Values*, *Limits*, and *Increments*. READ ∗ statements permit expressions.
3. DATA statements require that there be a one-to-one correspondence between the items in the *Variable List* and the items in the *Constant List*. Read ∗ statements permit more or less *List* items than data items.
4. A logical variable must be assigned to .TRUE. or .FALSE., not T or F.

The DATA statement has the same effect as a sequence of assignment statements. The subtle difference is that the variables in a DATA statement are preassigned during translation and the variables on the left sides of assignment statements are given their values at execution time (e.g., the assignment statement

$$S = 3.9$$

causes 3.9 to be moved from one memory location to another at execution). This difference is ordinarily unimportant to the high-level language programmer. What is important is the convenience offered by DATA statements. Not only do they permit several assignments to be made with a single statement, they may also include implied DO loops, something that is not available in assignment statements. Assignment statements do have the advantage of being able to reassign values to variables, whereas DATA statements (since they act during the translation stage) can only make initial assignments. DATA statements must be placed toward the beginning of a program (see Sec. 5-3).

Some examples of DATA statements are

```
DATA X, I, CS /-1.29, 52, 'ID NUMBER'/
DATA (A(J), J=1,3,2), N /1.0, 5.0, 0/
DATA LOG, DP, COMPLX /.TRUE., 0.1D-1, (1.0,2.0)/
```

where CS, LOG, DP, and COMPLX are assumed to be of the character, logical, double-precision, and complex types, respectively. The variables X, I, and N and the array A are assumed to be implicitly typed. These statements have the same effect as the statements

```
X = -1.29
I = 52
CS = 'ID NUMBER'
A(1) = 1.0
A(3) = 5.0
N = 0
LOG = .TRUE.
DP = 0.1D-1
COMPLX = (1.0,2.0)
```

A feature that is helpful in assigning several identical constants to consecutive items in the *Variable List* is the repeat factor notation. An item in the *Constant List* may have the form

r ∗ Constant

where *r* is a positive integer, called the *repeat factor*, and *Constant* is the quantity being assigned. This form has the same effect as repeating the *Constant r* times. The statement

DATA I, X, Y, Z, J /0, 3∗5.1, 2/

is equivalent to

DATA I, X, Y, Z, J /0, 5.1, 5.1, 5.1, 2/

(FORTRAN 77 also allows the repeat factor notation to be used with input data for a READ ∗ statement. It was not mentioned earlier because of its limited usefulness in inputting data.)

The repeat factor notation is particularly applicable to initializing arrays. The statement

DATA (A(I), I=1,5) /5 ∗ 1.0/

would cause the first five elements of A to be filled with 1.0, and the statement

DATA IARY /9 ∗ 0/

where it is assumed that IARY has nine elements, causes the entire array IARY to be initialized to 0.

EXERCISES

1. Give a sequence of statements that types X as double precision, I as complex, and TITLE as a character string, and causes X to represent the constant −1.05D-6, I to represent the constant (−1.6, 6.51), and TITLE to represent the string constant 'AJAX COMPANY'.

2. Describe the results of the statements

```
CHARACTER X*5, Y*10
INTEGER A, B
PARAMETER (X='HELLO', A=5)
PARAMETER (B=A-2, Y=X//' MARY')
```

3. Describe the differences and similarities of assignment statements and DATA statements.

4. Give a DATA statement that will assign:
   (a) −1 to I, 5.6 to TIME, and 'PRESSURE' to CSP.
   (b) 5 to IFLAG, −6.5 to A(1), 7.2 to A(2), and 0.0 to A(3).
   (c) 0.0 to the first 100 elements of BARR.
   (d) 0.0 to all elements in array DIST, which has 100 elements.

5. Describe the action caused by each statement.

   (a) DATA X, J, (A(I), I=1,50)/6.2E7, 2, 50*0.0/

   (b) DATA CS, VOLT/'VOLTAGE', (−1.0, 2.5)/

   (Assume that CS and VOLT have been explicitly typed to match their corresponding constants.)

6. Use a PARAMETER statement to give 100 the name N and a DATA statement to pre-assign 0.0 to the first 50 elements of an array A.

5-3 STATEMENT ORDERING

There are two general categories of statements; *nonexecutable statements*, which do not result in any action being taken at the time the program is running, and *executable statements*, which translate into the machine language program. The nonexecutable statements serve only to give directions to the translator (e.g., the DIMENSION statement informs the translator that the names in its list are array names and reserves the necessary memory space for these arrays). A complete listing of the FORTRAN 77 nonexecutable and executable statements is given in Fig. 5-6. The statements given above the heavy line have already been discussed and those below the line are yet to be considered.

The rules of FORTRAN dictate a partial ordering of the statements. Within a main program or subprogram there is normally an opening statement that includes

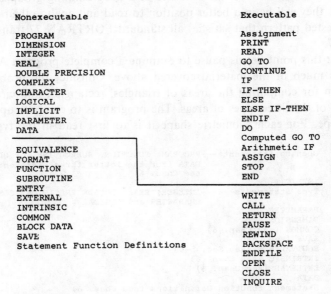

Nonexecutable	Executable
PROGRAM	Assignment
DIMENSION	PRINT
INTEGER	READ
REAL	GO TO
DOUBLE PRECISION	CONTINUE
COMPLEX	IF
CHARACTER	IF-THEN
LOGICAL	ELSE
IMPLICIT	ELSE IF-THEN
PARAMETER	ENDIF
DATA	DO
	Computed GO TO
EQUIVALENCE	Arithmetic IF
FORMAT	ASSIGN
FUNCTION	STOP
SUBROUTINE	END
ENTRY	
EXTERNAL	WRITE
INTRINSIC	CALL
COMMON	RETURN
BLOCK DATA	PAUSE
SAVE	REWIND
Statement Function Definitions	BACKSPACE
	ENDFILE
	OPEN
	CLOSE
	INQUIRE

Note: Statement types appearing above the line have already been introduced.

FIGURE 5-6 *Complete listing of FORTRAN 77 statements broken down into nonexecutable and executable sublists.*

a name, and the closing statement END. Generally, the nonexecutable data-related statements must appear just after the opening statement so that the translator will know the variable types, constant names, storage allocation, and so on, before it translates the executable statements. These are normally followed by the EXTERNAL and INTRINSIC statements (which are discussed in Chap. 6). Because DATA statements are for preassigning values and serve the same purpose as simple assignment statements, they are usually given just prior to the executable statements. Next, there are the executable statements whose presence determines the actions taken by the program. The ordering of the executable statements must satisfy the structuring rules of the FORTRAN language, but are otherwise determined by the algorithm being programmed. In subprograms the executable statements may be interspersed with ENTRY statements (see Chap. 6). FORMAT statements, which are used to specifically designate I-O formats (see Chap. 7), may also be interspersed with the executable statements; however, for reasons discussed later, the author suggests that they be grouped immediately before the END statement.

The FORTRAN 77 standard contains a set of rules for ordering statements in a program. In general, except for ENTRY and FORMAT statements, the nonexecutable statements must appear first. Their exact ordering depends on their content and on the particular translator. It is best if a programming group chooses a set pattern for the nonexecutable statements. If an individual programmer uses a set pattern, habits will form and these statements will be written instinctively, thus errors will be reduced. If all members of a programming group use the same convention, they will be in a better position to read and analyze their colleagues' work. A suggested pattern that satisfies all standard FORTRAN 77 translators is given in Fig. 5-7.

At this point, let us pause to examine a complete program AREAS that summarizes much of the material covered above. Consider the problem of writing a program for computing the areas of triangles, rectangles, and circles and the sum of each of the three types of areas. The program is to compute up to 1000 areas of each type. For each geometric shape it is to first read in the type (TRIANGLE,

```
Opening Statements---PROGRAM, FUNCTION, SUBROUTINE, or BLOCK
                     DATA (For the latter three statement types
                     see Chap. 6)
IMPLICIT
Type Statements------INTEGER, REAL, DOUBLE PRECISION, COMPLEX,
                     CHARACTER and LOGICAL
PARAMETER
DIMENSION
COMMON (see Chap. 6)
SAVE (see Chap. 6)
EQUIVALENCE (see Sec. 5-5)
INTRINSIC (see Chap. 6)
EXTERNAL (see Chap. 6)
DATA
Statement Function Definitions (see Chap. 6)
Executable statements and ENTRY statements (for ENTRY statements
                     see Chap. 6)
FORMAT (see Chap. 7)
END
```

FIGURE 5-7 *Suggested ordering for FORTRAN statements.*

RECTANGLE, or CIRCLE) and then read in its dimensions. If the dimensions are nonnegative, the program is to compute the area, store the result in the next available position in an array TA (for triangles), RA (for rectangles), or CA (for circles), and add the area to an accumulator TASUM, RASUM, or CASUM. If one of the dimensions is negative, then -1.0 is to be put in the next available position of TA, RA, or CA. The area computations are to continue until either 1000 geometric shapes have been processed or a type other than TRIANGLE, RECTANGLE, or CIRCLE is encountered. At this time the processing loop is to be exited and the areas and area sums are to be printed, with the areas and sum for triangles being output first, rectangles second, and circles third.

The output for triangles is to begin with the heading

TRIANGULAR AREAS ARE:

which is to be followed by a list of the areas. If an indicated area is not -1.0, an entry in the list is to be of the form

AREA (*Value of Index*) = (*Value of TA(Index)*)

Otherwise,

INVALID DIMENSIONS

is to be printed. The list is to be followed by

TOTAL AREA = (*Value of TASUM*)

The outputs for rectangles and circles are to be similar.

A fully commented program for solving this problem is given in Fig. 5-8. The program first explicitly types all variables and preassigns zeros to the indices and accumulators. It then enters a DO loop with a subscript limit of 1000. Each time the loop is traversed, a geometric type is read and a CASE is chosen according to the type. If the type is TRIANGLE, RECTANGLE, or CIRCLE, the necessary computations are made; otherwise, the loop is exited. After the loop is exited, either by the index reaching 1000 or by the exit condition, the data for the geometric types are printed. A representative set of test data is given in Fig. 5-9(a) and the corresponding output is shown in Fig. 5-9(b).

EXERCISES

1. Discuss why the FORTRAN statements in a program must be partially ordered.

2. Write a fully commented program for compiling data on three salespeople. Each salesperson is selling items whose identification numbers are 1 through 4. The prices of the items are stored in an array PRICE whose contents are preassigned to be $5.00, $8.50, $12.20, and $20.00 using a DATA statement. Each input record is to consist of the salesperson's name, which may be up to 20 characters long, and an item identification number. The program is to read input records and, for each salesperson, tabulate the number of

```
*****************************************************************************
*                           PROGRAM AREAS                                   *
* THIS PROGRAM USES DOUBLE PRECISION TO COMPUTE THE AREAS OF UP             *
* TO 1000 TRIANGLES, RECTANGLES, AND CIRCLES, AND THE TOTAL                *
* AREAS FOR EACH OF THESE THREE CATEGORIES.  THE VARIABLE AND              *
* ARRAY DEFINITIONS ARE:                                                    *
*     TA(1000)    - ARRAY FOR STORING TRIANGULAR AREAS                     *
*     RA(1000)    -   "     "     "      RECTANGULAR    "                   *
*     CA(1000)    -   "     "     "      CIRCULAR       "                   *
*     TASUM       - SUM OF TRIANGULAR AREAS                                 *
*     RASUM       -  "   "  RECTANGULAR AREAS                               *
*     CASUM       -  "   "  CIRCULAR AREAS                                  *
*     TIDX        - NO. OF TRIANGULAR AREAS                                 *
*     RIDX        -  "   "  RECTANGULAR  "                                  *
*     CIDX        -  "   "  CIRCULAR     "                                  *
*     AUX1, AUX2  - AUXILIARY VARIABLES FOR TEMPORARILY                    *
*                   HOLDING DIMENSIONS OF GEOMETRIC SHAPES                  *
*     AUXC        - AUXILIARY VARIABLE FOR TEMPORARILY                      *
*                   HOLDING TYPE OF AREA                                    *
*****************************************************************************

        PROGRAM AREAS

* DATA SPECIFICATION

        INTEGER TIDX, RIDX, CIDX
        DOUBLE PRECISION TA(1000), RA(1000), CA(1000), TASUM
             RASUM, CASUM, AUX1, AUX2, PI
        CHARACTER*9 AUXC
        PARAMETER (PI = 3.141592653589793)

* DATA PREASSIGNMENT

        DATA TASUM, RASUM, CASUM, TIDX, RIDX, CIDX /3*0.0, 3*0/

* I.   MAIN DO-LOOP FOR COMPUTING THE AREAS

        DO 10 I=1,1000
           READ *, AUXC
           IF (AUXC .EQ. 'TRIANGLE') THEN

* A. CASE 1:  TRIANGLE

              TIDX = TIDX + 1
              READ *, AUX1, AUX2
              IF (AUX1 .GE. 0.0 .AND. AUX2 .GE. 0.0) THEN
                   TA(TIDX) = AUX1*AUX2/2.0
                   TASUM = TASUM + TA(TIDX)
              ELSE
                   TA(TIDX) = -1.0
              ENDIF
           ELSE IF (AUXC .EQ. 'RECTANGLE') THEN
```

FIGURE 5-8 *Solution to the geometric-areas problem.*

each item sold and the gross sales for each item. This process is to continue until a fourth salesperson's name is encountered (thus permitting an exit on a sentinel such as XXXX), at which time the program is to compute, for each salesperson, the total gross sales and print a report of the following form:

REPORT FOR (Name of Salesperson)

ITEM NO.	NO. SOLD	GROSS SALES
1	*(Value)*	*(Value)*
2	*(Value)*	*(Value)*
3	*(Value)*	*(Value)*
4	*(Value)*	*(Value)*

TOTAL GROSS SALES *(Value)*

```
*     B. CASE 2:   RECTANGLE

                        RIDX = RIDX + 1
                        READ *, AUX1, AUX2
                        IF (AUX1 .GE. 0.0 .AND. AUX2 .GE. 0.0) THEN
                              RA(RIDX) = AUX1*AUX2
                              RASUM = RASUM + RA(RIDX)
                        ELSE
                              RA(RIDX) = -1.0
                        ENDIF
                  ELSE IF (AUXC .EQ. 'CIRCLE') THEN

*     C. CASE 3:   CIRCLE

                        CIDX = CIDX + 1
                        READ *, AUX1
                        IF (AUX1 .GE. 0.0) THEN
                              CA(CIDX) = PI*AUX1**2
                              CASUM = CASUM + CA(CIDX)
                        ELSE
                              CA(CIDX) = -1.0
                        ENDIF
                  ELSE

*     D. CASE 4:   CATCHALL -- EXIT LOOP

                        GO TO 20
                  ENDIF
      10    CONTINUE
      20    CONTINUE

* II.   OUTPUT CODE

*     A. OUTPUT FOR TRIANGLES

            PRINT *, 'TRIANGULAR AREAS ARE:'
            DO 30 I=1,TIDX
                  IF (TA(I) .EQ. -1.0) THEN
                        PRINT *, 'INVALID DIMENSIONS'
                  ELSE
                        PRINT *, 'AREA',I,' =',TA(I)
                  ENDIF
      30    CONTINUE
            PRINT *, 'TOTAL AREA =',TASUM
            PRINT *

*     B. OUTPUT FOR RECTANGLES

            PRINT *, 'RECTANGULAR AREAS ARE:'
            DO 40 I = 1, RIDX
                  IF (RA(I) .EQ. -1.0) THEN
                        PRINT *, 'INVALID DIMENSIONS'
                  ELSE
                        PRINT *, 'AREA',I,' =',RA(I)
                  ENDIF
      40    CONTINUE
            PRINT *, 'TOTAL AREA =',RASUM
            PRINT *

*     C. OUTPUT FOR CIRCLES

            PRINT *, 'CIRCULAR AREAS ARE:'
            DO 50 I = 1, CIDX
                  IF (CA(I) .EQ. -1.0) THEN
                        PRINT *, 'INVALID DIMENSIONS'
                  ELSE
                        PRINT *, 'AREA',I,' =',CA(I)
                  ENDIF
      50    CONTINUE
            PRINT *, 'TOTAL AREA =',CASUM
            END
```

FIGURE 5-8 (*Continued*)

```
TRIANGLE
2.0, 1.0
CIRCLE
10.0
CIRCLE
1.0
RECTANGLE
3.0, -2.0
RECTANGLE
2.0, 2.0
TRIANGLE
-1.0, 1.0
CIRCLE
-2.0
TRIANGLE
2.0, -1.0
RECTANGLE
4.0, 40.0
RECTANGLE
-2.0, 5.0
RECTANGLE
3.0, 4.0
FINISHED
```

(a)   Test data

```
TRIANGULAR AREAS ARE:
AREA       1 =  1.000000000000000
INVALID DIMENSIONS
INVALID DIMENSIONS
TOTAL AREA =  1.000000000000000

RECTANGULAR AREAS ARE:
INVALID DIMENSIONS
AREA       2 =  4.000000000000000
AREA       3 =  160.0000000000000
INVALID DIMENSIONS
AREA       5 =  12.00000000000000
TOTAL AREA =  176.0000000000000

CIRCULAR AREAS ARE:
AREA       1 =  314.1592653589793
AREA       2 =  3.141592653589793
INVALID DIMENSIONS
TOTAL AREA =  317.3008580125691
```

FIGURE 5-9 *Representative set of test data for the geometric-areas problems and the corresponding report.*

(b)   Report

The names of the salespeople may vary from one computer run to the next. If an invalid item number occurs, the program is to print

INVALID ITEM NO.

and continue. Also, prepare a set of test data for debugging the program.

5-4 HIGHER-DIMENSIONAL ARRAYS

We have seen the many advantages of the subscripting attribute of linear arrays and it may have occurred to the reader that double, triple, and so on, subscripting would also be beneficial. An array whose elements have n subscripts is called an n-dimensional array. Standard FORTRAN 77 accommodates up to seven subscripts, and hence up to seven-dimensional arrays.

216

A two-dimensional array is the most frequently encountered higher-dimensional array and is often referred to as a *matrix*. A two-dimensional array would apply to any situation that requires a table, and a three-dimensional array would apply where a family of similar tables is needed. For a two-dimensional array the first subscript indicates the row and the second the column, and for a three-dimensional array the first subscript indicates the row, the second the column, and the third the table; see Fig. 5-10. An example of a two-dimensional array would be a

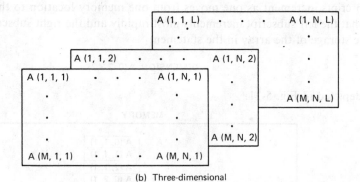

FIGURE 5-10 *Graphical illustration of 2- and 3-dimensional arrays.*

table for recording the grades of several students on each of several quizzes. The students could correspond to the rows and the quizzes to the columns. If such tabulations were to be made for several classes, each having several quizzes, a three-dimensional array would be needed in which the first subscript would indicate the student, the second the quiz, and the third the class. Arrays with more than three dimensions are seldom required, but there are certainly applications in which families of tables are needed with each family being described by more than one parameter (e.g., there is a type versus physical attributes table for each state and each geological area within the state).

The dimensioning of higher-dimensional arrays is similar to that of linear arrays except that limits must be specified for each dimension; for example,

DIMENSION HDARY(0:3,−1:5,8)

indicates that the first subscript may vary from 0 to 3, the second from -1 to 5, and the third from 1 to 8. (Recall that if a lower limit is not given, its value is 1.) Type statements may also be used to dimension higher-dimensional arrays. When an element of an array appears in an assignment or any other statement, the rules for specifying each subscript are the same as for specifying the single subscript in a linear array; that is, each subscript must be an expression which evaluates to an integer within the range of the subscript. For example, the following assignment statements are valid:

$$A(I,J) = B(1,I+1,J-1) + X$$
$$X = Y(INT(SQRT(W))+1,I*K,2)$$
$$K = INC(I,2,3*J) + 15$$
$$N(3*J-INT(S)) = SIN(X(I,J)-0.5)$$

All arrays are stored in consecutive memory locations. With linear arrays the ordering in memory is straightforward, the first array element is stored in the first memory location assigned to the array, the second element is stored in the second location, and so on. For higher-dimensional arrays there is a question as to how the subscripts increment as one moves from one memory location to the next. The rule is that the left subscript increments most rapidly and the right subscript most slowly. The storage of the array in the statement

DIMENSION A(0:2,3,2)

is depicted in Fig. 5-11.

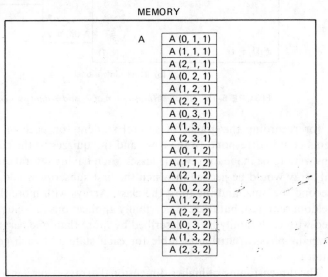

FIGURE 5-11 *Ordering of an array in memory.*

If the lower and upper ith subscript limits of an array X are L_i and U_i, respectively, then for a two-dimensional array the position of the element $X(I_1, I_2)$ is

$$(I_2 - L_2)(U_1 - L_1 + 1) + I_1 - L_1 + 1$$

For a three-dimensional array the position of the element $X(I_1, I_2, I_3)$ is

$$((I_3 - L_3)(U_2 - L_2 + 1) + (I_2 - L_2))(U_1 - L_1 + 1) + I_1 - L_1 + 1$$

As an example, consider the array in the statement

DIMENSION B(0:2,−1:5,4)

The position of the element B(1, 3, 3) is

$$((3 - 1)(5 - (-1) + 1) + (3 - (-1)))(2 - 0 + 1) + 1 - 0 + 1$$
$$= (2 \times 7 + 4)3 + 1 + 1 = 56$$

The general formula for n-dimensional arrays is

$$((\ldots((K_n J_{n-1} + K_{n-1})J_{n-2} + K_{n-2})J_{n-3} + \ldots)J_2 + K_2)J_1 + K_1 + 1$$

where

$$K_i = I_i - L_i$$
$$J_i = U_i - L_i + 1$$
$$\qquad i = 1, \ldots, n$$

The importance of being able to compute the position of an element within an array will become more evident later when the COMMON and EQUIVALENT statements are discussed.

From the preceding paragraphs it is seen that dimensioning tells the translator three things:

1. The given symbol is an array name.
2. The number of dimensions.
3. The subscript limits so that the proper amount of storage can be reserved and the positions of the elements can be computed.

For linear arrays the third item is needed only for allocating storage, but for higher-dimensional arrays the limits of the subscripts must also be known by the program so that the positions of the elements relative to the beginning of the array can be computed while the program is executing. (These computations are automatically translated into machine language instructions and need not concern the programmer.)

Just as with linear arrays, a problem arises with regard to preassigning, inputting, and outputting higher-dimensional arrays, and just as with linear arrays the solution lies in the application of implied DO loops. Nested implied DO loops are permissible and a three-dimensional array could be output with a statement such as

PRINT *, (((P(I,J,K), I=1,2), J=1,2), K=1,2)

Because the innermost loop would increment most rapidly and the outer loop most slowly, the printed values would be ordered as follows:

P(1,1,1), P(2,1,1), P(1,2,1), P(2,2,1),
P(1,1,2), P(2,1,2), P(1,2,2), P(2,2,2)

Therefore, the elements of P would be output in the same order they appear in memory. If the statement

PRINT *, (((P(I,J,K), K=1,2), J=1,2), I=1,2)

were executed, the order in which the elements of P would be printed is

P(1,1,1), P(1,1,2), P(1,2,1), P(1,2,2),
P(2,1,1), P(2,1,2), P(2,2,1), P(2,2,2)

Thus, the first memory location associated with P would be output first, but the fifth location would be output second.

Both of the statements above would print all the values on the first line if it were sufficiently large to contain all the values. If it were not, successive lines would be used. Blindly printing array data on successive lines usually results in output that is hard to read. Because the higher-dimensional arrays are normally viewed as consisting of rows, columns, and tables, it is more appealing to print one row per line. To force the one row per line format, the output statements must be written so that the PRINT * statement is reencountered for each row. This suggests that, for a two-dimensional array, the output should use an implied DO loop nested inside a regular DO loop. For outputting an array C with eight rows and six columns the program segment

```
      DO 10 I=1,8
        PRINT *, (C(I,J), J=1,6)
   10 CONTINUE
```

could be used. If only the first M rows and N columns were to be output, these statements could be changed to

```
      DO 10 I=1,M
        PRINT *, (C(I,J), J=1,N)
   10 CONTINUE
```

If, for some reason, the columns were to be printed across the page, the loop indices could be interchanged to give

```
            DO 10 J=1,N
              PRINT *, (C(I,J), I=1,M)
        10 CONTINUE
```

Finally a program segment for providing a row-by-row output of L tables with a title being printed at the beginning of each table is

```
            DO 20 K=1,L
              PRINT *
              PRINT *, 'TABLE NO.',K
              PRINT *
              DO 10 I=1,M
                PRINT *, (ITN(I,J,K), J=1,N)
        10      CONTINUE
        20 CONTINUE
```

A typical output for L = 3, M = 2, and N = 4 is shown in Fig. 5-12.

```
        TABLE NO.      1

                2       15      -11      3
                4      721       -6      4

        TABLE NO.      2

                0        1       -7      0
                1        1        1      1

        TABLE NO.      3

                0        2      -72      1
               -1        0       25      1
```

FIGURE 5-12 *Typical three-dimensional output.*

Several valid program segments involving DATA and list-directed I-O statements with implied DO loops are given in Fig. 5-13. The column on the right gives a verbal description of the input or output. In particular, note the second and last examples, which involve entire arrays. In such cases, the action taken is to preassign, read, or print the whole array in the order that the elements appear in memory (i.e., with the first subscript varying most rapidly, etc.).

Consider the problem of writing a program to solve the equations

$$A_{11}X_1 + A_{12}X_2 + A_{13}X_3 = B_1$$

$$A_{21}X_1 + A_{22}X_2 + A_{23}X_3 = B_2$$

$$A_{31}X_1 + A_{32}X_2 + A_{33}X_3 = B_3$$

```
READ *, (X(K),(I(J,K),J=1,2),K=1,2)     Reads X(1),I(1,1),I(2,1),
                                        X(2),I(1,2),I(2,2).


READ *, D                               If D is an array with two
                                        rows and two columns, D(1,1),
                                        D(2,1), D(1,2), and D(2,2)
                                        will be read.


READ *, (A(I),I=1,1000)                 Reads A(1), ..., A(1000)
                                        from successive input records
                                        until the list is exhausted.
                                        More than one datum may appear
                                        in a record.


DO 5 L=1,2                              Reads from:
    DO 4 I=1,2                          1st record-Y(1,1),T(1,1,1),T(1,2,1)
        READ *, (Y(I,L),(T(I,II,L),     2nd record-Y(2,1),T(2,1,1),T(2,2,1)
:                   II=1,2)             3rd record-Y(1,2),T(1,1,2),T(1,2,2)
4       CONTINUE                        4th record-Y(2,2),T(2,1,2),T(2,2,2)
5 CONTINUE


DO 5 I=1,2                              Prints L, S(1,1), S(1,3) on first
    PRINT *, L,(S(I,K),K=1,3,2)         line and L, S(2,1), S(2,3) on
5 CONTINUE                              second line.


PRINT *, (L,(X(I,J),J=1,2),            Prints L, X(1,1), X(1,2), L, X(2,1)
:           I=1,2),P                    X(2,2), and P.


DATA ((A(M,N),N=1,2),M=1,3) /6*0.0/    Preassigns 0.0 to the first three
                                        rows and two columns of A.


DATA I /1,2,3,4/                        If I is an array with two rows and
                                        two columns, 1, 2, 3, and 4 will be
                                        preassigned to I(1,1), I(2,1),
                                        I(1,2), and I(2,2), respectively.
```

FIGURE 5-13 *Examples of I-O and DATA statements involving higher-dimensional arrays.*

The program is to:

1. Read the coefficients into a two-dimensional array A such that one row (the coefficients for one equation) is input per input record.

2. Print the coefficients one row per line under the title

THE COEFFICIENTS ARE:

3. Read the values that the linear expressions are equal to into a linear array B.

4. Print the array B on one line under the title

THE B ARRAY IS:

5. If the absolute value of the determinant of coefficients is less than 10^{-20}, print

DEPENDENT EQUATIONS

and stop. Otherwise, compute the unknowns, put the results in a linear array X, and print the results, one element per line, under the title

THE SOLUTIONS ARE:

A solution to this problem is given in Fig. 5-14.

```
      PROGRAM SIMEQ
      REAL A(3,3), B(3), X(3), DET
      PRINT *, 'THE COEFFICIENTS ARE:'
      DO 10 I=1,3
          READ *, (A(I,J), J=1,3)
          PRINT *, (A(I,J), J=1,3)
   10 CONTINUE
      READ *, (B(I), I=1,3)
      PRINT *
      PRINT *, 'THE B ARRAY IS:'
      PRINT *, (B(I), I=1,3)
      DET = A(1,1)*(A(2,2)*A(3,3)-A(3,2)*A(2,3))
    :     -A(2,1)*(A(1,2)*A(3,3)-A(3,2)*A(1,3))
    :     +A(3,1)*(A(1,2)*A(2,3)-A(2,2)*A(1,3))
      IF (DET .EQ. 0.0) THEN
          PRINT *, 'DEPENDENT EQUATIONS'
      ELSE
          X(1) = (B(1)*(A(2,2)*A(3,3)-A(3,2)*A(2,3))
    :         -B(2)*(A(1,2)*A(3,3)-A(3,2)*A(1,3))
    :         +B(3)*(A(1,2)*A(2,3)-A(2,2)*A(1,3)))/DET
          X(2) = (A(1,1)*(B(2)*A(3,3)-B(3)*A(2,3))
    :         -A(2,1)*(B(1)*A(3,3)-B(3)*A(1,3))
    :         +A(3,1)*(B(1)*A(2,3)-B(2)*A(1,3)))/DET
          X(3) = (A(1,1)*(A(2,2)*B(3)-A(3,2)*B(2))
    :         -A(2,1)*(A(1,2)*B(3)-A(3,2)*B(1))
    :         +A(3,1)*(A(1,2)*B(2)-A(2,2)*B(1)))/DET
          PRINT *
          PRINT *, 'THE SOLUTIONS ARE:'
          DO 20 I=1,3
              PRINT *, X(I)
   20     CONTINUE
      ENDIF
      END
```

FIGURE 5-14 *Program for solving three simultaneous equations.*

A second example program, one that involves a three-dimensional array, is shown in Fig. 5-15. This program simply inputs production data for several plants and generates a report. It assumes that four items are being produced, the number of departments in the Kth plant is M(K), and the number of plants is L. The number of plants and the number of departments in each plant are input first, and then the data for each plant are read. The input for each plant is to consist of the plant name in the first record followed by the production quantities for each department. A production record for a department is to consist of four numbers, with these numbers being the quantities of the four production items. The production quantity input records are assumed to be ordered by department. A report which is output by the program has the form shown in Fig. 5-16.

```
PROGRAM REPORT
INTEGER Q(20,4,10), M(10), L
CHARACTER*20 PNAME(10)
CHARACTER*50 HDNGS
PARAMETER (HDNGS =
:          '                BOLTS    NUTS    WASHERS   SCREWS')
READ *, L, (M(K), K=1,L)
DO 20 K=1,L
      READ *, PNAME(K)
      DO 10 I=1,M(K)
          READ *, (QUAN(I,J,K), J=1,4)
10    CONTINUE
20 CONTINUE
PRINT *, '                    PRODUCTION REPORT'
DO 40 K=1,L
      PRINT *
      PRINT *
      PRINT *, 'DATA FOR PLANT ', PNAME(K)
      PRINT *
      PRINT *, HDNGS
      PRINT *
      DO 30 I=1,M(K)
          PRINT *, '   DEPARTMENT', I, (QUAN(I,J,K), J=1,4)
30    CONTINUE
40 CONTINUE
END
```

FIGURE 5-15 *Program for report-generating example.*

PRODUCTION REPORT

DATA FOR PLANT (*Name of Plant*)

		BOLTS	NUTS	WASHERS	SCREWS
DEPARTMENT	1	*Value*	*Value*	*Value*	*Value*
DEPARTMENT	2	*Value*	*Value*	*Value*	*Value*

DATA FOR PLANT (*Name of Plant*)

		BOLTS	NUTS	WASHERS	SCREWS
DEPARTMENT	1				
	.				
	.				
	.				

FIGURE 5-16 *Output format for program given in Fig. 5-15.*

EXERCISES

1. Describe the information given to the translator by each statement.
   (a) INTEGER A(0:5,0:3,4), I(1,2)
   (b) CHARACTER*2 J, ST(3,7,2)
   (c) COMPLEX XXX(−5:5,−5:5), FREQ(2,2,5), VOLT
   (d) DIMENSION X(2,3,4,10,10,5,2)
   (e) DATA (((A(I,J,K), I=1,5), J=1,3), K=1,4) /60*0.0/
   (f) X(I+1,I−1) = A(I)*B(J,INT(P)−1)

2. Give FORTRAN statements that will dimension:

    (a) A double-precision four-dimensional array with subscript limits from -5 to 5 for the first subscript, 0 to 3 for the second, 1 to 10 for the third, and 1 to 50 for the fourth.

    (b) A real linear array with subscript limits of 0 and 5, and a two-dimensional real array with limits of 1 and 10 for the first subscript and 1 and 1000 for the second subscript.

    (c) A character two-dimensional array whose elements are 20 characters long and that has limits from 0 to 5 for the first subscript and 0 to 10 for the second subscript.

3. Give a memory diagram (see Fig. 5-11) to show how each of the following statements assigns the elements of the given arrays to memory locations.

    (a) DIMENSION X(2,3,2)

    (b) REAL A(0:1,0:2,−1:1)

    (c) INTEGER P(0:4,2)

    (d) REAL CRNT(2,2,2,2)

4. Describe the output resulting from each program segment.

    (a) PRINT *, (((A(I1,I2,I3), I1=1,2), I2=1,2), I3=1,2)

    (b) CHARACTER C(3,2,2)
```
      DO 2 J=1,2
         PRINT *, ((C(I,J,K), I=1,3), K=1,2), 'LINE', J
    2 CONTINUE
```

    (c)
```
      DO 7 I=1,3
         PRINT *, (X(I,J), J=1,2)
    7 CONTINUE
```

5. Give program segments that will:

    (a) Read the first M rows and N columns of a two-dimensional array by inputting one row per input record.

    (b) Read the first M rows and N columns of a two-dimensional array by inputting one column per input record.

    (c) Read a three-dimensional array consisting of 10 tables with five rows and 20 columns in each table. The input is to be accomplished by reading pairs of input records, with each record containing 10 elements of a row and each pair of records containing a row.

    (d) Preassign 0 to all elements in a two-dimensional array with five rows and eight columns.

6. Write a program that will input M and N, input M rows and N columns of a two-dimensional array A, add the elements in each row and put the results in a linear array RSUM, add the elements in each column and put the results in a linear array CSUM, add all of the elements and put the result in S, and print the arrays A, RSUM, and CSUM and the sum S in the form

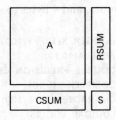

7. Write a program for printing the results of a political survey. Up to 1000 people in up to 50 states are asked 10 questions to which they answer Y (for yes) and N (for no). The program is to read in the number of states polled, the names of the states, the number of people polled in each state, and the answers for each person (one set of answers per input record). It is then to compute the percent of yes answers for each question and each state and output a report with the following form:

                          POLITICAL POLL

        (Name of State)
                          QUESTION 1   *(Percent Yes)*
                          QUESTION 2   *(Percent Yes)*
                              .
                              .
                              .

        (Name of State)
                          QUESTION 1   *(Percent Yes)*
                          QUESTION 2   *(Percent Yes)*
                              .
                              .
                              .

5-5 EQUIVALENCE STATEMENTS

Although programmers sometimes treat computer memories as if they are infinite, memories are often very limited. In fact, until the mid 1970s a computer's memory was frequently its most expensive component, and expanding the memory was a serious consideration. Even though recent developments have lowered memory costs to small fractions of what they were, these costs are still not insignificant and many applications require judicious use of the available memory space. Also, many small computers can support only a relatively small amount of memory, and many large computers are operated with several programs in memory at a time, with each program being limited to only a part of the memory.

Most programs are such that a large fraction of the memory they use is allocated to their arrays. The total amount of memory assigned to the arrays can easily be determined by multiplying, for each array, the number of bytes per element times the number of elements, and then summing over the arrays. If 1 byte is needed to store a character, 4 bytes to store an integer or real number, 8 bytes to store a double-precision or complex number, and 4 bytes to store a logical value, then the statements

```
INTEGER  X(10), Y(100)
REAL  A(10,10)
DOUBLE  PRECISION  C(2,10),  D(2,5,4,50)
COMPLEX  F(5,10)
CHARACTER*20  S(100)
LOGICAL  LOG(25)
```

would reserve

$$4 \times 10 + 4 \times 100 + 4(10 \times 10) + 8(2 \times 10) + 8(2 \times 5 \times 4 \times 50)$$
$$+ 8(5 \times 10) + 20 \times 100 + 4 \times 25$$
$$= 40 + 400 + 400 + 160 + 16000 + 400 + 2000 + 100$$
$$= 19,500 \text{ bytes}$$

The principal means of reducing the amount of memory required by a program is to reuse arrays where possible. If a program needs 40,000 bytes to store weights and 20,000 bytes to store costs, but is such that by the time costs enter into the process the weights are no longer needed, then the costs could use the same memory as the weights. At this point in our studies, the only way the two quantities could share an area of memory is to give the area a name and have both quantities be denoted by that name. This is not very satisfactory because, if two distinct quantities have the same name, it would lead to considerable confusion. The solution to the problem is to include in the language a means of assigning two names to the same area of memory. In FORTRAN the EQUIVALENCE statement is used for this purpose.

The EQUIVALENCE statement has the form

EQUIVALENCE (*Equivalence Class 1*), . . . , (*Equivalence Class N*)

where each *Equivalence Class* has the form

Name 1, . . . , *Name M*

with each *Name* being the name of a variable or array element. If an unsubscripted array *Name* appears, the first element of the array is assumed, and if a subscripted element appears, the subscripts must be constants (or names of constants). The effect of an EQUIVALENCE statement is to cause all the variable and array element names in each *Equivalence Class* to be assigned to the same memory location. For example,

EQUIVALENCE (I,X(1),Y(3,1))

would cause I, the first element of X, and the third element of Y to be assigned to the same memory location.

This process of assignment is called *equivalencing*. Variables and arrays of different types may be equivalenced, except that character variables and arrays cannot be equivalenced to variables and arrays of the other types. Clearly, conflicting EQUIVALENCE statements which are impossible to satisfy are not allowed.

Because elements within arrays are consecutive, putting one element from each array in an equivalence class is sufficient to equivalence all the elements in the arrays. The statement

EQUIVALENCE (C(1),D(1))

not only results in C(1) and D(1) being associated with the same memory location, but also C(2) and D(2), C(3) and D(3), and so on, are assigned the same locations. Several EQUIVALENCE statements and their resulting alignments are illustrated in Fig. 5-17. From Fig. 5-17(c) and (d) it is seen that arrays having different numbers

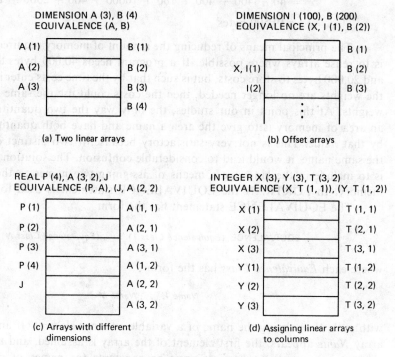

FIGURE 5-17 *Alignment of equivalenced arrays.*

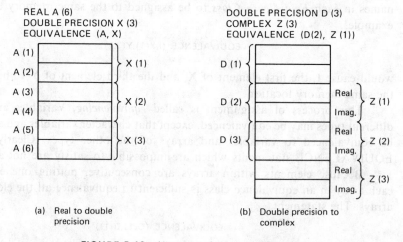

FIGURE 5-18 *Alignment of arrays of different types.*

of dimensions may be equivalenced. This is one of the reasons it is important to know the exact arrangement of higher-dimensional arrays within memory. Figure 5-17(d) shows how linear arrays can be made to correspond to the columns of a two-dimensional array.

When variables and arrays of different types are equivalenced and the alignment is to be determined, one must take into account the lengths of the different types. For the real and integer types there is no problem because they have the same length, but if a real array is equivalenced to a double-precision array, as shown in Fig. 5-18(a), the fact that the elements of the double-precision array are twice as long as the real elements must be kept in mind. Figure 5-18(b) gives the alignment of a double-precision array with a complex array.

EXERCISES

1. What is the principal reason for equivalencing arrays?

2. Given that a character occupies 1 byte, an integer or real number occupies 4 bytes, a double-precision or complex number occupies 8 bytes, and a logical value occupies 4 bytes, determine the amount of storage reserved by each statement.
   (a) DIMENSION I(4,4), X(0:1,−1:1)
   (b) REAL A(2,3,4,5)
   (c) CHARACTER S(2,3,4)
   (d) CHARACTER S(2,2)*8, I(3,2)*5
   (e) DOUBLE PRECISION Y, W(2,3), J(2,5)
   (f) LOGICAL T(2,2,2,3), U(0:10)
   (g) COMPLEX W(2,5), Z(0:5,−2:2)

3. Draw diagrams similar to those in Figs. 5-17 and 5-18 to show the array alignments that result from each program segment.
   (a) REAL A(3), B(5)
       EQUIVALENCE (I,A(1),B(2))
   (b) INTEGER X(6), B(3,2)
       EQUIVALENCE (X,B), (JVAR,PVAR)
   (c) INTEGER C(4,2)
       REAL A(4), B(4)
       EQUIVALENCE (A,C(1,1)), (B,C(1,2))
   (d) REAL X(8)
       DOUBLE PRECISION D(3)
       EQUIVALENCE (D,X(3))
   (e) REAL X(6)
       DOUBLE PRECISION N(3)
       COMPLEX V(3)
       EQUIVALENCE (X,N,V)
   (f) REAL A(2,3), B(3,4), C(2,2,2), D(2,2,2), E(2,2,2,2)
       EQUIVALENCE (A,B), (C,E), (D,E(1,1,1,2))

PROGRAMMING PROBLEMS

1. Complex numbers can be used to represent forces by letting the real parts represent the horizontal components of the forces and the imaginary parts represent the vertical components. Write a program that sums the forces that are input to it and produces a resultant force. The program is to first input an integer to CODE, print the headings

INPUT FORCES

HORIZONTAL COMPONENT   VERTICAL COMPONENT

if CODE is 0 and

INPUT FORCES

MAGNITUDE   ANGLE

if CODE is not 0, and then enter a loop. Inside the loop, the program is to input a force as a complex number (rectangular format), add it to an accumulator, print it out as a complex number in rectangular form if CODE = 0 and otherwise convert it to its polar form and then print it. The loop is to continue executing until a force of 0 is encountered, at which time the loop is to be exited and

RESULTANT FORCE = (*Complex value of resultant force*)

is to be printed if CODE = 0 and

RESULTANT FORCE:

MAGNITUDE = (*Mag. of resultant*)   ANGLE (*Angle of resultant*)

is to be printed if CODE $\neq$ 0. Use the forces

$$(3,4), \ (5,5), \ (1,5), \ (0,4), \ (-3,0)$$

and test the program twice, once with CODE = 0 and once with CODE = 1.

2. The transmittance of a laser beam (i.e., the fraction of the transmitted laser radiation that is received) through a gas is given by the equation

$$\tau = \exp\left[-\frac{DZ}{\pi} \sum_{i=1}^{N} S_i \frac{A_i P \sqrt{296.0/T}}{(F - F_i)^2 + A_i^2 P^2 (296.0/T)}\right]$$

where: D = density of gas
                Z = length of path
                N = number of effective absorbing lines for the gas being considered
                F_i = frequency of ith absorbing line
                S_i = intensity of ith absorbing line
                A_i = broadening of ith absorbing line
                T = temperature
                P = pressure
                F = frequency of laser

Write a program that inputs values into D, T, P, F, and N and then inputs the molecular line data into a two-dimensional array LDATA with the frequencies stored in the first column, the intensities in the second column, and the broadening values in the third column. It is to then input a maximum value of Z into ZM and a number of Z points into M and fill a linear Z array using the equation

$$Z(I) = I*ZM/M \quad I = 1, \ldots, M$$

Finally, the program is to compute the values of transmittance, put them in a linear array TAU, and print a report of the following form:

```
DENSITY = (Value of D)
TEMPERATURE = (Value of T)
PRESSURE = (Value of P)
FREQUENCY = (Value of F)
                   LINE DATA
FREQUENCY      INTENSITY      BROADENING
(Frequencies)   (Intensities)    (Broadenings)
         TRANSMITTANCE DATA
PATH LENGTH              TRANSMITTANCE
(Lengths from Z)          (Transmittances from TAU)
```

The program is to be run twice, once using single-precision variables and once using double-precision variables. The test data to be used are:

$$D = 3.62 \times 10^{17} \quad T = 300.00 \quad P = 0.982 \quad F = 1225.000$$

$$N = 10 \quad ZM = 10000.0 \quad M = 10$$

Frequencies	Intensities	Broadenings
1224.7134	0.474E-26	0.055
1224.7335	0.242E-25	0.055
1224.8101	0.133E-23	0.040
1224.8406	0.397E-23	0.041
1224.9501	0.897E-22	0.072
1225.0439	0.265E-21	0.072
1225.1712	0.242E-25	0.055
1225.1910	0.475E-26	0.055
1225.5300	0.785E-22	0.066
1225.6057	0.322E-26	0.069

3. Write a program that will successively input character strings of up to 80 characters into CHAR (one string per input record) and count the total number of times the letter "a" (or "A") occurs, the letter "b" (or "B") occurs, and so on through "z." The counts are to be put in an integer array NALPHA. The process is to stop when a blank string is read. The program is also to count the number of periods NPER, number of commas NCOM, number of semicolons NSEMI, number of blanks NBLANK (with multiple blanks counting as one blank), total number of characters NCHAR, and number of strings NSTRG. Assuming that only letters, periods, commas, semicolons, and blanks occur, the program

is to compute the average word length AWL, the standard deviation of the word length SDWL, the average sentence length ASL, and the standard deviation of the sentence length SDSL. (*Note:* In calculating the average word length, remember that each end-of-line is an end-of-word and only one space at the beginning or end of a line should be counted.) The program is to print the strings as they are input and the table

DISTRIBUTION OF LETTERS AND PUNCTUATION MARKS

LETTER	COUNT
A	(*Value of NALPHA(1)*)
B	(*Value of NALPHA(2)*)
.	.
.	.
.	.

followed by

WORD LENGTH:	MEAN = (*Value of AWL*)
	STANDARD DEVIATION = (*Value of SDWL*)
SENTENCE LENGTH:	MEAN = (*Value of ASL*)
	STANDARD DEVIATION = (*Value of SDSL*)

Test the program by applying it to the first paragraph of Sec. 5-1.

6

SUBPROGRAMS

The importance of subdividing a program into tasks, or *modules*, was discussed in Secs. 1-9-5 and 3-1. This chapter introduces the FORTRAN facilities for aiding the subdivision process and the terminology associated with these facilities. Although modularity could be attained by breaking a program into a simple sequence of tasks, each of which consists of a logically coherent group of statements, it is often advantageous to have a form of modularity that gives a greater degree of module independence than a simple sequence can provide. What is needed is a means of subdividing a program into modules in such a way that the modules can be conveniently used as many times as desired, and can be designed and written with only a general knowledge of the overall program.

The underlying definitions that are needed at this point are those of a program unit and an executable program. A *program unit* is a set of valid FORTRAN statements and comments that are ordered according to the rules of FORTRAN and include exactly one END statement. A collection of program units for which one program unit, called the *main program*, is such that all other program units, called *subprograms*, are subordinate to it is called an *executable program*, or simply a *program*. The previous programs we have studied have consisted of only a main program and, perhaps, one or two intrinsic functions. With the introduction of subprograms we may begin to build hierarchical structures of program units such as the one shown in Fig. 6-1. Within such a structure, if a program unit uses a subordinate program unit it is referred to as the *calling program* and the subordinate unit is referred to as the *called program*.

There are two major types of subprograms: executable subprograms and BLOCK

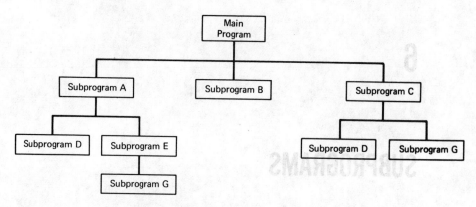

FIGURE 6-1 *Organizational structure of a typical program.*

DATA subprograms. An *executable subprogram* (or *procedure*) is one that contains executable statements, and a *BLOCK DATA subprogram* is one that contains only data-related nonexecutable statements. The purpose of a BLOCK DATA subprogram is to preassign values to areas of memory that may be shared by several program units, areas that are discussed in detail in the latter part of the chapter.

The first section of this chapter discusses modularity, defines the concept of scope, and examines the effects of scope on the independence of program units. The second section introduces the basic features of subprograms and relates these features to the two main types of executable subprograms, functions and subroutines, which are then examined in detail. This section also describes the linkage that exists between program units. Section 6-3 discusses the various processes for creating and using subprograms under both batch and interactive systems. Section 6-4 provides a detailed example of a system of subprograms and Sec. 6-5 considers the special aspects of dimensioning arrays within subprograms. The remainder of the chapter discusses a variety of subprogram-related topics which increase the flexibility of the way in which FORTRAN subprograms may be used.

6-1 MODULARITY AND SCOPE

The primary reasons for subdividing a program into modules are to:

1. Simplify the initial design and reduce the number of errors.
2. Permit common sets of instructions to be conveniently reused several places within a program.
3. Facilitate program documentation.
4. Make the program easier to maintain and update.
5. Allow the programming to be divided among several people.

234

With regard to the first of these reasons, the human mind is capable of grasping only so much information at one time. By breaking a program into tasks the programmer can attack a complex problem one piece at a time, and if the tasks are small enough to be fully comprehended, the opportunity for errors is significantly reduced. The tasks must be such that they can be neatly defined and logically fit together to form the overall program. Each task must perform an easily discernible function that meshes naturally with the remainder of the program. The modular approach blends well with the mind's ability to understand simple well-defined tasks and to form a hierarchical structure from these tasks.

As we have seen with intrinsic functions, it is often necessary to perform the same task at several points within a program. Therefore, modules are needed that can be easily referenced as many times as desired. In addition, a modular program can be easily documented by stating the purpose of the overall program, describing the function of each module and how the modules fit together, and then describing each of the modules. Such a program can be corrected or updated more easily because the affected modules can be isolated and modified without disturbing the remainder of the program. A properly designed modular program can also be conveniently broken down into programming tasks which may then be assigned to members of a programming group. Each group member would need a general understanding of the program as a whole and a detailed understanding of only his or her tasks.

Generally, modules should be selected so that the interaction, or *coupling*, between them is minimized. There are three basic types of coupling that need to be considered here. They are:

Control Coupling—The degree to which actions in one module affect the actions in another module.

Data Coupling—The amount of data that is passed between two modules.

Common Coupling—The amount of data that is shared by two modules through the use of a memory area that is accessible to both modules.

(The distinction between data coupling and common coupling will become clearer as we proceed.) The reasons for choosing modules so as to minimize coupling are obvious. If two modules are closely coupled they are not really distinct, and this implies that a thorough knowledge of one module must be accompanied by a considerable knowledge of the closely coupled module, thus defeating the principal advantages of modularity.

Another key concept with regard to the segmentation of a program is that of scope. The *scope* of a name or label is the range over which it has a fixed meaning. The scope of a FORTRAN variable name, array name, or label is the program unit in which it is contained. If the variable name X appears in two different program units, it may be associated with two different memory locations, but all occurrences of X within a given program unit must refer to the same memory location. Similarly, the statement label 10 may be used in more than one program unit but cannot appear more than once within a given program unit. In contrast, it will be seen that the scope of a subprogram name is the entire program. If the scope of a name is limited to a program unit, it is said to be *local*; if it is the entire program, it is said to be *global*. Variable and array names are local and subprogram names are global.

There are two principal ways of segmenting a FORTRAN program. One is to use a simple sequence and the other is to use subprograms, and all but very small programs involve a combination of the two types of modularization. The three chief advantages of subprograms are:

1. They permit the same code to be reused as many times as desired. This not only saves the programming time needed to rewrite and debug the same code over and over, but also saves memory space because the instructions need to appear only once.

2. They may be placed in libraries on mass storage devices, and incorporated into several different programs (e.g., a subprogram could be written to solve simultaneous equations and used in any program that requires the solution of such equations, regardless of the physical entities represented by the equations).

3. As program units, they limit the scope of the variable names, array names, and labels. Therefore, a subprogram may be called by another program unit without the person writing the calling program being concerned about using the same names and labels as are in the subprogram. This is very helpful when several people are working on a program, and is a requirement when putting subprograms in libraries. When a library subprogram is called the user seldom knows the internal workings of the subprogram, but knows only enough about the subprogram to communicate with it.

The primary disadvantage of subprograms is that data must be communicated between them and their calling programs. Depending on the degree of data and common coupling, the communication of data can be a nontrivial operation. As a non-trivial operation, it opens the door for errors and increases the time needed to execute a program. Consequently, the trade-off between simply labeling sections of a program as separate modules and splitting the sections off as subprograms must be studied carefully. Ordinarily, these decisions are based on coupling and scope. The typical program consists of a main program and several subprograms, each of which is made up of a simple sequence of modules that perform specific tasks.

EXERCISES

1. Discuss the effects of coupling on modularization.
2. Discuss the advantages of names and labels having limited scope.

6-2 EXECUTABLE SUBPROGRAMS

When using subprograms one must know how to:

1. Call a subprogram.
2. Return from a subprogram.
3. Communicate with the subprogram.

To accomplish the first two of these actions is generally a matter of learning a few elementary rules for writing the necessary statements. Just how these statements cause the program to branch to the subprogram and the subprogram branch back to the calling program at the point from which the call was made is unimportant to high-level language programmers.

On the other hand, to communicate among program units is more complicated and requires some understanding of the process. The problem in passing information between program units arises because program units are translated separately. As explained in Secs. 1-6, 1-7, and 1-8, program units are translated into separate object modules and it is left to the linker to put them together. The point is that the addresses associated with variables and array names in program units other than the one currently being translated are not known. Therefore, either extra information must be made available to the linker so that it can piece things together, or the necessary addresses must be passed between the program units at execution time.

There are three fundamental methods for providing communication between program units. One is to have the program units share specified areas in memory, a method that is examined in detail in Sec. 6-9. A second is to use a CPU register, in which case the transfer is incidental to the programmer. The other method is to have the calling program store the addresses of the data being communicated in a special area in memory, and then relay the location of the special area to the subprogram via a CPU register.

There are two basic types of executable subprograms in FORTRAN and they are distinguished by the ways they are called from and communicate with other program units. A *subroutine subprogram* is called by including its name in a CALL statement and passes information either through shared memory or by passing addresses. A *function subprogram* is called by the appearance of its name in an expression. Although the method of communicating information is system-dependent, a function subprogram's arguments are usually conveyed to it through passed addresses and the result is usually returned to the calling program through a CPU register. A function subprogram may also use shared memory. Both subroutines and functions use the same instructions for returning to the calling program. The rules regulating the names of subprograms are the same as the rules for variables and arrays: that is, subprogram names consist of up to six alphanumeric characters, the first of which must be alphabetic.

All subprograms must obey the following important rule:

> *A FORTRAN subprogram, say subprogram C, cannot call itself, and any subprogram that may directly or indirectly call subprogram C cannot be called by subprogram C.*

If subprogram A calls subprogram B and subprogram B calls subprogram C, then A could call C, but C could not call A, B, or itself.

6-2-1 Subroutines

Execution of a subroutine is initiated by a statement of the form

CALL Name (Argument List)

where *Name* is the name of the subroutine and *Argument List* is a list of the items, or *arguments*, whose addresses are to be passed to the subroutine. The arguments are separated by commas and may be any valid expressions, including variable names, array names, array element names, constants, and valid combinations of these entities. If an array name is an argument, the address that is passed to the subroutine is the address of the first element in the array. For expressions, they are evaluated and the result is put in a temporary location, and it is the address of this location that is passed. The *Argument List* may be void, in which case the parentheses may also be deleted. (Arguments may also be subprogram names or asterisks followed by labels; see Secs. 6-6 and 6-7.)

The structure of a subroutine is

SUBROUTINE Name (Parameter List)

.
.
.

END

where *Name* is the name of the subroutine and *Parameter List* is a list of variable and array names, called *parameters* (or *dummy arguments*). The parameters are in one-to-one correspondence with the arguments in the CALL statement, with the first parameter being associated with the first argument, and so on. Corresponding parameters and arguments must be of the same type with integer variables matched with integer quantities, real variables matched with real quantities, arrays matched with arrays, and so on. Although the corresponding pairs of arguments and parameters must be of the same type, they do not have to have the same name. In fact, it has been seen that an argument may be an expression. (Parameters may also be subprogram names or asterisks; see Secs. 6-6 and 6-7.)

The column of dots represents the body of the subroutine, which is essentially the same as the body of a main program. Constants, variables, and arrays are typed, dimensioned, and preassigned just as they are in a main program. Because subprograms are translated separately, variables and arrays that appear in the *Parameter List* must be assigned the appropriate data types (unless they are implicitly typed) and/or dimensioned even though their corresponding arguments have been assigned data types and dimensioned in the main program. Dimensioning within a subprogram is more flexible than dimensioning within a main program, and it is considered in detail in Sec. 6-5. For the moment, we will assume that the rules for dimensioning are the same as for a main program and that parameter arrays are dimensioned with the same subscript limits as their corresponding arguments.

Subroutines, as with all program units, must end with an END statement. This statement not only informs the translator that it is through translating the current program unit, but also causes a return branch (back to the calling program) to be inserted as the last instruction in the program unit. Statements of the form

RETURN

may also be used to insert return branches at one or more points in a subprogram; however, an END statement must still be included as the last statement.

When a subroutine begins execution, the values of the parameters are the values of the corresponding arguments at the time the call is made. If an argument has not been given a value at the time the subroutine is entered, the corresponding parameter must be given a value before it is used in the subroutine.

As an example, consider the main program given in Fig. 6-2(a) and the subroutine given in Fig. 6-2(b). The main program reads three numbers into A, B and

```
PROGRAM MAIN1
REAL A,B,C,X
READ *, A,B,C
CALL LINSOL(A,B,C,X)
PRINT *, 'SOLUTION=',X
END
```

(a) Main program, one CALL

```
SUBROUTINE LINSOL(A1,A2,A3,Y)
REAL A1,A2,A3,Y
IF (A1 .EQ. 0.0) THEN
      PRINT *, 'NO SOLUTION'
      STOP
   ELSE
      Y = (A3-A2)/A1
ENDIF
END
```

(b) Subroutine

```
PROGRAM MAIN2
READ *, A,B,C
CALL LINSOL(A,B,C,X)
PRINT *, 'X=',X
CALL LINSOL(A,B,X,Y)
PRINT *, 'Y=',Y
END
```

(c) Main program, two CALLs

FIGURE 6-2 *Example of a subroutine and two calling programs.*

C, calls the subroutine LINSOL to solve the linear equation

$$AX + B = C$$

and prints out the solution X. While the subroutine is executing, the values of A1, A2, and A3 are the values of *A*, *B*, and *C*, respectively, and the value of Y is returned to the main program as the value of X. Just as in a main program, if the STOP statement in the subroutine is executed, the program (the *entire* program, not just the subroutine) will be terminated.

Figure 6-2(c) gives a different main program that uses the subroutine LINSOL twice, once to solve

$$AX + B = C$$

and once to solve

$$AY + B = X$$

Note that in the second subroutine call, *X* matches A3 and *Y* matches Y. (Although corresponding parameters and arguments do not have to have the same name, they may have the same name.) Also, note that in this main program *A*, *B*, *C*, *X*, and *Y* are implicitly typed. This is acceptable provided that the types of the parameters and arguments still match. Subprograms may also use implicit typing.

To communicate effectively with a subprogram through *Argument* and *Parameter Lists* it is helpful to understand the process by which addresses are passed and why the two lists must be properly aligned. There is more than one way in which the addresses can be passed, but the procedure most commonly employed by FORTRAN translators is depicted in Fig. 6-3. The procedure is to have the calling program put the addresses of the arguments in a table (the table being an array) and put the address of the table in a CPU register; then the subprogram can retrieve the address of the table from the register and, knowing the address of the table, thereby retrieve the addresses of the arguments.

The retrieved addresses are the addresses associated with the corresponding parameters; therefore, an argument and its corresponding parameter are associated with the same memory location. The correspondence of arguments and parameters is achieved through simple ordering. The arguments are put into the table in order and the subprogram uses the first address in the table as the address of the first parameter, the second address in the table as the address of the second parameter, and so on. The fact that a parameter and its corresponding argument actually refer to the same memory location explains why they must be of the same type.

If an array name appears in the argument list, only the address of the first element, called the *base element*, is passed; all other addresses are computed from the subscript limits (see Sec. 5-4). Such address computations are automatically inserted in the subprogram machine language code and need not concern the high-level language programmer. If an array element appears, the address of the element is passed. When an expression is used as an argument, it is evaluated, the result is temporarily stored, and the address of the temporary location is passed. Addresses of constants are passed in the same way as the addresses of variables. This introduces

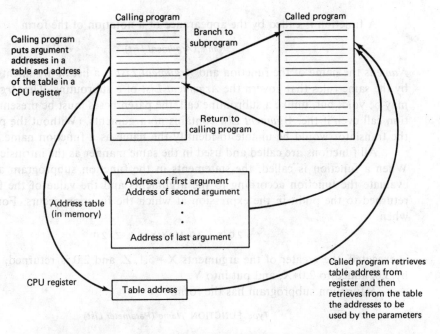

Calling program

Calling program
puts argument
addresses in a
table and address
of the table in a
CPU register

Branch to
subprogram

Called program

Return to
calling program

Address table
(in memory)

Address of first argument
Address of second argument
•
•
•
Address of last argument

CPU register

Table address

Called program retrieves
table address from
register and then
retrieves from the table
the addresses to be
used by the parameters

FIGURE 6-3 *Procedure for passing data between FORTRAN program units.*

a potential hazard, because a constant argument must be matched with a parameter variable name. Therefore, the constant is treated as a variable in the subprogram and may be changed. This could have undesirable effects in the calling program, which assumes that the constant cannot be changed. To avoid errors that may be very difficult to detect, *care should be exercised when using constant arguments, and their matching parameters should never be changed within the subprogram.*

The actions taken by the calling program to build the argument address table and by the subprogram to retrieve these addresses are due to machine language instructions that result from the translation of the CALL and SUBROUTINE statements. Because the instructions are generated automatically by the translator, the FORTRAN programmer does not need to be concerned with the details of the process. However, it is important that programmers understand the general nature of the process because it obviates the need to memorize a seemingly complicated set of rules. By understanding the process, the rules make sense and can be deduced.

6-2-2 Functions

There are two fundamental types of functions: intrinsic functions and external functions. The *intrinsic functions*, which have been introduced in previous chapters, are a part of FORTRAN and the programmer only needs to know how to reference them. *External functions* are those that are written by a programmer and are not part of FORTRAN.

A function is called by the appearance of a notation of the form

Name (Argument List)

Name is the name of the function and *Argument List* is a list of arguments governed by the same rules that govern the *Argument List* of a subroutine. The *Argument List* may be void, but, unlike a subroutine call, the parentheses must be present in a function call even if the *Argument List* contains no arguments. (Without the parentheses the translator would be unable to identify the name as a function name.)

All functions are called and used in the same manner as the intrinsic functions. When a function is called, the statements in the function subprogram are used to evaluate the function according to the arguments and the value of the function is returned to the point in the expression at which the function occurs. For example, when

$$Y = 2.0*X + 3.0*MAX(X+5.1, Z, 2.0)$$

is executed, the greater of the arguments $X+5.1$, Z, and 2.0 is returned, multiplied by 3.0, added to $2.0*X$, and put into Y.

A function subprogram has the form

Type FUNCTION *Name (Parameter List)*
.
.
.
END

where *Name* is the name of the function and *Parameter List* serves the same purpose and is governed by the same rules as a subroutine's *Parameter List*. *Type* specifies the type of the value returned and is optional. If *Type* does not appear, it is determined implicitly by the function name. In this case, a function name that begins with I through N returns an integer value and one that begins with any other letter returns a real value. Functions that are to have double precision, complex, logical, or character values must have explicitly declared types (i.e., *Type* must be included). In addition, if a function name does not follow the rules of implicit type declaration, the calling program must include a type declaration statement containing the name of the function. Because the calling program and the function are translated separately, both must indicate and agree on the type of a function; otherwise, the calling program may not interpret the returned value properly. For example, no confusion would result from the specifications shown in Fig. 6-4(a), but if, as shown in Fig. 6-4(b), the type of COUNT were not declared, the function would return an integer value and the calling program would erroneously use it as a real value.

The *Type* specification in the FUNCTION statement of a character function may or may not include a length. The default length is 1. The statement

CHARACTER*12 FUNCTION NAME (X,Y)

would cause a 12-character string to be returned and the statement

CHARACTER FUNCTION CONVRT (A)

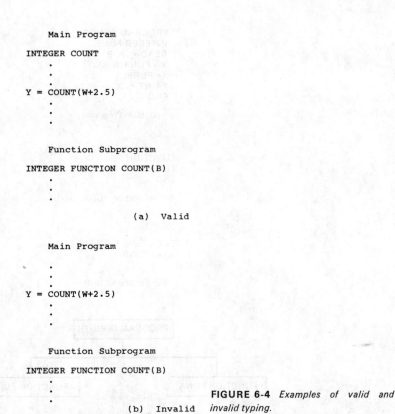

```
              Main Program
      INTEGER COUNT
                    .
                    .
                    .
      Y = COUNT(W+2.5)
                    .
                    .
                    .


              Function Subprogram
      INTEGER FUNCTION COUNT(B)
                    .
                    .
```

                         (a)   Valid

```
              Main Program
                    .
                    .
                    .
      Y = COUNT(W+2.5)
                    .
                    .
                    .


              Function Subprogram
      INTEGER FUNCTION COUNT(B)
                    .
                    .
                    .
```

                       (b) Invalid

FIGURE 6-4 *Examples of valid and invalid typing.*

would result in only a single character being returned. If a calling program refers to NAME and CONVERT, it must contain the statements

```
              CHARACTER*12 NAME
              CHARACTER CONVRT
```

The result of a function is passed back to the calling program through either a CPU register or memory location that is associated with the function name. The exact communication process depends on the translator and is not important. What is important is that the function name is associated with a location and that location must be filled during the execution of the function. This is accomplished by having the function name appear as a variable name within the function subprogram and *demanding* that at least one statement within the subprogram be such that it assigns a value to the function name. This statement could be an assignment statement or a READ statement.

Figure 6-5(a) gives a main program that calls two functions, Figs. 6-5(b) and (c) give the two functions, and Fig. 6-5(d) shows the hierarchical structure of the overall program. Although these program units are trivial, they demonstrate several of the points discussed above. One of the subprograms assigns the function value with an assignment statement and the other uses a READ statement. Also note the typing:

```
PROGRAM DONOTH
INTEGER FUNB
READ *,  A, B
X = FUNA(A, B)
J = FUNB( )
PRINT *,  X, J
END
```

(a) Main Program

```
FUNCTION FUNA (X, Y)
FUNA = X + Y**2
END
```

(b) Function FUNA

```
INTEGER FUNCTION FUNB( )
READ *,  FUNB
END
```

(c) Function FUNB

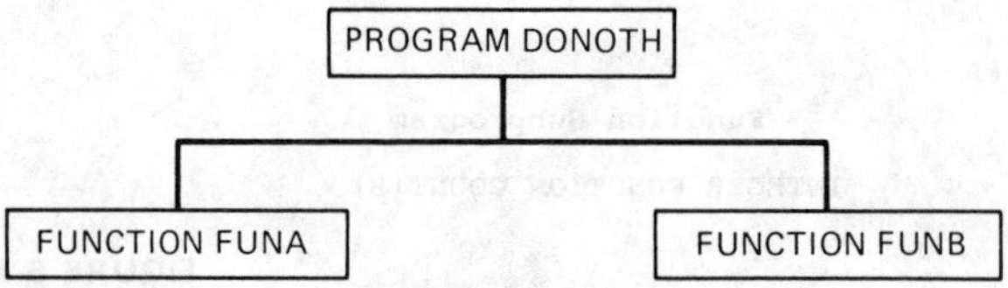

(d) Hierarchical diagram

FIGURE 6-5 *System of program units involving function sub-programs.*

FUNA utilizes implicit typing and FUNB utilizes explicit typing. FUNB provides an example of a function with no arguments.

Except for the rule that the *function name must be assigned a value within the body of a function subprogram*, the rules regarding the bodies of function subprograms are the same as those for subroutine subprograms. An END statement must be the last statement in a function subprogram and will insert a return instruction as well as terminate the translating process for the program unit. RETURN statements may also be used to cause returns from one or more points within a function.

Let us now consider an example that involves a main program, a function, and a subroutine that calls a second function. Suppose that a company manufactures two types of memory components, either of which may be used to fill the orders received by the company. Because the two types are produced by different processes, their cost versus quantity curves are different and the company would, of course, like to fill each order at the minimum cost. Assume that each cost curve is constructed from a base cost plus an incremental cost. This means that the cost curves are straight lines and, as illustrated in Fig. 6-6, the base costs are the cost axis intercepts and the incremental costs are the slopes. As the manufacturing processes change, the base

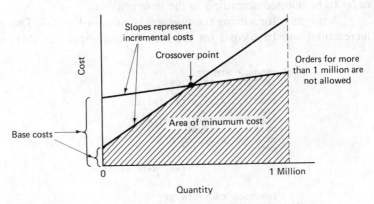

Production costs for the two component types

Slopes represent
incremental costs

Crossover point

Orders for more
than 1 million are
not allowed

Cost

Area of minumum cost

Base costs

0   1 Million

Quantity

FIGURE 6-6 *Production costs for the problem of minimizing memory com-*
ponent costs.

and incremental costs change and, therefore, may be considered constants for only
one set of orders. Orders for over 1 million components are disallowed.

The problem is to write a program that will input a set of orders and produce
a report that indicates, for each order, the order number, the type of memory component to be used to fill the order, the quantity, and the cost of filling the order. If
an order is for less than 0 or more than 1 million components, the program is to
print the order number followed by the message INVALID QUANTITY. Also,
the total cost of filling all orders is to be printed.

A hierarchical diagram for a solution to this problem is shown in Fig. 6-7.
This diagram indicates a main program that reads in the necessary data, uses a
function to compute the crossover point of the two cost curves, and calls a subroutine
to compute the costs and print the report. If the cost curves are parallel (i.e., the
slopes are the same), a crossover point that is greater than the greatest allowable

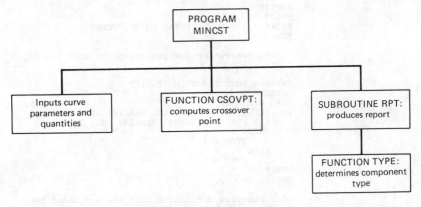

FIGURE 6-7 *Hierarchical diagram of the solution to the memory component cost*
program.

245

quantity (greater than 1 million) is assigned. This causes the component type for the order to be selected according to the base price only.

A program for solving the problem is given in Fig. 6-8. This program reads the incremental and base costs for the type 1 component into A(1) and B(1), and the

```
PROGRAM MINCST
INTEGER N, QUAN(100)
REAL A(2), B(2), XP
READ *, (A(I),B(I), I=1,2)
READ *, N
READ *, (QUAN(I), I=1,N)
XP = CSOVPT(A,B)
CALL RPT(A,B,QUAN,N,XP)
END
```

(a) Main program

```
FUNCTION CSOVPT(M,B)
REAL M(2), B(2)
IF (M(2) .EQ. M(1)) THEN
        CSOVPT = 2.0E 6
    ELSE
        CSOVPT = (B(1) - B(2))/(M(2) - M(1))
ENDIF
END
```

(b) Function for finding the crossover point

```
SUBROUTINE RPT(M,B,Q,N,XP)
INTEGER N, J, TYPE, Q(100)
REAL M(2), B(2), XP, TCOST
PRINT * '   MEMORY COMPONENT COST REPORT'
PRINT *
TCOST = 0.0
DO 10 I=1,N
    IF (Q(I) .LT. 0 .OR. Q(I) .GT. 1000000) THEN
            PRINT *, 'ORDER NO.',I,'   INVALID QUANTITY'
        ELSE
            J = TYPE(B,Q(I),XP)
            C = M(J)*Q(I) + B(J)
            PRINT *, 'ORDER NO.',I,'    TYPE',J,
      :          '   QUANTITY',Q(I),'    COST',C
            TCOST = TCOST + C
    ENDIF
10  CONTINUE
PRINT *
PRINT *, '         TOTAL COST', TCOST
END
```

(c) Subroutine for producing the cost report

```
INTEGER FUNCTION TYPE (C,D,XP)
INTEGER D
REAL C(2), XP
IF ((C(1) .LT. C(2) .AND. REAL(D) .LT. XP) .OR.
:  (C(1) .GE. C(2) .AND. REAL(D) .GE. XP))
:    THEN
        TYPE = 1
    ELSE
        TYPE = 2
ENDIF
END
```

(d) Function for determining the component type

FIGURE 6-8 *Program for solving the memory component cost problem.*

incremental and base costs for type 2 into A(2) and B(2). It then reads the number of orders into N and the sizes of the orders into QUAN. The crossover point is computed using the function CSOVPT and the result is put in XP. The data in A, B, QUAN, N, and XP are passed to the subroutine RPT, which generates the required report using the function TYPE to determine the type of component selected to fill each order.

This solution is designed to demonstrate as many of the rules for linking program units as possible, and is not an optimal programming solution. For example, different argument and parameter names have been used, although it would have been both possible and less confusing to use the same names. What should be noted is the hierarchical structure of the program, the correspondences between the parameters and the arguments, and the type declarations for the functions, one of which is implicitly typed and the other of which is explicitly typed.

EXERCISES

1. What are the principal differences between subroutines and functions?
2. After considering the way in which argument addresses are passed, state why constants and array elements cannot appear as parameters, and why corresponding arguments and parameters must agree in type.
3. Determine which of the following statements are invalid. For those that are invalid, state what is wrong with them and, if possible, rewrite them in a correct form.
   (a) SUBROUTINE INPUT (A,B,I,X+20.2,SIN(Y))
   (b) SUBROUTINE OUTPUT
   (c) REAL SUBROUTINE COMP (A,4,B(I),I)
   (d) DOUBLE PRECISION FUNCTION ADD (A,B)
   (e) FUNCTION VELOCITY (X,A,B)
   (f) REAL FUNCTION MAST
   (g) CALL SUBROUTINE INCTAX (A,B)
       where A is an array
   (h) CALL COMP (A,4,B(I),I)
       where A is an array
   (i) Z(I+1) = 3.2 + ADD(Y(3),SIN(X))
   (j) J = 5 + TYPE(MAX(I,J,K),A)
       where A is an array
   (k) CALL PMULT (SIN(X),4,X)
4. In each of the following situations, find the values of the arguments after the subroutine has executed.
   (a) DATA A,B /1.0,3.0/
       CALL SUBA (A,B,C)
       SUBROUTINE SUBA (X,Y,Z)
       X = Y+3.0
       Z = X**2
       END

    (b) DATA (J(I), I=1,5) /2,1,2,3,4/
       K = 3
       CALL SUBB (J,K)
       SUBROUTINE SUBB (A,M)
       INTEGER A(5)
       IF (M .LT. 5) THEN
           DO 5 I=1,M
               A(I) = A(M)
    5   CONTINUE
         ELSE
           A(5) = M
       ENDIF
       M = 4
       END

    (c) Replace K=3 with K=5 and rework part (b).

5. Given the function

```
CHARACTER*2 FUNCTION SS (STRG,N)
INTEGER N
CHARACTER*5 STRG
SS = STRG(N:N)//'A'
END
```

find the values of the function and of CS after the execution of each of the following:

    (a) CHARACTER*5 CS, CHR
        CHARACTER*2 SS
        DATA CHR /'HELLO'/
        CS = SS(CHR,4)//'P '
    (b) CHARACTER CS(5)
        CHARACTER*2 SS
        DO 5 K=1,5
           CS(K) = SS('HELLO',K)
     5 CONTINUE

6. Write a subroutine SUMZER that will add all of the elements in the first $M \leq 50$ rows and $N \leq 15$ columns of an array A, put the sum in SUM, zero the first M rows and N columns of A, and then return to the main program. The names A, SUM, M, and N are to appear as parameters. Give a CALL statement that will use SUMZER to add the first KK rows and N columns of array ARRY and return the sum to X.

7. Write an integer function CNT that will count the number of negative elements in a four-dimensional argument array, and return the count to the main program. All subscript limits are to be 0:2.

8. Write a subroutine TRANS that will transpose the first N rows and N columns of a two-dimensional array A by interchanging A(I,J) and A(J,I), for all $I \leq N$ and $J \leq N$. The parameters are to be A and N.

9. Write a function DIST that will compute the double-precision distance between any two points in three-dimensional space. Write a calling subroutine TDIST that uses DIST to find the distance along a path that is defined by fewer than 100 straight-line segments. The segment end points are to be in a two-dimensional array D that is dimensioned D(3,100). Write a main program that uses TDIST to compute the lengths of L ≦ 10 paths. The main program is to input the points in the paths to an array P, which is dimensioned P(3,100,10), and put the results in an array PLEN. The main program is to also print the results.

10. Write a companion set of subroutines that will modify a linear character (length 5) array A with N ≦ 100 elements as follows:

Subroutine INSERT—Moves the Ith through Nth elements to the I+1th through N+1th elements, inserts X in the Ith element, and increases N by 1. If the increased value of N exceeds 100, the subroutine is to print

ARRAY SIZE EXCEEDED

and the entire program is to stop. The parameters are to be A, N, I, and X.
Subroutine DELETE—Moves the I+1th through Nth elements to the Ith through N−1th elements and decreases N by 1. The parameters are to be A, N, and I.
Subroutine CHANGE—Replaces the Ith element with X. The parameters are to be A, N, I, and X.
Subroutine EXCHNG—Transposes the Ith and Jth elements. The parameters are to be A, N, I, and J.

In all the subroutines, if I is nonpositive or greater than N, the subroutine is to set I to −1, print

INDEX OUT OF RANGE

and return to the calling program without taking any action.

11. Write a function Y1 that receives an argument through the parameter X and computes the functional value using the graph

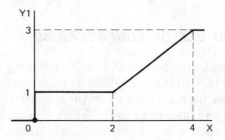

Give a PRINT * statement that outputs

W = (Value of 3.0 times Y1 evaluated at V)

12. Write a subroutine that reverses all the elements in a linear array whose subscript limits are −10 and 10.

13. Write a subroutine that adds the first N ≦ 100 elements of array A to the corresponding elements of array B if ICODE is zero, and subtracts the corresponding elements of array

B if ICODE is nonzero. In either case the results are to be put in the first N elements of C. The names A, B, C, N, and ICODE are to be the parameters. Also give a CALL statement that will add the first 10 elements of X to the first 10 elements of Y and put the results in Z.

14. Develop a system of program units for computing the net pay of up to 1000 employees. The main program PAY is to call a subroutine INP to input the name, age, hourly rate, and hours worked. It is then to compute the gross pay for all employees, assuming time and a half for all hours over 40 hours, and call a subroutine NET to compute the net pay for all employees. The net pay is to be computed by deducting $30 for medical insurance and deducting life insurance and income tax according to the following graphs:

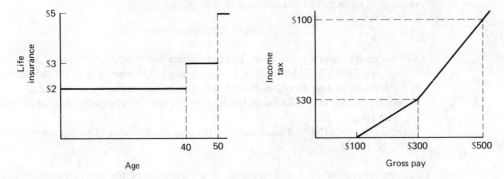

The net pay cannot be negative and it is assumed the company will pay for insurance shortages for those employees who have worked an insufficient number of hours. The life insurance and tax deductions are to be computed by function subprograms. After the net pay for each employee has been found, the main program is to call a subroutine PRT to print the name and net pay for each employee. If an employee's pay is 0.0, PRT is to follow the net pay with a string of 10 asterisks. First sketch a hierarchical diagram that matches this description and then write the necessary program units.

6-3 CREATION AND USE OF SUBPROGRAMS

Let us now consider the process of creating and using subprograms by reexamining the portion of Fig. 1-10 that is modified and redrawn in Fig. 6-9. The program units within a program, the main program and its subprograms, may be created as separate source modules and introduced to the system in sequence. As explained in Chap. 1, after the source modules have been translated into object modules, the object modules are joined together by the linker to form a load module that is ready to be loaded and executed. While the load module is being constructed by the linker, other object modules, such as those of the intrinsic functions, may be brought in from libraries and attached to the program being created. Some of these libraries contain only system subprograms and can be changed only by system programmers, but it is possible for users to create and utilize private libraries.

On a card-oriented system, each program unit is punched into cards and has a suitable opening statement (PROGRAM, SUBROUTINE, FUNCTION, or

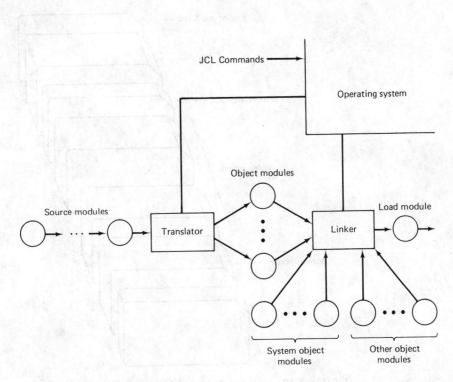

FIGURE 6-9 *Creating a program using a batch system.*

BLOCK DATA) as its first statement and an END statement as its last statement. Exactly how the program units are stacked together with the JCL and data cards to form the overall deck depends on the system, but a typical deck is shown in Fig. 6-10. In this deck structure, the introductory JCL cards are followed by the main program and all its subprograms. Then the data-related JCL cards are inserted and are followed by all the card data that will be needed during the execution of the program. Note that all the data that appear on cards, whether they are brought in by the main program or a subprogram, are ordered according to the sequence in which they are input and are grouped at the last of the deck. The last card in the deck is, as always, an end-of-job card.

If library subprograms, other than system subprograms, are to be attached to the program units included in the deck, extra JCL cards will be needed to inform the operating system and linker where to find these subprograms. Because of the variety of available systems and the differences in JCL from one system to the next, it would not be fruitful to give an example here. The reader should refer to the appropriate manuals for the system being used. There are also the questions of how to create a library and then add to, delete from, and modify the subprograms in the library. Building and modifying libraries also primarily involve knowing the proper JCL and, therefore, is left to system manuals.

The procedure for building programs on an interactive system is similarly dependent on the system being used. Figure 6-11 illustrates the most frequently

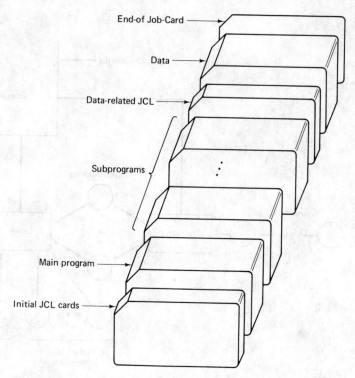

FIGURE 6-10 *Typical deck structure for a card-oriented batch system.*

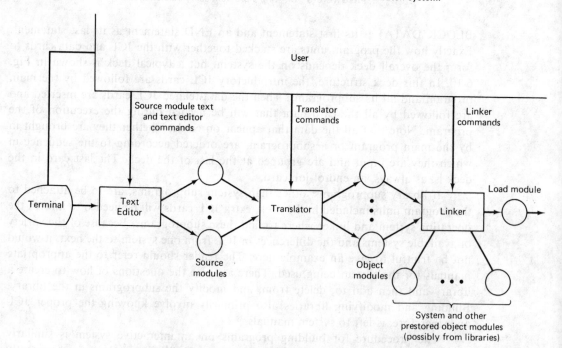

FIGURE 6-11 *Creating a program using an interactive system.*

encountered process for creating program units and forming programs from these units. The program units are created using a text editor and are stored as source module files on a mass storage device. After all the source modules have been generated, they are translated into object modules and linked together to form the load module. The linking process may include object modules that were created and stored during previous programming sessions or that have been placed in libraries. If object modules from libraries or mass storage locations that are normally inaccessible to the user are to be linked, special notations may be needed in the command given to the linker. The formats of the linker commands are very system-dependent and cannot be discussed in detail here.

Most interactive systems include a system program called a *librarian* for building and modifying libraries. The librarian is similar to the translators and linker in that it is executed by giving the proper command to the operating system and, during execution, performs its duties by receiving specially coded commands from the user. Commands to a librarian would indicate which object modules are to be grouped together to form a library, or which modules are to be added to or deleted from an existing library. As with linker commands, it would serve no purpose to provide even an example of a librarian command, and the reader must refer to the manuals for the specific system being used.

In summarizing the foregoing discussion, it is seen that subprograms may be classified as follows:

Subroutine
    System—in a system library
    User written
        Predefined—in a user library
        Submitted with the job (batch) or exists
            as a separate file (interactive)
Function
    Intrinsic—in system library and incorporated into the translator
    External function—user written
        Predefined—in user library
        Submitted with the job (batch) or exists
            as a separate file (interactive)

For a batch system, if a subprogram is submitted in the same deck as the main program, it is simply inserted in the deck as shown in Fig. 6-10; otherwise, the proper JCL may be needed to bring in the subprogram from a library. For an interactive system, the linker command must include the names of the object modules or of the libraries containing the object modules. Normally, a JCL or linker command that refers to a library causes that library to be searched for the needed object modules and the names of these object modules do not need to be listed individually in the command. (This is a principal advantage of subprogram libraries.)

6-4 EXAMPLE—RATIONAL FUNCTION ARITHMETIC

A rational function is a function that can be expressed as the quotient of two polynomials. Rational functions occur quite often in the solutions to engineering and scientific problems, and being able to conveniently execute the arithmetic operations on such functions would be useful in many situations. Therefore, let us suppose that an engineer or scientist is confronted with a problem that involves rational functions and has decided to write a collection of subroutines for equating, negating, adding, subtracting, multiplying, reciprocating, and dividing rational functions and for multiplying rational functions by constants. In addition, a function is needed to evaluate a rational function at a given point. Once the necessary subprograms are developed, they could be put in a library and accessed at will.

Subordinate to performing the operations on rational functions is performing them, except for reciprocation and division, on polynomials. For this reason, let us first develop a collection of subprograms for manipulating polynomials and then use this collection to produce the needed rational function subprograms.

First we must contemplate the question:

How can one store a polynomial in a computer?

keeping in mind that a computer can store only numbers. The answer is that a polynomial is completely defined by its coefficients and its degree, all of which are numbers. For example, the polynomial

$$-1.0 + 2.5X + 3.2X^3$$

is completely defined by the real numbers $-1.0, 2.5, 0.0$, and 3.2, and the integer 3. Note that all coefficients up to and including the leading coefficient (the coefficient of the highest power of X) must be part of the defining sequence of numbers, with zero being assigned to the missing terms. The degree is needed to indicate the highest nonzero coefficient. The conclusion is that an arbitrary polynomial

$$A_0 + A_1 X + \ldots + A_N X^N$$

can be stored in a computer by putting N in an integer location and A_0 through A_N in the elements A(0) through A(N) of a real array.

The next question is:

How can the computer perform the arithmetic operations on polynomials?

The answer to this question is found by examining the algebraic rules for carrying out the arithmetic operations on polynomials. Assuming that the degrees of the operand polynomials are N and M, these rules are:

Equation (the assignment of a polynomial to a second set of variables)—
Equate the coefficients and degrees.

Negation—Negate the coefficients. The degree is not affected.

Addition—Add the corresponding coefficients. The degree of the result is less than or equal to the larger of N and M, and must be found by determining the power of the highest nonzero term.

Subtraction—Subtract the corresponding coefficients. The degree of the difference is less than or equal to the larger of N and M and must also be determined.

Multiplication—Unless one of the factors is the polynomial that is identically 0, the degree of the product is $N + M$. If $A_0, \ldots, A_N$ are the coefficients of one of the factors, $B_0, \ldots, B_M$ are the coefficients of the other factor, and $C_0, \ldots, C_{N+M}$ are the coefficients of the product, then for $i = 0, \ldots, N + M$:

$$C_i = A_0 B_i + A_1 B_{i-1} + \ldots + A_{i-1} B_1 + A_i B_0$$

Multiplication by a Constant—Multiply each coefficient by the constant. Unless the multiplying constant is 0, the degree of the result is the same as that of the polynomial being multiplied.

For convenience, the polynomial that is identically 0 is assigned a degree of -1. Any other constant polynomial has a degree of 0.

The subroutines needed to perform these operations are given in Fig. 6-12(a) through (f). For equation, the coefficient arrays and degrees of the polynomials to be equated are the arguments, and the subroutine merely equates the degrees and the elements of the coefficient arrays. Negation is similar, except that one array is negated as it is equated to the other array. For addition, subtraction, and multiplication, the coefficient arrays and degrees of both operands and the result must be passed to the subroutine. Subtraction is performed by negating the subtrahend using PNEG and adding the result to the minuend using PADD. The subroutine PCMULT, which is for multiplying a polynomial by a constant, receives five arguments, the constant multiplier, the coefficient array being multiplied and its degree variable, and the coefficient array and degree variable for the result.

Observe that the application of PADD in PSUB uses duplicate arguments, thus causing one of the operands and the sum to share the same coefficient array and degree variable. Duplicate arguments could be used when calling any of these subroutines (e.g., the statement

CALL PNEG (P,K,P,K)

would cause P to be negated and put back into P). However, if the arguments are distinct, the operands will be left unchanged by the operation. Note that because polynomial multiplication must reuse the operand coefficient arrays as the product array is being computed, an auxiliary array must be used to store the product temporarily. Otherwise, duplicate argument arrays could not be permitted.

By assigning all coefficient arrays 21 elements, the polynomials have been limited to having degrees of 20 or less. To assure that this restriction is maintained, a subroutine DEGCHK, given in Fig. 6-12(g), is called at the beginning of each operation

```
              SUBROUTINE PEQ(A,N,C,L)
              INTEGER N,L
              REAL A(0:20), C(0:20)
              CALL DEGCHK(A,N)
              L = N
              IF (N .EQ. -1) C(0) = 0.0
              DO 5 I=0,N
                  C(I) = A(I)
        5     CONTINUE
              END
```

(a) Equation

```
              SUBROUTINE PNEG(A,N,C,L)
              INTEGER N,L
              REAL A(0:20), C(0:20)
              CALL DEGCHK(A,N)
              L = N
              IF (N .EQ. -1) C(0) = 0.0
              DO 5 I=0,N
                  C(I) = -A(I)
        5     CONTINUE
              END
```

(b) Negation

```
              SUBROUTINE PADD(A,N,B,M,C,L)
              INTEGER N,M,L
              REAL A(0:20), B(0:20), C(0:20)
              CALL DEGCHK(A,N)
              CALL DEGCHK(B,M)
              IF (N .LT. M) THEN
                      DO 5 I=0,M
                              IF (I .LE. N) THEN
                                  C(I) = A(I) + B(I)
                              ELSE
                                  C(I) = B(I)
                              ENDIF
        5             CONTINUE
                      L = M
              ELSE IF (M .LT. N) THEN
                      DO 6 I=0,N
                              IF (I .LE. M) THEN
                                  C(I) = A(I) + B(I)
                              ELSE
                                  C(I) = A(I)
                              ENDIF
        6             CONTINUE
                      L = N
              ELSE
                      IF (N .EQ. -1) C(0) = 0.0
                      DO 7 I=0,N
                          C(I) = A(I) + B(I)
        7             CONTINUE
                      L = N
                      CALL DEGCHK(C,L)
              ENDIF
              END
```

(c) Addition

```
              SUBROUTINE PSUB(A,N,B,M,C,L)
              INTEGER N,M,L
              REAL A(0:20), B(0:20), C(0:20)
              CALL PNEG(B,M,C,L)
              CALL PADD(A,N,C,L,C,L)
              END
```

(d) Subtraction

```
              SUBROUTINE PMULT (A,N,B,M,C,L)
              INTEGER N,M,L
              REAL A(0:20), B(0:20), C(0:20), T(0:20)
              CALL DEGCHK(A,N)
              CALL DEGCHK(B,M)
              IF (N .EQ. -1 .OR. M .EQ. -1) THEN
                      L = -1
                      C(0) = 0.0
                      RETURN
```

FIGURE 6-12 Subprograms for performing the arithmetic operations on polynomials.

```
                ELSE IF (N+M .GT. 20) THEN
                    CALL DEGCHK (C,N+M)
                ELSE
                    L = N+M
        ENDIF
        DO 6 I=0,L
            T(I) = 0.0
            DO 5 J=0,I
                IF (J .LE. N .AND. I-J .LE. M) THEN
                    T(I) = T(I) + A(J)*B(I-J)
                ELSE
                ENDIF
    5       CONTINUE
    6   CONTINUE
        DO 7 I=0,L
            C(I) = T(I)
    7   CONTINUE
        END
```

(e) Multiplication of polynomials

```
        SUBROUTINE PCMULT(D,A,N,C,L)
        INTEGER N,L
        REAL A(0:20), C(0:20), D
        CALL DEGCHK(A,N)
        IF (N .EQ. -1 .OR. D .EQ. 0.0) THEN
            L = -1
            C(0) = 0.0
        ELSE
            L = N
            DO 5 I=0,N
                C(I) = D*A(I)
    5       CONTINUE
        ENDIF
        END
```

(f) Multiplication by a constant

```
        SUBROUTINE DEGCHK(C,L)
        INTEGER L
        REAL C(0:20)
        IF (L .LT. -1) THEN
            PRINT *, 'INVALID DEGREE'
            L = -1
            C(0) = 0.0
        ELSE IF (L .GT. 20) THEN
            PRINT *, 'DEGREE TOO LARGE'
            STOP
        ELSE
        ENDIF
        K = L
        DO 5 I=K,0,-1
            IF (C(I) .EQ. 0.0) THEN
                L = L-1
            ELSE
                GO TO 6
            ENDIF
    5   CONTINUE
    6   CONTINUE
        END
```

(g) Program for checking degree

```
        FUNCTION PEVAL(A,N,X)
        INTEGER N
        REAL A(0:20),X
        CALL DEGCHK(A,N)
        IF (N .EQ. -1) THEN
            PEVAL = 0.0
        ELSE
            PEVAL = A(N)
            DO 5 I=N-1,0,-1
                PEVAL = PEVAL*X + A(I)
    5       CONTINUE
        ENDIF
        END
```

(h) Polynomial evaluation   FIGURE 6-12 (Continued)

to verify that the degrees of the operands are acceptable. If a degree greater than 20 is detected, DEGCHK prints

DEGREE TOO LARGE

and terminates the entire program. If a degree less than -1 is found, the warning message

INVALID DEGREE

is printed, the degree is set to -1, and the program continues.

Although none of the subroutines could produce a degree less than -1, the subroutines may be called by a variety of calling programs and need to be protected from these programs. It is possible for a calling program to assign an invalid degree mistakenly, and a well-written general-purpose subprogram should be designed to notify the user of such errors. Sometimes the subprogram should print a warning, make an intelligent guess at correcting the error, and then continue. This is done for degrees less than -1. Other times, it would be futile to continue and a descriptive message should be printed and the program terminated—as in the case of the degree being too large.

DEGCHK also verifies that the degree agrees with the coefficients by testing the leading coefficient. If the leading coefficient is zero, the degree is decremented and the next lower coefficient is tested. This continues until a nonzero coefficient is found. Because an addition may result in a lower degree than either of the operands if the degrees of the operands are equal, DEGCHK is called by PADD to readjust the degree of the sum. Subtraction may also result in a degree that is less than the degree of either operand, but recall that subtraction is performed by adding the negative of the subtrahend. Therefore, the degree check for subtraction is done when PADD is called.

The function PEVAL for evaluating a polynomial at a given point is given in Fig. 6-12(h). It receives three arguments, the coefficient array and degree variable of the polynomial being evaluated, and the point at which the polynomial is to be evaluated. PEVAL is based on Horner's rule,

$$A_N X^N + \ldots + A_1 X + A_0 = ((\ldots (A_N X + A_{N-1}) X + \ldots) X + A_1) X + A_0$$

It also uses DEGCHK to verify the degree of the polynomial being operated on.

Figure 6-13(a) gives a subroutine RFADD for adding two rational functions. Because a rational function consists of two polynomials, a numerator polynomial and a denominator polynomial, a two-dimensional coefficient array with two columns is needed to store the coefficients and a two-element linear array is needed to store the degrees. The subroutine RFADD assumes that the first column of the coefficient array and the first element of the degree array correspond to the numerator polynomial, and the second column and element correspond to the denominator polynomial. In order to apply the polynomial arithmetic subroutines the two-dimensional arrays are equivalenced to linear arrays. RFADD uses the polynomial arithmetic

```
SUBROUTINE RFADD (AR,NR,BR,MR,CR,LR)
INTEGER NR(2), MR(2), LR(2)
REAL AR(0:20,2), BR(0:20,2), CR(0:20,2)
REAL P(0:20), Q(0:20), R(0:20), S(0:20), U(0:20), V(0:20)
EQUIVALENCE (P,AR(0,1)), (Q,AR(0,2)), (R,BR(0,1)), (S,BR(0,2)),
:      (U,CR(0,1)), (V,CR(0,2))
CALL PMULT (P,NR(1),S,MR(2),U,LR(1))
CALL PMULT (Q,NR(2),R,MR(1),V,LR(2))
CALL PADD (U,LR(1),V,LR(2),U,LR(1))
CALL PMULT (Q,NR(2),S,MR(2),V,LR(2))
CALL ZCHK (LR(2))
END
```

(a)   Addition

```
SUBROUTINE ZCHK(N)
INTEGER N
IF (N .LT. 0) THEN
        PRINT *, 'DENOMINATOR POLYNOMIAL IS ZERO'
        STOP
    ELSE
ENDIF
END
```

(b)   Zero check

FIGURE 6-13 *Subroutines for adding rational functions and checking for zero denominators.*

subroutines and the equations

$$\frac{P}{Q} + \frac{R}{S} = \frac{PS + QR}{QS} = \frac{U}{V}$$

to find the sum. It then checks for a zero denominator polynomial by calling the subroutine ZCHK given in Fig. 6-13(b). A hierarchical diagram for RFADD is given in Fig. 6-14.

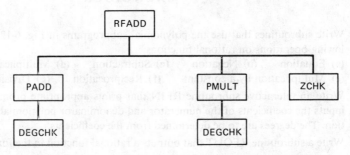

FIGURE 6-14 *Hierarchical diagram for the subroutine RFADD.*

Subroutines for performing the other rational function arithmetic operations have been left to the exercises. However, assuming the existence of the subroutines RFIN, RFOUT, RFADD, RFSUB, RFMULT, and RFDIV for inputting, output-ting, adding, subtracting, multiplying, and dividing rational functions, respectively, Fig. 6-15 gives an interactive program RATCAL for executing these operations. The program first asks which operation is to be performed and the user is to respond with "+", "−", "*", or "/". RATCAL then calls RFIN to input the two operands. Pre-sumably, RFIN asks for and inputs the numerator and denominator polynomials.

```
        PROGRAM RATCAL
        INTEGER NR(2), MR(2), LR(2)
        REAL AR(0:20,2), BR(0:20,2), CR(0:20,2)
        CHARACTER*1 TC
5     PRINT *, 'OPERATION?'
        READ *, TC
        IF (TC .NE. '+' .AND. TC .NE. '-' .AND. TC .NE. '*'
:         .AND. TC .NE '/') GO TO 10
        PRINT *, 'INPUT FIRST OPERAND'
        CALL RFIN (AR,NR)
        PRINT *, 'INPUT SECOND OPERAND'
        CALL RFIN (BR,MR)
        IF (TC .EQ. '+') THEN
                CALL RFADD (AR,NR,BR,MR,CR,LR)
            ELSE IF (TC .EQ. '-') THEN
                CALL RFSUB (AR,NR,BR,MR,CR,LR)
            ELSE IF (TC .EQ. '*') THEN
                CALL RFMULT (AR,NR,BR,MR,CR,LR)
            ELSE
                CALL RFDIV (AR,NR,BR,MR,CR,LR)
        ENDIF
        CALL RFOUT (CR,LR)
        GO TO 5
10    CONTINUE
        END
```

FIGURE 6-15 *Program for performing arithmetic on rational functions.*

Next RATCAL performs the requested operation, outputs the result, and returns to the statement that asks for an operation. The loop continues to be executed until the operation question is answered with something other than "$+$," "$-$," "$*$," or "$/$", at which time the program terminates.

EXERCISES

1. Write subroutines that use the polynomial subprograms in Fig. 6-12 to perform the following operations on rational functions.
   (a) Equation   (b) Negation   (c) Subtraction   (d) Multiplication
   (e) Multiplication by a constant   (f) Reciprocation   (g) Division

2. Write an interactive subroutine RFIN that prints appropriate prompting messages and inputs the coefficients of the numerator and denominator polynomials of a rational function. The degrees are to be determined from the coefficients.

3. Write a subroutine RFOUT that outputs a rational function in the form

   NUMERATOR COEFFICIENTS
   (List of numerator coefficients beginning with
   the constant term)
   DENOMINATOR COEFFICIENTS
   (List of denominator coefficients beginning with
   the constant term)

4. Assume the existence of RFADD and the subprograms requested in Exercises 1 through 3, and draw a complete hierarchical diagram of the program RATCAL given in Fig. 6-15.

5. Write a function subprogram that will evaluate a rational function at a given point.

6. RFADD cannot put the result in either operand. Why? Modify RFADD so that this problem is avoided.

7. The equivalencing in Fig. 6-13 could not be made to work properly if AR, BR, and CR had been dimensioned (2,0:20) instead of (0:20,2). Why?

6-5 DIMENSIONING PARAMETERS

It has been mentioned that the reasons for dimensioning are:

1. To inform the translator that a name is an array name.
2. To specify subscript limits so that element addresses can be computed.
3. To allocate the proper amount of memory space.

It has also been stated that arrays whose names appear as parameters in the opening statement of a subprogram must be dimensioned in the subprogram (as well as those whose names are not in the parameter list). Only the first two of the reasons above apply in this case because the space has already been reserved. Recall that an array reference causes both the calling program and the subprogram to access the same area of memory, and the subprogram knows where to find that area because the base element address is passed to it via the argument table.

The fact that only the base element address of a higher-dimensional array is received by the subprogram creates a problem. The calling program will use the subscript limits given by its dimensioning statements to compute the element addresses, and the subprogram will use the subscript limits in its dimensioning statements. Given:

Calling program	Subprogram
REAL X(3,2)	SUBROUTINE SUBR (Y) REAL Y(2,2)
. . CALL SUBR (X)	.

the alignment would be

```
X (1, 1)  ┌──────┐  Y (1, 1)
X (2, 1)  ├──────┤  Y (2, 1)
X (3, 1)  ├──────┤  Y (1, 2)
X (1, 2)  ├──────┤  Y (2, 2)
X (2, 2)  ├──────┤
X (3, 2)  └──────┘
```

which is likely to be different from the intended alignment. The conclusion is that, except possibly for the rightmost subscript, the same subscript limits should always be used in both the calling program and the subprogram. The problem is compounded if higher-dimensional character arrays are being related because the lengths of the elements must also be considered.

The FORTRAN 77 rules are quite loose in allowing array reconfiguration to occur when passing from a calling program to a subprogram, but reconfiguration *should not be practiced.* An array dimensioned by

DIMENSION A(10,20)

in the calling program could be matched with an array dimensioned by

DIMENSION B(40,5)

in the subprogram, but such a reconfiguration would lead to confusion. The only rule that is required is that the total number of elements in the array in the calling program must be greater than or equal to the total number of elements in the corresponding subprogram array. (Even this rule is seldom enforced because the calling program and the subprogram are translated separately, thus making enforcement difficult.)

Since the subscript limits for parameters are needed solely for the purpose of locating array elements and not for reserving space, it is possible to allow variable dimensioning within subprograms. *Variable dimensioning* means that the subscript limits may be integer expressions that include integer variables, and *fixed dimensioning* means that the subscript limits must be integer constants. Variable dimensioning is done according to the following rules:

1. The subscript limit expressions may include only integer constants and integer variables; integer-valued functions and integer array element names are not permitted.
2. All variables appearing in the subscript limit expressions must also appear as parameters and must be given values by program units higher in the hierarchy. The values of these variables must not be changed within the subprogram.
3. Fixed dimensions must be given to the array by a program unit that is higher in the hierarchy than the subprogram.

As an example:

Calling program	Subprogram
PROGRAM MAIN	SUBROUTINE SUBR(J,Y,L)
REAL I(4), X(3,4)	REAL J(0:L-1), Y(3,L)
N=3	.
.	.
.	.
.	
CALL SUBR (I,X,N)	

I (1)		J (0)		X (1, 1)		Y (1, 1)	
I (2)		J (1)		X (2, 1)		Y (2, 1)	
I (3)		J (2)		X (3, 1)		Y (3, 1)	
I (4)				X (1, 2)		Y (1, 2)	
				X (2, 2)		Y (2, 2)	
				X (3, 2)		Y (3, 2)	
				X (1, 3)		Y (1, 3)	
				X (2, 3)		Y (2, 3)	
				X (3, 3)		Y (3, 3)	
				X (1, 4)			
				X (2, 4)			
				X (3, 4)			

FIGURE 6-16 *Example of the alignment of arrays.*

would cause the array J to have three elements and the array Y to have nine elements. The alignment of the arrays is illustrated in Fig. 6-16.

Allowing variable dimensioning is very important. The reason is that many subprograms may be called by a variety of calling programs, some of which are written by people who know little about the subprogram. For example, suppose that a subprogram is written to solve 10 equations and 10 unknowns, and therefore uses the statement

```
DIMENSION A(10,10)
```

to dimension the coefficient array. It would be possible to use the subprogram only to solve exactly 10 equations. However, if the statement

```
DIMENSION A(N,N)
```

were used, where N is determined by the main program, the subprogram (if written properly) could be employed to solve any number of equations. The dimensioning in the subprogram would no longer be a limiting factor.

In the same vein, if the subroutine PNEG in Fig. 6-12b had begun with

```
SUBROUTINE PNEG (A,N,C,L,K)
INTEGER N,L,K
REAL A(0:K), C(0:K)
            .
            .
            .
```

the calling program would have control over the maximum degree that could be accommodated. All the subprograms given in Fig. 6-12 could be similarly altered and the result would be a much more useful polynomial arithmetic package.

Another possibility permitted by FORTRAN 77 is to leave the upper limit of the rightmost subscript unspecified by placing an asterisk in its position in the dimensioning notation. If the statement

```
DIMENSION A(*)
```

were in a subprogram, the size restriction caused by fixing the limit could be avoided without passing an extra variable to specify the limit. This procedure provides some flexibility in a few situations, but has many disadvantages. It can seldom be helpful when applied to higher-dimensional arrays because an asterisk can replace only the rightmost upper subscript limit. Also it cannot be used if other references in the subprogram, either explicit or implicit, must be made to the unspecified limit; for example, the statement

READ *, A

where A is an array with an unspecified limit, could not be used in the subprogram. Finally, a programmer should consciously specify limits, because not specifying a limit leads to carelessness which, in turn, leads to errors.

    Asterisks may also replace length specifiers in CHARACTER statements that are contained in subprograms. A statement of the form

CHARACTER*(*) List

would cause the items in the *List* to assume the same length as the matching variables or arrays in the calling program. The matching variables and arrays must, of course, be of the character type and all have the same length. In the following situation:

Calling program	Subprogram
CHARACTER*5 A,B(10),C(6),D(8)	SUBROUTINE SUBR (X,Y,Z,W,Q,K)
CHARACTER*2 P(10)	CHARACTER*(*) X,Y(7),Z(*),W(K)
M=4	CHARACTER*2 Q(K)
⋮	⋮
CALL SUBR (A,B,C,D,P,M)	

X and all the elements of Y, Z, and W are five characters long. The number of elements in the Y array is seven, in Z is unspecified, and in W is four. The array Q has four elements, each consisting of two characters.

    The restrictions regarding the use of character arguments are:

1. The length of a parameter variable may not be more than that of the argument. For arrays this statement applies to the elements.

2. The total length of a parameter array (length of each element in characters times the number of elements) cannot exceed the total length of the matching argument.

3. A character-type parameter with an assumed length (by means of an asterisk) cannot be used in a concatenation except on the right side of an assignment statement.

EXERCISES

1. Discuss the way in which a subprogram would assign the element locations for the arrays that are dimensioned by:
   (a) DIMENSION A(4)
   (b) DIMENSION X(N)
   (c) DIMENSION P(*)
   (d) DOUBLE PRECISION B(3,3)
   (e) DIMENSION L(M,N,K)
   (f) CHARACTER*3 C(N)
   (g) CHARACTER*(*) V(3,*)

2. Given that M corresponds to N, for each of the following pairs of matching arrays, show how they are aligned in memory.

	Calling program	Subprogram
(a)	DIMENSION A(4,4)	DIMENSION B(4,3)
(b)	N=3	
	DIMENSION X(4,4), A(3,3)	DIMENSION Y(M,4), B(M,M)
(c)	DIMENSION U(5), V(5,3)	DIMENSION U(*), V(5,*)
(d)	N=3	
	DIMENSION A(4,4)	DIMENSION B(4,M:M+2)

3. Assume a linear character array and an associated linear real array. Write a subroutine SEARCH that will sequentially search the character array for a given name and, if the name is found, will set a flag to 1 and pass to the calling program the flag and the corresponding entry in the real array. If the name is not found, the subprogram is to set the flag to 0. The parameters are to be the character array, the real array, the number of entries in the arrays, the variable that contains the name that is being searched for, the variable for returning the corresponding real number, the dimension of the character and real arrays, and the flag. The length of the elements in the character array and the name are to be assumed from the calling program, and variable dimensioning of the arrays is to be used. Also write a calling program that will use the subroutine to search a list of minerals for a given mineral and return that mineral's density. The calling program is to reserve 10 characters for the mineral names and enough space for 100 minerals, but the actual number of minerals in the array is to be input by the user together with the name of the mineral to be found.

6-6 EXTERNAL STATEMENTS

It was indicated earlier that names of executable programs could also appear as arguments and parameters. This would permit a subprogram to call another subprogram whose name is given to it by a calling program. Figure 6-17 shows a main program, a subprogram SUBR, and two other subprograms PROA and PROB that may be called by SUBR. The first time the main program calls SUBR, the name

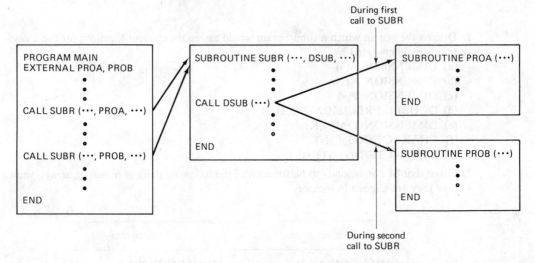

FIGURE 6-17 *Use of subprogram names as parameters.*

PROA is given to SUBR through the parameter DSUB, and PROA is called by SUBR. In the second call to SUBR the name PROB is passed and SUBR calls PROB.

We have seen that for data-related arguments their addresses are placed in a table and thereby passed to the subprogram. However, for a subprogram name an address is not put in the argument table and the translator must have an explicit means of identifying the arguments that are subprogram names. This identification is provided by an EXTERNAL statement which has the form

EXTERNAL *Subprogram Name List*

where the *Subprogram Name List* consists of subprogram names that appear as arguments. All subroutine or external function names that are included in an argument list of a subprogram call within a given program unit must also appear in an EXTERNAL statement within that unit. Note that in Fig. 6-17 an EXTERNAL statement is included in the main program but not in the subprogram SUBR. EXTERNAL statements must be placed before the first executable statement in a program unit.

Any subroutine or external function name may appear as an argument. Most intrinsic functions may appear as arguments, but if they do, they must also be included in an INTRINSIC statement (instead of an EXTERNAL statement). An INTRINSIC statement has the same form as an EXTERNAL statement. Not all intrinsic functions can appear in argument lists, and those whose names cannot appear are INT, IFIX, IDENT, REAL, FLOAT, SNGL, ICHAR, CHAR, MIN, MAX, DBLE, CMPLX, LOG, and LOG10. (*Warning:* This list is for standard FORTRAN 77, but in general it may be system-dependent.)

To demonstrate the use of function names as arguments, suppose that a chemical process produces products A and B from a type of oil. The total output quantity equals the input quantity, and the ratio of the amounts of the two products depends on the grade of the oil, 1 or 2, and on the pressure applied during processing. The problem is to write a program that computes the income derived from these products given that the oil costs $1 per liter, product A sells for $2 per liter, and product B sells for $3 per liter. If P is the pressure, the fractional part of grade 1 oil that is converted into product A is determined by

$$F = 1 - e^{-P}$$

and the fractional part of grade 2 oil that is converted into product A is given by

$$F = \tfrac{1}{2} \arctan (P)$$

A solution to the problem is given in Fig. 6-18. The main program inputs the quantity of grade 1 oil, the quantity of grade 2 oil, and the pressure into QUAN1, QUAN2, and P. It then calls the function INCOME twice, once for each grade of

```
PROGRAM MAIN
REAL INCOME, QUAN1, QUAN2, AMT, P
EXTERNAL G1, G2
READ *, QUAN1, QUAN2, P
AMT = INCOME(G1,QUAN1,P) + INCOME(G2,QUAN2,P)
PRINT *, 'TOTAL INCOME',AMT
END
```

(a) Main program

```
REAL FUNCTION INCOME(G,Q,P)
REAL Q,P
INCOME = (2.0*G(P) + 3.0*(1-G(P)) - 1.0)*Q
END
```

(b) Function INCOME

```
FUNCTION G1(P)
REAL P
G1 = 1.0 - EXP(-P)
END
```

(c) Function G1

```
FUNCTION G2(P)
REAL P
G2 = 0.5*ATAN(P)
END
```

(d) Function G2

FIGURE 6-18 *Solution to the chemical process example.*

oil. The first time INCOME is called, it is given the function name G1 and G1 is called from INCOME to compute the fractional amount of product A that is produced. During the second call, G2 is passed and used.

EXERCISES

1. Usually, programs can be written just as easily, and in a more straightforward structure, without using subprogram names as arguments. Rewrite the program in Fig. 6-18 so that subprogram names do not appear as arguments.
2. Write a main program MAIN, a subroutine SUBR, and two functions POLA and POLB. SUBR is to have the parameters P, X, A, and ICODE, and is to compute

$$A = EXP(P(X))$$

where P is either POLA or POLB. SUBR is to set ICODE = 0 if A > 5, and otherwise set ICODE = 1. MAIN is to read a number into X, compute A and ICODE using SUBR and POLA, and print

VALUE OF A = (*Value of A*)

If ICODE is 0, A and ICODE are to be recomputed using SUBR and POLB; otherwise, no further action is to be taken. POLA and POLB are to have a single parameter S and are to be such that

POLA = 3.0∗S − 2.0
POLB = SIN(S) + 1.2

6-7 PROGRAMMING EXCEPTIONS

A type of situation that arises quite often is one in which a subroutine must produce a code value in addition to its other duties. The code value indicates one of several cases that are related to the actions taken by the subroutine. Then, upon the return to the calling program, a branch is taken to one of several program segments depending on the value of the code. Under such circumstances, a combination such as

CALL (. . . , CODE)
CASE *Structure* − CODE *Condition*

could be used. The CASE structure could be implemented with either an IF block or a computed GO TO.

One application of this procedure is in programming exceptions. An *exception* is a case that does not normally occur (e.g., a subscript that is out of range). Murphy's law states that if anything can go wrong it will, and a well-designed subprogram should take all possibilities into account. This is particularly true if the subprogram may be used in different programs written by different people. Subprograms that are not designed to detect improper inputs or results may allow errors to propagate into the calling program structure, and the cause of such errors may be very difficult to find.

Although inputs could be checked for incorrect values before entering a subprogram, this is not a good technique. The reason is that the checking would have to be repeated for each call. Also, if the programmer has not written the subprogram, he or she may mistakenly assume that the testing is done inside the subprogram. The other possibilities are to (1) test and take corrective actions within the subprogram, and (2) test within the subprogram and take corrective actions after the subprogram has returned to the calling program. The first possibility has the disadvantage that it does not give control of the corrective actions to the calling program. It is utilized primarily by functions because a function can appear in the middle of an expression. If the corrective actions were taken outside the function, the corrective actions could be taken only after the expression is evaluated. Also, the code could be returned only by changing an argument, and this practice is not encouraged. The second possibility is the normal procedure for subroutines. The subroutine provides the protection and, by the existence of the code argument, indicates to the person that is programming the calling program that corrective actions are needed. The person writing the calling program can decide what the corrective actions should be.

For example, suppose that a subroutine LIMAVE is to average the first $N \leq$ 1000 numbers in an array G that are nonnegative and less than or equal to UL. The parameters are to be G, N, AVE, UL, and CODE. If N is less than 1 or greater than 1000, CODE is to be set to 1 and the subroutine is to return without taking further action. If a number in G is outside the interval 0 through UL, the number is to be left out of the average and CODE is to be set to 2, but the subprogram is to continue its processing. Otherwise, CODE is to be set to 0 and the average is to include all the numbers in G.

Figure 6-19(a) gives a subroutine that satisfies these requirements and Fig. 6-19(b) gives a segment of a calling program that uses the subroutine to average grades that range from 0 through 100. Upon being returned to from the subroutine, the calling program tests CODE. If CODE is 1, the message

SUBSCRIPT OUT OF RANGE

is printed and the program stops. For the CODE=2 case, the message

INVALID GRADE OCCURRED – AVERAGE = (*Value of average*)

is printed, but the program continues. Otherwise, the calling program prints

AVERAGE = (*Value of average*)

FORTRAN 77 also allows another method for providing multiple branching upon the return from a subroutine. The method involves arguments that are asterisked labels and matching asterisk parameters. However, it also involves multiple

```
          SUBROUTINE LIMAVE (G,N,AVE,UL,CODE)
          INTEGER N, CODE, M
          REAL G(1000), AVE, UL
          IF (N .LT. 1 .OR. N .GT. 1000) THEN
                    CODE = 1
          ELSE
                    AVE = 0.0
                    CODE = 0
                    M = 0
                    DO 5 I=1,N
                      IF (G(I) .LT. 0.0 .OR. G(I) .GT. UL) THEN
                            CODE = 2
                      ELSE
                            AVE = AVE + G(I)
                            M = M + 1
                      ENDIF
5                 CONTINUE
                  IF (M .EQ. 0) THEN
                        PRINT *, 'NO VALID VALUES'
                  ELSE
                        AVE = AVE/REAL(M)
                  ENDIF
          ENDIF
          END
```

(a) Subroutine

```
          CALL LIMAVE (GRADE,M,AVE,100.0,CODE)
          IF (CODE .EQ. 1) THEN
                    PRINT *, 'SUBSCRIPT OUT OF RANGE'
                    STOP
          ELSE IF (CODE .EQ. 2) THEN
                    PRINT *, 'INVALID GRADE OCCURRED -- AVERAGE =',AVE
          ELSE
                    PRINT *, 'AVERAGE =',AVE
          ENDIF
```

(b) Typical calling sequence

FIGURE 6-19 *Example of using a code to identify exceptions.*

RETURN statements within the subroutine and results in a structuring nightmare. Therefore, it should not be used and is not discussed in this book. It is mentioned only to warn the reader of its existence.

EXERCISES

1. Why is it inconvenient to use a code to pass an exception identification from a function to a calling program?

2. Write a subroutine that will sort the first $M \leq 50$ character strings in an array C into ascending order. If M is less than 1 or greater than 50, CODE is to be set to 1. If a character string is found that begins with a character other than a letter, CODE is to be set to -1, but sorting is to continue. Otherwise, CODE is to be set to 0. The parameters are to be C, M, and CODE. Assume the ASCII code; see Fig. 5-4. Also write a calling sequence that, after the call, causes

STRING SUBSCRIPT ERROR

to be printed and the program to stop if CODE$=1$, causes

INVALID STRING OCCURRED

to be printed and the program to continue if CODE$=-1$, and simply continue if CODE$=0$.

6-8 ENTRY STATEMENTS

As illustrated in Fig. 6-20, most versions of FORTRAN permit subprograms to be entered at points other than the beginning. This is done by inserting statements of the form

ENTRY Name (Parameter List)

where *Name* is the name of the entry point. The *Name* can be any valid subprogram name except that the names of the subprogram and entry points within a program unit must not be duplicated. The *Parameter List* for an ENTRY statement can be completely different from the *Parameter Lists* in the opening statement of the subprogram and the other ENTRY statements. An ENTRY statement is branched to by a CALL statement or function reference in the same way as a SUBROUTINE or FUNCTION statement. An ENTRY statement is nonexecutable and execution actually begins at the first statement after the ENTRY statement. All type declaring, dimensioning, and so on, must be done at the beginning of the subprogram. The

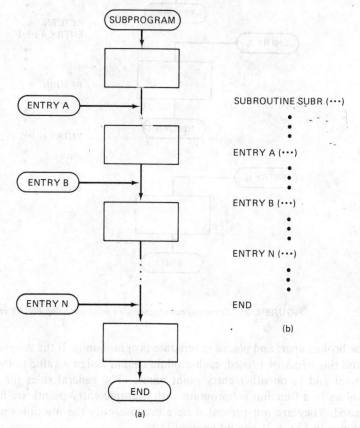

FIGURE 6-20 *Multiple entry points.*

only nonexecutable statements that may occur after the first executable statement in a program unit are ENTRY and FORMAT statements.

The structure indicated in Fig. 6-20 violates the single-input, single-output rule for structured programming and, therefore, *should not be used.* (An exception to the rule might be justified when writing a system subprogram that must be designed for efficiency, but system programs are beyond the scope of this book.) Multiple entry points can be used, however, to essentially group several subprogram-like modules within a single program unit. This structure is depicted in Fig. 6-21 and does not allow any branching between modules. The modules are such that they could easily

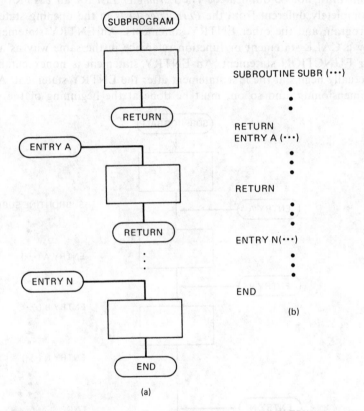

```
                    SUBROUTINE SUBR (···)
                        •
                        •
                        •
                    RETURN
                    ENTRY A (···)
                        •
                        •
                        •
                    RETURN
                        •
                        •
                    ENTRY N(···)
                        •
                        •
                        •
                    END

                                    (b)
```

(a)

FIGURE 6-21 *Grouping subprogram-like modules using ENTRY statements.*

be broken apart and placed in separate program units. If the subprogram is a function and this structure is used, each module should assign a value to the name of its entry point and to no other entry point name. (The general rules for assigning function values in a function subprogram with multiple entry points are flexible but complicated. They are not presented here because only the multiple-entry-point structure shown in Fig. 6-21 should be used.)

EXERCISES

1. Explain the statement: The structure indicated in Fig. 6-20 violates the single-input, single-output rule of structured programming.

2. Use the structure shown in Fig. 6-21 to rewrite and group the subroutines in Fig. 6-12(a) through (f) into a single subroutine with six entry points. Note that PSUB must be rewritten so that it does not call PNEG or PADD and that DEGCHK cannot be included in the grouping. Why? Also, PEVAL cannot be included. Why? If the subroutines in Fig. 6-12(a) through (g) are to be combined and included as a system subroutine, the user would not be concerned with the internal structure of the subroutine. Therefore, the single-input, single-output rule could be broken. Using as few statements as possible, combine these subroutines into a single subroutine with multiple entry points. Discuss the effect of this structure on scope.

6-9 COMMON

The other principal method for transferring information between program units is to assign special data areas in memory, called *common areas*, that can be accessed by several program units. Figure 6-22 shows the relationship between program units and a common area. Common areas have the advantage that the data in them can be referred to directly without the program having to first retrieve an address from an argument table. Also, by putting data in common areas, one can reduce the sizes of *Argument* and *Parameter Lists*. As we will soon see, the major disadvantage is that the programmer must be concerned with alignment.

In FORTRAN, there are two types of common areas, unnamed common and named common. Within a given program there can be only one *unnamed common*

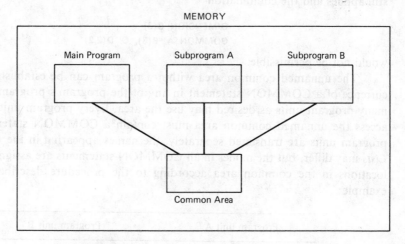

FIGURE 6-22 *Relationship of a common area to program units.*

area and it is established by the appearance of a statement of the form

COMMON *Common Data List*

where *Common Data List* is a list of variable and array names. The assignment of the names in the *Common Data List* to the memory locations in the unnamed common area is done in order. The first variable or array element is assigned to the first memory location, the second to the second memory location, and so on. The statements

DIMENSION B(3), D(2,2)
COMMON A, B, C, D

would associate the names A, B, C, and D with memory locations as shown in Fig. 6-23.

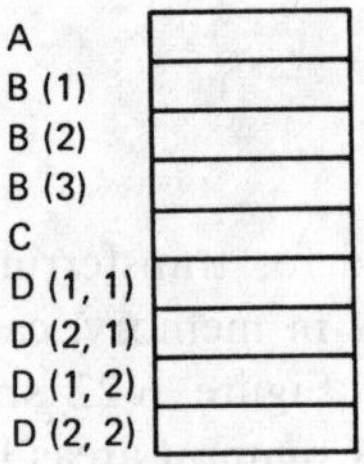

A
B (1)
B (2)
B (3)
C
D (1, 1)
D (2, 1)
D (1, 2)
D (2, 2)

FIGURE 6-23 *Assignment of variables and array elements to a common area.*

Dimensioning may also be accomplished with a COMMON statement and the two statements above could be combined into the single statement

COMMON A, B(3), C, D(2,2)

However, the rule that an array cannot be dimensioned by more than one statement still applies and the combination

DIMENSION B(3)
COMMON A, B(3), C, D(2,2)

would not be permissible.

The unnamed common area within a program can be established by the occurrence of a COMMON statement in any of the program's program units, and as many program units as desired may use the area. Every program unit that needs to access the unnamed common area must contain a COMMON statement. Because program units are translated separately, the names appearing in the *Common Data Lists* may differ, but the names in all COMMON statements are assigned to memory locations in the common area according to the procedure described above. For example:

Program unit A	Program unit B
COMMON F, X, Y(4), Z(2,2)	COMMON G, A(2), B, C(3)

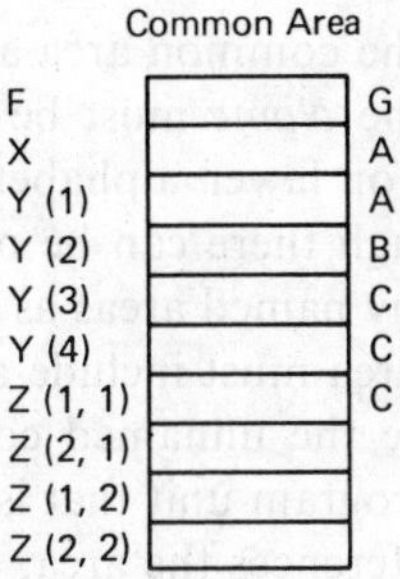

F		G
X		A (1)
Y (1)		A (2)
Y (2)		B
Y (3)		C (1)
Y (4)		C (2)
Z (1, 1)		C (3)
Z (2, 1)		
Z (1, 2)		
Z (2, 2)		

FIGURE 6-24 *Assignment of a common area by different program units.*

would result in the alignment shown in Fig. 6-24. Note that for unnamed common the numbers of memory locations assigned by COMMON statements in different program units may be different.

Clearly, the types specified by two program units for names that refer to the same location in a common area must agree. The assignments

Main program	Subprogram
INTEGER P	REAL A
COMMON P, Q, X	COMMON A, B, C

would not be allowed because P and A would occupy the same memory location. On the other hand, variables may be aligned with array elements of the same type, and arrays of the same type but of different dimensions may be aligned.

Numerical and logical names can be assigned to the same common area, but a bothersome limitation is that a common area must consist entirely of character-type variables and arrays or of variables and arrays that are of other types. The assignments

```
INTEGER P, I
REAL B(3)
DOUBLE PRECISION X, Y(2,3)
LOGICAL A
COMMON A, B, X, P, I, Y
```

would be valid, but

```
INTEGER A
CHARACTER C
COMMON A, C
```

would be invalid.

Named (or *labeled*) common is established by a statement of the form

COMMON /Name/ Common Data List

where *Name* is the name of the common area and the *Common Data List* must obey the rules discussed above. The *Name* must be constructed under the same rules as the name of a variable: six or fewer alphabetic and numeric characters, with the first being alphabetic. Although there can be only one unnamed common area in a program, there can be as many named areas as desired. Any program unit that needs to access a named common area must include a COMMON statement that contains the name of the area. Unlike the unnamed common area, a named common area should only be related to a program unit that is lower in the program hierarchy than the program unit that first references the area.

Figure 6-25 depicts a typical subprogram hierarchy and corresponding common structure. For this structure, the main program must contain the COMMON statements

COMMON ...
COMMON /CA1/ ...

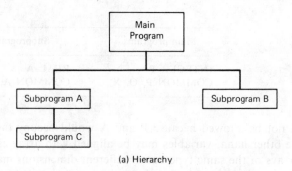

(a) Hierarchy

MEMORY

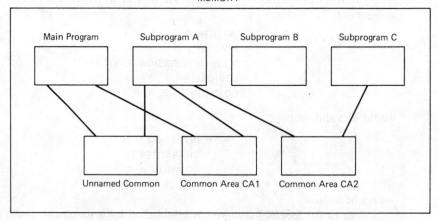

(b) Common structure

FIGURE 6-25 *Typical common structure.*

subprogram A must contain

```
COMMON ...
COMMON /CA1/ ...
COMMON /CA2/ ...
```

and subprogram C must contain

```
COMMON /CA2/ ...
```

where the ellipses represent *Common Data Lists*. Subprogram B does not refer to any of the common areas and, therefore, does not need to include any COMMON statements. If it contained the proper COMMON statements, it could reference the unnamed common area and the area named CA1 because they first appear in the main program. However, subprogram B should not reference CA2 because this could result in errors even if it contained the statement

```
COMMON /CA2/ ...
```

The alignment process is the same as for unnamed common areas, but the *Common Data Lists* for a named common area must all correspond to *exactly the same number* of memory locations. Even though the *Common Data Lists* in the statements

Program unit A	Program unit B
COMMON /AREA1/ W,X,Y,Z	COMMON /AREA1/ P,Q,R

would be acceptable for unnamed COMMON, they are not acceptable for named COMMON.

If the COMMON statements for the structure shown in Fig. 6-25 were

Main program	Subprogram A	Subprogram C
COMMON A, B, C, D, E	CHARACTER*4 F, G(2)	CHARACTER*2 R(3), H(3)
COMMON /CA1/ X, Y(2), I(2,2)	COMMON A, B, U(2)	COMMON /CA2/ R, H
	COMMON /CA1/ P(2), Q, J(4)	
	COMMON /CA2/ F, G	

where only the dimensioning shown is to be assumed, the alignment would be as illustrated in Fig. 6-26. Note that subprogram A does not use all the unnamed common area, but the named common areas have exactly the same amounts of memory assigned to them by both of the program units that access them. Also, note that the

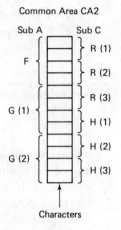

FIGURE 6-26 *Alignments of several common areas within a single program.*

unnamed common area and the common area CA1 consist entirely of noncharacter data, and area CA2 consists entirely of character data. As mentioned above, mixing the two categories is not allowed.

Both common areas and *Argument Lists* can be used to communicate with a subprogram. The statements

Calling program	Subprogram
COMMON A(100), B	SUBROUTINE SUBR (P,Q)
	COMMON A(100), C
·	·
·	·
·	·
CALL SUBR (X,Y)	·

would cause the variables X, Y, and B and the array A to be available to the subprogram. The variables X and Y would be referred to in the subprogram as P and Q and the variable B would be referred to as C.

Although the examples above have aligned variables with arrays and have overlapped arrays, such practices would obviously lead to confusion and should be used only under very special circumstances. The examples were designed to demonstrate what is possible. Normally, common areas are used only in programs that are written by a single programmer or a closely knit group of programmers and, for each area, the same names are assigned in the same order. Each area serves as a block of memory locations which are referenced in the same way by all the program units that access the block. Confusion should be minimized, with the naming and alignment of the areas being done in the most straightforward manner possible.

Common areas should not be employed to pass information to and from general-purpose subprograms that may be attached to a variety of programs. The reason is that a knowledge of the ordering of the common areas would be required and this would mean extra descriptive information and a greater chance for misunderstanding. General-purpose subprograms should rely only on *Argument Lists* for communication.

A frequent pitfall occurs when a program unit needs to access only some of the variables and arrays in a common area, but these variables and arrays are not contiguous in memory. Suppose that program unit A needs to use arrays W, X, Y, and Z and program unit B needs to use only W and Z. If the COMMON statements were

Program unit A	Program unit B
COMMON W(2), X(2), Y(2), Z(3)	COMMON W(2), Z(3)

the alignment would be

```
W (1)  ┌────────┐  W (1)
W (2)  │        │  W (2)
X (1)  │        │  Z (1)
X (2)  │        │  Z (2)
Y (1)  │        │  Z (3)
Y (2)  │        │
Z (1)  │        │
Z (2)  │        │
Z (3)  └────────┘
```

which is not the desired alignment. By adding the dummy array DUMMY as a spacer, the COMMON statement in program unit B becomes

COMMON W(2), DUMMY (4), Z(3)

and the proper alignment is obtained. When dummy arrays are inserted, the space they are to occupy must be computed carefully and they should be given distinctive names. An alternative would be to use the same COMMON statements to guarantee the proper correspondence, but this is deceptive because it makes it difficult to identify which arrays are actually used by the various program units. However, COMMON statements are often duplicated, particularly during the early stages of development (unless the different program units are designed to use different variable and array names).

EQUIVALENCE statements can refer to names that appear in Common Data Lists, but such references are discouraged. If an EQUIVALENCE statement is used in conjunction with a COMMON statement, it should be done in such a way that the alignment is clear. Ambiguities are not allowed, e.g.,

COMMON A, B, C
EQUIVALENCE (A,C)

is invalid, and the size of a common area should not be indirectly increased by an EQUIVALENCE statement (even though the rules of FORTRAN permit some extensions of unnamed common).

EXERCISES

1. Find the errors in each of the following corresponding pairs of COMMON statements (assume implicit-type declaration unless explicit-type declaration is indicated):

	Program unit A	Program unit B
(a)	COMMON A, B(10)	COMMON /CAREA/ C, D(2,5)
(b)	COMMON /S/ X(100)	COMMON /S/ A(5)
(c)	CHARACTER C(5)	
	COMMON C	COMMON C(5)
(d)	DOUBLE PRECISION B	DOUBLE PRECISION W
	COMMON /T/ A, B, C	COMMON /T/ U, V, W
(e)	COMMON X, I, N	COMMON Y, Z, N

2. Given the following common area definitions, show the alignments of the variables and arrays:

Main program	Subprogram A	Subprogram B
CHARACTER*4 D(0:1,2)	COMMON F(3,2)	CHARACTER*16 CS
COMMON A, B(3), C(2)	COMMON /T/ J(5)	COMMON W(2)
COMMON /S/ D		COMMON /S/ CS
COMMON /T/ I, J(4)		

3. Consider the arrays that are dimensioned as follows:

U(10), V(2,4), X(-2,2), Y(2,2,2)

where Y is a character array with the elements being two characters long. Assume that the main program references U, V, and Y, subprogram A references V, X, and Y, subprogram B references U and X, and subprogram C references U, V, and X, and provide a consistent set of COMMON statements for the program units. Answer the question in such a way that no more than two common areas are needed. Why are two common areas required?

6-10   BLOCK DATA

Although some enhanced versions of FORTRAN may permit the preassignment of common areas, in standard FORTRAN 77 common areas cannot be preassigned with DATA statements that are included in executable program units, but locations associated with *named* common areas can be preassigned from within a BLOCK DATA program unit. A BLOCK DATA program unit has the form

```
BLOCK DATA Name
Type Statements
COMMON Statements (for named common areas)
DATA Statements
END
```

where *Name* is the name of the BLOCK DATA program unit and is optional. A typical BLOCK DATA program unit is

```
BLOCK DATA
INTEGER I(3)
REAL A, B(2)
CHARACTER*4 C(2)
COMMON /AREA1/ I, A, B
COMMON /AREA2/ C
DATA I,A,(B(J), J=1,2) /3*0,2.5,-1.0,0.0/
DATA C(2) /'GOOD'/
END
```

An *unnamed* common area cannot normally be preassigned by a BLOCK DATA program unit.

6-11   SAVE STATEMENTS

Standard FORTRAN 77 does not require that the contents of the local variables and arrays be saved while a subprogram is not executing, in which case they must be assigned values each time the subprogram is entered. This can be overcome by including in the subprogram statements of the form

SAVE List

where *List* is a list of the local variables and arrays to be saved. Then, for all executions other than the first, the local variables in the *List* will contain the values left in them by the previous execution of the subprogram. A detailed discussion of the use of SAVE statements is not given in this book, and their introduction has been included only for completeness and to make the reader aware of their existence.

6-12 STATEMENT FUNCTIONS

A statement function is not a subprogram, but is included in this chapter because it is referenced in the same way as a function subprogram. A statement function is defined by placing a statement of the form

Name (Parameter List) = Expression

before the first executable statement of a program unit. *Name* can be any valid subprogram name and may have its type declared either implicitly or explicitly. The *Parameter List* is governed by the same rules that apply to subprograms except that only variable names are permitted. The *Expression* can be any expression that could appear on the right side of an assignment statement. It can include both parameters as variables and other variables that are contained in the program unit. Just as with function subprograms, the parameters are matched with the arguments in the function call according to their order. All variables in the *Expression* must be given values before the statement function is called. A statement function is only locally defined (i.e., it can be used only in the program unit in which its defining statement appears).

A typical application of a statement function is given in Fig. 6-27. The program shown in the figure computes the total distance traveled when traversing straight-line segments between N points in three-dimensional space. It also computes the distance between the origin and the point that is farthest from the origin. The distance between any two points is calculated by the statement function LENGTH, which includes a scale factor A that allows for a change in units (e.g., feet to meters). Note that only three of the variables in the expression are parameters; A is a variable in the program.

```
            PROGRAM PATH
            INTEGER N
            REAL A, XT, YT, ZT, X, Y, Z, TDIS, MAXDIS, LENGTH
            LENGTH(U,V,W) = A*SQRT(U**2 + V**2 + W**2)
            READ *, A
            READ *, N
            READ *, XT, YT, ZT
            TDIS = 0.0
            MAXDIS = LENGTH(XT, YT, ZT)
            DO 5 I=2,N
                READ *, X,Y,Z
                TDIS = TDIS + LENGTH(X-XT, Y-YT, Z-ZT)
                IF (LENGTH (X,Y,Z) .GT. MAXDIS) THEN
                        MAXDIS = LENGTH(X,Y,Z)
                    ELSE
                ENDIF
                XT = X
                YT = Y
                ZT = Z
          5 CONTINUE
            PRINT *, 'MAXIMUM DISTANCE=', MAXDIS
            PRINT *, 'TOTAL DISTANCE=', TDIS
            END
```

FIGURE 6-27 *Application of a statement function.*

During translation, the machine language instructions that are needed to evaluate the expression in a statement function are inserted at the point of each reference. Therefore, statement functions are unlike subprograms, which consist of reusable instructions. Statement functions do not save memory space or facilitate modularity; they are simply a laborsaving device that a programmer can use to write an expression only once and then reference it by its name as many times as desired.

EXERCISES

1. Identify the errors (if there are any) in the following statement function definitions.
   (a) FN(X,Y(I)) = SIN(X) + Y(I)
   (b) FUNPOLY(X) = 3.1*X**2 + 2.0*X + 1.5
   (c) FUNCTION POLY(X) = X**2 − 1.0
   (d) POLY(X) = A*X**2 + B*X

2. Find the value of X resulting from each program segment.
   (a) FUNC(U,V) = ATAN(U/V)**2/V
      A(1) = 1.0
      A(2) = A(1)**2 + 1.0
      X = FUNC(A(1),A(2))
   (b) FNA(X) = 5.0 + EXP(A*X)
      A = −1.0
      X = 2.0
      X = 1.0 + FNA(X)

3. Write a program that inputs the end points of an interval and finds the maximum value of the expression

$$-X^2 + 2X + 1$$

within that interval. This is to be done by comparing the results obtained by evaluating the expression at the end points and, if 1.0 lies within the interval, at the point $X = 1.0$. Evaluation of the expression is to be done by a statement function.

PROGRAMMING PROBLEMS

In addition to solving the following problems, give a hierarchical diagram of the solution.

1. A method for approximating functions by applying only the four arithmetic operations is to use continued fraction expansions. As an example, a continued fraction expansion approximation for e^X, which for $|X| \leq 1$ is good to seven significant figures, is

$$e^X = 1 + \cfrac{X}{1 - 0.5X + \cfrac{X^2}{12 + \cfrac{X^2}{5 + \cfrac{X^2}{28}}}}$$

Using this approximation and the fact that for any X there is an integer M and a fraction Z such that

$$e^X = e^M e^Z \qquad (e^M = 2.7182818^M)$$

write a function subprogram EX that will accept a value for X and return the value of e^X.

Also write a main program that will input N, XL, and XH, print the headings

X   EXP(X)   EX(X)   EXP(X) – EX(X)

and then compute and print the values of X, EXP(X), EX(X), and EXP(X)–EX(X) for $X = XL + I*(XH - XL)/N$, $I = 0, \ldots, N$. Test the program with N=50, XL=−5.0, and XH=5.0. Test the program again with N=50, XL=−50.0, and XH=50.0.

2. The probability (or chance) of an event occurring is the theoretical ratio of the number of times the event will occur to the number of opportunities for it to occur (e.g., the probability that a coin toss will be heads is 0.5). Quite often an uncertainty is described numerically (e.g., the length of time required to complete a task) and is represented by a symbol called a *random variable*. When this is the case, the probability of the event that the random variable will be less than or equal to a specified amount X is a function of X. This function is called the *probability distribution function* of the random variable and is written $P(X)$. As X increases from the lowest to highest possible value for the random variable, $P(X)$ increases from 0 to 1. Two example distribution functions are given below.

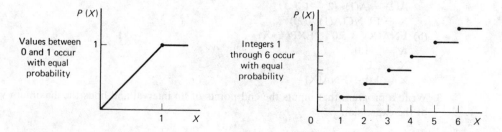

Because computers must follow fixed rules, it is impossible for them to produce numbers that are truly random, but programs are available for simulating random occurrences. A subprogram for generating seemingly (or pseudo) random numbers is called a *random number generator*. These are function subprograms that can be used by other programs to simulate the rolling of dice, times to complete tasks, and so on. Most random number generators are written to produce pseudo random numbers between 0 and 1 with equal probability. The design of a random number generator is dependent on the computer being used. A random number generator for a 32-bit computer (such as the IBM 360/370) is

```
FUNCTION RANDOM (SEED)
INTEGER SEED
SEED = 843314861*SEED+453816693
IF (SEED .LT. 0) THEN
        SEED = (SEED+2147483647)+1
    ELSE
ENDIF
RANDOM = SEED*0.4656612E−9
END
```

(If this subprogram does not execute properly on the system being used, refer to the appropriate manual—the system may include a random number generator.) The integer SEED is called the *seed* and at the beginning of the main program the seed is usually input from the user, a mass storage device, or a special memory location. If the same seed is input with each execution of a program the random number generator would always generate the same sequence of pseudo-random numbers. Therefore, normally different seeds are input for different executions.

Write a program that simulates N rolls of two dice. RANDOM must be executed twice for each roll, once for each die, and in each case the result must be converted to an integer from 1 through 6. This can be done by letting the roll be 1 if the result is less than or equal to $\frac{1}{6}$, 2 if the result is greater than $\frac{1}{6}$ but less than or equal to $\frac{2}{6}$, and so on. The input is to be N and an initial value for the seed and the output for each roll is to be:

DIE 1: *(1st result)*   DIE 2: *(2nd result)*   SUM: *(Sum of results)*

3. Extending the concepts presented in Programming Problem 2, suppose that the random variable can take on values other than those from 0 through 1 and does not take on values with equal likelihood. When this is the case, the output of the random number generator must be transformed to match the desired probability distribution. This transformation is accomplished by using the inverse of the desired probability distribution, as shown below.

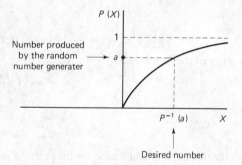

Write a subroutine RANNUM that uses the function RANDOM requested in Programming Problem 2 to return pseudo-random numbers according to a probability distribution that is passed to it via a common area array PROD. The common area is to also contain the SEED that is needed by RANDOM. The array PROD is to have two columns, with the first column containing values of X and the second containing values of the probability distribution $P(X)$. Linear interpolation is to be used for finding values between the values of X given in the first column of PROD, and this interpolation is to be done by a function subprogram LININT. The subroutine RANNUM is to have two parameters, the random number and a flag. Before computing the random number to be returned to the calling program, RANNUM is to verify that the values of $P(X)$ in the second column of PROD are in the interval 0 through 1 and are in ascending order. If these values are not valid distribution values, RANNUM is to set the parameter FLAG (which is to be a character string) to 'NOT VALID' and return without computing a random number. (FLAG is to be set to 'VALID' at the beginning of the subroutine.)

Finally, write a program that uses RANNUM to estimate the number of alpha particles N given off by a spherical mass in time TF, given that the time T between alpha particles is described by the distribution

$$1 - e^{-RT}$$

where R is the radius of the mass. The distribution is to be approximated by 11 evenly spaced points from $RT = 0$ through 2 with the distribution at $RT = 2$ being approximated by 1.0. The inputs are to be R, TF, and M, where M is to be used as the seed, and the output is to be

> ESTIMATED NO. OF ALPHA PARTICLES GIVEN
> OFF BY A SPHERE OF RADIUS (*Value of R*) CENTIMETERS
> IN (*Value of TF*) MICROSECONDS IS (*Value of N*)

Draw a hierarchical diagram of the program. Test the program using the values

$$R = 2.0 \qquad TF = 10.0$$

4. Gaussian elimination is a method for solving simultaneous linear equations which proceeds by eliminating one variable at a time by multiplying equations by constants and adding them to the other equations. The procedure can be reduced to the tabular method, which is outlined as follows. Given the equations

$$a_{11}x_1 + \cdots + a_{1n}x_n = b_1$$
$$\vdots \qquad\qquad \vdots \qquad\qquad \vdots$$
$$a_{m1}x_1 + \cdots + a_{mn}x_n = b_m$$

create an array of the form

$$
\begin{array}{ccc}
a_{11} & \cdots & a_{1n} \quad b_1 \\
\vdots & & \vdots \quad\ \vdots \\
a_{m1} & \cdots & a_{mn} \quad b_m
\end{array}
$$

Begin with the first column and scan it for the nonzero value with the greatest magnitude. Assuming that the greatest nonzero value is in the rth row, the first element in the rth row is called the pivot element. Interchange the rth row with the first row. Divide the new first row by the pivot element. For all other rows, replace each existing element with

$$a'_{ij} = a_{ij} - a_{i1} a'_{1j} \qquad i = 2, \ldots, m; \quad j = 1, \ldots, n$$

where a'_{1j} is the jth element in the new first row. For the new table, exclude the first row and choose the element in the second column which has the greatest magnitude, and let it be the new pivot element. Interchange the pivot element row with the second row and divide it by the pivot element. Replace the element in all the rows except the second row using the equation

$$a''_{ij} = a'_{ij} - a'_{i2} a''_{2j} \qquad i = 1, 3, \ldots, m; \quad j = 1, \ldots, n$$

Repeat the process for the third column through the nth column. If at any stage, say the kth stage, the kth through the mth elements are all zeros, skip the column and go to the next column (but choose the pivot element from the same set of rows, just as if a column had not been skipped). If after the nth column has been considered, there is a row containing only zeros in the first n columns but a nonzero number in the "b" column, the equations have no solution. Otherwise, the solution is constructed from the "b" column by taking the elements of this column in order, except that zeros are to be assigned to the x_j's corresponding to the columns that were skipped. As an example, for

$$x_1 \qquad + \; x_3 + 2x_4 = -2$$
$$2x_1 + 3x_2 + 5x_3 - \; x_4 = \; 1$$
$$x_1 + \; x_2 + 2x_3 + \; x_4 = \; 2$$

the following sequence of arrays is produced:

$$
\begin{array}{rrrrr}
1 & 0 & 1 & 2 & -2 \\
\textcircled{2} & 3 & 5 & -1 & 1 \\
1 & 1 & 2 & 1 & 2
\end{array}
\longrightarrow
\begin{array}{rrrrr}
1 & \frac{3}{2} & \frac{5}{2} & -\frac{1}{2} & \frac{1}{2} \\
1 & 0 & 1 & 2 & -2 \\
1 & 1 & 2 & 1 & 2
\end{array}
\longrightarrow
\begin{array}{rrrrr}
1 & \frac{3}{2} & \frac{5}{2} & -\frac{1}{2} & \frac{1}{2} \\
0 & \textcircled{-\frac{3}{2}} & -\frac{3}{2} & \frac{5}{2} & -\frac{5}{2} \\
0 & -\frac{1}{2} & -\frac{1}{2} & \frac{3}{2} & \frac{3}{2}
\end{array}
$$

$$
\begin{array}{rrrrr}
1 & 0 & 1 & 2 & -2 \\
0 & 1 & 1 & -\frac{5}{3} & \frac{5}{3} \\
0 & 0 & 0 & 1 & \frac{7}{2}
\end{array}
\longleftarrow
\begin{array}{rrrrr}
1 & 0 & 1 & 2 & -2 \\
0 & 1 & 1 & -\frac{5}{3} & \frac{5}{3} \\
0 & 0 & 0 & \textcircled{\frac{2}{3}} & \frac{7}{3}
\end{array}
\longleftarrow
\begin{array}{rrrrr}
1 & \frac{3}{2} & \frac{5}{2} & -\frac{1}{2} & \frac{1}{2} \\
0 & 1 & 1 & -\frac{5}{3} & \frac{5}{3} \\
0 & -\frac{1}{2} & -\frac{1}{2} & \frac{3}{2} & \frac{3}{2}
\end{array}
$$

$$
\begin{array}{rrrrr}
1 & 0 & 1 & 0 & -9 \\
0 & 1 & 1 & 0 & \frac{15}{2} \\
0 & 0 & 0 & 1 & \frac{7}{2}
\end{array}
\longrightarrow
\quad x_1 = -9 \quad x_2 = \frac{15}{2} \quad x_3 = 0 \quad x_4 = \frac{7}{2}
$$

If there is a solution and (1) $m < n$ or (2) $m \geqq n$ and more than $m - n$ columns have been skipped, the solution is just one of an infinite number of solutions.

    Write a subroutine SIMUL that accepts a two-dimensional coefficient array A, a linear array B, and integers K and L (where K and L are used to set the subscript limits on A and B) and computes the corresponding solution using the procedure described above. If there is more than one solution, the subroutine is to print the message

INFINITE NO. OF SOLUTIONS

and continue, and if there is no solution the subroutine is to print

NO SOLUTION

and stop.

    Also write a main program that inputs the number of equations to be solved into M, the number of unknowns into N, and values into the A and B arrays; prints the contents of the A and B arrays under suitable titles; uses SIMUL to compute the solution; and prints

THE SOLUTION IS:

followed by the elements of the solution, one element per line. Test the program by using it to solve the equations

$$2x_1 + 5x_2 + 2x_3 + 3x_4 = 4$$
$$2x_1 + 3x_2 + 3x_3 + 4x_4 = 0$$
$$3x_1 + 6x_2 + 3x_3 + 2x_4 = 4$$
$$4x_1 + 12x_2 \qquad\quad + 8x_4 = 0$$

(The answer is: $x_1 = -7$, $x_2 = 3$, $x_3 = 3$, and $x_4 = -1$). Suggest other sets of data for testing the program more thoroughly.

5. Suppose that a metallurgical process receives three elements (1, 2, and 3) and an inert substance (4) and produces four minerals (1, 2, 3, and 4) as well as passing the inert matter without chemical change. Let A, B, C, and D represent the fractional amounts of the elements and inert matter entering the system and W, X, Y, Z, and D the fractional amounts of the minerals leaving the system. The problem is to determine W, X, Y, and Z from A, B, C, and D by forming a set of linear mass-balance equations. One of the equations simply equates the input noninert mass to the output noninert mass and is

$$W + X + Y + Z = 1 - D$$

The other equations are obtained by performing a mass balance on the individual elements. The result is the system of equations

$$R_{11}W + R_{12}X + R_{13}Y + R_{14}Z = A$$
$$R_{21}W + R_{22}X + R_{23}Y + R_{24}Z = B$$
$$R_{31}W + R_{32}X + R_{33}Y + R_{34}Z = C$$
$$R_{41}W + R_{42}X + R_{43}Y + R_{44}Z = 1 - D$$

where $R_{41} = R_{42} = R_{43} = R_{44} = 1$ and

$$R_{ij} = \frac{\text{molecular weight of } i\text{th element in mineral } j}{\text{molecular weight of } j\text{th mineral}} \qquad \begin{array}{l} i = 1, 2, 3 \\ j = 1, 2, 3, 4 \end{array}$$

Write a program that inputs values to A, B, C, and D, inputs the molecular weights of the three elements in each of the four minerals to a two-dimensional array E, inputs the molecular weights of the minerals to a linear array M, computes the elements of the array R, uses the subroutine SIMUL written in Programming Problem 4 to solve the equations, and prints the results in the following form:

FRACTIONAL AMOUNT OF:

MINERAL NO.	AMOUNT
1	(*Value of W*)
2	(*Value of X*)
3	(*Value of Y*)
4	(*Value of Z*)

Test the program assuming that the input elements are copper, iron, and sulfur and the output minerals are $CuFeS_2$, Cu_2S, Cu_5FeS_4, and FeS_2. For these process elements and outputs the computer inputs are to be

$$A = 0.339 \quad B = 0.245 \quad C = 0.332 \quad D = 0.084$$

$$E(1,1) = 63.54 \quad E(1,2) = 127.08 \quad E(1,3) = 317.7 \quad E(1,4) = 0.0$$

$$E(2,1) = 55.85 \quad E(2,2) = 0.0 \quad E(2,3) = 55.85 \quad E(2,4) = 55.85$$

$$E(3,1) = 64.128 \quad E(3,2) = 32.064 \quad E(3,3) = 128.256 \quad E(3,4) = 64.128$$

$$M(1) = 183.52 \quad M(2) = 159.18 \quad M(3) = 501.81 \quad M(4) = 119.98$$

(The answer is: $W = 0.361$, $X = 0.165$, $Y = 0.130$, and $Z = 0.261$).

6. Assume the following electric power network:

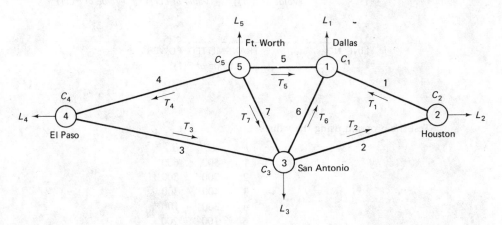

where the numbers in the circles are the numbers associated with the generating stations in the network and the numbers beside the connecting lines are those of the transmission lines. The ith station has a capacity of C_i megawatts and must supply a demand load of L_i megawatts, $i = 1, \ldots, 5$. If P_i is the power generated by the ith station, $i = 1, \ldots, 5$, and T_i is the power sent over the ith transmission line, $j = 1, \ldots, 7$, the problem is to find the P_i's and T_i's such that all the loads are satisfied but none of the capacities are exceeded. One procedure for solving the problem is to:

1. Check $C_1 + \ldots + C_5 \geq L_1 + \ldots + L_5$. There is a solution if and only if this inequality is true.
2. If there is a solution, let $P_i = C_i$ for all cases for which $L_i \geq C_i$.
3. Note that for each station there is an equation of the form

$$P_i + \sum \pm T_j = L_i$$

where the summation is over the transmission lines connected to the station and $+$ or $-$ is chosen according to the direction of flow. Use the subroutine SIMUL requested in Programming Problem 4 to solve the system of station equations for the T_js and the P_is not already assigned in step (2).
4. If the solution results in some of the stations exceeding their capacities, their generated powers are to be set to their capacities and step 3 is to be repeated, or if any of the P_is are negative equate them to their loads and repeat step (3). Otherwise, a solution has been found.

Write a program that sets the capacities with a DATA statement, inputs the demand loads, computes a valid set of values for the P_i's and T_i's, and prints

WARNING: NETWORK OVERLOADED

if there is insufficient overall capacity. If there is sufficient capacity, then the program is to print a report of the following form:

LOADING AND TRANSMISSION TABLE

STATION NO.	CAPACITY	LOAD	GENERATED POWER
1	*(Value of C(1))*	*(Value of L(1))*	*(Value of P(1))*
.	.	.	.
.	.	.	.
.	.	.	.

LINE NO.	TRANSMITTED POWER
1	*(Value of T(1))*
.	.
.	.
.	.

Test the program using the values:

i	C_i	L_i
1	500	600
2	700	800
3	400	300
4	300	100
5	100	200

7

FORMATTED INPUT-OUTPUT

The list-directed I-O that we have used until now is limited to the field lengths and format that are fixed by the design of the FORTRAN translator. Although it does afford a means of providing both numeric and alphanumeric input and output, it may not input or output information in the form that is most appealing to the user. The user may get more decimal places than desired, or may be forced into reading an E-format when the normal decimal format would be much better. To get around this problem the programmer needs to have some kind of format control.

FORTRAN provides such control by permitting the programmer to note I-O patterns using format specifications. When this is done there exists a three-way correspondence among the I-O list, the format specification, and the format of the input or output. The generalizations of the I-O statements introduced in Chap. 2 are

READ 'Format Specification', Input List

and

PRINT 'Format Specification', Output List

where in each case the * has been replaced with a *Format Specification* that determines the pattern to be used by the I-O operation. The patterns resulting from the *Format Specifications* are stored with the program and when a READ or PRINT statement is encountered, the pattern directs the use of the columns of the input or output media (cards or lines).

Even more general forms of the I-O statements are

READ (Control List) Input List

and

WRITE (Control List) Output List

where the *Control List* includes not only a format specification, but also a device specification and certain I-O control parameters. The *Control List* permits the use of I-O devices other than card readers, line printers, and terminals and allows the program to execute predefined branches if certain events occur during an I-O operation (e.g., the end-of-job card is encountered).

The purpose of this chapter is to introduce the various types of I-O statements that are available in FORTRAN, with particular attention being given to the formatting patterns. Section 7-1 discusses the structure of *Format Specifications* and how they are used to determine the records being input or output. Section 7-2 examines the inclusion of *Format Specifications* in the READ and PRINT statements and describes the list–pattern–record relationship that is associated with an I-O operation. The third section discusses the application of a line printer as a graphics device. Section 7-4 briefly considers *Control Lists* and the most general forms of the FORTRAN I-O statements, although a detailed discussion of these topics is left to the chapter on file processing, Chap. 8. The last section examines the overall I-O process and introduces internal files which provide a means of changing the form of internal data.

7-1 FORMATTING AND FORMAT CODES

The READ and PRINT statements used in the examples in this section have the form

> READ *'Format Specification', Input List*

and

> PRINT *'Format Specification', Output List*

where the *Format Specifications* consist of format codes, repeat factors, string constants, commas, and grouping symbols, and the *Input* and *Output Lists* are constructed as described in Chap. 2. The *Format Specifications* set up patterns that are scanned at execution time and direct the transformation between the internal and external data formats. An I-O record may be treated as a set of character positions (or columns) that is divided into fields, and the purpose of the *Format Specification* is to designate the number of columns in each field and how these columns are used.

The simplest *Format Specifications* appear as follows:

> *(Format Code 1, . . . , Format Code N)*

where each *Format Code* corresponds to an item in the *Input* or *Output List* and determines:

1. The number of character positions in the field.
2. The exact manner in which these character positions are to be used.

The correspondence is such that *Format Code* 1 relates to the first item being input or output, *Format Code* 2 relates to the second item, and so on. The first several subsections given below primarily describe the available *Format Codes* and concentrate on this simple formatting pattern. The latter subsections, except for the last subsection, are concerned with the rules regarding the list–pattern–record relationships. The last subsection summarizes the format codes that are used only in special cases.

7-1-1 Numeric Format Codes (I, F, E, G, and D)

A numeric format code has the form

Letter w.d.

where the *Letter* indicates the type of code, w indicates the field width in character positions, and d, which is not present in integer format codes, indicates the number of decimal places or significant figures. The types of numeric format codes are summarized in Fig. 7-1. The rightmost column in the figure describes the output that

Type	Format Code	Example	Comments on Output
Integer	Iw	I3	Integer is right justified in a field of w columns.
Real	Fw.d	F6.3	Real number is right justified in a field of w columns. It is printed to d decimal places using the normal decimal format (or F-format). If the magnitude is less than 1, a 0 is placed to the left of the decimal point.
Real	Ew.d	E12.3	Real number is right justified in a field of w columns. It is printed to d significant figures using the E-format d digits $\overbrace{\hspace{2cm}}$ S0.XX...XESXX where S is a blank (for plus) or a minus, and the X's are decimal digits.
Real	Gw.d	G10.2	Real number is printed in a field of w columns. If the magnitude of the number is > 0.1 and $< 10^d$, then it is printed right justified to d significant figures, but with four trailing blanks, using an F-format. Otherwise, it is printed right justified using the Ew.d format.
Double-Precision	Dw.d	D20.12	Double-precision number is right justified in w columns. It is printed to d significant figures using the same format described above for the E-format code.

FIGURE 7-1 *Summary of the numeric format codes.*

would result if the format code were to appear in a PRINT statement. If a numeric format code is of integer type (I), its corresponding input or output list item must be of integer type, and if the format code is of a real or double-precision type, the list item must be of real or double-precision type. (Note, however, that the D format code may be used with single-precision list items and the F, E, and G format codes may be used with double-precision list items.) Negative numbers are preceded by a minus sign and nonnegative numbers are printed with no sign. Because the normal decimal format is printed using an F format code, such a format is called an *F-format*.

The list–pattern–record relationship for the statement

PRINT '(I3,F5.2,I4,E10.2)', K,X,J,Y

is depicted in Fig. 7-2. As this statement is executed the pattern

I3,F5.2,I4,E10.2

is scanned, causing the integer in K to be printed in the first three columns, the real number in X to be printed to two decimal places in the next five columns, the integer in J to be printed in the next four columns, and the real number in Y to be printed

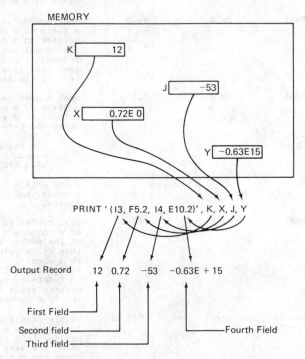

FIGURE 7-2 *An illustration of the list-pattern-record relationship.*

to two significant figures in the succeeding 10 columns. All numbers will be printed right-justified. *Note that columns must be reserved for the signs, decimal points, and the letter E as well as the required digits.*

As we have seen, if w reserves more columns than are needed, the number is right-justified. On the other hand, if w is not large enough and the number requires more columns than have been reserved, *the entire field is filled with asterisks.* For example, if I = −5, J = 67821, K = 2, and X = −26.321 and the statement

PRINT '(I3,I4,I3,F6.3)', I,J,K,X

is executed, the output would be

−5**** 2****** ···

(Note that there is no ambiguity in a variable I using an I format code.)

Although real and double-precision numbers may be stored in memory to several significant figures, the output is determined by the format code and rounding. If 6.6257 is stored in X, the statement

PRINT '(F8.2)', X

will cause X to be rounded and the output to be

6.63 ···

In all of the preceding examples the first field was sufficiently large that the first column was always blank. As discussed later (Sec. 7-1-8), the first column in a printed output record is used for vertical spacing control and a blank in this first column results in single spacing. Therefore, prior to Sec. 7-1-8 all the examples will result in blanks in the first column. In the next subsection it will be seen that a T or TR format code may be used to guarantee that a blank will occur in the first column.

Figure 7-3 shows several additional output examples which involve the I, F, and E format codes. The advantage of the F format code is that it results in a more readable output than does the E format code. Its disadvantages are that it guarantees only a specified number of decimal places, not a specified number of significant figures, and that it may result in output that exceeds the field size. From the third example in Fig. 7-3 it is seen that if the F format code is used, a small number may cause only zeros to be printed and a large number may cause only asterisks to be printed. The advantages of the E format code are that it always prints a designated number of significant figures and, provided that $w \geq d + 7$, will always reserve enough space. The price is, of course, reduced readability due to fraction-exponent pair.

In an attempt to reap the good aspects of both the F and E format codes, the G format code has been made available. It causes *d* significant figures to be printed in an F-format when the magnitude of the number being output is > 0.1 or < 10^d,

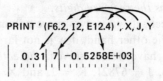

X = 0.312   Y = −525.8   Z = 0.0048   I = −32   J = 7

PRINT ' (F6.2, I2, E12.4) ', X, J, Y

```
 0.31| 7|−0.5258E+03|
```

PRINT ' (F6.0, E11.4, I3)', Y, X, I

```
−526.| 0.3120E+00|−32|
```

PRINT '(F7.2, F6.2)', Z, Y

```
 0.00|******|
```

PRINT ' (I5, F8.2, E15.5)', I, J, X

No output — error because a format code type and a variable type do not match.

FIGURE 7-3 *Output examples using the I, E, and F format codes.*

and otherwise prints the number in an E-format. When printing a number in an F-format, the G format code appends four trailing blanks to the number before it is printed right-justified in its field. Therefore, if a column of numbers is being output using a G format code, those numbers printed in an E-format will stand out. For example, the statements

```
DATA (W(I), I=1,4) /−231.0, 7560.0, 0.123, −0.01352/
DO 5 I=1,4
    PRINT '(G11.3)', W(I)
5 CONTINUE
```

would result in the output

```
       −231.
     0.756E+04
       0.123
    −0.135E−01
```

296

Number	G10.3 Output	G11.4 Output
0.05787	0.579E-01	0.5787E-01
0.5787	0.579	0.5787
57.87	57.9	57.87
0.5787E3	579.	578.7
0.5787E4	0.579E+04	5787.
0.5787E5	0.579E+05	0.5787E+05
-7852.6	-0.785E+04	-7853.

FIGURE 7-4 *Output examples using the G format code.*

Several other examples of the appearance of numbers output using the G-format are given in Fig. 7-4.

> *Warning: The exact rules regarding the G-format have not been standardized and vary from one FORTRAN translator to the next. However, G-formats do not vary significantly from the one described above.*

For output from either a single-precision or double-precision variable, any one of the F, E, G, or D format codes may be used. However, the D format code will cause a D to be printed instead of an E, thus permitting easy identification of double-precision output (provided that it is used with and only with double-precision variables). The G format code always prints the letter E regardless of the variable type. In general, the *d* value given in the format code should never exceed the precision of the variable being output, for this could mislead the user into believing that there are more significant figures than actually exist.

For complex output, any of the real format codes may be used, but it takes a pair of format codes to print a complex value, one for the real part and one for the imaginary part. (Clearly, this is an exception to the one-to-one correspondence between format codes and list items.) For example, if

$$FREQ = (2.566, -0.732)$$

then the statement

    PRINT '(F8.2,F8.2)',FREQ

will cause the output

    2.57   -0.73

The rules for formatted inputting are summarized in Fig. 7-5. In particular, note rules 4, 5, and 6. Quite often, integer data are input incorrectly because the data are not right-justified and trailing blanks, which are normally interpreted as zeros, increase the magnitude of the input quantity. Also, the rules regarding the input of single- and double-precision numbers are very liberal with respect to both the type of format code and the form of the input datum. Several input examples are given in Fig. 7-6. Note especially that, because the *d* in the format code is ignored if a decimal point is present, the numbers being input are not truncated or rounded according to the value of *d*.

1. The sign of the number must appear first in the field and if there is no sign, a plus is assumed. Blanks may appear before or after the sign.

2. Fields that consist entirely of blanks result in zero being input.

3. Blanks that appear after the first digit in a field are interpreted as zeros.

4. Fields that are not blank must contain at least one digit.

5. Integers must be right-justified in the field. No error will occur, but the trailing blanks will be interpreted as zeros and incorrect input may result.

6. A single- or double-precision number may be read into either a single- or double-precision variable using any one of the F, E, G, or D format codes.

7. A number being read using an F, E, G, or D format code may appear in any form that can be used to express a real or double-precision constant in a program statement. In addition, it may or may not include a decimal point. If there is a decimal point in the field (which is usually the case) the d part of the format code is ignored. If there is not a decimal point, then for the F-format the decimal point is assumed to be d places to the left of the right side of the field, and for the E- and D-formats it is assumed to be d places from the right after the number is converted to the F-format. In any case, a d value must appear in the format code.

8. Numbers with decimal points that are input using an F, E, G, or D format code may appear anywhere within the field.

FIGURE 7-5 *Summary of the rules for formatted input.*

READ '(I4, F8.2, F9.3)'. I, X, Y

```
 -18┊3.1     ┊    7.3142┊
 ^  ┊^  ^^^^^^^^^^
```

Variable contents after input:
I = − 18   X = 3.1   Y = 7.3142

READ '(I1, F7.4, E10.3)' L, S, T

```
3┊ 3.2E −1┊ −2.15     ┊
 ┊^       ┊^      ^^^^┊
```

Variable contents after input:
L = 3   S = 0.32   T = −2.15

READ '(F6.2, I3, E10.3)', W, N, X

```
  3212┊   ┊    -53.213┊
^ ^   ┊^^^^^^^^
```

Variable contents after input:
W = 32.12   N = 0   X − 53.213

READ '(F6.2, E10.4, F4.0)', A, B, C

```
      ┊   3568E −1┊23.5 ┊
^^^^^^^^^^
```

Variable contents after input:
A = 0.0   B = 0.03568   C = 23.5

FIGURE 7-6 *Examples of formatted input.*

For input, the *Format Specification* causes the columns in the input record to be divided into fields, and when reading into a variable *only the columns in the field corresponding to the variable are examined*. If the information in a field does not obey the rules given in Fig. 7-5, an error message is printed, but if the rules have not been violated, the input will be made *even if the data are incorrect*. Examples of inputs that are either invalid or result in incorrect values are given in Fig. 7-7.

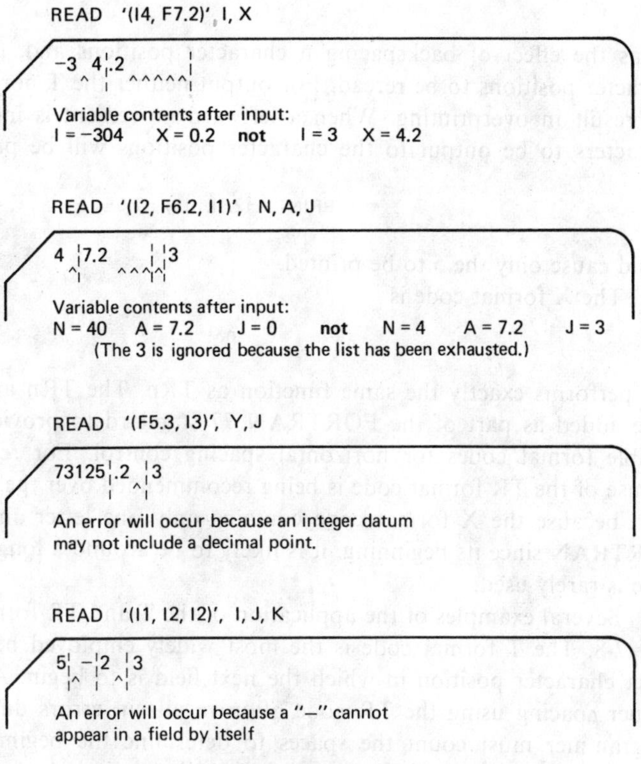

READ '(I4, F7.2)', I, X

-3 4.2

Variable contents after input:
I = −304   X = 0.2 **not** I = 3   X = 4.2

READ '(I2, F6.2, I1)', N, A, J

4 7.2 3

Variable contents after input:
N = 40   A = 7.2   J = 0 **not** N = 4   A = 7.2   J = 3
     (The 3 is ignored because the list has been exhausted.)

READ '(F5.3, I3)', Y, J

73125.2 3

An error will occur because an integer datum
may not include a decimal point.

READ '(I1, I2, I2)', I, J, K

5 −2 3

An error will occur because a "−" cannot
appear in a field by itself

FIGURE 7-7 *Examples of incorrectly formatted inputs.*

7-1-2 Horizontal Spacing Format Codes (T, TR, TL, and X)

There is a need for a convenient way of inserting blanks and backspacing while outputting, and skipping and rereading columns while inputting. The T, TR, TL, and X format codes serve this purpose. The T format code appears as follows:

$$Tn$$

where n is the column in the I-O record in which the next format code is to *begin*. The TR (move right) format code has the form

$$TRn$$

where, for input, n is the number of character positions to be skipped and, for output, n is the number of blanks to be inserted. A character position outside the record may result without an error occurring provided that a subsequent format code does not attempt to use the invalid character position.

The TL (move left) format code has the form

$$TLn$$

It has the effect of backspacing n character positions and, for input, it causes n character positions to be reread. For output neither the T nor the TL format codes will result in overprinting. When a leftward movement is indicated, only the last characters to be output to the character positions will be printed. The statement

PRINT '(I2,TL1,I1)', 7,5

would cause only the 5 to be printed.

The X format code is

$$nX$$

and performs exactly the same function as TRn. The TRn and TLn format codes were added as part of the FORTRAN 77 standard to provide a consistent set of flexible format codes for horizontal spacing control. For reasons of consistency, the use of the TR format code is being recommended over the X format code. However, because the X format code contains only one letter and has been a part of FORTRAN since its beginning, it is likely to be around a long time. The TL format code is rarely used.

Several examples of the application of the T and TR format codes are given in Fig. 7-8. The T format code is the most widely employed because it indicates the exact character position in which the next field is to begin. Attempting to provide proper spacing using the TR code often results in errors due to the fact that the programmer must count the spaces to determine the beginning position of each field. The T format code leaves no doubt about where the next field is to start.

Recall that the first column in an output record is for vertical control and, if single spacing is desired, this column should be blank. It was mentioned in the preceding section that if the w part of the first format code is large enough, the first column will be blank and single spacing will result, but if a very large number were to be unexpectedly output, unwanted vertical spacing could occur. By placing a T, TR, or X format code first in a *Format Specification*, one can guarantee a blank in the first column. For example, both of the following statements provide the needed blank (i.e., both cause the first numeric field to begin in column 2):

PRINT '(TR1,I2,F8.2)',ITEM,COST
PRINT '(T2,E12.5)',PWR

As an example, suppose that the lengths, widths, and thicknesses of M sample

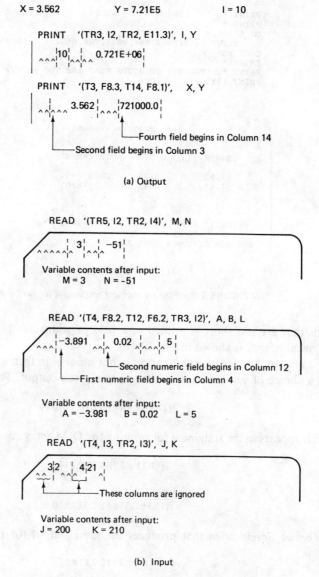

X = 3.562   Y = 7.21E5   I = 10

PRINT   '(TR3, I2, TR2, E11.3)', I, Y

∧∧∧|10|∧∧|∧∧ 0.721E+06|

PRINT   '(T3, F8.3, T14, F8.1)', X, Y

∧∧|∧∧∧ 3.562|∧∧∧|721000.0|

———Fourth field begins in Column 14
—Second field begins in Column 3

(a) Output

READ   '(TR5, I2, TR2, I4)', M, N

∧∧∧∧∧|∧ 3|∧∧|∧ -51|

Variable contents after input:
  M = 3   N = -51

READ   '(T4, F8.2, T12, F6.2, TR3, I2)', A, B, L

∧∧∧|-3.891|∧∧|∧ 0.02|∧|∧∧∧|∧ 5|

———Second numeric field begins in Column 12
——First numeric field begins in Column 4

Variable contents after input:
  A = -3.981   B = 0.02   L = 5

READ   '(T4, I3, TR2, I3)', J, K

3|2|∧∧|4|21 |∧|

———These columns are ignored

Variable contents after input:
J = 200   K = 210

(b) Input

FIGURE 7-8   *Examples involving the T and TR format codes.*

2 in. × 4 in. × 8 ft studs from a lumber-cutting process are in the first, second, and third columns of a two-dimensional array DIM, respectively, and that the number of boards that are too short is kept in ICNT. A program segment for printing these data with suitable headings is given in Fig. 7-9(a). The lengths and widths are printed to two decimal places in fields of eight columns, and the thicknesses are printed to three significant figures in fields of 10 columns. The first numeric field begins in column 3 and four blanks are inserted between the numeric fields. The number of

```
PRINT *, '   LENGTH       WIDTH       THICKNESS'
PRINT *
DO 5 I=1,M
   PRINT '(T3,F8.2,TR4,F8.2,TR4,E10.3)', (DIM(I,J), J=1,3)
5  CONTINUE
PRINT *
PRINT *, 'THE NO. OF STUDS THAT ARE TOO SHORT:'
PRINT '(T16,I5)', ICNT
   .
   .
   .
```

(a) Program segment

```
   LENGTH        WIDTH      THICKNESS

    7.92         3.35       0.157E+01
    7.43         3.41       0.146E+01
     .            .            .

     .            .            .
    8.11         3.52       0.151E+01
```

THE NO. OF STUDS THAT ARE TOO SHORT:
            57

(b) Typical output

FIGURE 7-9 *Program segment and output for lumber statistics.*

studs that are too short is printed in a field of width five beginning at column 16.
A typical output is shown in Fig. 7-9(b).

   Format Specifications are certainly not unique. In fact, a programmer generally
has a choice of several ways of producing a given output. The *Format Specification*

$$(T3,F8.2,TR4,F8.2,TR4,E10.3)$$

which appears in the statement for printing the DIM array could be replaced by either

$$(TR2,F8.2,TR4,F8.2,E14.3)$$

or

$$(T3,F8.2,T15,F8.2,T27,E10.3)$$

A *Format Specification* that produces the same output for reasonable data is

$$(F10.2,F12.2,E14.3)$$

It is subtly different, however, in that it could cause unwanted vertical spacing and
would permit longer lengths and widths to be printed before outputting asterisks.

7-1-3 *Logical Format Code (L)*

   Formatted I-O of logical values is accomplished through the use of the format
code

$$Lw$$

302

where w is the width of the field in columns. Formatted logical output consists of a T (for true) or an F (for false) being printed right-justified in the field.

Logical input must be such that the first nonblank character, except for an optional period, is a T or an F. The characters to the right of the T of F are ignored, but for ease of identification it is suggested that either TRUE and FALSE or .TRUE. and .FALSE. be used. Also, consistency is important.

7-1-4 Alphanumeric Format Code (A)

Formatted I-O of character strings is done through the use of the format code

$$Aw$$

where w is optional. If the w is present, it indicates the number of columns in the field, and if it is absent, the number of columns is the same as the length of the corresponding list item.

For output, the list item corresponding to an A format code must be a character expression. When a w is specified in an output format code and the number of characters in the list item is more than w, the output item will be truncated from the right and only the first w characters in the string will be printed. If w is larger than the number of characters in the list item, the datum is padded on the left with blanks and printed right-justified in its field. For example,

PRINT '(T2,A,A4,A3,A7)', 'ITEM NO. ',S1,'COLOR',S2

where S1 = 'SIZE' and S2 = 'WEIGHT', would result in the output

ITEM NO. SIZECOL WEIGHT

For input, the corresponding input item must be a character string variable or array element. If the number of characters in the list item is greater than w, the input datum is padded on the right with blanks before being put in the list item. On the other hand, if the number of characters in the list item is less than w, the datum is truncated from the left and only the last w characters are input. If the card

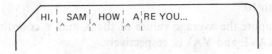

HI, SAM HOW ARE YOU...

is input by

READ '(A3,A4,A,A2)', A,B,C,D

where A is 3 characters long, B is 2 characters long, and C and D are 4 characters long, the values of the variables will become

A = 'HI '   B = 'AM'   C = ' HOW'   D = ' A'

```
CHARACTER*5, CS
DATA CS, AMT / 'H20', 52.586/
PRINT   '(T2, A, A10, F10.3)','MOLUCULE: ' CS, AMT
```

```
 MOLECULE:        H20        52.586
```

```
CHARACTER X*3, Y*4, Z*6
READ   '(T2, A, T5, A5, A5)', X, Y, Z
```

```
R ENT  FOOD  CLOT HES
```

```
X = 'ENT'      Y = 'FOOD'        Z = ' CLOT '
```

```
CHARACTER*5, CLOTH(3)
READ '(A4, TR4, A4, TR4, A4)', (CLOTH(J),   J = 1, 3)
PRINT '(T2, A4, TR2, A4, TR2, A4)', (CLOTH(J),   J= 1. 3)
```

```
COTT ON   WOOL      SAT IN
```

```
CLOTH(1) = 'COTT '    CLOTH(2) = 'WOOL '    CLOTH(3) =   ' SAT '
```

```
 COTT  WOOL   SAT
```

FIGURE 7-10 *Examples involving A format codes.*

The 'RE YOU' will be ignored because the list is exhausted. Other examples of
alphanumeric I-O are given in Fig. 7-10.

As an example of the use of formatted I-O to generate a report, consider the
problem of writing a program PLOC to tabulate particle locations. The program
is to:

1. Input from the first record a particle name into PNAME and a particle type
   into PTYPE, where PNAME and PTYPE are character strings.

2. Input from the second record an integer N from columns 5 through 7.

3. Input N X-Y coordinate pairs by placing each coordinate in a field of
   width 10.

4. Compute the average values of the X and Y coordinates and put these values
   in XAVE and YAVE, respectively.

5. Print

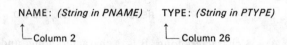

   NAME: *(String in PNAME)*   TYPE: *(String in PTYPE)*

   └─Column 2   └─Column 26

6. Print the title

                    TABLE OF PARTICLE LOCATIONS

beginning in column 35, and the headings

X DISTANCE　　　　　Y DISTANCE

beginning in columns 31 and 51, respectively.

7. Print one coordinate pair per line with each line having the form

POINT NO. *(Index I)*　　　*(Value of X(I))*　　　*(Value of Y(I))*

└─Column 5

The rightmost columns in the three numeric fields are to be 17, 40, and 60, and the values of X(I) and Y(I) are to be printed to four decimal places in fields of width 10.

8. Print

AVERAGE X = *(Value of XAVE)*
AVERAGE Y = *(Value of YAVE)*

└─Column 25

with five significant figures of XAVE and YAVE being output to fields of width 14.

The program for solving this problem is given in Fig. 7-11. The third READ statement will bring in pairs of coordinates from successive input records until the input list is exhausted. The T format code is used in several of the print statements to tab to the desired columns and the A format code is used to print the character strings.

```
PROGRAM PLOC
REAL X(100), Y(100)
CHARACTER*10, PNAME, PTYPE
READ '(A10,A10)', PNAME, PTYPE
READ '(T5,I3)', N
READ '(F10.3,F10.3)', (X(I), Y(I), I=1,N)
SX = 0.0
SY = 0.0
DO 5 I=1,N
    SX = S1 + X(I)
    SY = S2 + Y(I)
5   CONTINUE
XAVE = SX/REAL(N)
YAVE = SY/REAL(N)
PRINT '(T2,A,A12,T26,A,A12)', 'NAME:',PNAME,'TYPE:',PTYPE
PRINT *
PRINT '(T35,A)', 'TABLE OF PARTICLE LOCATIONS'
PRINT *
PRINT '(T31,A,T51,A)', 'X DISTANCE', 'Y DISTANCE'
PRINT *
DO 10 I=1,N
    PRINT '(T5,A,I4,T31,F10.4,TR10,F10.4)', 'POINT NO.',I,X(I),Y(I)
10  CONTINUE
PRINT *
PRINT '(T25,A,E14.5)', 'AVERAGE X=', XAVE
PRINT '(T25,A,E14.5)', 'AVERAGE Y=', YAVE
END
```

FIGURE 7-11 *Program for solving the particle-location problem.*

The F format code is used to obtain exactly four decimal places and the E format code appears in the last two PRINT statements so that XAVE and YAVE will be printed to five significant figures.

7-1-5 *Record Termination Format Code (/)*

In this book it has been assumed that card reader input records are 80 character positions (or columns) in length, line printer output records are 132 character positions in length, and terminal records are 80 character positions long for both input and output. Information is taken from or put into records from left to right. For list-directed input a new record is begun each time a READ * statement is encountered and successive records are brought in until the list is used up. Similarly, list-directed output initiates a new output record with each PRINT * statement and will continue to output records until there are no more items in the output list. In either case, the only control list-directed I-O has over the grouping of information into records is to force the beginning of a new record by encountering, or reencountering, a READ * or PRINT * statement.

Executing a formatted I-O statement also forces the initiation of a new record. However, with the ability to format records one would expect to be able to use the *Format Specification* to terminate a record at any desired point and continue the I-O operation with a succeeding record. This is accomplished with the slash (/) format code. The appearance of a / in a *Format Specification* causes the current I-O record to be terminated and a new record to be begun. Unlike the previous format codes, which must be separated by commas, commas before and after the slash are optional and normally are not used. Because an I-O statement always causes a new record to be started, if the first or last format code is a slash, then an input record will be skipped or a blank output record will be inserted. Also, two or more consecutive slashes will cause records to be skipped or blank records to be inserted.

One must keep in mind that while outputting to a line printer or terminal the first character in the record determines the vertical control and, for single spacing, the T, TR, or X format code should be used to force a blank after a slash. When a slash is the last format code in a specification, the next record is skipped and the additional vertical control is determined by the next I-O statement. Examples of the use of the slash format code in formatted PRINT statements are given in Fig. 7-12 together with the outputs produced by the indicated I-O statements. Input examples and their resulting input values are provided in Fig. 7-13.

A set of format codes for a single record is scanned from left to right. If the total number of character positions accounted for by the format codes corresponding to a record is less than the number of positions in the record, blanks are put in the remaining positions. If the total number of positions indicated by the format codes for a record is greater than the number of positions available in the record, an error will occur. This is true whether the set comprises an entire *Format Specification* or consists of a set of format codes delimited by slashes. For example, assuming that an

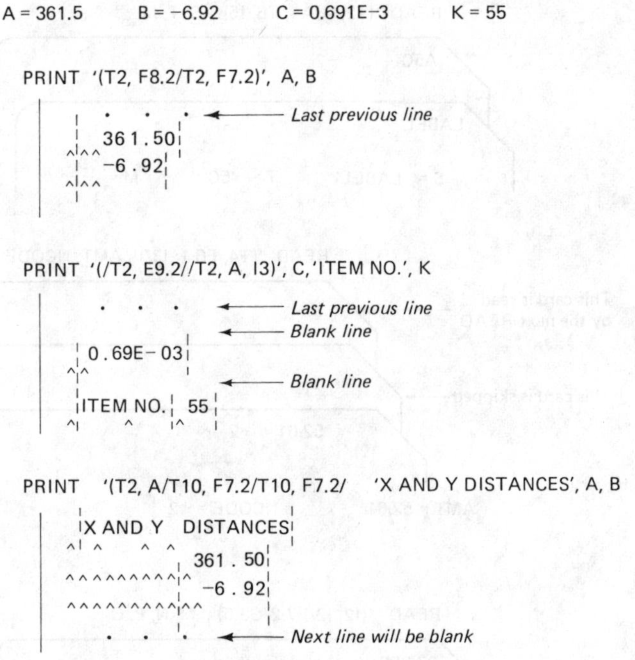

A = 361.5   B = −6.92   C = 0.691E−3   K = 55

```
PRINT  '(T2, F8.2/T2, F7.2)',  A, B
```

```
PRINT  '(/T2, E9.2//T2, A, I3)',  C, 'ITEM NO.', K
```

```
PRINT    '(T2, A/T10, F7.2/T10, F7.2/   'X AND Y DISTANCES', A, B
```

FIGURE 7-12 *Output examples involving the "/" format code.*

80-column card reader is being input from, the *Format Specification* in the statement

READ '(T11,F10.2/T5,A40,A40)',X,A,B

would allot the character positions for the first record satisfactorily, but would result in an error because the set of format codes associated with the second record would require

$$4 + 40 + 40 = 84 > 80$$

character positions. (*Exception:* Some translators may permit trailing TR or X format codes to extend beyond the number of available character positions.)

7-1-6 Repeat Factors and Grouping

In the foregoing examples, if a format code was needed more than once in succession, it was simply written the required number of times. This inconvenience can be avioded by using repeat factors. A *repeat factor* is a number that is written to the immediate left of a format code and causes the format code to be used the number of times specified; for example,

PRINT '(T3,3I5,2F8.2)', J,K,L,X,Y

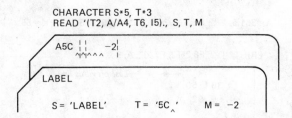

```
CHARACTER S*5, T*3
READ '(T2, A/A4, T6, I5)., S, T, M
```

S = 'LABEL'   T = '5C_'   M = −2

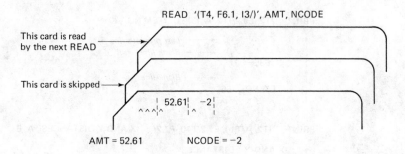

```
READ '(T4, F6.1, I3/)', AMT, NCODE
```

This card is read by the next READ

This card is skipped →

AMT = 52.61   NCODE = −2

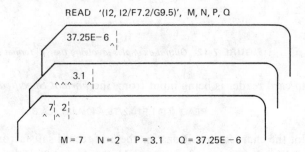

```
READ '(I2, I2/F7.2/G9.5)', M, N, P, Q
```

M = 7   N = 2   P = 3.1   Q = 37.25E − 6

FIGURE 7-13 *Input examples involving the "/" format code.*

would have the same effect as

PRINT '(T3,I5,I5,I5,F8.2,F8.2)', J,K,L,X,Y

To make repeat factors even more useful, they may be applied to groups of format codes by enclosing the groups in parentheses and preceding each group with the desired repeat factor. The *Format Specification*

(T3,2F5.0,3(I2,G10.2),I6)

would be equivalent to

(T3,F5.0,F5.0,I2,G10.2,I2,G10.2,I2,G10.2,I6)

In addition, groups may be nested so that the *Format Specification*

(2(2I2,F10.2,2(I3,I4)),D15.9)

is equivalent to

$$(I2,I2,F10.2,I3,I4,I3,I4,I2,I2,F10.2,I3,I4,I3,I4,D15.9)$$

A program segment that uses repeat factors for printing students' names, their final letter grades, and their numeric and letter grades for two tests is given in Fig. 7-14(a). A typical output resulting from this segment is given in Fig. 7-14(b).

```
      REAL  G(100,2)
      CHARACTER*12  NAME(100)
      CHARACTER  FGRADE(100), LG(100,2)
           .
           .
           .
      DO 20 I=1,N
         PRINT '(T6,A12,TR2,A1,2(F8.1,TR2,A1))', NAME(I),
     :         FGRADE(I),(G(I,J), LG(I,J), J=1,2)
   20 CONTINUE
```

                (a) Program segment

```
      MARY JONES     A   98.6 B  100.0 A
      SAM SMITH      B   81.2 B   90.6 A
                    .
                    .
                    .
      SUE LARK       D   70.5 C   55.7 F
```

             (b) Typical output

FIGURE 7-14 *Example that applies a repeat factor to a group of format codes.*

7-1-7 Rescanning and the Colon Format Code

If after taking into account the repeat factors, there are not enough format codes, then the ones that are present are reused. The simplest case is the one in which there is no grouping within the *Format Specification*; then the format codes are rescanned from the beginning. If there is a grouping, the following rule prevails:

Rescanning begins with the outermost left parenthesis that is used for grouping (this excludes the left parenthesis that opens the Format Specification) or, if there is one, with the repeat factor associated with this parenthesis.

In either case a rescan *always initiates a new record.* Two examples are given in Fig. 7-15, one that does not include a grouping and one that includes a nest of groups. Note particularly the rescan points and how they affect the outputs.

If there are more format codes than are needed by the list, the rule is:

The scan (or rescan) will continue until the first I, F, E, G, D, or A format code or a colon (:) format code is encountered. The purpose of the colon format code is to terminate a scan or rescan, and it is ignored if the list is not exhausted. The ":" is not normally separated from the other format codes by commas.

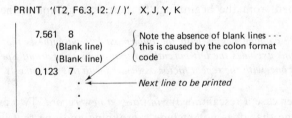

```
                    ┌── Rescan Point
                    │
                    ▼
PRINT    '(T2, 2F6.2)',  (A(I),  I = 1, 6)

        −5.12      0.63
        25.06      0.00
        −7.00     −0.07


                        ┌── Rescan Point
                        │
                        ▼
PRINT    '(T2, I2, (T4,  (TR2, I3, I4)), E10.2)' , N,
             ( (M(I, J),  I = 1, 2), X(J),  J = 1, 2)


     |51|  |  7| −15|  −0.76E − 10|
     ^ |  ^ ^|^ ^  |  ^          |

        |  | 75|  0|  0.22E + 05|
     ^ ^ ^|^ ^|  ^|  ^          |
```

FIGURE 7-15 *Examples of rescanning.*

Therefore, /, T, TR, and X format codes will be recognized for all rescans until the list is used up, then they will have an effect only until a numeric, alphanumeric, or colon format code is encountered. Examples demonstrating the use of the colon format code are given in Fig. 7-16.

```
PRINT '(T2, F6.3,I2//) ', X, J, Y, K

    7.561  8
          (Blank line)
          (Blank line)
    0.123  7
          (Blank line)
          (Blank line)
       •  ◄─────── Next line to be printed
       •
       •


PRINT '(T2, F6.3, I2: / / )',  X, J, Y, K

    7.561  8              ┌ Note the absence of blank lines - - -
          (Blank line)    { this is caused by the colon format
          (Blank line)    └ code
    0.123   7
       •  ◄─────── Next line to be printed
       •
       •
```

FIGURE 7-16 *Demonstration of the effect of the colon format code.*

7-1-8 Vertical Control

As has been mentioned several times, the first character position of an output record is not actually printed but is used for vertical control. It has been seen that a blank in the first position indicates single spacing, but what characters can be used to cause other types of vertical spacing? A list of these characters and the actions associated with them are given in Fig. 7-17. Overprinting, which results from placing a $+$ in the first character position, causes no line feed before the output record is printed and, therefore, the record is printed over the previous record. Overprinting is most often used for shading or filling in numbers when utilizing the line printer for graphics applications. A "0" in the first character position will insert a blank line before outputting the record, and a "1" will cause the printer to skip to the top of the next page before printing the record.

Character Code in First Character Position	Vertical Control Action
$+$	Overprint
(blank)	Single spacing
0 (zero)	Double spacing
1	Skip to top of next page

FIGURE 7-17 *Summary of the vertical control character codes.*

For example, if $P = $ '$+$', and CS1 and CS2 are character strings, then

$$\text{PRINT '(T2,A)',CS1}$$
$$\text{PRINT '(P,A)',CS2}$$

would print CS2 over CS1. If P were '0', a blank line would be inserted between CS1 and CS2, and if P were '1', CS1 would be printed on the next available line and CS2 would be printed at the top of the next page.

7-1-9 Designing Format Specifications

Formatting is a tedious and error-prone task. Although there are numerous rules concerning the format codes, experience is a good teacher and these rules are learned through usage. Proper formatting is a matter of discipline and a programmer should develop a set routine for writing *Format Specifications*. There are several commercially available forms for aiding the formatting process. These forms consist primarily of a large quadruled area with numbered columns, and they provide a convenient means of diagramming the *Format Specifications* so that they can be verified. Without such verification, errors will almost certainly occur, even for relatively simple formatting requirements.

Consider the problem of outputting a set of $L \leq 10$ tables from a three-dimensional array for which the third subscript indicates the table number. The overall title is to be

TABULAR OUTPUT

and is to appear beginning with the sixteenth column. The first line of each table is to consist of the string S = "TABLE" in columns 2 through 6, the table number in columns 8 and 9, and the first row of the table in fields of 10 beginning in column 11. The other lines in a table are to contain only the remaining rows, one row per line,

1	2	3	4	5	6	7	8	9	10	11	12	13	14	15	16	17	18	19	20	21	22	23	24	25	26	27	28	29	30	31	32	33	34	35	36	37	38	39	40	41	42	4
															T	A	B	U	L	A	R		O	U	T	P	U	T														
	T	A	B	L	E			1						X	.	X	X	X	X					X	.	X	X	X	X					X	.	X	X	X	X			
														X	.	X	X	X	X					X	.	X	X	X	X					X	.	X	X	X	X			
														X	.	X	X	X	X					X	.	X	X	X	X					X	.	X	X	X	X			
	T	A	B	L	E			2						X	.	X	X	X	X					X	.	X	X	X	X					X	.	X	X	X	X			
														X	.	X	X	X	X					X	.	X	X	X	X					X	.	X	X	X	X			
	T	A	B	L	E			3						X	.	X	X	X	X					X	.	X	X	X	X					X	.	X	X	X	X			
														X	.	X	X	X	X					X	.	X	X	X	X					X	.	X	X	X	X			

FIGURE 7-18 *Use of a formatting form in solving the table-output problem.*

with the entries being aligned with those of the first row. All entries are to be to four decimal places. All tables are to have three columns and the Kth table is to have $N(K) \leqq 100$ rows (for $K = 1, \dots, L$). There is to be a blank line before each table, including the first table.

A formatting form for the problem is shown in Fig. 7-18 and a program segment for producing the required format is given in Fig. 7-19. The program segment can be verified by simulating the program's actions while examining the formatting form.

```
      REAL T(100,3,10)
      CHARACTER*5  S
      DATA S /'TABLE'/
              .
              .
              .
      PRINT '(T16,A)', 'TABULAR OUTPUT'
      DO 5 K=1,L
          PRINT '(/T2,A5,I3,(T11,3F10.4))', S,K,(T(I,J,K), J=1,3), I=1,N(K))
    5 CONTINUE
                         └─ Rescan point
```

FIGURE 7-19   *Program segment for the table-output example.*

7-1-10   Other Format Codes

This subsection includes several format codes and format code modifiers that provide additional formatting capability, but are used so seldom that an individual discussion of each of them is not justified in an introductory text. These codes and code modifiers are included only for completeness. They are:

m modifier—may be appended to an I-format code as follows:

$$Iw.m$$

It forces at least m digits to be printed even if leading zeros are required. It is ignored if it is attached to an input format code.

Ee modifier—is appended to E, G, and D format codes to form

$$Ew.dEe \qquad Gw.dEe \qquad Dw.dEe$$

It causes e exponent digits to be printed instead of the normal two digits. The Ee modifier is ignored for input operations.

kP format code—specifies a scale factor k and affects only those format codes that follow it in a *Format Specification*. For output it affects the format codes F, E, D, and G as follows:

F—causes the printed value to be 10^k times the internal value.

E or D—k must be such that $-d < k \leqq d + 1$. If $k \leqq 0$, there will be $|k|$ leading zeros and $d - |k|$ significant digits after the decimal point. If $k > 0$, there will be k significant figures to the left of the decimal point and $d - k + 1$ significant figures to the right of the decimal point.

G—whether the F- or E-format is to be used is determined before the scale factor k is taken into account. If the F-format is used, k is ignored; otherwise, the E-format is printed as described above.

For input the P format code affects only input data with no decimal points or explicit exponents and, for such data, the data are multiplied by 10^{-k} before they are stored.

S, SP, and SS format codes—plus signs may appear in certain places or be implied by a blank. An SP format code forces plus signs to be printed for all I, F, E, G, and D format codes that follow it and appear prior to an SS or S format code. Similarly, an SS code forces plus signs to be represented by blanks. The S format code returns the choice to the FORTRAN translator (which normally prints blanks for plus signs). By default, the S mode is automatically assumed at the beginning of all *Format Specifications*. These format codes are ignored for input operations.

BN and BZ format codes—have no effect on output operations. On input BN and BZ codes affect only the I, F, E, G, and D format codes that follow them in a *Format Specification*. The BN code causes blanks to be ignored (deleted from the input data), and BZ causes the blanks to be interpreted as zeros.

EXERCISES

1. For each of the following I-O statements, describe how the fields are assigned and how the data are placed in these fields within the I-O record.
   (a) PRINT '(T2,I2,F10.3,E12.4)', I,X,Y
   (b) PRINT '(T2,F8.2,TR2,F8.2,TR2,G15.7)', A,B,C
   (c) PRINT '(T11,D20.12,T41,D20.12)', DIST,FRCE
   (d) PRINT '(T2,A,A10,A5)', S1,S2,'WEIGHT'
       given that S1 and S2 are 6 characters long
   (e) READ '(I5,F8.2,F9.3)', L,A,B
   (f) READ '(T21,D25.15,G10.3)', X,Y
   (g) READ '(A,A6,A4)', S,T,U
       given that S, T, and U are five characters long
2. Give formatted I-O statements that will:
   (a) Print the value of K in columns 7 through 10, the value of X to four decimal places in columns 11 through 20, and the value of Y to four significant figures in columns 40 through 55.
   (b) Print the string constant 'DISTRICT NO.' in columns 11 through 22, the value of I in columns 25 and 26, and the character string SCHNAM (whose length is 20) beginning at column 42.
   (c) Read the first 10 columns into X, the next 15 columns into the string variable SV (whose length is 20), and columns 51 through 60 into W.

3. Given that

$$X = -5.653 \qquad Y = 15.2E-6 \qquad I = 10 \qquad J = -7$$

show the output resulting from each statement.

(a) PRINT '(T8,F10.8,I3/T5,F8.0,I4)',X,I,Y,J

(b) PRINT '(/T2,G10.4,G10.5/)',X,Y

(c) PRINT '(T2,I3///T2,I3)',I,J

4. Given the card input

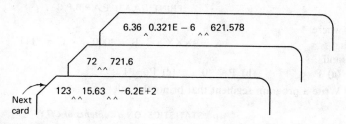

```
            6.36  0.321E - 6    621.578
                  ^         ^ ^

      72   721.6
         ^ ^

 123   15.63    -6.2E+2
    ^ ^     ^ ^
```

Next
card

determine the contents of the list variables after each of the following statements is
executed.

(a) READ '(I4,F8.1,F8.2/I3,E10.3/F5.0,F9.2,E12.4)',
:   I,X,Y,J,Z,A,B,C

(b) READ '(/I4,F7.2,F9.3/F4.2,E10.3,D11.1)', I,A,B,C,D,E

(c) READ '(F4.2,F8.3/I2/D4.3)',X,Y,K,Z

(d) READ '(T2,I3//TR4,F10.3/)',I,F

(e) READ '(2I4/I4//)',J,K

5. Given the card input

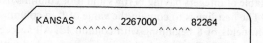

```
 KANSAS        2267000      82264
       ^^^^^^^        ^^^^^
```

determine the contents of the list variables after each of the following statements is
executed.

(a) CHARACTER*12 STATE
    READ '(A,I8,TR2,F8.0)',STATE,IPOP,AREA

(b) CHARACTER S(12)
    READ '(12A,I8,T23,F9.1)', (S(I), I = 1,12),IP,A

(c) CHARACTER*10 S,P,A
    READ '(A8,A12,A10)',S,P,A

6. Given that

$$X(1) = 5.6812 \qquad X(2) = 7.9551 \qquad X(3) = -7.21 \qquad A = 782.1$$
$$B = 0.3E-2 \qquad K=0 \qquad J(1) = 5 \qquad J(2) = -6 \qquad J(3) = 2$$
$$C = \text{'HELIUM'}$$

determine the output resulting from each of the following PRINT statements (also indicate blank lines).

(a) PRINT '(T2,3F8.2,3I4)', (X(I), I=1,3), (J(I), I=1,3)

(b) PRINT '(T2,3(F8.2,I4))', (X(I), J(I), I=1,3)

(c) PRINT '(2X,3E11.3,F8.2,I1,2X,G10.2)', (X(I), I=1,3), B,K,A

    (d) PRINT '(T2,F8.2,I2)', (X(I),J(I), I=1,3)

    (e) PRINT '(T2,A,I3/T2,A)', 'QUANTITY',K,'REORDER'

    (f) PRINT '(T2,A/T5,3I4//T2,A/T5,3G9.2)', 'J ARRAY',

       :   (J(I), I=1,3), 'X ARRAY', (X(I), I=1.3)

    (g) PRINT '(T2,E10.2://)',A,B

    (h) PRINT '(T5,A,A6)', 'ELEMENT: ', C

7. Describe the output caused by the statement

PRINT '(A,A3)',P,A,P,B,P,C

where

$$A = \text{'XXX'} \qquad B = \text{'000'} \qquad C = \text{'111'}$$

and

    (a) P = '+'   **(b)** P = '0'   **(c)** P = '1'

8. Write a program segment that prints the title

STATISTICS ON *(Contents of CITY)*

where CITY is a character string containing 12 characters, then prints the headings

YEAR   AREA   POPULATION

Column 10   Column 20   Column 40

and then prints the contents of the linear arrays IY, AR, and IP in columns below these headings. There are to be two blank lines after the title and one blank line after the headings.

9. Write a program segment that will print an integer label from the variable L, and then print a table of integers having N rows and four columns from the two-dimensional array NTAB. The first line is to contain the value of L in columns 6 and 7, and the first row of NTAB in fields of 8 beginning with column 12. All succeeding lines are to contain the other rows of NTAB such that the columns are aligned with the array entries printed on the first line.

10. Write a program REPORT that will input a title to a string variable TLE, integers into M and N, M heading titles into the first M elements of a linear string array HTLE, and N rows of a two-dimensional logical array into LA, M entries per row and one row per card. The program is to then print the title, skip three lines, print the headings, skip one line, and print the logical values in LA, one M-entry row per line, properly aligned under the headings.

7-2 FORMATTED READ AND PRINT STATEMENTS

Format Specifications may be associated with READ and PRINT statements in three fundamental ways. READ and PRINT statements may be viewed as having the forms

READ *Format Identifier, Input List*

and

PRINT *Format Identifier, Output List*

where the *Format Identifier* may be one of the following:

  *—Indicates list-directed I-O

  Character String—A string constant or variable that contains any valid *Format Specification*. (It could even be a character string expression, provided that the expression does not include a concatenation of variable-length operands.) Section 7-1 was concerned with the string-constant case.

  Label—Matches the *Label* of an associated FORMAT statement which includes the *Format Specification* to be used.

All FORTRAN 77 translators have incorporated into them a procedure for constructing *Format Specifications* from default format codes, and if the *Format Identifier* is an *, the default procedure is used. Application of the default procedure is called *list-directed I-O*. Because the default format codes depend on the translator, a standard set could not be given in Chap. 2 and a typical set was assumed.

7-2-1   Character String Formatting

In the preceding section the *Format Identifiers* were string constants and that is the reason the *Format Specifications* were enclosed in single quotes. Clearly, greater flexibility can be achieved by using character string variables. By using a string variable the *Format Specification* may be preassigned with a DATA statement, determined by an assignment statement at execution time, or input at execution time using a previously encountered READ statement. All three possibilities serve to separate the formatting function from the I-O statement. This permits the *Format Specifications* to be grouped together and allows a single *Format Specification* to be used by several I-O statements.

  An application of the ability to use a *Format Specification* by more than one I-O statement is found in reproducing input data at the output. The statements

```
FS = '(T2,I4,F10.2)'
READ FS, NUM, WGT
PRINT FS, NUM, WGT
```

would cause NUM and WGT to be read and printed in the same format, the output would be an image of the input. As mentioned in Chap. 4, printing the image of an input record is called *echo printing* and is used extensively during the debugging phase of a program's development. Usually, all input data are echo printed immediately during this stage to assure that they are being read correctly. Keep in mind that, because not all incorrect data are necessarily invalid from a syntax standpoint, an error in spacing can cause incorrect data to be input without causing an error message.

  Being able to separate *Format Specifications* from the I-O statements permits *Format Specifications* to be pooled. A group of assignment or DATA statements at the beginning of the program could assign character variable names to the *Format*

Specifications and then only the variables would need to appear in the I-O statements. If

$$FS1 = '(T2,F10.2,3I3)'$$
$$FS2 = '(I7,E12.5,E15.7)'$$
$$FS3 = '(T2,F8.0/3(I2,F6.1)'$$

were the first executable statements in the program and no other *Format Specifications* are needed by the program, the *Format Identifiers* could all be FS1, FS2, or FS3. Although this approach improves the appearance of the program by removing the *Format Specifications* from the processing part of the program, it creates the inconvenience of not having the *Format Specification* beside its associated I-O list. This trade-off is considered further in the discussion of FORMAT statements given below.

A feature that is provided by using a character string variable to store a *Format Specification* is that of inputting to the variable at execution time. This gives the user the ability to dictate some of the I-O formats as the program is running. Although this capability is not often utilized, it makes it possible for the programmer to give some of the I-O format control to the user. The reason *Format Specifications* are not input very often is that this might give the user more control than he or she wants or should have. *Format Specifications* are complex and are extremely prone to errors. If format control needs to be given the user, a much more reasonable approach would be to include in the program a set of choices and allow the user to select one of these choices by inputting a code. A program segment that demonstrates this technique is given in the next subsection.

7-2-2 Format Statements

The third means of designating a format is to use a FORMAT statement. This is done by letting the *Format Identifier* be the *Label* of a FORMAT statement and including the *Format Specification* in the FORMAT statement. A FORMAT statement has the form

Label FORMAT *Format Specification*

where the *Label must be present*. Figure 7-20 gives several I-O statements and their equivalent statement pairs that include FORMAT statements. (Note the absence of the enclosing single quotes in the FORMAT statements.)

```
PRINT '(T2,I3,F8.2)', I,X          PRINT 10, I,X
                                10 FORMAT (T2,I3,F8.2)

PRINT '(T2,A/T2,F9.3)','TEST',Y     PRINT 5, 'TEST',Y
                                 5 FORMAT (T2,A/T2,F9.3)

READ '(16I5)', (L(I), I=1,N)        READ 7, (L(I), I=1,N)
                                 7 FORMAT (16I5)

READ '(A20,TR10,I5)', ST,M          READ 1, ST,M
                                 1 FORMAT (A20,TR10,I5)
```

FIGURE 7-20 *I-O statements and their equivalent statement pairs using FORMAT statements.*

Even though FORTRAN 77 offers new alternatives in format designations, the FORMAT statement, which was among the first FORTRAN statements, is likely to continue as the most prominent method for conveying *Format Specifications*. It provides for the separation of the specification and the list, and thus avoids exceedingly long I-O statements. It also permits the pooling concept discussed above. Unlike the use of assignment statements to associate string variables with *Format Specifications*, FORMAT statements include the keyword FORMAT that makes them easy to identify. In addition, an assignment statement must appear in a program unit before the string variable is used in an I-O statement. A FORMAT statement may be placed anywhere between the opening and END· statements of a program unit, although *it must be in the same program unit as the I-O statements that reference it.*

Whether FORMAT statements are pooled or are placed with the I-O statements that use them is a decision a programmer or programming group should make in advance, and once the decision is made, consistency should be the rule. The advantage of placing the FORMAT statements next to the corresponding I-O statements is that the *Format Specifications* and *Lists* can be easily compared and verified. It should be remembered, however, that several I-O statements may refer to a single FORMAT statement and, therefore, mandatory juxtaposition may require unnecessary duplication of FORMAT statements. The advantage in pooling FORMAT statements is that it improves readability by preventing them from detracting from the flow of the program. If they are pooled, the authors recommend that they be placed last so that they are separated from the data-type declaration, allocation, and preassignment statements.

A program segment that allows the user to select from one of three possible output formats is given in Fig. 7-21. This segment utilizes a FORMAT statement pool and a CASE structure with a different PRINT statement in each CASE. Note that people using the program do not need to know anything about FORTRAN formatting; they would only need to know the printed formats produced by the various code values (presumably, this information would be available in a user's manual).

```
          INTEGER CODE
                 .
                 .
                 .
          READ 100, CODE
          IF (CODE .EQ. 0) THEN
                  PRINT 101, 'SALES DATA', I,X
              ELSE IF (CODE .EQ. 1)
                  PRINT 102, 'SALES DATA', I,X
              ELSE
                  PRINT 103, 'SALES DATA', I,X
          ENDIF
               .
               .
               .
      100   FORMAT (I5)
      101   FORMAT (T2,A,I2,F8.2)
      102   FORMAT (T2,A/T2,I2,F8.2)
      103   FORMAT (T2,A/T2,I2/T2,F8.2)
          END
```

FIGURE 7-21 *Example that permits the user to select the output format.*

7-2-3 String Constants in Format Specifications

String constants may be placed in the *Format Specifications* of a PRINT statement, as well as in the *Output List*. This is done by simply placing the string constant, enclosed in single quotes, in a format code position. Then, as the *Format Specification* is scanned from left to right, the string constant is printed in its turn. For example, if I = 4 and X = 77.98, the statements

```
                    PRINT 15, I,X
                15 FORMAT (T2,'ITEM NO.',I4,TR6,'COST',F8.2)
```

would print

```
                ITEM NO.  4    COST 77.98
```

One important application of placing string constants in *Format Specifications* is in providing vertical control. The statements

```
                        PRINT 25, CS1
                    25 FORMAT ('1',A)
```

would cause the contents of the string variable CS1 to be printed at the top of the next page, and the statements

```
                        PRINT 31, CS1,CS2
                    31 FORMAT (T2,A/'+',A)
```

would result in CS2 being printed over CS1.

Although string constants may be placed in any *Format Specification*, such placement is usually done in FORMAT statements and not when the *Format Specification* is itself a character string. One of the main reasons for this is that FORMAT statements are used to shorten I-O statements, and placing the string constants in the FORMAT statement helps by removing them from the I-O statement. Another reason string constants are not normally found in *Format Specifications* that are themselves string constants is that a string constant must be enclosed in single quotes and consecutive single quotes are needed to represent single quotes in a string constant. For example,

```
            PRINT (T5,A,I4), 'IT''S TOO HIGH',N
```

could be written

```
            PRINT '(T5,"IT""''S TOO HIGH'',I4)', N
```

but the latter is harder to read and is more subject to errors. In most situations the form

```
                    PRINT 8, N
                8 FORMAT (T5,'IT''S TOO HIGH',I4), N
```

would be preferred over both of the other choices.

In general, the FORMAT statement approach to designating formats is predominant, with the other choices being used only in special cases in which the *Format*

Specification is short or the I-O statement is to be included only during the debugging phase. If an I-O statement is to be part of a program only temporarily, it would be better to have the *Format Specification* included in the I-O statement so that only one statement would need to be removed. Also, because FORMAT statements may be associated with more than one I-O statement, the deletion of a FORMAT statement could cause an unexpected error.

Included in the ANSI 1966 standard FORTRAN, but not in FORTRAN 77, is an alternative means of inserting a string constant in a *Format Specification*. It is the H format code, which has the form

nH *String Constant*

where n is the number of characters in the *String Constant*. Since the H format code is not permitted in FORTRAN 77, it is mentioned here only because it appears in old programs.

EXERCISES

1. Give three equivalent ways of providing the I-O described below, one way using a string constant, one using a string variable, and one using a FORMAT statement.
   (a) Input the string in columns 6 through 16 into ST1, the integer in columns 19 and 20 into L, and the real number in columns 23 through 35 into V.
   (b) Input the integers in the first four fields of width 5 into M(1) through M(4), and the real number in columns 21 through 30 into X.
   (c) Print the integer in J in columns 5 through 8 on one line and the real number in W in columns 11 through 25 on the next line.
   (d) Skip to the top of the next page and print the headings DISEASE and SYMPTOMS beginning in columns 5 and 80, respectively.

2. Give I-O and FORMAT statement pairs that will:
   (a) Print the first 10 elements of array A in columns 11 through 25 to four significant figures. The elements are to be printed on every other line.
   (b) Skip to the top of the next page and print

THE TEMPERATURE IS: *(Value of T)*

   The string constant is to begin in column 10 and the value of T is to be printed to four decimal places in columns 31 through 40.
   (c) Read the two-dimensional array ARR from fields of 10. Assume that ARR has eight columns and 10 rows.

3. Given

$$X = 1.5216 \qquad Y = 7.921 \qquad Z = 3.52E15 \qquad I = 2 \qquad J = 7$$

and the statement

PRINT 90, X,Y,Z,I,J

show the output resulting from each of the following FORMAT statements (note any errors that may be present):

(a) 90 FORMAT (T2,3F12.4,T30,2I3)
(b) 90 FORMAT ('1',3(F8.6,I3))
(c) 90 FORMAT (T10,3F8.6///(T20,I5))
(d) 90 FORMAT ('1',3E15.5/'0',2I5)
(e) 90 FORMAT (' ',3F8.0/'0',I2/' ',I2)

4. Given the input cards

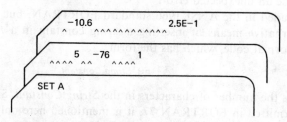

determine the contents of the list variables after each of the following pairs is executed
(ST is a string variable of length 6).

(a)   READ 55, ST,(N(I), I=1,4), (X(I), I=1,3)
       55 FORMAT (A/4I5/3F8.2)
(b)   READ 16, LIM,AMT
       16 FORMAT (/T5,I3/T7,2F10.0))
(c)   READ 23, ST,(N(I), I=1,3), X,Y,Z
       23 FORMAT (A5,3I5,3F8.2)

5. Given that $M = 3$ and $N = 4$ and that the array K has 10 rows and 10 columns with
each element being the sum of its subscripts, show the output resulting from each of the
following program segments.

(a)   PRINT 8, ((K(I,J), I=1,M), J=1,N)
       8 FORMAT (T5, 'THE MATRIX K IS:' /(T2,10I5))
(b)   PRINT 12, ((K(I,J), J=1,N), I=1,M)
      12 FORMAT (10I5)
(c)   DO 5 I=1,M
           PRINT 3, (K(I,J), J=1,N)
     3   FORMAT (T2,10I5)
     5 CONTINUE
(d)   DO 5 I=1,M
           DO 3 J=1,N
               PRINT 2, K(I,J)
     2   FORMAT (10I5)
     3   CONTINUE
     5 CONTINUE
(e)   PRINT 10,K
     10 FORMAT (10I5)

6. Write a program segment that will skip to the top of the next page and write one X on the
first line, two Xs on the second line, and so on, until 50 Xs are written on the last line.
All lines are to begin in column 11.

7. Write a program segment that will read a title consisting of 50 characters or less into
TLE and print it out centered on a 132-column page.

8. Write a program segment that will input 80-column lines of text, search them for the substring DOG, and replace DOG with CAT. Each line is to be brought in, corrected, and output before the next line is read, and the process is to cease when a blank line is encountered.

9. Write a program segment that will read an 80-column record into a string variable NAME whose length is 20, an integer ID, and a real number AMT. The first 20 columns are to be read into NAME, columns 31 through 35 are to be read into ID, and columns 41 through 55 are to be read into AMT. Then the segment is to read in and echo-print records with the same format as described above until a line is found whose first 20 columns match the contents of NAME. This record is not to be echo-printed; instead, the contents of NAME, ID, and AMT are to be output. This output is to use the same format as described above, except that asterisks are to be printed in columns 71 through 80. The segment is to then continue echo-printing until a blank record is found, at which time the process is to cease. If no input record is such that its first 20 columns match the contents of NAME, then when the blank record is encountered the program is to print

(Contents of NAME) NOT FOUND.

10. Write a program that will input geological information (that has been taken from several areas) and produce a report summarizing the information. The input is to be 80-column records that are formatted as follows:

20 cols.	14 cols.	12cols.	12 cols.	12 Cols.	10 cols.
Type of rock	Weight	X-coordinate	Y-coordinate	Elevation	Area no.

For each area, the report is to contain a table of the following form:

	STATISTICS ON AREA NO. *(Area No.)*			
TYPE OF ROCK	TOTAL WEIGHT	MEAN X	MEAN Y	MEAN ELEVATION
(Type of Rock)	*(Weight)*	*(Mean X)*	*(Mean Y)*	*(Mean Elev.)*
.	.	.	.	
.	.	.	.	
.	.	.	.	

Input is to stop when a blank card is found. Assume that the input is ordered numerically by area number and alphabetically by rock type and that the output is to be similarly ordered.

11. Rewrite your solution to Exercise 10 assuming that the input is not ordered but that the output is to be ordered.

7-3 LINE PRINTER GRAPHICS

Although tables can be used to display numerical information to practically any required amount of detail, they are not always the best way of presenting such information. Often, graphs, histograms, and pictures can adequately summarize the data in such a way that the essential information can be absorbed more quickly. Although such illustrations do not give the information to a specified number of significant figures or decimal places, precise knowledge of the data may not be required and an illustrative form may be more suitable.

There are numerous pieces of equipment (plotters, graphics terminals, etc.) specifically designed for displaying information in pictorial forms and most of them are accompanied by software packages that provide users with an easy means of using the equipment. Because there are so many different types of equipment and software packages available, it would be fruitless to present an example in detail. However, a line printer or printing terminal can be used to provide limited graphics capability and it is worthwhile to examine this possibility. Many of the concepts associated with line printer graphics are also encountered when designing or using software packages for other graphics equipment.

Computer graphics is a very complex subject and space prevents more than a limited introduction to it here. Histograms and pictures are considered in the Exercises and Programming Problems, and the discussion below is primarily concerned with X-Y plots. Shaded pictures are obtained by dividing the given area into small subareas called pixels, selecting a darkness for each pixel, and then outputting the pixels. If a line printer is being used, the amount of ink determines the shading and different characters can be used to represent the various degrees of darkness. A blank would obviously produce the lightest shade, a period would be slightly darker,

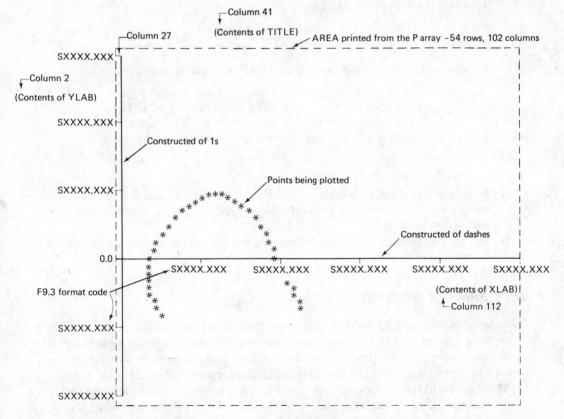

FIGURE 7-22　*Format of the plots produced by the plotting program in Fig. 7-23.*

and so on. Overprinting characters on other characters may be used to produce the very dark shades.

The precision with which a point in a graph may be placed is called the *resolution of the graph*. Most plotters are designed so that points can be assigned to the nearest $\frac{1}{100}$ of an inch or less, but most line printers output 10 characters per inch horizontally and six characters per inch vertically. Because a FORTRAN program can only print characters from a given character set, a FORTRAN program for outputting X-Y plots on a line printer or terminal is limited to a horizontal resolution of $\frac{1}{10}$ in. and a vertical resolution of $\frac{1}{6}$ in. Although this restriction is severe, it does permit the output of graphs that satisfy many requirements.

To demonstrate some of the salient points of line printer plotting, let us study a subprogram that produces an X-Y plot of the form shown in Fig. 7-22. The subprogram itself is given in Fig. 7-23. Although writing a plotting program may at

```
****************************************************************
*                        SUBPROGRAM PLOT                       *
* SUBPROGRAM PLOT RECEIVES THE TITLE, AXIS LABELS, MAXIMUM AND  *
* MINIMUM X AND Y COORDINATE VALUES, AND POINTS TO BE PLOTTED   *
* FROM THE MAIN PROGRAM, AND CONSTRUCTS A PLOT OF UP TO 500     *
* POINTS BY FILLING IN AND PRINTING FROM A 54 ROW BY 102 COLUMN *
* ARRAY P.  THE Y-AXIS IS ALWAYS PLACED TO THE FAR LEFT.  THE   *
* Y-AXIS IS ADJUSTED SO THAT, IF 0 IS IN THE Y-RANGE, 0 WILL    *
* BE AT ONE OF THE TICK MARKS.  THE PLOT IS FORMED BY           *
* OVERLAYING THE ARRAY USING THE ORDER:  (1)  Y-AXIS,           *
* (2)  X-AXIS, (3)  POINTS TO BE PLOTTED, (4)  Y-AXIS TICK      *
* MARKS, (5)  X-AXIS TICK MARKS, (6)  BLANKS FOR THE X-AXIS     *
* COORDINATES, AND (7)  X-AXIS LABEL.  OVERPRINTING IS USED TO  *
* INSERT THE Y-AXIS LABEL, Y-AXIS COORDINATES, AND X-AXIS       *
* COORDINATES.                                                  *
*          TITLE    -  TITLE OF PLOT                            *
*          XLAB     -  X-AXIS LABEL                             *
*          L        -  LENGTH OF X-AXIS LABEL                   *
*          YLAB     -  Y-AXIS LABEL                             *
*          XMIN     -  MINIMUM X-COORDINATE                     *
*          XMAX     -  MAXIMUM X-COORDINATE                     *
*          YMIN     -  ORIGINAL MINIMUM Y-COORDINATE            *
*          YMAX     -  ORIGINAL MAXIMUM Y-COORDINATE            *
*          N        -  NUMBER OF POINTS TO BE PLOTTED           *
*          X(500)   -  ARRAY OF X-COORDINATES                   *
*          Y(500)   -  ARRAY OF Y-COORDINATES                   *
*          XT(6)    -  ARRAY OF X-AXIS COORDINATES              *
*          YT(6)    -  ARRAY OF Y-AXIS COORDINATES              *
*          YCODE    -  CODE INDICATING POSITION OF X-AXIS       *
*                   DEL - AUXILIARY VARIABLE                    *
****************************************************************

      SUBROUTINE PLOT(TITLE,XLAB,L,YLAB,XMIN,XMAX,YMIN,YMAX,X,Y,N)

* STORAGE ASSIGNMENT

      INTEGER YCODE, N, L
      REAL X(500),Y(500),XT(6),YT(6),XMIN,XMAX,YMIN,YMAX,DEL
      CHARACTER TITLE*40, XLAB*15, YLAB*15
      CHARACTER P(-3:50,-1:100)

* I.  COMPUTES X-AXIS COORDINATES

      DEL = (XMAX - XMIN)/5.0
      DO 5 I=1,6
          XT(I) = XMIN + REAL(I-1)*DEL
    5 CONTINUE
```

FIGURE 7-23 *Subprogram for plotting coordinate pairs.*

```
* II. ADJUSTS Y-AXIS AND COMPUTES Y-AXIS COORDINATES

                DEL = (YMAX - YMIN)/5.0
                YT(1) = YMIN
                YT(6) = YMAX
                IF (YMIN .LT. 0.0 .AND. YMAX .GT. 0.0) THEN
                        IF (DEL .GT. -YMIN) THEN
                                YT(1) = -YMAX/4.0
                                YCODE = 1
                        ELSE IF (2.0*DEL .GT. -YMIN) THEN
                                YT(1) = -2.0*YMAX/3.0
                                YCODE = 2
                        ELSE IF (3.0*DEL .GT. -YMIN) THEN
                                YT(1) = -3.0*YMAX/2.0
                                YCODE = 3
                        ELSE IF (4.0*DEL .GT. -YMIN) THEN
                                YT(6) = -2.0*YMIN/3.0
                                YCODE = 3
                        ELSE
                                YT(6) = -YMIN/4.0
                                YCODE = 4
                        ENDIF
                ELSE IF (YMIN .GT. 0) THEN
                        YCODE = 0
                ELSE
                        YCODE = 5
                ENDIF
                DEL = (YT(6) - YT(1))/5.0
                DO 10 I=2,5
                        YT(I) = YT(1) + REAL(I-1)*DEL
        10      CONTINUE

* III. CONSTRUCTS P ARRAY

*       A.   FILLS P ARRAY WITH BLANKS

                DO 20 I=-3,50
                        DO 15 J=-1,100
                                P(I,J) = ' '
        15              CONTINUE
        20      CONTINUE

*       B.   OVERLAYS Y-AXIS

                DO 25 I=0,50
                        P(I,0) = '1'
        25      CONTINUE

*       C.   OVERLAYS X-AXIS

                DO 30 J=0,100
                        P(10*YCODE,J) = '-'
        30      CONTINUE
```

FIGURE 7-23 *(Continued)*

first seem straightforward, it can actually be quite complex. There are numerous questions that must be resolved before writing such a program, some of which are:

1. How are the physical dimensions of the plotting area specified?
2. What are the maxima and minima X and Y values to be included in the graph?
3. How are the axes to be placed?
4. How closely are the tick marks (i.e., marks indicating important abscissas and ordinates) to be spaced?

```
*       D.    DISCRETIZATION AND OVERLAYING OF POINTS TO BE PLOTTED

              XF = 100.0/(XT(6) - XT(1))
              YF = 50.0/(YT(6) - YT(1))
              DO 35 I=1,N
                 P(NINT(XF*(X(I)-XT(1)), NINT(YF*(Y(I)-YT(1)))) = '*'
       35  CONTINUE

*       E.    OVERLAYS Y-AXIS TICK MARKS

              DO 40 I=0,50,10
                 P(I,-1) = '-'
       40  CONTINUE

*       F.    OVERLAYS X-AXIS TICK MARKS

              DO 45 J=0,100,20
                 P(10*YCODE-1,J) = '1'
       45  CONTINUE

*       G.    OVERLAYS BLANKS FOR X-AXIS COORDINATES

              DO 55 J=20,100,20
                 DO 50 K=-5,3
                    P(10*YCODE-2,J+K) = ' '
       50     CONTINUE
       55  CONTINUE

*       H.    OVERLAYS X-AXIS LABEL

              DO 60 K=1,L
                 P(10*YCODE-3,K+111) = XLAB(K:K)
       60  CONTINUE

* IV.  OUTPUTS PLOT

              PRINT 100, TITLE
              DO 70 I=50,-3,-1
                 PRINT 101, (P(I,J), J=-1,100)
                 IF (I .EQ. 45) PRINT 102, YLAB
                 IF (MOD(I,10) .EQ. 0) PRINT 103, YT(1+I/10)
                 IF (I .EQ. 10*YCODE-2) THEN
                    IF (YCODE .EQ. 0) THEN
                          PRINT 104, (XT(I), I=1,6)
                    ELSE
                          PRINT 105, (XT(I), I=2,6)
                    ENDIF
                 ELSE
                 ENDIF
       70  CONTINUE

* FORMAT SPECIFICATIONS

      100  FORMAT ('1',T41,A40/)
      101  FORMAT (T26,102A)
      102  FORMAT ('+',T2,A)
      103  FORMAT ('+',T17,F9.3)
      104  FORMAT ('+',T22,F9.3,5(TR11,F9.3))
      105  FORMAT ('+',T31,5(TR11,F9.3))
           END
```

FIGURE 7-23 (*Continued*)

5. Which tick marks are to have coordinate labels?

6. How many significant figures or decimal places are to be included in the coordinate labels?

7. Is there to be a title and, if so, where is it to be placed?

8. Are there to be axis labels and where are they to be placed?

9. When there is a conflict among the items to be printed, how are these conflicts to be resolved (e.g., is a plot point to take precedence over a tick mark)?

10. Which of the answers to the foregoing questions are to be built into the program and which are to be answered by the user at execution time?

For the plotting subprogram being considered, the

Physical dimensions of the plotting area
Placement of the axes
Spacing and coordinate labeling of the tick marks
Format of the tick mark coordinate labels
Placement of the title
Placement of the axis labels
Conflict precedence

are built into the subprogram, but the

Maxima and minima X and Y coordinates
Contents of the title
Contents of the axis labels

are passed to the subprogram by the calling program together with the data to be plotted. Whether the user is given control over any of the last three items is determined by the calling program.

The function of the subprogram is to adjust the axes according to the maximum and minimum X and Y values, put in the axes, plot the points, put in the tick marks, put in the title and axis labels, and insert the tick mark coordinate labels. The minimum X, maximum X, minimum Y, and maximum Y coordinates are input to the subprogram through the variables XMIN, XMAX, YMIN, and YMAX, respectively. The number of points to be plotted is in N and the points are in the X and Y arrays. The title of the plot and the X- and Y-axis labels are in the string variables TITLE, XLAB, and YLAB. The number of characters in the X-axis label is in L. The reason the number of characters in the X-axis label is in L is that this label may appear in the plotting area and should not block out more space than is necessary; thus only the first L characters of XLAB are printed.

The plotting area consists of 54 rows and 102 columns, with the Y-axis always appearing at the far left, regardless of the range of the X-coordinate. The X-axis, however, is placed according to the Y-axis zero. Each axis includes six evenly spaced tick marks which, for the X-axis, are determined directly from XMIN and XMAX. For the Y-axis the tick marks are determined directly from YMIN and YMAX if the Y-range does not include 0, but if this range does include 0, then either YMIN or YMAX is adjusted so that 0 will fall on one of the tick marks. The X-axis is then placed at this tick mark.

The plot is constructed by placing symbols in a character string array P whose elements are single characters. The array P has 54 rows and 102 columns and is first filled with blanks. It is then partially filled with the Y-axis (1's), X-axis (−'s), the points to be plotted (∗'s), Y-axis tick marks (−'s), X-axis tick marks (1's), and the X-axis label. Blanks are reinserted where the X-axis tick mark coordinates are to be placed.

The subprogram utilizes both overlaying and overprinting. The P array is first blanked and then the Y-axis, X-axis, the plot, Y-axis tick marks, X-axis tick marks, blanks for the X-axis coordinates, and the X-axis label are overlaid in that order. The order of overlaying determines the order of precedence because the last character put in an element of P is the one that is printed. If there is a conflict between, say, a point to be plotted and an axis symbol, the point takes precedence because it is overlaid after the axes have been inserted. While the plot is being printed, overprinting is used to insert the Y-axis label and tick mark coordinates.

An important point is that the elements of the P array must be initially blanked by an assignment statement, not a DATA statement. The subroutine may be used several times within a program and the P array must be blanked every time the subroutine is entered. A DATA statement would only preassign blanks to P at the time the subroutine is translated.

EXERCISES

1. Write a program that will use the subroutine in Fig. 7-23 to plot the sine of X from 0 to X_{max} degrees, where X_{max} is read in at execution time. The title is to be THE SINE OF X and the X- and Y-axis labels are to be Y = SIN(X) and X IN DEGREES.

2. Modify the subroutine in Fig. 7-23 so that the number of X-axis tick marks is variable and is passed from the calling program.

3. Write a program that will print an 8-in.-diameter circle in the middle of a 66-line, 132-column page. Assume 10 characters per inch horizontally and six characters per inch vertically.

4. Write a program that will print your initials in a form such as

```
MMM                MMM      GGGGGGGG
 MMM              MMM       GG
 MM  M          M  MM       GG
 MM    M      M    MM       GG   GGGG
 MM      M  M      MM       GG     GG
 MM       M M      MM       GG     GG
MMM        MMM     MMM      GGGGGGGG
```

5. Write a subroutine LINE that will accept the coordinates of two points and print asterisks that lie (as closely as possible) on a straight line between the points. Other parameters to be passed to the subroutine are the X and Y values corresponding to the edges of the plotting area. The plotting area is to consist of 55 rows and 125 columns. If one of the points is out

of bounds, the subroutine is to print INVALID POINT, set a flag, and return to the calling program. Also write a program TRIANG that reads in three coordinate pairs and the X and Y boundary values, and uses the subroutine LINE to draw the best straight line approximation of the three points—see Programming Problem (9) in Chap. 2. If the "invalid point" flag is set by the subroutine, the program is to simply stop.

6. Write a program that prints a rectangle that becomes continually darker from left to right and from top to bottom, with the darkest position being at the lower right. The rectangle is to have eight rows and eight columns; therefore, 15 intensity levels are needed. Use overprinting to obtain a sufficient differential between intensity levels. For example, a blank could be the lowest intensity, and an O, X, and 8 could be superimposed to provide the highest intensity.

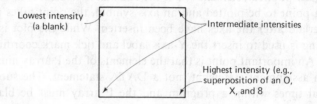

Lowest intensity (a blank)

Intermediate intensities

Highest intensity (e.g., superposition of an O, X, and 8

7-4 GENERAL READ AND WRITE STATEMENTS

In the preceding material the READ and PRINT statements contained no reference to the device with which the I-O was being conducted. It was assumed that for batch processing the input device was a card reader and the output device was a line printer, and for an interactive system the user's terminal provided both the input and output. This is certainly not always the case, the most obvious example being line printer output from an interactive system. Also, I-O with mass storage devices, paper tape equipment, and special-purpose I-O equipment must be accommodated. To add the flexibility needed to communicate with a variety of I-O and mass storage devices, the I-O statements that were used heretofore have been generalized to include a list of control specifiers.

The general forms of the I-O statements are

READ (Control List) Input List

and

WRITE (Control List) Output List

where the *Input* and *Output Lists* are defined as before. The *Control List* is made up of from one to five specifiers separated by commas. A list of the specifiers and their formats are given in Fig. 7-24. In the specifiers,

Unit is either a nonnegative integer that identifies a device or an internal file identifier. The set of possible *Unit* device numbers depends on the computer system. An internal file identifier is a string variable, array, or array element name, or substring. Internal files are discussed in Sec. 7-5.

Format Specification is as defined previously.

Specifier	Possible Forms			
Unit[1]	UNIT = *Unit*		UNIT = *	*Unit* *
Format[2]	FMT = *Format Spec.*		FMT = *	*Format* *
Record[3]	REC = *Record Number*			
I–O Status[3]	IOSTAT = *I–O Status Variable*			
Error[3]	ERR = *Label*			
End[4]	END = *Label*			

[1] Must be present and must be first if an abbreviated
form is used.

[2] Must be present if I–O is formatted, and must be
second if an abbreviated form is used.
Cannot be abbreviated unless the unit
specifier is abbreviated. Is not present
for unformatted I–O, which is discussed
in Chap. 8.

[3] Optional specifier

[4] Optional, but cannot be present if there is a
record specifier.

FIGURE 7-24 *Summary of the I-O specifiers.*

Record Number is a positive integer that identifies a record (see Chap. 8).

I-O Status Variable is an integer variable that, upon completion of an I-O operation, will contain an I-O status condition (see Chap. 8).

Label is a statement label.

The *Control List* must include a unit specifier and, for formatted I-O, a format specifier, but these specifiers may be written without their keywords UNIT and FMT and the associated equal signs. Either the *Unit* or the entire unit specifier may be represented by an asterisk, in which case the appropriate system default device will be used. (The system default devices are the ones used by the READ * and PRINT * statements.) Either the *Format Specification* or the entire format specifier may be represented by an asterisk, in which case the I-O is to be list-directed. If the *full* unit specifier format is not used, the unit specifier must appear first in the *Control List;* if the *full* format specifier is not used, the format specifier must appear second. Also, the "FMT = " notation may be deleted only if the "UNIT = " notation is deleted.

The other specifiers are optional, but cannot be abbreviated. Of these, only the end specifier is considered further at this point; the others are discussed in Chap. 8. An end specifier cannot be present if there is a record specifier.

Some examples of READ and WRITE statements are given in Fig. 7-25. If it is assumed that the default input device is *Unit* 5 and the default output device is *Unit* 6, the statements in the left column are equivalent to the corresponding statements in the right column.

Records that are stored on mass storage devices such as disks and tapes are grouped into files and at the end of some of these files, special indicators, called *end-*

```
READ (UNIT=5,FMT=9,ERR=70,END=90) A      READ (5,9,ERR=70,END=90) A

WRITE (UNIT=6,FMT=100) X                 WRITE (6,100) X

READ (UNIT=5,FMT=100) K,(B(I),I=1,N)     READ (*,100) K,(B(I),I=1,N)

WRITE (6,FMT=*) S,T,U                     WRITE (*,*) S,T,U

WRITE (*,*) (X(I,J), J=1,50)              PRINT *, (X(I,J), J=1,50)

READ (*,50) A,B,C                         READ 50, A,B,C

WRITE (6,FMT='(T2,I5)') 2*(I+K)           PRINT '(T2,I5)', 2*(I+K)

WRITE (6,FMT=*) 'MESSAGE'                 PRINT *, 'MESSAGE'
```

FIGURE 7-25 *Examples of general READ and WRITE statements. If* Unit 5 *is the standard input device and* Unit 6 *is the standard output device, the corresponding statements in the two columns are equivalent.*

of-file (EOF) markers, are inserted to denote the ends of the files. Also, when inputting from devices such as card readers, paper tape readers, and so on, special EOF indicators are placed at the end of data sets to separate the data sets. When performing interactive processing a special character may represent an EOF, and for batch processing the end-of-job card may be interpreted as an EOF. The purpose of the end specifier is to detect an EOF and take special action when one is found. In particular, the end specifier causes a branch in the program to the statement whose label is the *Label* included in the specifier.

The reason for considering the end specifier at this point is that it offers an alternative way of terminating the input of a set of data. Previously, the input was stopped either by first informing the computer how many records were to be read, or by examining each input record and terminating the input when a sentinel was found. These two approaches are illustrated in Fig. 7-26(a) and (b). The other possible procedure, which is to stop the input when an EOF is detected, is shown in Fig. 7-26(c). The third choice has the advantages that:

1. The number of records does not need to be known and input separately.

2. A special value does not need to be reserved as the sentinel.

3. An IF statement that checks the input is not needed because the end specifier automatically checks for the EOF.

However, if the end specifier technique is used and the number of input records must be known later in the program, they must be counted as they are read. This feature is included in Fig. 7-26(d).

To exhibit the application of the end specifier to inputting from the default input device, assume batch processing and that the end-of-job card is interpreted as an EOF. Now consider two simple programs, one that brings in one number per record, adds the numbers, and prints the sum, and the other, which is the same except that it also computes the average of the numbers. The two programs are given in Fig. 7-27(a) and (b), respectively, and represent the two cases illustrated in Fig. 7-26(c) and (d). Although this technique is frequently used, one should beware of a

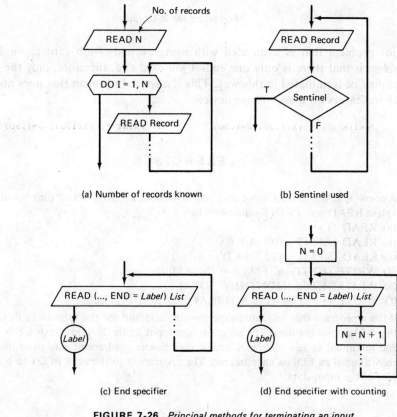

(a) Number of records known   (b) Sentinel used

(c) End specifier   (d) End specifier with counting

FIGURE 7-26 *Principal methods for terminating an input.*

```
      PROGRAM SUM
      SUM = 0.0
    5 READ (*,100,END=10) X
          SUM = SUM+X
          GO TO 5
   10 CONTINUE
      WRITE (*,101) SUM
  100 FORMAT (F10.3)
  101 FORMAT (T10, 'SUM=', F10.3)
      END
```

                    (a) Without counting

```
      PROGRAM AVE
      SUM = 0.0
      N = 0
    5 READ (*,100,END=10) X
          N = N+1
          SUM = SUM+X
          GO TO 5
   10 CONTINUE
      AVE = SUM/REAL(N)
      WRITE (*,101) SUM, AVE
  100 FORMAT (F10.3)
  101 FORMAT (T10, 'SUM=', F10.3, TR5, 'AVERAGE=', F10.3)
      END
```

                    (b) With counting

FIGURE 7-27 *Programs for demonstrating the use of the end specifier.*

333

major problem that is associated with using an end-of-job card as an EOF. The problem is that there is only one end-of-job card and, therefore, only the last set of data may be terminated in this way. This is a special problem that does not apply to EOF indicators on mass storage devices.

EXERCISES

1. Assume that the default input and output devices are *Unit* 5 and *Unit* 6 and give equivalent READ and PRINT statements for:
   (a) READ (*,*) X
   (b) READ (*,FMT=100) A,B,C
   (c) READ (5,FMT='(T5,10F8.2)') (X(I), I=1,N)
   (d) WRITE (UNIT=6, FMT=*) (X+15.0)/Y
   (e) WRITE (6,210) 'MONTHLY TOTAL:',T
   (f) WRITE (*,FMT='(T40,A /T38,A)') 'TABLE I',TITLE

2. Write a program that will input experimental data and use the subroutine PLOT given in Fig. 7-23 to plot the data. The program is to input a title, X- and Y-axis labels, maximum and minimum values for the X and Y coordinates, and coordinate pairs (one pair per record) until an EOF is encountered. The program is to then call PLOT to print an X-Y plot of the input data.

7-5 THE I–O PROCESS AND INTERNAL FILES

At this point, it is helpful to consider the processes that take place while I-O is being conducted. Such a discussion will not only aid in the understanding of the previous material, but is necessary to the introduction of the internal file concept.

All I-O is performed using special areas in memory, called *buffers*. On input the information is first transferred from the I-O device to a buffer and is then passed to the *Input List* variables; on output this process is reversed. There are two basic types of I-O, unformatted I-O, shown in Fig. 7-28(a), and formatted I-O, shown in Fig. 7-28(b). For *unformatted I-O* there is no conversion of the 0-1 combinations being input or output; an image of the information is transferred to or from the I-O device. Mass storage devices such as magnetic tape and disk units can handle such direct transfers because they simply magnetically implant the 0-1 combinations on the storage medium. (Unformatted I-O is considered further in Chap. 8.) On the other hand, devices such as card readers, line printers, and terminals are only capable of encoding and/or decoding information that is in an alphanumeric code and require that the external appearance of the information be readable. This means that an extra step, called *formatting*, is needed to provide spacing and to convert the numerical data into character strings before they are input from or output to these devices. Formatting is done according to the *Format Specification* and is performed while passing the information between the program and the I-O buffer.

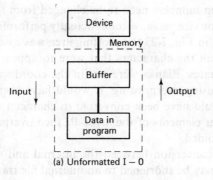

(a) Unformatted I – 0

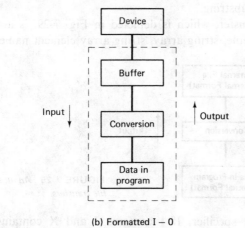

(b) Formatted I – 0

FIGURE 7-28 *The two basic types of I-O.*

For example, if N contains −52 and X contains 73.51, when the statements

PRINT 60,N,X
60 FORMAT (T2,I4,F6.1)

are executed, blanks are inserted in the first and second character positions in the buffer; the binary equivalent of −52 is converted to the character string '−52', which is placed in the third, fourth, and fifth positions; blanks are inserted in the sixth and seventh positions; and the 0–1 combination for 73.51 is converted (after rounding) to the character string '73.5', which is placed in the eighth through eleventh positions. The contents of the buffer are then transmitted to the line printer or user's terminal and

−52   73.5

is printed.

The formats used to store numbers in memory, the integer and real formats, are called the *internal formats* of the numbers. The character string equivalents of these numbers are called their *external formats*.

There are times when numbers need to be changed from their internal formats to their external formats, or vice versa, without actually performing an I-O operation. In the subprogram PLOT in Fig. 7-23 the plotting area was associated with an array P, and P was filled with all the characters that were to appear in the plotting area except the X-axis coordinates. Blanks were put in the coordinate positions and the coordinates were output using overprinting. It would have been more convenient if the X-axis coordinates could have been converted to character strings and the characters placed in the proper elements of the array P; then overprinting the X-coordinates could have been avoided.

To accomplish the conversion between the internal and external formats, the formatted I-O processes may be shortened to an internal file transfer. An *internal file* is an I-O buffer area that has been associated with a string variable, string array, string array element, or substring.

An internal file transfer, which is depicted in Fig. 7-29, is accomplished by substituting a string variable, string array, string array element name, or substring,

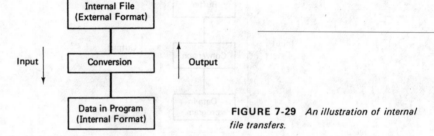

FIGURE 7-29 *An illustration of internal file transfers.*

for the *Unit* in the unit specifier. If I contains 7 and X contains -52.89, the statements

```
CHARACTER*20 STEQ
              .
              .
              .
WRITE (UNIT=STEQ, FMT=100) I,X
100 FORMAT (I5,E12.4)
```

would cause the string

$$'_{\wedge\wedge\wedge\wedge}7_{\wedge}-0.5298E+02_{\wedge\wedge\wedge}'$$

to be placed in STEQ. The character positions in STEQ are filled from left to right just as columns in a printed line are filled. On the other hand, if CSTG contains

$$'NO._{\wedge\wedge\wedge}15_{\wedge}-731'$$

then the statements

```
READ (UNIT=CSTG(4:13), FMT=110) M,N
110 FORMAT (2I5)
```

would cause the internal formats of 15 and -731 to be put in M and N.

If the internal file identifier is a string variable name, string array element name, or substring, the internal file transfer is made as if a single I-O record were being transferred, but if the identifier is a string array name, each element in the array is treated as a separate record. This is demonstrated by the statements

```
          CHARACTER*10 B(2)
                  .
                  .
          WRITE (UNIT=B, FMT=105) L1,L2
    105 FORMAT (I5)
```

which cause the external formats for L1 and L2 to be put in the rightmost five columns of B(1) and B(2), respectively. If the WRITE and FORMAT statements were replaced with

```
          WRITE (UNIT=B(1), FMT=105) L1,L2
    105 FORMAT (I5,I5)
```

the external formats of L1 and L2 would be placed side by side in B(1).

Other important rules regarding the use of internal files are:

List-directed formatting cannot be specified for an internal file transfer.

The string variable name, string array name, or other name that is used as the internal file identifier can also appear in other FORTRAN statements wherever strings or substrings are appropriate.

I-O operations are conducted between internal files and formatted external devices using alphanumeric formatting (A-format).

The last of these rules permits an I-O operation to be divided into two distinct steps: the conversion step and the I-O step. To demonstrate the last two rules, consider the following program segment:

```
          CHARACTER*80 BUFF
                  .
                  .
          READ (*,100) BUFF
    100 FORMAT (A80)
          READ (UNIT=BUFF, FMT=101) W
    101 FORMAT (T51,E12.4)
          X = W**2
          WRITE (UNIT=BUFF, FMT=102) X
    102 FORMAT (T66,E12.4)
          BUFF(1:10) = 'X AND X**2'
          WRITE (*,103) BUFF
    103 FORMAT (A80)
```

This segment inputs an 80-character line from the default input device to an internal file BUFF, converts the real number in character positions 51 through 62 to internal form, squares the number, converts the square to external form and puts it in positions 66 through 77 of BUFF, changes the first 10 characters of BUFF to ' X AND X**2', and outputs BUFF to the default output device.

EXERCISES

1. Give detailed descriptions of the actions taken by each of the following sets of statements.
   (a)   READ (*,90) (X(I), I=1,4)
          90 FORMAT (4F12.4)
   (b)   WRITE (*,10) I
          10 FORMAT (I5)
   (c)   READ (UNIT=BUFF, FMT=50) X,Y
          50 FORMAT (F12.5,TR2,F12.5)
   (d)   WRITE (UNIT=STR, FMT=80) 'ATOMIC NO.',I
          80 FORMAT (A10,I5)
   (e)   CHARACTER*5 A(10)
          N = 7
          .
          .
          .
          WRITE (UNIT=A, FMT=85) (L(J), J=1,N)
          85 FORMAT (T2,I4)

2. Write a program segment that will input an 80-character record from the default input device to the internal file TEMP, replace the characters in positions 11 through 23 of TEMP with the string 'BATCH NUMBER ', replace the integer in positions 26 through 30 of TEMP with that integer plus 2, and print the first 30 characters of TEMP followed (on the same line) by five blanks and the string 'BATCH NO. CORRECTION'.

3. Write a program segment that will convert the first 10 numbers in the array F to character strings using the F9.2 format code and put the resulting strings in the corresponding elements of the string array NUM.

4. Modify the subprogram PLOT in Fig. 7-23 so that, instead of overprinting, an internal file is used to print the X-axis coordinates.

PROGRAMMING PROBLEMS

1. Write a program that inputs a string to CHS (length 10) and prints the characters in CHS in block form in columns 2 through 80. The characters must be digits or blanks and each character must occupy seven columns and nine lines as follows:

```
2222222
      2
      2
      2        The digit "2"
2222222        in 9 × 7 block form
      2
      2
      2
2222222
```

Side-by-side characters are to be separated by a single blank column. The program is to first call a logical function subprogram CHECK to make sure that CHS consists of only digits and blanks. If CHECK returns the truth value .TRUE., the program is to proceed; otherwise, it is to print

INVALID STRING

and stop. A subroutine LINE that receives CHS and a line index (1 through 9) as arguments is to be used to form each line of print. A preassigned array is to be used to store the patterns needed to form the various characters. Test the program with 23 592.

2. Write a subroutine HIST that will print a histogram. It is to accept a set of years through an integer array Y and a set of corresponding real quantities through an array Q. The number of years is to be in a parameter N and the name of the quantities is to be in a parameter LABEL. There are to be six evenly spaced vertical scale quantities in a parameter array VS. The histogram bars are to be vertical and contained in 50 rows. Each bar is to consist of five columns of X's and the bars are to be separated by five blanks. The contents of LABEL and a scaled vertical axis made up of 1s are to appear on the left. The bars are to be underscored with a solid line of dashes and the year corresponding to each bar is to be printed below the bar. The word YEAR is to be printed on the line following the years printed below the bars. If there are too many bars to fit in the available columns, the program is to print

TOO MANY BARS

and stop.

Also write a program that inputs a number of years to M, a set of years to Y and a corresponding set of percentages to P; and uses HIST to print a histogram having the label 'PERCENT OF GNP' and the vertical scale quantities 0.0, 20.0, . . . , 100.0. Test the program with N = 4 and

Years	1980	1981	1982	1983
Percentage	12.9	15.1	18.2	22.2

3. The fraction S of a group of organisms that survive a dosage D of radiation is often described by the sigmoid survival function, which has the form

$$S = 1 - (1 - e^{-KD})^N$$

where N and K are experimentally determined constants. Write a program that uses the subroutine PLOT in Fig. 7-23 to plot S as a function of D. The program is to input K, N, M (the number of dosages to be plotted), D (a linear array containing the dosages), TITLE (the title of the graph), DTLE (the title for the horizontal axis), and STLE (the title for the vertical axis). It is to then determine the value of DMAX (maximum value of D), let SMAX (maximum value for S) be 1.0, let DMIN and SMIN (the minimum values of D and S) be 0.0, determine the number of characters in DTLE, and compute the entries in S. Finally, the program is to call PLOT and produce the desired graph. Test the program using the data

$$K = 0.4 \times 10^4 \qquad N = 1.15 \qquad M = 101$$
$$D(I) = I \times 10^{-5} \qquad I = 0, \ldots, 100$$

TITLE = 'VIRUS TYPE B – GAMMA RADIATION'

DTLE = 'DOSE – RADS'

STLE = 'FRACTION'

4. Suppose that a computer is being used as a message concentrator in a communications network. The messages are sent to the computer from terminals and are temporarily put in a queue in the computer's memory until they can be transmitted over a communications link to a central computer for processing.

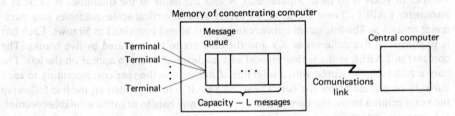

It is assumed that the messages arrive at random and that they have random lengths. For certain commonly used arrival and length statistics it is known that the average time a message spends in the queue is given by the equation:

$$T = \frac{1}{M_A}\left[\frac{\rho}{1 - \rho} - \frac{(L + 1)\rho^{L+1}}{1 - \rho^{L+1}}\right]$$

where $\rho = M_A M_L / R$, L is the queue capacity in messages, M_A the average arrival rate in messages per second, M_L the average length of a message in characters, and R the rate at which messages can be sent over the communications link in characters per second. The probability that the queue will overflow upon arrival of the next message is given by

$$P_0 = \frac{1 - \rho}{1 - \rho^{L+1}}\rho^L$$

(For a discussion of probability, see Programming Problem 2 at the end of Chap. 6.) The problem is to compute, for a fixed value of L and for various values of M_A and M_L, the probabilities of the queue overflowing and the average time spent in the queue as functions of *R*. These functions will then aid in the design of the concentrating computer and its communication equipment.

Write a program that will read a title of up to 40 characters into TITLE, three values into each of the linear arrays MA and ML, a value for the queue length into L, lower and upper limits on the communication rate into R1 and R2, and the number of evenly spaced rates to be examined into NR. The input records are to be according to the following table:

Input record no.	Record description
1	Title beginning in column 1.
2	Average arrival times MA to two decimal places in fields of width 10, with the first field beginning in column 11.
3	Average message lengths ML to three significant figures in fields of width 12 beginning in column 6.
4	Queue length L in a field of width 5 beginning with column 1.
5	Rate limits R1 and R2 to two decimal places in fields of width 10 beginning in column 1, and the number of rates NR in a field of width 6 beginning at column 26.

The program is to use function subprograms to compute T and P0 as functions of R at

$$R = R1 + I*DELR \qquad I = 0, \ldots, NR-1$$

where

$$DELR = (R2-R1)/(NR-1)$$

for all combinations of nonzero values in the MA and ML arrays. Finally, the program is to print a report of the following form:

←Top of page

    ┌──Column 15
    ↓
    (Contents of TITLE)–QUEUE CAPACITY *(Value of L)*

┌──Column 10
↓
AVERAGE ARRIVAL TIME = *(MA(1) to 2 places in field of 10)*
AVERAGE MESSAGE LENGTH = *(ML(1) to 3 significant figures in field of 12)*

  ┌──Column 15   ┌────Column 40   ┌────Column 62
  ↓   ↓   ↓

COMMUNICATION RATE	AVERAGE WAITING TIME	PROB. OF OVERFLOW
(Column of rates	*(Column of times to*	*(Column of probabilities*
to 2 decimal places	*4 significant figures*	*to 3 significant figures*
in fields of width	*in fields of width 14,*	*in fields of width 12,*
10, ending in column 30)	*ending in column 57)*	*ending in column 74)*

Skip to top of next page
      Repeat for each combination MA(I) and ML(J)

Test the program by letting

TITLE = 'CONCENTRATOR DESIGN STUDY'

$$MA(1) = 0.50 \qquad MA(2) = 0.75 \qquad MA(3) = 1.00$$

$$ML(1) = 0.400E2 \qquad ML(2) = 0.600E2 \qquad ML(3) = 0.800E2$$

$$L = 10$$

$$R1 = 100.00 \qquad R(2) = 200.00 \qquad NR = 6$$

8

FILE PROCESSING

Although the instructions being executed and data being operated on must be in memory, for most applications the memory is not large enough to contain all the data at one time. Also, the contents of memory are not retained when the computer is shut down (except in special cases), and memory cannot be used to transport information from one computer system to another. For these reasons, there must be a means of storing information outside the computer's memory and then inputting the information as it is needed. Until now, only card reader and terminal input and printer and terminal output have been considered. Terminal input requires that the data be typed each time the program is run and could only be used if the amount of input is small. Card input does utilize a medium that can be reread, but cards are bulky, require considerable storage space, are expensive (because they are not re-usable), and can be read only at relatively low speeds. Neither a printer nor a terminal provides output on a medium that can be input directly by the computer at a later time.

What is needed is a means of storing data that satisfies the following requirements:

1. Has a large capacity.
2. Is inexpensive and reusable.
3. Can be quickly input from or output to (i.e., has a low access time).
4. Is portable from one computer system to another (even between systems manufactured by different companies).

The generic name for equipment that fulfills these needs is *mass storage*, and the primary mass storage devices are magnetic tape and disk units. Although disks are not always portable and magnetic tapes are not fast enough for some applications, these types of mass storage do meet the foregoing requirements to varying degrees, depending on the specific equipment.

The purpose of this chapter is to examine how information is stored on magnetic tapes and disks and how it is brought into or output from the computer's memory where it is used. Because mass storage holds so much information, a variety of schemes are used to structure the information so that it can be readily accessed. Most of these schemes are similar to those used to file information in a library or office, but are complicated by the hardware and speed requirements of computer systems. The data arrangements are normally hierarchical and designed so that selected portions of the data can easily be found, changed, added, or deleted. FORTRAN is designed to access information that is divided into files, which are subdivided into records, which are, in turn, subdivided into fields. Each file is identified by a name and each record is found by its position within its file. The fields within a record are dependent on the structure of the record.

Accessing data on a mass storage device is a complicated operation that involves two types of identifiers. The *logical identifier* is the one used to reference the file from within the program. In FORTRAN the logical identifier is the *Unit* given in the unit specifier and is a nonnegative integer. The *physical identifier* specifies precisely where in the computer system the file is located. At some time before or during the execution of the program the logical identifiers must be associated with the physical identifiers. When a logical file identifier is associated with a physical file identifier it is said that *the logical file is connected to the physical file.* The logical/ physical connections are used during the execution of a program as indicated in Fig. 8-1. The operating system records the connections in a table and when a program refers to a file by its logical identifier, the operating system looks up the physical identifier in the table and the access is made. If a connection is made by system (or JCL) commands prior to the execution of the program, it is called a *preconnection.* The reason for having logical identifications is to divorce the programmer from being concerned with the actual location of the data. Physical positioning of the data is quite complex and is left to the operating system.

In FORTRAN 77 the OPEN statement, which is discussed in Sec. 8-3, is for making connections from within a program. The OPEN statement also performs other functions and, therefore, may be used even if a file has been preconnected. Although the FORTRAN 77 standard sets forth the rules for OPEN statements, there are no rules regulating preconnections. Preconnection is entirely system-dependent and is governed by the requirements for giving commands to the operating system being used. Some systems require preconnection whereas in others preconnection is optional. Because of the variety of available operating systems and their commands, it would not be practical to give a detailed discussion of preconnection here, but it is important to note the distinction between connection from within the program and preconnection.

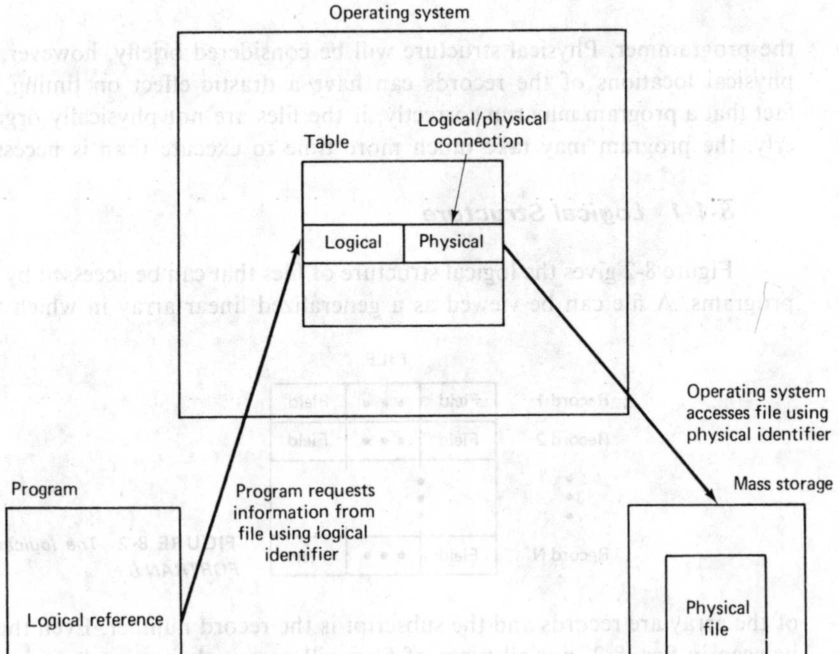

Operating system

Table

Logical/physical
connection

Logical | Physical

FILE

	Field	• • •	Field
Record 1	Field	• • •	Field
Record 2			
Record N		• • •	Field

Program

Program requests
information from
file using logical
identifier

Logical reference

Operating system
accesses file using
physical identifier

Mass storage

Physical
file

FIGURE 8-1 *Relationship between a logical identifier and a physical identifier.*

Section 8-1 discusses the elementary file concepts, including file structures and the fundamental attributes of files. The next section introduces the fundamental types of files and considers the advantages and disadvantages associated with them. The third section defines the OPEN and CLOSE statements for connecting and disconnecting files from a program. Section 8-4 discusses file I-O and some of the problems related to accessing files, and Sec. 8-5 introduces the INQUIRE statement for checking the attributes of a file. The last section outlines some of the organizational aspects of file systems.

8-1 ELEMENTARY FILE CONCEPTS

In addition to having both logical and physical file identifiers, the file itself may have both a logical structure and a physical structure. The *logical structure* is the format visualized by the programmer as he or she writes the statements needed to access the file. The *physical structure* is the way in which the records in the file are located on the physical medium (i.e., the tape or disk). We will be concerned primarily with the logical structure because the operating system handles the transformations required to communicate with the physical file and these transformations are incidental to the programmer. Physical structure will be considered briefly, however, because the physical locations of the records can have a drastic effect on timing. Despite the fact that a program may run correctly, if the files are not physically organized properly, the program may take much more time to execute than is necessary.

8-1-1 Logical Structure

Figure 8-2 gives the logical structure of files that can be accessed by FORTRAN programs. A file can be viewed as a generalized linear array in which the elements

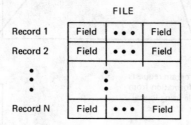

FIGURE 8-2 *The logical structure of a FORTRAN file.*

of the array are records and the subscript is the record number. Even though, as will be seen in Sec. 8-2, not all types of files will permit their records to be accessed by record numbers, it is still helpful to view the file as a sequence of numbered records. Each record is, in turn, broken into fields, with each field containing a datum. The assignment of the data items to the fields is very flexible and is determined by the WRITE statement that is used to output the record. The overall length of a record is also determined by the outputting WRITE statement and may in some cases vary from record to record within a file.

Files are accessed by reading or writing records as a whole using the READ and WRITE statements considered in Sec. 7-4. Even when a READ statement *Input List* refers to only some of the fields, the physical transfer will bring all the information into the I-O buffer area and then pass on only the listed items to the variable locations. The fields in a record are ordered and during a read the contents of the first field are input to the location of the first list item, the second field to the location of the second item, and so on. The input from a general record is analogous to the input from a card. Similarly, output operations transfer information to the fields in order. Exactly what happens during a write depends on the type of file. The actions taken while executing READ and WRITE statements are discussed in detail later.

Which record is currently being accessed is determined by an entity called a *pointer*. The pointer is essentially an integer variable that contains the number of the record. At the time a read or write is made, the pointer can be viewed as pointing to the record being accessed. The programmer is given a means of adjusting the value of the pointer (i.e., determining the point in the file to be accessed), but these means are dependent on the type of file and will not be discussed until Sec. 8-2.

8-1-2 Physical Structure

A magnetic tape is a strip of plastic that has been coated with a magnetic substance. Tapes are typically 1/2 in. wide by 2400 ft long and are wound on a reel that is 10 in. in diameter (see photograph in Fig. 1-4(a)). The physical structure of a file on a magnetic tape is similar to the logical structure shown in Fig. 8-2 except that fields as well as the records are placed longitudinally along the tape. The physical arrangement of the fields is unimportant, however, because records are accessed only in their entirety. A magnetic tape often contains only one file, but may contain several files. Figure 8-3 shows a typical file and record disposition along a magnetic tape. As indicated in the figure, there are blank spaces, called *record gaps*, between

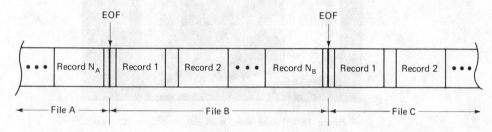

FIGURE 8-3 *Format of a magnetic tape.*

the records. Between the files are EOF indicators. Just what these indicators are physically depends on the system and is unimportant to the programmer. (In addition to the data records, most files begin, and perhaps end, with special records called *file labels* or *data set labels*. These records are not shown because they are used only by the system and the programmer can always assume they are not present. They do occupy space, but the amount of space is insignificant.)

A magnetic tape unit operates by passing the tape over a read/write head that magnetically transfers the information to or from the coating on the tape. Most tapes travel from 45 to 250 inches per second (ips) and are capable of holding from 800 to 6250 bits per inch (bpi). There are enough bits positioned laterally across the tape to form a byte, so that the information density is 800 to 6250 bytes/in. Assuming a tape speed of 75 ips, it would take

$$12 \times 2400/75 = 384 \text{ s} = 6 \text{ min } 24 \text{ s}$$

to traverse the entire length of a 2400-ft tape. If the storage density were 1600 bpi and there were no record gaps, a tape would hold

$$1600 \times 12 \times 2400 = 46,080,000 \text{ bytes}$$

Because the number of record gaps depends on the lengths of the records, the actual amount of information on a tape varies considerably and the figure given above serves only as an upper limit.

347

Pertec T8000 tape drive with mounted tape (Courtesy, *Pertec Computer Corporation*).

Even more important to a programmer is the amount of time it takes to find a record or set of records and the rate at which the information in the records can be transferred into the computer once it is found. Once again assume a tape speed of 75 ips and a density of 1600 bpi. If the tape must traverse one-tenth of its length while searching for a needed record, the required time would be

$$(12 \times 2400/75) \times (1/10) = 38.4 \text{ s}$$

The transfer rate after the data has been found would be

$$75 \times 1600 = 120,000 \text{ bytes/s}$$

In addition to the read/write speed, tape units have a higher rewind speed, typically between 150 and 600 ips. If in the example above the tape had to be rewound from its midpoint before the record search began and the rewind speed was 200 ips, the total time required would be

$$12 \times 1200/200 + 38.4 = 110.4 \text{ s}$$

The purpose of this discussion has been to give the reader a feeling for the amount of time it takes to perform tape operations. An operation that requires a lot of rewind and search time but transfers only a few records is relatively slow. An operation that starts at the beginning of a tape and reads or writes all the records in sequence is relatively fast. This has a direct bearing on the types of applications for which tapes are used. A typical application is one that involves a single large file, such as the medical histories of hundreds of people, that must be updated periodically. The data tape would be mounted on one tape unit and a blank tape would be mounted

348

on a second unit. As the original file is transferred from the old data tape to the new data tape, the updating information could be input from cards or a disk file and the necessary changes could be made. The whole operation would require one pass with no intervening rewinding.

Another important point regarding magnetic tapes is that information cannot be positioned at an exact point. The mechanical movement of the tape cannot be precisely controlled. Therefore, tape records are not changed in place, but changes are made as a tape is copied onto another tape. This reinforces the reasons for limiting tape usage to those applications for which the records are accessed in order.

The construction of a typical disk pack is shown in Fig. 8-4. A disk pack con-

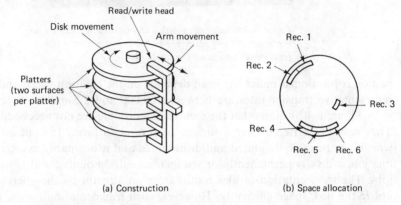

(a) Construction   (b) Space allocation

FIGURE 8-4 *Construction of a disk and allocation of disk space to a file.*

sists of one or more metal disks, called *platters*, mounted on a cylindrical core. Each platter is covered on both sides with a magnetic coating. A movable-head disk drive, which is by far the most popular, is constructed so that there is a read/write head for each surface of each platter, and the heads are mounted on fingers that are interleaved with the disks. The fingers are attached to an arm assembly that moves in and out. The information is placed in concentric circles, called *cylinders*, on the platters and, by rotating the disk pack and laterally moving the arm containing the heads, any area on the disk can be accessed. The number of platters, number of cylinders, and amount of information that can be stored in a cylinder vary drastically, but typical multiplatter disks hold from 20 to 500 million bytes. (See photo, p. 350.)

The access time of a disk depends on both the rotation speed and the speed with which the arm can move in and out. Rotation speeds are usually between 2250 and 3600 revolutions per minute (rev/min) and the average arm movement time (the time it takes to traverse half of the disk) is normally from 0.01 to 0.1 s. Assuming a rotation speed of 3600 rev/min (or 60 rev/s) and an average arm movement time of 0.05 s, the average access time would be

$$0.05 + (1/60) \times (1/2) = 0.0583 \text{ s}$$

The multiplier $1/2$ accounts for the fact that on the average only one-half of a revolution will occur before the needed data are found. The transfer rate after the infor-

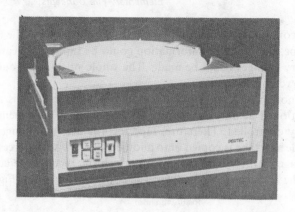

Pertec D 3400 disk drive with a 25 million byte capacity on 4 platters, 3 fixed platters, and 1 removable platter (Courtesy, *Pertec Computer Corporation*).

mation is positioned under the head depends on the rotation speed and density, and representative transfer rates are between 100,000 and 2.5 million bytes per second.

Figure 8-4(b) shows that the records in a disk file are not necessarily contiguous. They may be scattered over a surface or several surfaces. In contrast with a tape, which may be easily mounted and dismounted and is ordinarily associated with only one job, a disk is permanently or semipermanently mounted and is used by several jobs. The fragmentation of files results from an attempt by the operating system to utilize the disk space efficiently. However, such fragmentation results in more head movement when several records are being accessed and, consequently, the total access time is increased. Thus there is a trade-off between time efficiency and space efficiency, a trade-off that often occurs in computer work. Although a FORTRAN program cannot control the location of disk records, most systems include operating system commands that can be used in conjunction with preconnection to force records to be contiguously grouped. For applications involving a lot of disk accesses, a programmer may want to examine this possibility.

It is seen that because a disk access includes two movements and may involve several surfaces, records do not need to be passed sequentially over a read/write head in order to find a particular record. This increases the speed substantially and broadens the field of applications. Unfortunately, disks are much more expensive than tapes and, even if they are removable, they are more cumbersome to store or ship. Because tapes are inexpensive, different files are often put on different tapes even if they occupy only a small fraction of a tape's capacity. Among other things, this separability provides security and convenience. Tapes are used primarily in applications for which the records are operated on in sequence and for storing or transporting large quantities of data. Disks are used when records are not accessed in order and for storing information that is continually being updated. Frequently, a program will transfer a file from a tape to a disk, interact with the disk, and then transfer the information back to a tape.

When a tape should be used, a disk should be used, or the two should be used together must be decided after carefully studying an application. It is hoped that this brief discussion and the material in the succeeding sections will aid in making such decisions.

8-1-3   File Attributes

The major attributes of a file at any given time are:

1. Its type (sequential or direct—discussed in Sec. 8-2).
2. Its form (formatted or unformatted).
3. Whether it is connected or not connected.
4. Whether it is existing or not existing.
5. Whether it is a named file or a scratch file.

As discussed earlier, a file may be preconnected by a system command before a program is executed or it may be connected during the execution of the program by an OPEN statement. If a file is either preconnected or connected, it is connected; otherwise, it is not connected. Similarly, a file may preexist, meaning that it is a reality before the program is run, or it may be created by the program. In either case, once it is created it is said to *exist*; otherwise, it does *not exist*. The existence of a file means that it can be recognized by a program; it does not necessarily mean that it contains any data.

A file may be a named file or a scratch file. A named file may be saved and used by future program runs or by other programs. A scratch file is for the temporary use of the program that creates it and does not exist after the program has completed its run.

EXERCISES

1. Describe the logical structure of a FORTRAN accessible file and the purpose of the pointer.

2. If a tape drive is such that its:

> Read/write speed is 100 ips
> Rewind speed is 300 ips
> Density is 6250 bpi
> Length is 2400 ft

what is the maximum capacity of the tape? What is its transfer rate once a record is found? How much time would be needed to rewind the entire tape? How much time would be needed to rewind one-third of the tape, search forward one-fourth of the tape, again rewind the tape, and search forward through one-half of the tape? If each record is 3125 bytes long and a record gap is 0.3 in. long, how many records could be stored on the tape and what percentage of the tape would consist of record gaps?

3. Suppose that a disk rotates at 2400 revolutions per minute and the average arm movement time is 0.03 s. What is its average access time? Assuming that the read time is insignificant when compared to the access time, find the total amount of time it would take to read:
   (a) Six randomly distributed records.
   (b) Six records that are randomly distributed in pairs.
   (c) Six contiguous records.

4. On a disk, the read/write head can access only one bit at a time. If the bits on a disk are spaced at 20 kb track and the disk rotates at 2400 revolutions per minute, what is the transfer rate in bytes per second once a record is under the read/write head? (Assume 8 bits per byte.) A *track* is that portion of a cylinder that is on a single surface.

5. What are the advantages and disadvantages of tapes versus disks?

8-2 FILE CLASSIFICATIONS

Files are classified in two ways. They are classified by the way they are accessed and according to the form of their data. With regard to access, a file may be a sequential file or a direct file and its classification as sequential or direct is called its *type*. As discussed later, a file must be accessed using the proper type indicator or an error will occur. The characteristics of the two types of files are summarized in Fig. 8-5.

As indicated by the figure, the types of files differ primarily in the need for an EOF indicator, the record length requirements, and the way in which the pointer is changed. An EOF is required for a sequential file, but cannot be placed at the end of a direct file. Record lengths may vary within a sequential file, but records in a direct

Sequential	Direct
A complete sequential access file must terminate with an EOF indicator, although it may temporarily not have an EOF while it is being created or expanded.	A direct access file has no EOF indicator.
Records may differ in length.	Records must all have the same length
A BACKSPACE statement will cause the pointer to decrement (i.e., to move backward one record).	Prior to an I-O operation, the pointer may be moved to any record by specifying a record number in the READ or WRITE statement (see Sec. 8-4).
A REWIND statement causes the pointer to return to record 1.	The BACKSPACE and REWIND statements do not apply to direct files.
An I-O operation, a BACKSPACE, or a REWIND are the only means of moving the pointer. Record numbers may not appear in the READ or WRITE statement.	A record specifier appearing in a READ or WRITE statement is used to point to the record.
May be stored on tape or disk.	May be stored only on disk.

FIGURE 8-5 *Summary of the characteristics of the two types of files.*

file must all have the same length. Finally, the most significant difference lies with the movement of the pointer. For a direct file the pointer can be moved to any record in the file by giving a record specifier in the READ or WRITE statement, but for a sequential file the pointer can be changed only by an I-O operation (which increments the pointer), a BACKSPACE statement (which decrements the pointer), or a REWIND statement (which sets the pointer to record number 1). When a sequential file is opened, the pointer is set to 1. As shown in Fig. 8-6, a read or write will cause the pointer to move forward so that after the operation it will point to the next record in sequence. A backspace causes the pointer to move back one record and a rewind

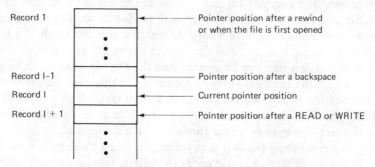

FIGURE 8-6 *Pointer movement within a sequential file.*

results in a return to the first record. When tape is being used the pointer value indicates the physical position of the read/write head with respect to the file.

The BACKSPACE and REWIND statements have the forms

$$\text{BACKSPACE } \textit{(Unit)}$$

and

$$\text{REWIND } \textit{(Unit)}$$

where *Unit* is the logical identifier associated with the file when it is connected. If the pointer contains a 1 at the time a BACKSPACE statement is executed, the statement has no effect.

Sequential files tend to be used more in situations in which the records are accessed in order, in applications in which a file is updated and used only periodically (e.g., once a day). Direct files are better adapted to situations in which the records are randomly accessed, such as in interactive applications. For example, an inventory program that is updated continually from interactive terminals would take advantage of the random pointer movement of a direct file. Note that direct files can be stored *only* on disks. One reason for this is that the random pointer movement is of little value unless it is coupled with the random-accessing nature of a disk. Sequential files may be stored on disk, but on disks they are only logically sequential. Physically they are scattered, but the operating system causes them to appear sequential to the programs that use them. The programmer must cause an EOF indicator to be placed at the end of each sequential file and this is done using a statement of the form:

ENDFILE *(Unit)*

The other principal means of classifying files is by the way the data are stored. Some files, called *formatted files*, store data as character strings, and others, called *unformatted files*, store data as images of their 0–1 combinations. As explained in Sec. 7-5 and illustrated in Fig. 7-28, data being transmitted between a card reader, terminal, or printer must be in an alphanumeric format even if they are numeric data. The conversion of the numeric data to the bit patterns of the integer, real, double-precision, and complex formats occurs as the data are transferred between the I-O buffer and the locations associated with the list items. The same process can be used when communicating with a tape or disk file and the result is a formatted file. On the other hand, tape and disk files do not have to be stored in an alphanumeric code. The conversion step can be deleted and the file can consist of the same bit patterns that are in the list item memory locations. In this case the file is unformatted. The classification of a file with respect to its format is called its *form* and if a file is accessed using the incorrect form specifier, an error will occur (see Sec. 8-3). Both sequential and direct files may be either formatted or unformatted.

In comparing the two data forms, the thing to keep in mind is that formatted data consist of alphanumeric codes for letters, numbers, punctuation marks, blanks, and so on, and they are transmitted to and from a mass storage device just as they are communicated when a card reader, terminal, or printer is used. As a result, such data can be visualized as if it were a line of print.

The advantages of formatted files are:

1. They are transportable between computer systems, even systems produced by different manufacturers.
2. They can be accessed by programs written in different languages.
3. They are more easily transmitted between mass storage devices and devices that can handle only alphanumeric data (card readers, etc.)

Unformatted data depend on the internal formats of the computer system, and unformatted data created by one system may not make sense to another system. Single-precision real numbers occupy 4 bytes on an IBM-370 and 5 bytes on a DEC System 10. Also, the exponent-fraction formats for real numbers on these systems are different. Therefore, the real numbers stored by an IBM-370 would be incorrectly interpreted by a DEC System 10. On the other hand, if two systems use the same alphanumeric code, a FORTRAN program run on one system can read formatted data that are written by a FORTRAN program on the other system. Similarly, although most high-level language programs can perform I-O with alphanumeric data that are formatted by a FORTRAN program, they may not be able to communicate with FORTRAN-created unformatted data.

With regard to the third advantage, by using a string variable or array it is possible to transmit data between a formatted mass storage file and a card reader, terminal, or printer without performing any conversion. When this is done, the A format code is used in the format specification of both the READ and WRITE statements. For example, if a connection has been made and the pointer is initially at 1, the program segment

```
CHARACTER*80 BUFF
        .
        .
        .
        DO 15 I=1,N
          READ (*,100) BUFF
          WRITE (22,100) BUFF
     15 CONTINUE
    100 FORMAT (A80)
```

would cause the information on N data cards to be transferred to the file whose logical identifier (as indicated in the unit specifier) is 22. No conversion would be needed during the transfer.

The advantages of the unformatted form are:

1. It saves memory space.
2. It eliminates conversions between the internal and external formats, thereby saving time and preserving accuracy.

If the number −3.592 were output using the format code F10.3, it would occupy 10 bytes even though it is stored in 4 bytes of memory. For massive amounts of data this can be significant, particularly if a disk is the storage device. Disk space is expensive, but even for magnetic tape the use of an unformatted file instead of a formatted file could avoid the inconvenience of more than one tape. In addition, the compactness of unformatted data would mean shorter search times.

Avoiding conversions would clearly save computer time and this could be noticeable for extremely large files. Also important is the fact that, by not converting the data, their internal accuracy is maintained. Suppose that a computer stores numbers in the real format to seven significant figures and the contents of X are written to a formatted file using the format code E12.4. The data are stored to only four significant figures and that is all that will be available when the data are accessed later. Even if E15.7 had been used, there may be some loss in accuracy due to the change from the binary internal format to the decimal external format.

List-directed I-O is a special case of formatted I-O, but it can be used only in communicating with sequential files. The reason is that the records in direct files have fixed lengths and the length resulting from a list-directed write is unpredictable. As a general rule, list-directed mass storage I-O should not be performed even with sequential files. Because the files on mass storage devices are not visible, it is best if the exact format is available through an explicit format specification.

Card readers, terminals, and printers are normally referred to as formatted sequential files, and from the computer's standpoint that is what they are. Each card or line is a formatted record and the records must be accessed in order, but there are some limitations. These devices cannot be backspaced or rewound and their record lengths are fixed. (We have assumed 80-character records for card readers and terminals and 132-character records for line printers.)

EXERCISES

1. Discuss the advantages and disadvantages of sequential versus direct files and relate the discussion to possible applications.
2. Summarize the advantages and disadvantages of formatted and unformatted files.
3. If X, Y, and I are output to a formatted file using the format specification '(F10.4, E11.3, I8)', how many bytes would be output? How many bytes would be output if these variables were put in an unformatted file? (As usual, assume that integer and single-precision numbers occupy 4 bytes.)
4. If A were a double-precision variable and a computer kept double-precision numbers to 17 significant figures, how many figures would be lost if A were put in a formatted file using the E25.12 format code and then later input using the same code? Input using the F15.2 format code? If A is output using the F20.17 format code, what could be said about the number of significant figures stored?

8-3 OPEN AND CLOSE STATEMENTS

As we have seen, before a file can be accessed it must be connected. This can be done:

1. Automatically by the operating system, such as for the default input and output devices.
2. By a command to the operating system.
3. By an OPEN statement.

Only the last of these alternatives can be done from within the program and it is the one of interest at this point. An OPEN statement has the form

OPEN *(Unit Specifier, Other Specifiers)*

where the *Other Specifiers* are as indicated in Fig. 8-7. The third column gives the type of entity that can be placed to the right of the = sign in the specifier and the fourth column gives the possible values the entity can become.

The *Unit* in the unit specifier is the logical identifier associated with the file. The *Other Specifiers* are separated by commas and are optional, except that the file specifier must be present if the file has not been preconnected. If both the unit specifier and the file specifier appear, then *Name* in the file specifier is connected to the Unit

Name	Format	*Specifier* Type	Possible *Specifier* Values
Unit	UNIT = *Unit* [1]	Integer exp.	Nonnegative integer, system-dependent
File	FILE = *Name*	Character exp.	Valid filename, system-dependent
Type	ACCESS = *Type*	Character exp.	'SEQUENTIAL' or 'DIRECT'
Form	FORM = *Form*	Character exp.	'FORMATTED' or 'UNFORMATTED'
Length	RECL = *Length*	Integer exp.	Positive integer
Status	STATUS = *Status* [2]	Character exp.	'OLD' or 'NEW', 'SCRATCH', or 'UNKNOWN'
I-0 Status	IOSTAT = *I-0 Status* [3]	Integer variable	Integer, system-dependent
Error	ERR = *Label* [4]	Statement label	Positve integer
Blank	BLANK = *Blank*	Character exp.	'NULL' or 'ZERO'

[1] Format may simply be the *Unit*.

[2] Exactly what is meant by 'UNKNOWN' depends on the system.

[3] Integer variable to receive the error code returned by the operation.

[4] Statement label branched to if an error occurs during open operation.

FIGURE 8-7 *Summary of the OPEN statement* Specifiers.

indicated by the unit specifier. In general a *Name* must be sufficient to point either implicitly or explicitly to the device containing the file and to the exact position of a file on the device.

The formats of Filenames are system-dependent and the reader must refer to the proper manuals for his or her system.

If a file specifier is given and the *Unit* is already connected to the file, the connection remains intact. If the *Unit* is connected to some other file, the old connection is canceled and the new connection is made.

After an OPEN statement has been executed the file referenced by the statement is said to be *opened*. Opening a file may include its connection, but it may also include other functions, such as:

1. Allocating space for a file that does not already exist, and thereby causes it to exist. (This would apply only to mass storage devices.)
2. Comparing a file's attributes to those given in the OPEN statement specifiers to make sure that they match. Mismatches may result in errors.

An internal file cannot be opened and, therefore, cannot appear as a *Unit* in an OPEN statement.

The type and form specifiers indicate the type and form of the file. If a file exists and the type or form indicated by these specifiers disagree with the actual type or form of the file, an error will occur. The length specifier gives the length of the records in the file and should only appear when a direct file is being opened. The status specifier can be present only if there is a file specifier, in which case it indicates whether the file is an existing file, is to be created, is to be treated as a scratch file, or has an unknown status. (What is meant by "unknown" depends on the system.) A *scratch file* is a temporary unnamed file that is set up by the system and exists only while the program is running. If a file exists and there is a conflict between the length or status specifiers and the actual characteristics of the file, an error will occur.

What happens in the event of an error depends on the system. When an I-O status specifier is given, some types of errors, such as incorrect matches for existing files, will cause a code value to be put in the *I-O Status* variable included in the specifier. Also, if an error specifier is included, some errors will cause a branch to the *Label* given in the error specifier.

> *To determine the I-O status code values and the types of errors that cause a branch to be taken by an error specifier, one should refer to the manual for the system being used.*

The blank specifier determines the interpretation of blanks that are embedded in or trail numbers that are being input. If this specifier indicates 'NULL' such blanks are ignored; if it indicates 'ZERO', they are treated as zeros. A blank specifier overrides all previous blank specifications for the file.

The requirements and defaults for the specifiers are summarized in Fig. 8-8. Note that the record length for unformatted (direct) files is given in system-dependent units. Normally, these units would be the size of a location needed to store an integer or real number. Because of the savings resulting from the elimination of conversions, unformatted files are primarily used for storing numerical data.

Several representative OPEN statements are given in Fig. 8-9. Which specifiers should be included in an OPEN statement depends on the situation. The OPEN statements given in the right column of the figure have the suggested formats for the situations indicated in the corresponding entries in the left column.

As mentioned previously, card readers, terminals, and printers can be viewed as files. In fact, FORTRAN treats all devices used for I-O as files and, except for the default input and output devices, they must be either preconnected or connected by an OPEN statement. Examples of such devices are card punches, paper tape readers and punches, and auxiliary terminals and line printers. To connect I-O devices as files they must have system-dependent names associated with them and, if they are connected with OPEN statements, these names must appear as *Names* in the file specifier. The last example in Fig. 8-9 shows how a line printer named 'DEVLP2' could be connected by an OPEN statement.

> *Warning: Some systems may require that files other than mass storage files be preconnected.*

Specifier	Requirements	Default
Unit	Required	
File	Required for mass storage files if file is not preconnected and is not a scratch file	System determined files
Type*	If file exists, types must agree	Sequential
Form*	If file exists, forms must agree	Formatted if sequential, unformatted if direct
Length*	For direct file only. In bytes if formatted, and system-dependent units if unformatted	
Status	If 'OLD', file must exist, and if 'NEW', file is created. Can be 'SCRATCH' only if there is no file specifier, and otherwise can appear only if there is a file specifier.	'UNKNOWN'
Blank	Will change old blank specification, even for default case	'NULL'

* May be established by preconnection, in which case, if the OPEN statement contains the specifier, the specification must agree. The default takes effect only if the specification is not made by either preconnection or by the apperance of the specifier.

FIGURE 8-8 *Requirements and default values for the OPEN statement specifiers.*

```
Situation                    OPEN Statement

File exists, no       OPEN (12, FILE='FILEA', ACCESS='SEQUENTIAL',
error recovery      :    FORM='FORMATTED', STATUS='OLD')

File exists, error    OPEN (12, FILE='FILEA', ACCESS='SEQUENTIAL',
recovery desired    :    FORM='FORMATTED', STATUS='OLD', IOSTAT=ICODE)

                      OPEN (15, FILE='A.SRC', ACCESS='DIRECT',
                    :    FORM='UNFORMATTED', STATUS='OLD', RECL=100,
                    :    IOSTAT=ICODE, ERR=200)

File being created    OPEN (7, FILE='TEXT', ACCESS='SEQUENTIAL',
                    :    FORM='FORMATTED', STATUS='NEW')

Scratch file          OPEN (10, ACCESS='SEQUENTIAL', FORM='UNFORMATTED',
                    :    STATUS='SCRATCH')

Nonstorage device     OPEN (31, FILE='DEVLP2', ACCESS='SEQUENTIAL',
(e.g., nondefault   :    IOSTAT=KCODE)
line printer)
```

FIGURE 8-9 *Representative OPEN statements.*

For a preconnected file, the extra functions performed by the opening process can be carried out automatically when the file is accessed by a READ or WRITE statement. If an OPEN statement is not used, either the attributes established by the preconnection or the default attributes are assumed. Even though OPEN statements are not necessary, *OPEN statements should be used to explicitly open all files* (*except the default input and output devices*). *It is recommended that the type and form attributes be given explicitly.* There are two reasons for this: (1) the OPEN statements provide a double check by comparing what the programmer thinks the attributes are with the actual attributes, and (2) the OPEN statements indicate the attributes of the files to anyone who reads the program.

The counterpart to opening a file is closing a file. *Closing* a file cancels the connection if there is one, and has no effect if there is no connection. A close is executed by a statement of the form

CLOSE *(Unit Specifier, Status Specifier)*

where the *Unit Specifier* is as defined for the OPEN statement and the *Status Specifier* is optional. The *Status Specifier* has the form

STATUS = *Status*

where *Status* is either 'KEEP' or 'DELETE'. If 'KEEP' is given, the file is saved for future reference; if 'DELETE' is indicated, the file ceases to exist. A 'KEEP' status may not be given for a scratch file. The default status for a scratch file is, of course, 'DELETE', and for all other files it is 'KEEP'. Error and I-O status specifiers can also be included in a CLOSE statement, but they are seldom used because few errors can occur during a close operation. If a file is not closed with a CLOSE statement, it is automatically closed using the defaults at the time the program is terminated. It is suggested that *all files be explicitly closed with a CLOSE statement and that the status specifier be used for all mass storage files except scratch files.* Typical CLOSE statements are shown in Fig. 8-10.

Both the OPEN and CLOSE processes are global. That is, they apply to all program units in a program regardless of which program unit initiates them. Because a *Unit* in a unit specifier can be a variable, it can be passed to a subprogram through a parameter.

```
        Situation                          CLOSE Statement

File needed for future use         CLOSE (15, STATUS='KEEP')

Nonstorage device or scratch       CLOSE (18)
file
```

FIGURE 8-10 *Representative CLOSE statements.*

1. What is the purpose of the OPEN statement? Of the CLOSE statement?

2. Give a statement that:
    (a) Opens an existing sequential formatted file SEQFIL and associates it with *Unit* 15.
    (b) Opens a scratch unformatted direct file with records of length 200 and associates it with *Unit* 23.
    (c) Opens a nonexisting sequential formatted file FILEN and associates it with *Unit* 10. If an error occurs, IC is to contain the error code and a branch is to be taken to the statement whose label is 500.
    (d) Closes the file associated with *Unit* 5 and causes it to be deleted.

3. State what each of the following statements do and, *if possible*, find the number of bytes reserved by them for each record.
    (a) OPEN (8, ACCESS='DIRECT', FORM='UNFORMATTED', RECL=200)
    (b) OPEN (15, FILE='FILE.DAT', ACCESS='DIRECT', RECL=200)
    (c) OPEN (10, ACCESS='DIRECT', FORM='FORMATTED', RECL=200)
    (d) OPEN (12, FILE='MT2', ACCESS='SEQUENTIAL', STATUS='NEW',
    :   IOSTAT=K, ERR=50, BLANK='ZERO')

8-4 FILE I-O

The actual accessing of a file is done by the general READ and WRITE statements introduced in Sec. 7-4. In that section the unit, format, and end specifiers were considered, but a discussion of record, I-O status, and error specifiers was delayed. From the foregoing discussion of OPEN statements it is clear that the record specifier indicates the length of the records in a direct file and the I-O status and error specifiers are for controlling a program's actions in the event of an error. If an I-O status specifier is given in the *Control List* of a READ or WRITE statement, a code value is returned to the integer variable that appears in the specifier. The code is set according to the rules:

Negative—an EOF was detected during the operation

0—neither an EOF nor an error was detected

Positive—an error was detected

The nonzero values that are returned are system-dependent. A −1 is normally used for signaling an EOF and the positive values indicate the various types of errors (e.g., hardware error during transmission could be 1, file not connected could be 2, etc.).

Note: The programmer must refer to the appropriate manual to find the meanings of the error codes for the system being used.

If an error specifier is included in the *Control List* and any type of error occurs, a branch will be taken to the *Label* appearing in the specifier.

```
INTEGER CODE
      .
      .
      .
WRITE (8, 100, IOSTAT = CODE)  (A(I), I = 1, 1000)
IF (CODE .LT. 0) THEN
      .
      .    }  Process EOF
      .
   ELSE IF (CODE .GT. 0) THEN
         CALL ERROR (8, CODE)
      ELSE
ENDIF
      .
      .
      .

END

SUBROUTINE ERROR (LOGID, CODE)
INTEGER LOGID, CODE
IF (CODE .EQ. 1) THEN
      .
      .    }  Process transmission error
      .
   ELSE IF (CODE .EQ. 2) THEN
         .
         .   }  Process file not connected error
         .
      ELSE
         .
         .   }  Process remaining errors
         .
ENDIF
END
```

Some of the CASEs may include STOP statements.

FIGURE 8-11 *Typical error processing using the I-O status variable.*

A common application of the I-O status specifier is depicted in Fig. 8-11. The WRITE statement is followed by a CASE structure which is based on the I-O status variable. If the I-O status variable is negative, a program segment for handling EOFs is executed. If the I-O status variable is positive, a subroutine ERROR is called that uses another CASE structure to analyze the I-O status variable further and take action depending on the type of error. Otherwise, the program continues in sequence.

It should be obvious that when inputting a record from a mass storage file the *Format Specification* in the READ statement must match the *Format Specification* used in the WRITE statement that output the record. It is strongly recommended that for most cases:

FORMAT statements be used to provide the Format Specifications and that the same FORMAT statement be used for the read as was used for the write.

The READ statement does not have to include all the list items that appear in the WRITE statement, but those that are included must be the first items in the

WRITE statement list and they must have the same order. For example,

```
WRITE  (8,100)  X,Y,Z
READ   (8,100)  X,Y
```

would be all right, but

```
WRITE  (8,100),  X,Y,Z
READ   (8,100)  Y,Z
```

would assign the value of X to Y and the value of Y to Z.

Let us now consider several representative examples, with each example being slightly more complicated than the previous one. All the examples are based on a single application, the manipulation of experimental biological data, and are designed to demonstrate how files are created, changed, and used. They are also designed to emphasize the strong points and weak points of sequential and direct files.

Accompanying each example program is a system flowchart. A *system flowchart* is a symbolic illustration of the flow of information while a program is executing. Figure 8-12 summarizes the system flowcharting symbols that are used in this book.

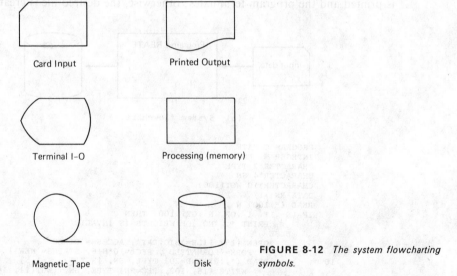

Card Input   Printed Output

Terminal I-O   Processing (memory)

Magnetic Tape   Disk

FIGURE 8-12 *The system flowcharting symbols.*

For a more extensive listing of system flowcharting symbols, see the reference *Tools for Structured Design* by Bohl in the Bibliography. System flowcharts are considerably different from the program flowcharts discussed earlier. System flowcharts are concerned with the flow of information within the system and program flowcharts illustrate the control flow within a program.

Suppose that a biological laboratory is studying the growth rates of several types of bacteria. In our first example we will assume an existing set of data that has been punched into cards. We will be concerned with programs for creating a mass storage file from the data and outputting the mass storage file to the line printer. Suppose that the bacteria in each sample have been weighed $N \leq 100$ consecutive days and that the experimental input data for each sample is to have the format

> First field—type, two characters, field width 2
>
> Second field—sample number, integer, field width 4 beginning in column 7
>
> N other fields—sample weights to two decimal places, real, field width 10

If $N > 7$, the data for a sample must be put on more than one card, in which case the continuation cards are to have blanks in the first 10 columns. The mass storage file is to be a formatted direct file, with each record being the data for a sample.

A system flowchart for creating the file is given in Fig. 8-13(a) and a corresponding program is given in Fig. 8-13(b). The program proceeds by first reading the number of weights associated with the samples into N. If the number is unacceptable, the message

NO. OF WEIGHTS IS INVALID

is printed and the program terminates; otherwise, the desired file is created. To keep

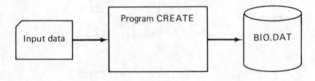

(a)   System flowchart.

```
PROGRAM CREATE
INTEGER N, RN
CHARACTER*2 TYPE
CHARACTER*4 SN
CHARACTER*10 WGT(100)
DATA RN /1/
READ (*,100) N
IF (N .LT. 1 .OR. N .GT. 100) THEN
        PRINT *, 'NO. OF WEIGHTS IS INVALID'
    ELSE
        OPEN (15, FILE='BIO.DAT', ACCESS='DIRECT',
    :        FORM='FORMATTED', RECL=10*N+6, STATUS='NEW')
10      READ (*,101,END=20) TYPE, SN, (WGT(I), I=1,N)
        WRITE (15, 102, REC=RN) TYPE, SN, (WGT(I), I=1,N)
        RN = RN+1
        GO TO 10
20      CONTINUE
        CLOSE (15, STATUS='KEEP')
    ENDIF
    PRINT *, 'TRANSFER COMPLETE, NO. OF RECORDS =',RN-1)
100 FORMAT (I3)
101 FORMAT (A2,T7,A4,(T11, A10))
102 FORMAT (A2,A4,100A10)
    END
```

(b)   Program

FIGURE 8-13 File creation example.

the program simple, error recovery has not been provided with the WRITE statement. Error recovery could be added by using the procedure shown in Fig. 8-11. The A format code is used to read and write the sample numbers and weights because the program does not use them as numbers and there is no reason to convert them on input and immediately reconvert them for formatted storage.

A system flowchart and a program for listing the BIO.DAT file are given in Fig. 8-14. The structure of the program is similar to that of CREATE except that the total number of records to be read is input to M and a DO loop is used to read and print the records. Once again, error recovery is not provided with the file access, but could easily be added. One weakness of the program is that N is checked only to ascertain that it is in the range 1 through 100; it is left to the user to know the exact number of weights in the records. Also, M is not checked and the user must know the

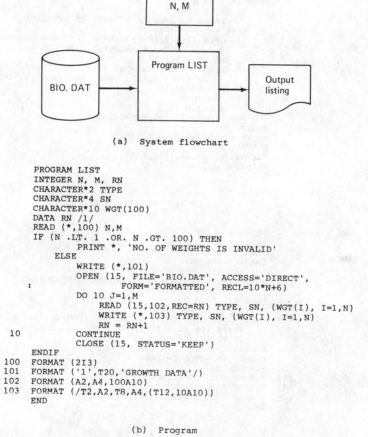

(a) System flowchart

```
PROGRAM LIST
INTEGER N, M, RN
CHARACTER*2 TYPE
CHARACTER*4 SN
CHARACTER*10 WGT(100)
DATA RN /1/
READ (*,100) N,M
IF (N .LT. 1 .OR. N .GT. 100) THEN
          PRINT *, 'NO. OF WEIGHTS IS INVALID'
     ELSE
          WRITE (*,101)
          OPEN (15, FILE='BIO.DAT', ACCESS='DIRECT',
     :              FORM='FORMATTED', RECL=10*N+6)
          DO 10 J=1,M
               READ (15,102,REC=RN) TYPE, SN, (WGT(I), I=1,N)
               WRITE (*,103) TYPE, SN, (WGT(I), I=1,N)
               RN = RN+1
   10          CONTINUE
          CLOSE (15, STATUS='KEEP')
     ENDIF
  100    FORMAT (2I3)
  101    FORMAT ('1',T20,'GROWTH DATA'/)
  102    FORMAT (A2,A4,100A10)
  103    FORMAT (/T2,A2,T8,A4,(T12,10A10))
     END
```

(b) Program

FIGURE 8-14 *File listing example.*

total number of records. The first problem could be circumvented by using an INQUIRE statement to obtain the record length (see Sec. 8-5). The second problem could be corrected by having CREATE put M, and only M, in the first record of BIO.DAT. Then LIST would not input M from a card; it would input it from the first record and the user would not need to know its value. The value of N could also be stored in and obtained from the first record if the file were sequential, but for a direct file the length of the records must be known when the file is opened.

Figure 8-15 shows how CREATE and LIST could be rewritten for a sequential file. The number N is stored in the first record and the EOF indicator, which is not available in direct files, is used in SLIST to detect the end of BIO.DAT. Therefore, M is not needed. Also, because N is stored in the file, SLIST assumes that it is correct

```
        PROGRAM SCREAT
        INTEGER N
        CHARACTER*2 TYPE
        CHARACTER*4 SN
        CHARACTER*10 WGT(100)
        READ (*,100) N
        IF (N .LT. 1 .OR. N .GT. 100)
                PRINT *, 'NO. OF WEIGHTS IS INVALID'
            ELSE
                OPEN (15, FILE='BIO.DAT', ACCESS='SEQUENTIAL',
            :           FORM='FORMATTED', STATUS='NEW')
                WRITE (15,100) N
    10          READ (*,101, END=20) TYPE, SN, (WGT(I), I=1,N)
                    WRITE (15,102) TYPE, SN, (WGT(I), I=1,N)
                    GO TO 10
    20          CONTINUE
                ENDFILE (15)
                CLOSE (15, STATUS='KEEP')
        ENDIF
        PRINT *, 'TRANSFER COMPLETE'
   100  FORMAT (I3)
   101  FORMAT (A2,T7,A4,(T11,A10))
   102  FORMAT (A2,,A4,100A10)
        END
```

(a)   Program SCREAT

```
        PROGRAM SLIST
        INTEGER N
        CHARACTER*2 TYPE
        CHARACTER*4 SN
        CHARACTER*10 WGT(100)
        OPEN (15, FILE='BIO.DAT', ACCESS='SEQUENTIAL,
    :           FORM='FORMATTED')
        READ (15,100) N
        WRITE (*,101)
    10  READ (15,102, END=30) TYPE, SN, (WGT(I), I=1,N)
            WRITE (15,103) TYPE, SN, (WGT(I), I=1,N)
            GO TO 10
    30  CONTINUE
        CLOSE (15, STATUS='KEEP')
   100  FORMAT (I3)
   101  FORMAT ('1',T20,'GROWTH DATA'/)
   102  FORMAT (A2,A4,100A10)
   103  FORMAT (/T2,A2,T8,A4,(T12,10A10))
        END
```

(b)   Program SLIST

FIGURE 8-15   *Creating and listing a sequential file.*

and the IF-THEN-ELSE structure is deleted. Because the file BIO.DAT is now sequential it could be stored on a magnetic tape. The fact that a tape can be dismounted and stored in the researcher's office gives tape storage a distinct advantage over disk storage.

It has been seen that for files whose records are accessed in order, sequential files offer the termination convenience of the EOF indicator, which can be used to automatically branch out of an input loop. This convenience can be simulated in a direct file by having the last record consist of a specially coded value and then exiting the loop when this record is detected. As with the special input values introduced in Chap. 2, such records are called *sentinels*.

The programs described above would furnish a means of creating a file and later examining it. The listing program could be changed to include some processing, such as computing the means and standard deviations for the various types and days, and either of the pairs of programs described above could serve as a basis for a reasonably useful system of programs. However, data must invariably be changed and the only means of altering even one weight using the programs described would be to change a card in the input file and recreate the entire file BIO.DAT. It would be much better if there were a program for correcting selected weights in the BIO.DAT file. What is needed is a program that would accept the corrections from a card reader or terminal, find the record that needs correcting, and then correct the record. This is a classic situation in which the set of corrections is referred to as the *transactions file* and the file to be corrected is referred to as the *master file*. If the master file is a direct file, it can be corrected in place, but if it is sequential, a new file that includes the corrections would need to be created. The updating of a sequential master file by a transaction file is illustrated in Fig. 8-16.

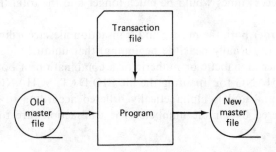

FIGURE 8-16 *Updating a sequential master file using a transaction file.*

Figure 8-17 offers a possible solution to the problem of making changes to a file. This process consists of reading a transaction (correction), sequentially searching the master file for the record to be changed, making the change, moving the master file pointer back to record 1, reading another transaction, and then, if the transaction is not an EOF, repeating the process. There is a serious problem with this approach. Suppose that there are 12,000 master file records and 1000 transactions and the transactions are randomly ordered. On the average, 6000 master file records would need to be examined per transaction. Even if only an average of 0.01 s is needed to

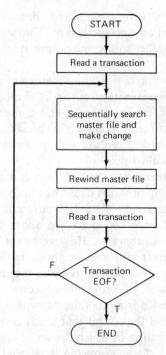

```
        ┌─────────────┐
        │    START    │
        └──────┬──────┘
               │
       ┌───────▼────────┐
       │ Read a transaction │
       └───────┬────────┘
               │
       ┌───────▼────────────┐
       │ Sequentially search │
       │   master file and   │
       │    make change      │
       └───────┬────────────┘
               │
       ┌───────▼────────┐
       │ Rewind master file │
       └───────┬────────┘
               │
       ┌───────▼────────┐
       │ Read a transaction │
       └───────┬────────┘
               │
          F    ▼
        ◄──◇ Transaction ◇
            ◇   EOF?     ◇
                │
                │ T
        ┌───────▼──────┐
        │     END      │
        └──────────────┘
```

FIGURE 8-17 *Example of a bad procedure for changing a file.*

access a record, the total master file read time needed to make the corrections would be

$$0.01 \times 1000 \times 6000 = 60{,}000 \text{ s} = 1000 \text{ min}$$

For a tape the average access times would be much longer and the total time would be extremely long.

The solution is to order both the master and transaction files according to keys. A *key* is a field in a record (usually near the beginning) that uniquely identifies the record. Keys may be either alphabetic or numeric or a combination of both. Figure 8-18 gives a program SCHANG for updating the file BIO.DAT. SCHANG assumes that BIO.DAT is sequential and is alphabetically ordered according to type and, within each type, is ordered by sample numbers. The transactions are to have the form

First field—type, two characters

Second field—sample number, integer, field of 4

Third field—weight to two decimal places, real, field of 10

Fourth field—position within the array of weights of the weight to be changed

It is assumed that the transactions are not input in order, but that there is a subroutine SORT for putting them in order. The transactions are first transferred from the card reader to an unformatted scratch file and then SORT is called to put the transaction records in order. SORT is not given (see Exercise 4) but it is assumed that it is a gen-

368

```
          PROGRAM SCHANG
          INTEGER P, TCODE, MCODE
          CHARACTER*2 T, TYPE
          CHARACTER*4 S, SN
          CHARACTER*8 FIN, FOUT
          CHARACTER*10 W, WGT(100)
          DATA TCODE, MCODE, T, TYPE /2*0,2*'ZZ'/
          OPEN (14, ACCESS='SEQUENTIAL', FORM='UNFORMATTED',
        :         STATUS='SCRATCH')
    10    READ (*,100, END=20) T,S,W,P
              WRITE (14) T,S,W,P
              GO TO 10
    20    CONTINUE
          ENDFILE (14)
          CALL SORT (14,6)
          READ (*,101) FIN, FOUT
          OPEN (15, FILE=FIN, ACCESS='SEQUENTIAL', FORM='FORMATTED',
        :         STATUS='OLD')
          OPEN (16, FILE=FOUT, ACCESS='SEQUENTIAL', FORM='FORMATTED',
        :         STATUS='NEW')
          READ (15,102) N
          READ (14) T,S,W,P
          READ (15,103) TYPE, SN, (WGT(I), I=1,N)
    30    IF (TCODE .EQ. -1 .AND. MCODE = -1) GO TO 40
              IF (T//S .EQ. TYPE//SN) THEN
                      WGT(P) = W
                      T = 'ZZ'
                      READ (14, IOSTAT=TCODE) T,S,W,P
                  ELSE IF (T//S .GT. TYPE//SN) THEN
                      WRITE (16,103) TYPE, SN, (WGT(I), I=1,N)
                      TYPE = 'ZZ'
                      READ (15,103, IOSTAT=MCODE) TYPE, SN, (WGT(I), I=1,N)
                  ELSE
                      PRINT '(5A)','TYPE: ',T,'    SAMPLE:',S,'    NOT FOUND'
                      T = 'ZZ'
                      READ (14, IOSTAT=TCODE) T,S,W,P
              ENDIF
              GO TO 30
    40    CONTINUE
          ENDFILE (16)
          REWIND (16)
          CLOSE (14, STATUS='DELETE')
          CLOSE (15, STATUS='DELETE')
          CLOSE (16, STATUS='KEEP')
          PRINT *, 'FILE UPDATE COMPLETE'
   100    FORMAT (A2,A4,A10,I5)
   101    FORMAT (2A8)
   102    FORMAT (I3)
   103    FORMAT (A2,A4,100A10)
          END
```

FIGURE 8-18 *Program for updating an ordered sequential file.*

eral-purpose subroutine with two parameters. The first parameter is to be the *Unit* associated with the file to be ordered and the second is to be the number of characters in the keys (which is six for the file BIO.DAT). The subroutine assumes the keys are at the beginning of the records. SORT also rewinds the scratch file so that it is positioned at record 1 when the return is made to the calling program. All comparisons are made alphanumerically despite the numerical ordering of the sample numbers. (The reader should verify that this is permissible.) Note that an EOF indicator must be added to the end of the newly created file. The program assumes that there is no type 'ZZ' and 'ZZ' will be the type when an EOF has been reached. Before each read the type variable (T or TYPE) is set to 'ZZ' and if it is not reset by the read, an EOF will have occurred. The fact that 'ZZ' is higher in the alphabet than any of the sample types is used in the *Conditions* in the CASE structure.

The whole process requires only one pass through the master file, and if the master file contains 12,000 records and the average access time is 0.01 s, the total master file read time would be 2 min. This is a substantial improvement over the procedure mentioned above, even though the transaction sort could require several minutes.

Let us now assume that BIO.DAT is an ordered direct file that is to be corrected from an interactive terminal. Suppose that the sample numbers are consecutive within each type grouping and the first record of the file contains the record number of the first record for each type. The first record is to have the structure

> Number of types—integer—L
> Name of first type—2 characters
> Record no. of first record of first type—integer
> Name of second type—2 characters
> Record no. of first record of second type—integer
>
> :
> :
>
> Name of Lth type—2 characters
> Record no. of first record of Lth type—integer
> The string '??'—2 characters
> Record no. of first record of Lth type + no. of samples for Lth type

The second record will now contain the number of weights in the records. The purpose of the first record is, of course, to aid in locating the remainder of the records in the file by providing the record number positions of the important groups of records within the file. A set of information that serves such a purpose is called a *directory*. A directory may be a special record in a file, a file by itself, or an array (or set of arrays) in memory. For the problem at hand, because the sample numbers are consecutive, the number of the record to be changed can be computed from the formula

$$M_I + S - 1$$

where M_I is the record number of the first record in the Ith type grouping and S is the sample number.

The interactive updating of a direct file is flowcharted in Fig. 8-19. A program CHANGE that permits an interactive user to change the records in the newly struc-

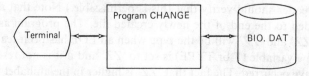

FIGURE 8-19 *Interactive updating of a direct file.*

```
      PROGRAM CHANGE
      INTEGER L, P, S, SN, N, RN, TIDX(11)
      REAL W, WGT(100)
      CHARACTER*2 T, TYPE, TID(11)
      CHARACTER*80 STR
      OPEN (15, FILE='BIO.DAT', ACCESS='DIRECT', FORM='FORMATTED',
     :           STATUS='OLD', RECL=1006)
      READ (15,100, REC=1) L,(TID(I),TIDX(I), I=1,L+1)
      READ (15,101, REC=2) N
10    PRINT *, 'ENTER NEXT CHANGE'
         READ (*,104) STR
         IF (STR(1:2) .EQ. 'NO') GO TO 20
         READ (STR,102) T,S,W,P
         CALL LOOKUP (L, T, TID, S, TIDX, RN)
         IF (RN .GT. 0) THEN
                 READ (15,103, REC=RN) TYPE,SN,(WGT(I), I=1,N)
                 WGT(P) = W
                 WRITE (15,103, REC=RN) TYPE,SN,(WGT(I), I=1,N)
         ELSE
         ENDIF
         GO TO 10
20    CONTINUE
      CLOSE (15, STATUS='KEEP')
100   FORMAT (I2,11(A2,I4))
101   FORMAT (I3)
102   FORMAT (A2,I4,F10.2,I5)
103   FORMAT (A2,I4,100F10.2)
104   FORMAT (A80)
      END
```

                    (a) Program CHANGE

```
      SUBROUTINE LOOKUP (L, T, TID, S, TIDX, RN)
      INTEGER L, S, TIDX(11), RN, K
      CHARACTER*2 T, TID(11)
      DO 10 I=1,L
         IF (T .EQ. TID(I)) THEN
                 K = TIDX(I+1) - TIDX(I)
                 IF (S .LE. K) THEN
                         RN = TIDX(I) + S - 1
                 ELSE
                         PRINT *, 'INVALID SAMPLE NO.--CANNOT EXCEED',K
                         RN = 0
                 ENDIF
                 RETURN
         ELSE
         ENDIF
10    CONTINUE
      PRINT *, 'INVALID BACTERIA TYPE'
      RN = 0
      END
```

                    (b) Subroutine LOOKUP

FIGURE 8-20 *Interactive updating of a file.*

tured BIO.DAT file is given in Fig. 8-20. Because the master file is a direct file the records may be changed in place. The program first brings in the directory and then enters a loop. The loop begins by printing the prompting message

                        ENTER NEXT CHANGE

The user is to input to an internal file STR the word 'NO' or the change in the form

                Type, Sample No., Weight, Position of Correction

If 'NO' is entered, the loop is exited; otherwise, the change is transferred from the internal file STR to the variables T, S, W, and P. A subroutine LOOKUP is called to search the directory for the type that matches the type entered with the change data and to put the record number of the first record of that type into RN. If there is a match, the subroutine checks the magnitude of the sample number to determine whether or not it exceeds the number of samples for the requested type. If it does, the message

INVALID SAMPLE NO. – CANNOT EXCEED *(Number of samples)*

is printed and RN is set to 0; otherwise, RN is set to the record number of the record to be changed. Note that the L+1th pair of entries in the directory is needed to compute the number of samples of the Lth type. If there is no match, the message

INVALID BACTERIA TYPE

is printed and RN is set to 0.

Upon return from the subroutine the value of RN is tested and if it is positive, the change is made. In either case a return is made to the beginning of the loop and the prompting message

ENTER NEXT CHANGE

is printed once again.

The examples above have presented some of the fundamental concepts of file I-O, but have left many questions unanswered. Some of these questions are:

How should a file be designed if information must be added to or deleted from its records?

How should a file be designed if new records may be added or deleted?

If the records are ordered and the file is added to or deleted from, how should the reordering be done?

If the file contains a directory, how should it be updated when records are added or deleted?

When should a directory be included and how should it be designed?

Although space does not permit a thorough examination of the problems related to answering these questions, some attention does need to be given to them. It should be understood that these questions do not have pat answers; the answers should be arrived at only after studying the application carefully.

First let us consider the problem of adding information to or deleting it from a record. For a sequential file the records may have different lengths, but the program must have a means of determining the lengths. The lengths could be input, but this is seldom practical. The solution is to put the length of a record in one of the first few fields of the record. In the file BIO.DAT the third field of each record could be used to store the number of weights in the record. Since all records must be at least three fields long, no error would occur if only the first three fields were read. Then, after the length is known, the entire record could be read. In SLIST in Fig. 8-15 the READ file statement and corresponding FORMAT statement could be replaced with

```
        READ (15, 102, END=30) TYPE, SN, N, (WGT(I) = 1,N)
                          .
                          .
                          .
        102 FORMAT (A2, A4, I4, 10A10)
```

Using this approach, BIO.DAT could be a dynamic file that would permit the addition and deletion of weights. The program SCHANG in Fig. 8-18 could also be easily modified to include this new flexibility (see Exercise 6).

This approach could not be used when working with direct files because all their records must have the same length and that length must be specified in the OPEN statement. However, the length is only a maximum that cannot be exceeded; the entire capacity of the record does not have to be used. The program CHANGE in Fig. 8-20 could add and delete weights as long as the maximum length of 1006 bytes is not exceeded. The disadvantage in using a direct file in an application in which the amount of data in the records can expand and contract is that much of the storage space may be wasted. (We saw a similar disadvantage in connection with dimensioning an array. When writing a DIMENSION statement a worst-case selection must be made.) In any case, having the number of weights in each record stored in the record would facilitate working with the records.

The problem with adding and deleting records can be much more difficult to solve. This is because:

1. The only way to delete a record is to copy the file.
2. Records cannot be added after a file is closed following its creation.
3. If there is a directory, it must be updated.

The outcome is that to add or delete a record requires that the file be copied and, if there is a directory, an algorithm for updating the directory must be programmed. Having determined that the file must be copied anyway, it is seen that inserting and deleting records in an ordered file is no more trouble (and may be less trouble) than making such changes in an unordered file. Assuming that the insert, change, and delete transactions are ordered, updating an ordered file would be a matter of monitoring the data stream as the records are being copied and performing the transactions at the proper time. For an unordered file, deletions could be made by inputting the set of keys for the records to be deleted and testing the key for each record against this set, and additions could be made by appending the added records to the end of the file.

Figure 8-21 shows a flowchart of a process for performing deletions, insertions, and changes to an ordered file as it is being copied. It assumes that the keys are in ascending order and that the transactions include a code to indicate the function to

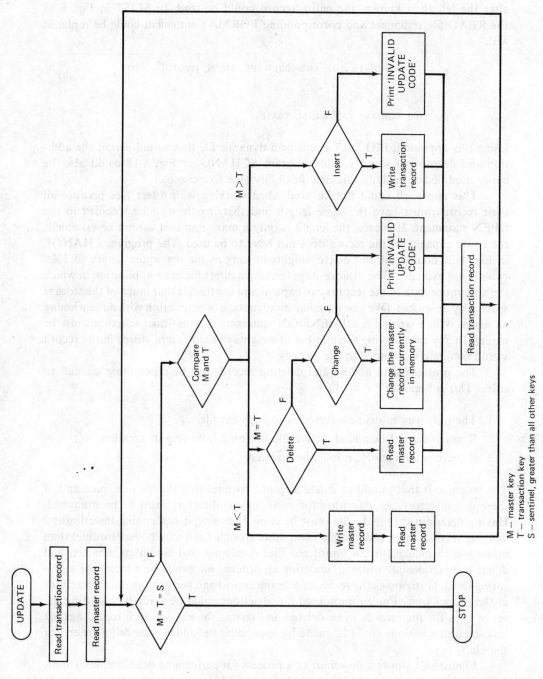

M – master key
T – transaction key
S – sentinel, greater than all other keys

FIGURE 8-21 Flowchart for updating an ordered sequential file.

be performed. The letters M and T represent, respectively, the keys of the master and transaction records that are currently in memory, and S represents a sentinel key which is greater than all other possible keys. (In Exercise 7 the reader is asked to write a program from this flowchart.)

Whether or not a directory should be included and how it should be designed and updated is very application-dependent. Because sequential files must be read in order, there is no advantage in having them include directories; it is just as efficient to use keys contained in the records and examine each record. It is advantageous to associate directories with direct files since they can be used to compute the record number. As shown in Fig. 8-22, directories are normally constructed of a pair of linear arrays, with one array containing the keys and the other containing the corresponding record number pointers. A direct file directory may contain a record num-

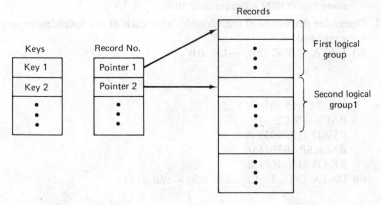

FIGURE 8-22 *Relationship between the keys and record number pointers in a directory and the records in a file.*

ber pointer to each record or may contain only pointers to logical groups of records (as in program CHANGE in Fig. 8-20). If there is a directory entry for each record, the directory may be quite large and may itself extend over several records. If a directory is very large, its keys should be ordered so that a binary search could be used to find the requested records. However, if there is a directory entry for each record, the records themselves would not need to be ordered. For the case in which the records are ordered and there is a directory entry for each record, the record number pointer array may not be needed because the record number is either the same as the index in the key array or can be computed from this index.

The size of the directory is important. If it can be stored in memory it can be searched much more quickly. For large files this may mean separating the records into groups with only the first record in each group having an entry in the directory. The disadvantage in this procedure is that it may then be necessary to search through the group being accessed, although it is sometimes possible to compute the position in the group from other information (once again refer to the program CHANGE).

EXERCISES

1. Give a statement that performs each of the following operations.
   (a) Reads the next record from *Unit* 8 into the entire array A using the FORMAT statement 100. If an error occurs, a branch is to be taken to the statement 400.
   (b) Reads record 52 from *Unit* 12 into the variable X and the first N elements of a linear array P using the FORMAT statement 105. The I-O status code is to be put in the variable K.
   (c) Writes an array JARY into record 71 of an unformatted file.
   (d) Backspaces *Unit* 5.
   (e) Rewinds *Unit* 6.
   (f) Puts an EOF indicator on *Unit* JUNIT.
   (g) Writes the number 9999 as a sentinel in record 100 of the file connected to *Unit* 7 using the FORMAT statement 105.

2. Determine the values of the variables after each of the following program segments have been executed.
   (a) DATA X,Y,Z /5.0, −1.0, 0.0/

   .
   .
   .

   WRITE (15,105) X,Y,Z
   BACKSPACE (15)
   READ (15, 105) A
   BACKSPACE (15)
   READ (15, 105) B
   (b) DATA (J(I), I=1,5) /2.0, 0.0, −1.0, 2∗1.0/

   .
   .
   .

   WRITE (16, 18, REC=8)(J(I), I=1,5)
   READ (16, 18, REC=8)(J(I), I=1,5,2)
   (c) The values in J if the statements

   WRITE (16, 18, REC=8)(J(I), I=1,5)
   READ (16, 18, REC=8)(J(I), I=5,1,−1)

   were appended to those in part (b).

3. Assume an array A with 100 rows and 100 columns.
   (a) Write a program segment, including the OPEN, CLOSE, and ENDFILE statements, that will write the first M rows and N columns of the array to a sequential formatted file MATRIX. The values of M and N are to be stored in the first record and the columns of the array are to be stored in the succeedings records.
   (b) Write a program segment that will list the contents of MATRIX.
   (c) Write a program that will change the element in the Jth row and Kth column of the array in MATRIX.
   (d) Assume that MATRIX is a direct file and modify the solution to part (c) accordingly.
   (e) Expand the answer to part (d) so that the segment can interactively change the elements of the array in MATRIX.

4. Write the subroutine SORT needed by the program SCHANG in Fig. 8-18. (*Hint:* Input only the keys and sort the keys using an insertion sort. As the sort proceeds, the association between the keys and the record numbers must be maintained. Then copy the original scratch file into a second scratch file using the record numbers that have been sorted according to their keys. Close the old scratch file and reopen the new scratch under the *Unit* associated with the old file.)

5. Assume that the sample types are ordered and rewrite the subroutine LOOKUP in Fig. 8-20 so that it uses a binary search instead of a sequential search.

6. Modify the program SCHANG so that it accommodates the addition and deletion of weights.

7. Use the flowchart in Fig. 8-21 to write a program UPDATE for updating a sequential formatted file MED.DAT. Assume that each master record consists of a four-character key followed by 100 integers, and that the transaction records consist of a key and one of the forms:

> Delete—A "D"
>
> Change—A "C" followed by the position of the change within the record and by the new integer
>
> Insert—An "I" followed by 100 integers

8. Write a program for changing ordered formatted direct files interactively. The files may contain up to 4000 records and are to begin with a directory which may be several records long. Each record is to consist of a character string of length 80. The directory is to be a single linear array with eight elements/record. The elements are to be keys that are ten characters long, and they are to be ordered in the same sequence as the records. The program is to first input the name of the file to be changed and then input the changes. The changes are to have the form

Record key	Position of first character to be changed	No. of characters to be replaced	Replacement string

The program is to continue to make changes until the command 'QUIT' is given.

9. Assume the files are not ordered, but that the directory includes a record number pointer array, and then modify the solution to Exercise 8 accordingly.

8-5 INQUIRE STATEMENT

The purpose of an INQUIRE statement is to examine the attributes of a *Unit* or file. It has the form

INQUIRE *(Unit or File Specifier,* ERR=*Label, Inquiry Specifiers)*

where a unit or file specifier, but not both, is given, the error specifier is optional, and the *Inquiry Specfiers* are as summarized in Fig. 8-23. The INQUIRE statement can be used to determine information about a *Unit* or about a file, even if the file is

Inquiry Specifier	Value Returned by INQUIRE Statement
IOSTAT = *I-O Status*	Same as for an OPEN statement
EXIST = *Exist*	Logical variable, becomes .*TRUE*. or .*FALSE*. depending on whether or not the *Unit* or file exists
OPENED = *Opened*	Logical variable, becomes .*TRUE*. or .*FALSE*. depending on whether or not the *Unit* or file is opened
NAMED = *Named*	Logical variable, becomes .*TRUE*. or .*FALSE*. depending on whether or not the *Unit* is connected to a named file
NUMBER = *Number*	Integer variable, becomes the *Unit* associated with the specified file
NAME = *Name*	String variable, becomes the name of the file connected to the specified *Unit*
ACCESS = *Access*	String variable, becomes the type, 'SEQUENTIAL' or 'DIRECT', of the specified *Unit* or file
SEQUENTIAL = *Seq.*	String variable, becomes 'YES' or 'NO' depending on the type of the specified file
DIRECT = *Direct*	
FORM = *Form*	String variable, becomes the form 'FORMATTED' of 'UNFORMATTED', of the specified *Unit* or file
FORMATTED = *Form*	String variable, becomes 'YES' or 'NO' depending on the form of the specified file
UNFORMATTED = *Unform*	
RECL = *Length*	Integer variable, becomes the record length for direct files
NEXTREC = *Pointer*	Integer variable, becomes the file pointer
BLANK = *Blank*	String variable, becomes 'NULL' or 'ZERO' according to the blank specifier

FIGURE 8-23 *Summary of the Inquiry Specifiers.*

not connected. For example, the need for an INQUIRE statement may arise because different files may be assigned to a *Unit* depending on the path taken through an IF block. After emerging from the IF block the program may need to know which file has been connected. The statement

INQUIRE (8, NAME = CSTRG)

would cause the name of the file connected to *Unit* 8 to be put in the string variable CSTRG.

A frequent application of the INQUIRE statement is to determine the record length of a direct file. In program LIST in Fig. 8-14 the record length had to be input by the user. The INQUIRE statement

INQUIRE (FILE = 'BIO.DAT', RECL=N)

could have been inserted in the program to put the record length in N.

8-6 FILE SYSTEMS

For the most part a FORTRAN programmer needs to know very little about how the system stores information, but because the programmer does get involved in giving system commands, punching JCL cards, and writing I-O statements, it is worthwhile to have an overall understanding of the way data and programs are typically stored and referenced. Figure 8-24 gives an overview of the normal organization of files (including programs) in a general-purpose computer system. This exact structure does not apply to all systems but it does encompass the fundamental concepts.

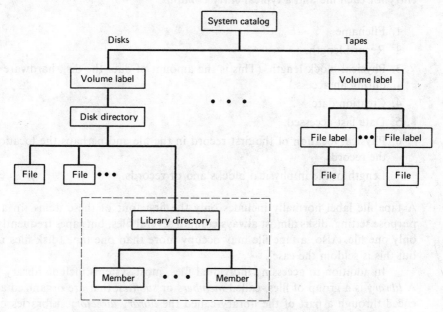

FIGURE 8-24 *Diagram of the organization of a system's data structure.*

A general-purpose system has one mass storage device, called the *system device*, which is for storing the programs and data that are basic to the operation of the system (e.g., the operating system). The key referencing mechanism, called the *system catalog*, is stored on the system device and is closely associated with the operating system. Each disk or tape (or other mass storage medium) that is mounted on a device in the system is called a *volume*, and each volume contains a set of data called a *volume label*, which includes an identifying name or number. For each file there is an entry in the system catalog which indicates:

1. The name of the file.
2. The volume name or number containing the file.
3. The type and/or name of the device on which the volume must be mounted.

Whenever a file is requested by either an executing program or a system command,

379

the operating system first references the system catalog to determine the device and then inputs the volume label from the device. (If necessary, the operating system will print a message to tell the computer operator to mount the needed volume.)

At this point, the action takes different courses according to the type of device. A disk is structured by having a device directory that points to its files, and a tape has its files longitudinally distributed along the tape with each file beginning with a file label. For a disk, the volume label also includes the location of its directory. A file is found on a disk by looking in its directory and is found on a tape by sequentially reading the tape file labels until the desired file is found. There is a disk directory entry for each file and a typical entry contains:

1. Filename.
2. Record length.
3. Physical block length. (This is the amount of data the disk hardware transfers during an access.)
4. Creation date.
5. Date last accessed.
6. Physical location of the first record in the file and perhaps the locations of all the records.
7. Length of file in physical blocks and/or records.

A tape file label normally includes only the first four of these items. In a general-purpose setting, disks almost always contain several files, but tapes frequently contain only one file. Also, a tape file may occupy more than one tape (disk files may, too, but this is seldom the case).

In addition to accessing individual files, most systems include library facilities. A *library* is a group of files, called *members* or *subfiles*, that are organized and referenced through a part of the library called the *library directory*. Libraries ordinarily consist of closely related files that need to be accessed as a group. There are both system libraries and user libraries. The intrinsic functions constitute the most familiar example of a system library. Libraries are almost always stored on disks.

Figure 8-25 depicts the overall referencing procedure. The only actions that involve the programmer are formulating the system commands or writing the file I-O program statements. Building a library is also a matter of providing the operating system with the proper commands. As mentioned before, the system commands vary considerably from one system to the next and a detailed discussion of them would not be practical here.

As a final note, it is important to protect against loss of data or programs due to a system malfunction. It is possible for disk heads to "crash" (scratch the recording surface) or for the transmission to a tape or disk write head to become garbled. Also, human errors may result in the wrong tape being mounted or the wrong files being erased. It is therefore important to keep at least one backup copy of the important files. Backup copies are normally stored on tape because tapes:

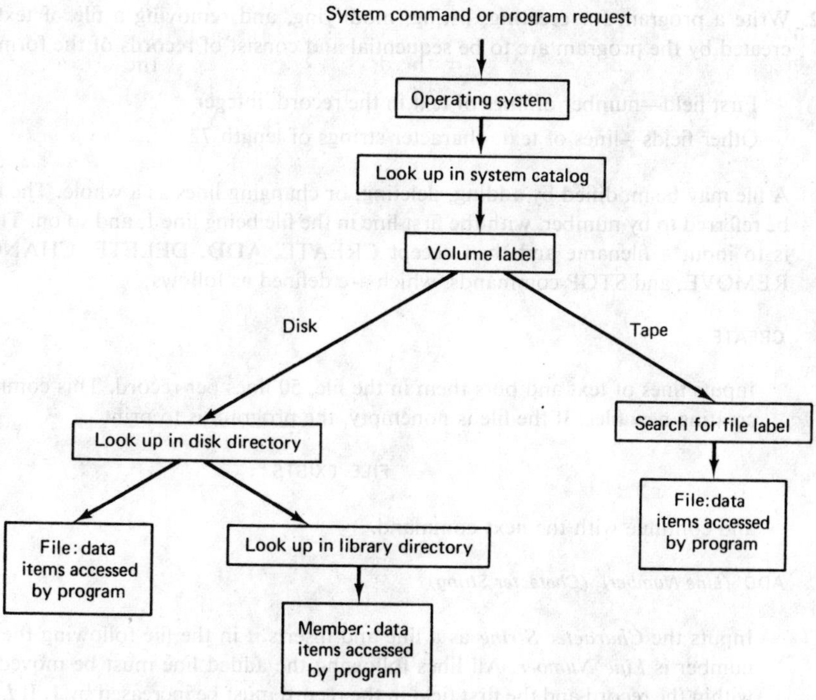

System command or program request

Operating system

Look up in system catalog

Volume label

Disk

Look up in disk directory

File: data items accessed by program

Look up in library directory

Member: data items accessed by program

Tape

Search for file label

File: data items accessed by program

FIGURE 8-25 *Typical system referencing procedure.*

1. Are inexpensive.

2. Can be dismounted and easily stored in a secure place.

3. Are normally updated by copying, thus the original information cannot be destroyed while the updating process is taking place.

4. Can be physically protected by a plastic ring, called a *write ring*, whose absence prevents the hardware from writing on the tape regardless of the command given to (or invented by) the computer.

Business, government, and research establishments normally have fixed procedures for backing up files. If the backup decisions are left to the individual, the only advice is: *Proceed at your own risk*.

PROGRAMMING PROBLEMS

1. Modify Programming Problem 1 at the end of Chap. 7 so that a direct file CHPAT is used to store the character patterns instead of a preassigned array. Also write a program for modifying and listing CHPAT.

2. Write a program for creating, listing, modifying, and removing a file of text. The files created by the program are to be sequential and consist of records of the form

    First field—number of lines of text in the record, integer

    Other fields—lines of text, character strings of length 72

A file may be modified by adding, deleting, or changing lines as a whole. The lines are to be referred to by number, with the first line in the file being line 1, and so on. The program is to input a filename and then accept CREATE, ADD, DELETE, CHANGE, LIST, REMOVE, and STOP commands, which are defined as follows:

CREATE

    Inputs lines of text and puts them in the file, 50 lines per record. This command is for creating new files. If the file is nonempty, the program is to print

                     FILE EXISTS

    and continue with the next command.

ADD *(Line Number) (Character String)*

    Inputs the *Character String* as a line and inserts it in the file following the line whose number is *Line Number*. All lines following the added line must be moved down one within the record and the first field in the record must be increased by 1. If *Line Number* is 0, the line is to be added to the beginning of the file.

DELETE *(Line Number)*

    Deletes the line whose number is *Line Number*. All lines following the deleted line must be moved up one within the record and the first field in the record must be decreased by 1.

CHANGE *(Line Number) (Character String)*

    Inputs the *Character String* and uses it to replace the line whose number is *Line Number*.

LIST

    Causes the entire file to be printed. If the file has been modified, the file is to be copied before it is printed.

REMOVE

    Causes the file to be deleted from the mass storage device.

STOP

    Causes the program to copy the remainder of the file, output an EOF, close the file, and terminate the program's execution.

The *Line Numbers* in sucessive ADD, DELETE, and CHANGE commands must be in ascending order. If a command is found to have a smaller *Line Number* than the previous command, the message

INVALID LINE NUMBER

is to be printed and the program is to continue with the next command. No single record is to exceed 100 lines and if an ADD command attempts to exceed this limit, the message

RECORD CAPACITY EXCEEDED

is to be printed and the program is to finish copying the file, add an EOF, close the file, and terminate. Test the program by first creating a file that contains the source code for the program. Then modify the file by adding, deleting, and modifying comment lines within the program. After the modifications have been made, list the program and then remove the file.

3. Write a program similar to the one described in Programming Problem 2, except that direct files are to be assumed. In addition to the filename the total number of records must be input. If this number is exceeded during an execution of the CREATE command, the message

FILESIZE EXCEEDED

is to be printed and the program is to terminate. Also, the first record is to be a directory which contains the line numbers of the first lines in the other records. The directory is to be brought into memory at the beginning of the program and must be updated during the execution of the CREATE, ADD, and DELETE commands.

9

PROGRAM DESIGN

Program design is the process of stating the structure and algorithms of a program to such a level that the coding of the program can proceed without further definition. The design and coding of a program should be directed at producing a "good" program, that is, one which has the following characteristics:

1. It works.
2. It is well documented and easily understood by other programmers.
3. It is easy to maintain or modify.

It is important to understand the meaning of a working program. The programmer may create a program that does what he or she intended it to do, but if the program does not meet the specifications to the expectation of the requestor, it is not a working program. For scientific programs, not only does the program need to proceed according to the intended algorithm, but it must be written so that the results are within the specified error limits.

If a program is not well documented and easily understood by other programmers, it has failed to provide for the basic needs of the organization that is to use and maintain it. In addition to working and being well documented, a good program must be designed so that modifications to the program, including new features, are easy to implement and corrections can be easily made.

Section 9-1 discusses top-down design and modular programming, and the following section describes how to document a program, including module documentation, file documentation, and documentation for the person who will use the program. Section 9-3 summarizes much of the information in Secs. 9-1 and 9-2 by providing an example of a top-down design for an inventory update program. Section 9-4 is primarily directed toward scientific applications and surveys the more prominent sources of numerical errors, errors that may occur due to the limitations of the computer and/or the algorithm used to write the program.

9-1　TOP-DOWN DESIGN

The top-down design technique is a widely accepted method of designing a program so that the result will meet the criteria listed in the introduction above. Top-down design is a natural way of designing a computer program or, for that matter, anything else. It involves taking a large problem and breaking it down into smaller and smaller pieces until it becomes a series of small, easily managed subproblems. Top-down design takes a general problem statement and produces a precise definition of:

1. The program inputs from mass storage files as well as terminal and card inputs.
2. The program outputs to mass storage files and printed reports.
3. The data used by the program and how they are stored both internally and externally.
4. The process for converting the input data into the desired results.

This design method defines the overall logical structure of a program before defining the detailed elements. By defining the logical structure (i.e., by completely specifying the inputs, the data, the outputs, and the process), the designer has structured a solution to the problem. By postponing the detailed elements, the designer is better able to keep the overall program in mind and thus better able to optimize trade-offs for the benefit of the program as a whole, rather than suboptimizing for only one small part of the program. Top-down design should be distinguished from structured programming (although both are important to a good program) in that top-down design is a method for arriving at a well-defined, complete specification of a program, whereas structured programming is a method for implementing the design.

9-1-1　Inputs to the Design Process

In the same manner that a program must have input data in order to produce an output, the design process must have input in order to produce a correct program design. This input consists of a general program specification in some form. The specification defines the requestor's needs, and it may be as simple as a verbal request or as detailed as the requestor desires. Who is the "requestor" of a program? It may be a systems analyst who has the job of defining many programs to complete a general function (such as inventory management), a user of the computer system who is entirely unfamiliar with computers, or another programmer who sees the need for a general subprogram that would be useful to all the programmers in a company or other organization. In any case, the general specification usually tells only what the program should do. The program designer must take this general specification, solidify it into specific, precise definitions, and add his or her own knowledge of programming to provide the complete set of information necessary to design the program.

What should be included in the general specification? Of course, it should be as precise as possible and should include a description of what the program is to do in as much detail as the requestor can provide, but only to the extent of defining what has to be accomplished by the program, not how the program should accomplish it. It should also include a description of all the files that are to be used by the program, both those that are already on the computer system and those that must be created before the program can be used. The general specification should not be considered "frozen" or final when the programmer receives it but should be viewed as a working document to be used as a means of communication between the requestor and the programmer. In addition to his or her own knowledge of programming or knowledge of the particular problem, the designer should consult reference material on the subject, such as other company or research records, or texts that contain information on the problem, and should consult with programmers who have worked on similar problems in the past.

9-1-2 The Method of Top-Down Design

As mentioned earlier, top-down design involves breaking a large problem into smaller subproblems that are easier to deal with. If FORTRAN had a statement

UPDATE INVENTORY

we would have no problem in writing a program to update an inventory file that would work on any system that has a FORTRAN compiler. Unfortunately, FORTRAN has no such statement, so we have to proceed to define subproblems that are simpler and can be more easily implemented in FORTRAN. One approach is to start the processing with functions that commonly appear when solving any programming problem. Figure 9-1 shows a typical breakdown of the modules that might exist in a program. Typically, a program has some form of initialization, such as DATA statements, PARAMETER statements, or assignment statements, as well as an OPEN statement for each file. Then the program performs a loop which includes reading a record, performing some computations, which may also involve reading records, and writing some type of output. Sooner or later the loop will be terminated either because a count has reached its limit or because an EOF or sentinel has been encountered. Then the program will perform some termination functions, such as printing totals or closing files. As illustrated in Fig. 9-1 by the blocks A, B, and C, the compute function (or any of the other functions) may be broken into smaller subproblems.

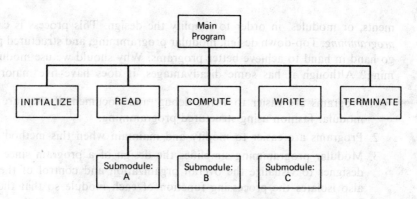

FIGURE 9-1 *The organization of a typical program.*

The most important part of the top-down design process is to make a rigorous and formal effort to specify the input, processing function, and output of each module at each level. The key to this methodology is that this specification be a formal, written document. Too often programmers fall into the trap of loose, informal specifications and assume that everything is defined, only to realize later that the whole design must be reconsidered and rewritten. The designer should not spend time on how the module will be written but concentrate on defining the input, processing function, and output of each module.

The input, process, and output of each module should be explained on a single sheet of paper. If this cannot be done in terms of the computation or operation involved (i.e., 30 to 50 pseuodcode statements or a short paragraph), explain it in terms of lower-level modules that will be called from this module. This effectively limits the sizes of the modules, and restricting the sizes of the modules is an important part of top-down design. The design of the data interface between a given module and other modules is also very important, because data are the communication link between the given module and the rest of the program.

As each level is designed, errors in the design of the next higher level may become apparent. At this point the higher-level modules should be reexamined and redesigned as necessary. This process is called *stepwise refinement.* This is the feedback mechanism in top-down design which allows the design to be refined gradually as it becomes more and more complete. When working at one level within a program, there is frequently a great temptation to become absorbed in the details of the lower levels. This urge should be resisted. The programmer should develop a discipline for concentrating on the current level and the stepwise refinement of the levels above it. If some aspect of the program that is crucial to the entire program must be developed out of order, one should develop it and then immediately return to the top-down design procedure. Too often, when it is essential that some small part of a program be designed in advance of its normal schedule, the programmer forgets about the top-down design process and proceeds randomly toward completing the design.

In the foregoing discussion we have divided the program into program segments, or modules, in order to simplify the design. This process is called *modular programming*. Top-down design, modular programming, and structured programming go hand in hand to achieve better programs. Why should we use modular programming? Although it has some disadvantages, it does have five major advantages:

1. Programs are easier to write, debug, and document if they are written in a modular fashion using structured programming.
2. Programs are easier to modify and maintain when this method is used.
3. Modular programming simplifies the design of a program since it allows the designer to visualize the overall organization and control of the program. It also isolates the processing function of each module so that the subproblem being addressed by the module is easier to solve.
4. The management of a large programming project is easier with modular programs since there is more flexibility in assigning the tasks.
5. Modular programming limits the communication between a module and the rest of the system to a well-defined interface. This limits the effect on other modules when one module is changed.

There are some disadvantages to modular programming, however, and these should be taken into consideration if they will seriously affect a project:

1. Modular programming requires that a program be carefully designed before it is coded into FORTRAN and, in some cases, this may cause an increase in programming time. However, this increase is usually more than offset by the decrease in maintenance time.
2. It can sometimes be less efficient in its utilization of computer processing time.
3. It may use slightly more computer memory space than is necessary.
4. It may not be feasible in real-time systems (those that require a response in a very short time, such as industrial manufacturing plant control systems) and on-line systems (those that require that a program be rapidly loaded and executed in order to respond quickly to a user's terminal, e.g., a bank teller machine). Time and memory space tend to be critical and, in such programs, time and space considerations may take precedence over having a well-structured modular design.

Even though these disadvantages exist, a programmer should look long and hard at a problem before deciding not to use modular programming.

    Deciding to divide a program into modules is one part of the solution to designing a program; the other part is deciding how the division is to be accomplished. The division of a program into modules may be based on program segment size, the processing functions to be performed, control coupling, data coupling, or some combination of these properties. Each module should be small, hopefully one page

(50 statements) or less, it should be relatively independent of the other modules so that it can be changed without significantly affecting the rest of the program, and it should be functional in that it performs a specific part of the overall processing task. Separating a program into modules by function is based on identifying all the tasks a program must accomplish and making each task a separate module. Some examples of separate functions are file searching, sorting, computational algorithms, and I-O tasks. I-O routines and computational routines should always be put into different modules. This will allow all I-O to be done in one place so that any program changes caused by changes in the files can be made easily. As mentioned in Chap. 6, control, data, and common coupling should also be taken into account. Too much control coupling leads either to an unstructured program or to an overreliance on flags. Too much data and common coupling may result in lengthy argument lists and/or a complicated assortment of common areas, either of which will increase the chance of error and reduce the program's readability and efficiency.

Modules can also be defined by the sequence of the program, by breaking the problem into the major activities to be performed sequentially from the start of the program. The best method is to combine functionality and sequence into a hierarchy of program flow so that each module is functional but also each is performed in sequence. Figure 9-1 is an example of this approach, in which the functions INI-TIALIZE, READ, COMPUTE, WRITE, and TERMINATE are separated into modules and these modules are executed in sequence (left to right), with READ, COMPUTE, and WRITE being included in a loop. If a choice must be made between functionality or sequence, functionality is preferable since this will allow for easier maintenance. Flowcharts are used primarily to indicate sequence and hierarchical diagrams show the functional modularity.

Some precautionary measures must be observed when breaking a program into modules. Do not overmodularize by creating very small modules (i.e., less than 10 statements). One or two small modules, if they perform a very specific function, would not cause problems, but if the entire program consists of small modules it will be very difficult for other programmers to understand and it may consume extra computer time. Try to use symbolic parameters (i.e., the PARAMETER statement) rather than constants since this allows for easier modification later should the values of the constants change. Do not share temporary or auxiliary storage locations between modules. *Temporary storage locations* are those used for intermediate computations and a problem arises if, while intermediate data are stored in the temporary location, another module is called which also uses the temporary storage location, thus destroying the data from the first module. This can be a very difficult bug to find.

As was discussed earlier, it is important that each module, at each level, be documented completely (see Sec. 9-2 on how to document a module). Incomplete specification and documentation at a level will invariably lead to a poor overall design and a false sense of security about the design.

9-1-3 Design Output

The output of the design process is a description of the overall organization of the program and a specification for each module. The overall program specification, which is discussed in detail in Sec. 9-2, should include:

1. A description of the files accessed by the program.
2. A list of the principal I-O with external devices.
3. A description of the common areas.
4. A discussion of the more important sets of data to be communicated between the modules.
5. A hierarchical diagram accompanied by a description of the method used by the program and a one sentence explanation of each module.
6. The module specifications.
7. A commented listing of the program.

Each module specification should include:

1. A title.
2. An entry name.
3. A description of inputs.
4. A description of outputs.
5. A description of errors detected.
6. A description of the algorithm used.

Every module in the program should have a one-line title that describes what the module does and, of course, an entry name (usually, this is also the module name) must be specified so that calling modules will be able to reference the module. The inputs to the module consist of the arguments passed into the module, the common areas used by the module, and the inputs from mass storage and external devices. The argument types should be clearly specified and the reasons why the arguments and common areas are needed should be given in the process description. Any files that are read by the module should be described only by their names, since file descriptions are given in the overall program specification.

The outputs of the module consist of a list of the arguments and common areas which are modified by the module and of the outputs to mass storage and external devices. Some of these outputs are modified inputs, whereas others are variables, arrays, and so on, that are initially assigned values within the module. For those that are modified inputs, a brief description of the modifications could be given, but detailed descriptions should be reserved for the description of the module's algorithm. As with input files, output files should be referred to only by their names in the module specification and detailed descriptions of the output files should be included in the overall program specification. Any error conditions that may be detected by the module should be listed together with descriptions of how they are processed and how the errors are indicated to the calling module or user. Error messages and their meanings should also be included in the specification.

The algorithm or process used by a module should be presented in two ways. A narrative description should be included for those programmers who will later be interested in how the module accomplishes its purpose, and a flowchart or set of pseudocode should be included so that the FORTRAN statements can be written without further decisions having to be made.

9-2 PROGRAM DOCUMENTATION

Program documentation is a set of descriptive material that provides both general and detailed information about a program. It should serve as a reference for:

1. Administrative purposes.
2. The program designer and those who are to maintain the program.
3. Those who are to use the program.

Good, accurate, and complete documentation is obtainable with a minimum amount of work if it is done with each step of the design and programming process.

Program documentation normally consists of two or three items, the program specification, the user's guide, and, perhaps, an operator's guide. The program specification not only tells the programmer how to write the program, but also tells other programmers, such as the maintenance programmer, how the program works and where to make changes in order to add new features. The user's guide is the document that tells someone other than the programmer how to use the program, as well as how to cope with any errors that may arise while it is being run. The third document is an operator's guide, which may be needed by the computer system operator, although is not usually required except in the case of large and complicated programs. The operator's guide should detail the requirements necessary for the program to run.

The program specification is the main working document for the programmers who write and maintain the program. It should include a title and perhaps a preface which describes how it is to be used. If a set specification format is consistently used throughout an organization, a preface may not be necessary. If the program has more than 10 modules, a table of contents should be included so that the information on a particular module is easy to find.

The specification should also include an introduction that describes, in general terms, what the program does and how it performs its job. The introduction should be complete but should not contain the detailed information found in later sections. It should provide an overview of the program, but no more.

All the files that are used by the program must be described; however, if the program is part of a system of programs and the files are described in the system documentation, the files need only be listed in the program specification. If the program is not part of a system, each input file should be described in detail in the program specification. The contents of a file description are shown in Fig. 9-2. Nor-

1. The file name.

2. The record length (both a minimum and maximum should be given if the record length can vary).

3. A description that indicates the following field attributes for each type of record:

    (a) The name of the field
    (b) The starting position of the field within the record
    (c) The length of the field
    (d) The type of data contained in the field (integer, real, etc.)
    (e) A description of the contents of the field (voltage, tax, temperature, etc.)

FIGURE 9-2 *Contents of a file description.*

mally, the description of the inputs also includes a description of any parameters that are passed into the program.

The description of the outputs should be similar to the description of the inputs. In addition to the output files, all reports, or printout, need to be specified in detail as to what is to be printed (field size, type, etc., just as for each file). Also, headings and titles should be indicated. Along with the report description a sample report is needed which includes representative data. If the program is an interactive program, each interactive message should be described, and a summary of the expected responses to each query must be given.

The overall process used by the program should be shown using three separate elements:

1. Brief narrative description
2. Hierarchical diagram
3. Module descriptions

The narrative description should be short (one page or less) and should describe what the program does, not how it does it (i.e., the program's objective). As explained in Chap. 3, the hierarchical diagram shows each module and its relationship to the other modules in the program. Figure 9-3 gives a typical hierarchical diagram. The uppermost box in this diagram shows the module that contains the PROGRAM statement, and the modules called by this module are shown in the second row of boxes. The third row of boxes contains the modules called by the modules shown in the second row, and so on. Notice that module G in Fig. 9-3 is called by three different modules (B, C, and E) and that it appears three times. Because the hierarchical

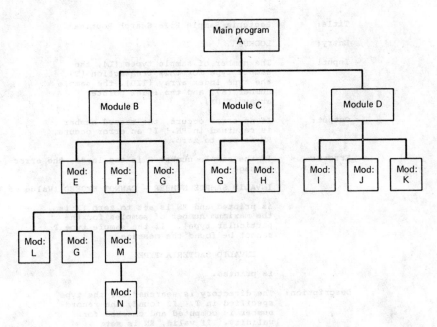

FIGURE 9-3 *Example of a hierarchical diagram.*

diagram is designed to show organization, a module is to appear each time that it is subordinate to another module.

A detailed description of each module should be included and Fig. 9-4 shows an example of a module description for the file search subroutine LOOKUP given in Fig. 8-20. The module description includes a one-line title which should describe the function performed by the module. It also includes the entry name, which in this case is also the name of the subroutine. The list of inputs to the module is to include the arguments passed into the module and all COMMON variables or arrays that are used by the module. As previously mentioned, files are not included here since these are shown elsewhere in the program specification. The list of outputs is to show any arguments or common areas which are modified, but again, files are not shown. All the errors that may occur within the module are listed and how each error is handled by the module is described together with how the error indication is returned to the calling program (e.g., RN set to zero). The description section includes the method (or algorithm) used by the module to perform its function. It should be as detailed as necessary to describe exactly how the module operates.

The last item in the program specification is to be a well-documented, current program listing. Providing good comments should become a habit with every programmer. It takes some extra work to create good comments, but if the comments are written along with the program, the amount of extra work is small. At the beginning of each program unit, there should be comments which explain the function of the program unit and the algorithm it uses to fulfill its function. These opening comments should include definitions for the variables that appear in the program unit.

```
Title:          Bacteria Sample File Search Routine

Entry:          LOOKUP

Input:          The number of sample types (L), the
                sample type for this transaction (T),
                the type index array (TID), the sample
                number (S), and the index pointer
                array (TIDX).

Output:         If no error occurs, the record number
                is returned in RN.  If an error occurs,
                RN is set to zero.

Errors:         If the sample number S is too large, the error
                message

                INVALID SAMPLE NUMBER - CANNOT EXCEED (Value of X)

                is printed and RN is set to zero (X is
                the maximum number of samples for the
                particular type).  If the sample type T
                cannot be found the message

                     INVALID BACTERIA TYPE

                is printed.

Description:    The directory is searched for the type
                specified in T.  If found, the record
                number is computed and checked for
                validity.  If valid, RN is set
                to the record number, and a RETURN
                statement is executed.  If not valid
                or if the sample type T is not found, then
                an error message is printed, RN is set
                to zero, and a RETURN is executed.
```

FIGURE 9-4 *Example of a module description.*

(The entire module description could be included as opening comments.) Comments that are interspersed with the program statements should have blank lines above and below them for readability. (Do not forget to include an * or other valid symbol in the first column.) The body of every IF and DO sequence needs to be indented two or more positions to the right of the IF or DO, and the ENDIF or CONTINUE statement which terminates the IF or DO should be aligned with the IF or DO (this practice has been followed in the examples in this book). Figure 9-5 shows a summary of the contents of the program specification.

In addition to the specification, most programs should have a user's guide for the person who only wants to know how to use the program and does not care how it performs its function. This manual must be written with the user in mind, and it should not require any reference to the specification; however, most of the information can be taken directly from the specification. Figure 9-6 shows a summary of the user documentation, which includes the title, preface, and introduction. The input required from the user must be described in detail. Each output report should be described in detail and a sample report should be included. Again, output files should be listed by name, but no detailed description given. All interactive messages should be shown together with a description of the expected responses to each message. If no response

```
Title
Preface (instruction on how to use the document)
Table of contents (programs with 10 or more modules)
Introduction
Inputs
        - variables and arrays
        - files
Outputs
        - files
        - reports
            - example report
Interactive messages - including expected responses
Method
        - narrative
        - hierarchical diagram
        - module descriptions
                - module title
                - entry name
                - inputs (parameters and COMMON variables)
                - outputs (modified parameters and COMMON variables)
                - errors
                - description of the process
Error messages and recovery procedures
Commented program listing
```

FIGURE 9-5 *Program documentation summary.*

```
Title
Preface (description of how to use the document)
Introduction
Input
        - describe user input in detail
        - list the files without description
Output
        - describe each report and show a sample
        - list the files without description
Interactive Messages
        - describe the necessary responses
Method (brief description only)
Error Messages
        - include a description of the expected responses
```

FIGURE 9-6 *User documentation summary.*

is needed, this should be indicated. The method used by the program needs to be briefly described only to the point of alerting the user if the method may produce results inconsistent with other data. Error messages and a recovery procedure for each type of error are very important to the user, and sufficient time must be spent on this area to ensure that the user is able to recover successfully from any error condition.

9-3 TOP-DOWN DESIGN EXAMPLE

As an example of a top-down design, let us consider a program that will allow an interactive user to update a simple inventory file. The purpose of this program is to allow a user to change any of the fields of an inventory record except the part number field. The program should validate, as much as possible, that the new information is correct. Figure 9-7 shows a description of the inventory record, including a description of each of the fields within the record. The PN field is the part number and it is also the record key of the inventory record (i.e., this is the record key to be used in

Position	Field Name	Description
1-5	PN	Integer part number, values 1 to 99999
6-10	QOH	Integer quantity on hand, values 0 to 99,999
11-15	QOO	Integer quantity on order, values 0 to 99,999
16-23	DATE	Date the part was added to the file or was last updated. Alphanumeric and in the format MM/DD/YY
24-53	DESC	Part description, alphanumeric
54-58	VEND1	Integer, vendor number for the primary vendor, value 1 to 99999
59-63	VEND2	Integer, vendor number for the second source, value 1 to 99999

FIGURE 9-7 *Record format for the inventory problem.*

the direct-access READ and WRITE statements). The QOH field holds the number of parts currently in the warehouse. This field can never be negative. The QOO field holds the number of parts currently on order and cannot be negative. The DATE field contains the date that this part was placed in the file or the date on which the specification for the part was last updated. The DESC field contains an English description of the part, padded with blanks to 30 characters. The two vendor fields (VEND1 and VEND2) contain the numbers of the vendors who normally supply the part.

The general specification given to us consists of the foregoing file description and the commands that should be allowed for updating the fields. In this section we define the program specification for the update program and write some modules in FORTRAN, leaving some parts of the specification and some FORTRAN coding as exercises for the reader.

Using the top-down design method, the top module is called INVUPD (inventory update). Let us proceed, as in Fig. 9-1, to define the functions that might be needed by INVUPD. Initialization and termination functions will be needed, but since only one file is involved, these functions may be performed by INVUPD rather than defining separate modules for them. If these functions prove to be too long, we can update the hierarchical diagram later. Certainly, inventory records have to be read and INVRD is included to perform this function. The record must be displayed or printed on the user's terminal so that the user can see the current contents of the record. This is done with the module named DISP. We also need a module that will print the necessary messages and read in the data needed to update the fields of the record; in other words, to query the user concerning the update information. The module for performing this task is given the name QUERY. After the updates have been done, a module is needed to rewrite the inventory record and it is given the name INVWRT. In addition to these main modules, we also need to perform numeric validation at several points in the program and a module NUMVAL has been included to perform this function. Figure 9-8 shows a hierarchical diagram for the inventory update program. Note that NUMVAL is used by INVUPD to validate the part number (which is

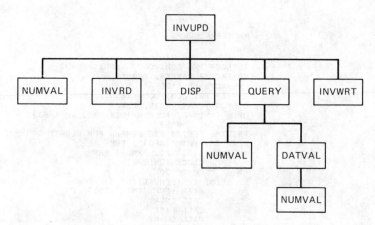

FIGURE 9-8 *Inventory update program hierarchical diagram.*

also the record number), by QUERY to validate QOH, QOO, VEND1, or VEND2, and by DATVAL to validate the month, day, and year of the date.

Figure 9-9 is the module specification for the INVUPD module. Note that this module performs the initialization for the program and it reads the part number from the user's terminal. It validates the part number (by calling NUMVAL) and then calls INVRD to read the record. If a record is found, it calls DISP to display (or print) the contents of the record on the user's terminal and then calls QUERY to update the fields of the record. When QUERY returns, INVWRT is called to

```
Title:          Top Level Update Module

Entry:          INVUPD

Input:          Inventory file.
                User terminal input.

Output:         Updated inventory file.
                Messages to the user's terminal.

Errors:         If no record having the given record number
                exists in the file, the error message

                INVALID DATA IN RECORD NUMBER

                is printed and the user is prompted
                for another record number.

Description:    A message is printed requesting the number
                of the record to be updated.  A record is
                read, NUMVAL is called to perform numeric
                validation, INVRD is called to read the
                record, DISP is called to display the
                record on the terminal, and QUERY is
                called to perform the update on the fields.
                After QUERY returns, INVWRT is called to
                rewrite the updated record back to the
                inventory file.  This module also
                performs all the program initialization
                and termination that is required.
```

FIGURE 9-9 *Module specification for INVUPD.*

```
PROGRAM INVUPD

            INTEGER PN, OOH, QOO, VEND1, VEND2
            CHARACTER DATE*8, DESC*30
            CHARACTER BUF*80
            COMMON PN, OOH, QOO, VEND1, VEND2
            COMMON /CHAR/ DATE, DESC
            OPEN (UNIT=8, ACCESS='DIRECT', RECL=63)
            DO 10 I=1, 99999
            PRINT*, 'ENTER REC NUMBER FOR UPDATE OR END'
            READ (*, FMT='(A80)') BUF
            IF (BUF(1:3) .EQ. 'END') THEN
                   CLOSE (UNIT=8)
                   GO TO 20
               ELSE IF (NUMVAL(BUF,5)) THEN
                   READ (BUF, FMT='(I5)') PN
                   CALL INVRD
                   CALL DISP
                   CALL QUERY
                   CALL INVWRT
               ELSE
                   PRINT*, 'INVALID DATA IN RECORD NUMBER'
            ENDIF
        10  CONTINUE
        20  CONTINUE
            END
```

FIGURE 9-10 *FORTRAN program for INVUPD module.*

rewrite the record on the inventory file. Figure 9-10 shows the FORTRAN statements for INVUPD. Figure 9-11 gives the module specification for the numeric validation routine and Figure 9-12 shows the FORTRAN statements for NUMVAL. NUMVAL examines each character of the input string to determine if the character is between 0 and 9 inclusive (spaces are ignored). It does not allow signs or decimal points since

```
Title:          Numeric Validation

Entry:          NUMVAL

Input:          A character string containing data to be
                validated and an integer containing the length
                of the string.

Output:         A logical value of .TRUE. or .FALSE. indicating
                whether the data contain only numbers.

Errors:         None

Description:    The character string is scanned character by
                character starting with the first character of
                the string.  Each character is checked to
                determine that it is between 0 and 9 inclusive.
                If any nonnumeric character (including a minus
                sign) is found, .FALSE. is returned, otherwise
                .TRUE. is returned.  Spaces are skipped.
```

FIGURE 9-11 *Module specification for NUMVAL.*

```
      LOGICAL FUNCTION NUMVAL (STRING, LENGTH)
      INTEGER LENGTH
      CHARACTER*(*) STRING
      NUMVAL = .TRUE.
      DO 10 I=1,LENGTH
          IF (STRING(I:I) .NE. ' ') THEN
                      IF (STRING(I:I) .LT. '0' .OR. STRING(I:I) .GT. '9')
     :                     NUMVAL = .FALSE.
              ELSE
          ENDIF
   10 CONTINUE
      END
```

FIGURE 9-12 *FORTRAN subprogram NUMVAL.*

the numbers involved must all be positive integers. Figure 9-13 gives the module specification for QUERY. This module performs the I-O and checking necessary to update each field of the inventory record.

Title: Field Update Module

Entry: QUERY

Input: Inventory record stored in COMMON.
               User terminal input on fields to update.

Output: Updated fields of the inventory record
               stored in COMMON.

Errors: Invalid numeric data in any field will cause
               an error message containing the field name
               and the invalid data to be printed. A new
               prompt for correct data will be printed, then
               new data will be read.

               Improper positioning of "/" in the date field
               will also generate a request for proper data.

Description: For each field in the record, a message requesting
               that the user update the field will be printed.
               Then update data are read. NUMVAL is called to
               validate all numeric fields and DATVAL is
               called to validate the DATE field. If invalid
               data is detected, an error message is printed
               and new data is requested for the field. If the
               data are correct, the field is updated (if
               no data are entered, the field is not changed)
               and a prompt for the next field is given until
               all fields are processed; then QUERY returns
               to the calling module.

FIGURE 9-13 *Module specification for QUERY.*

EXERCISES

1. Complete the program specification for the inventory program as described in Fig. 9-5.

2. Write the module specification and FORTRAN statements for DATVAL.

3. In Fig. 9-9 one of the errors occurs if no record having the given record number is found in the file. Since INVRD reads the file, how can INVUPD know that no record was found? (Examine Fig. 9-10.)

9-4 NUMERICAL ERRORS

In designing a program, particularly one that is to serve a scientific or engineering application, it is necessary to consider the numerical limitations introduced by the computer as well as those related to modeling and solving the problem. When solving a problem using a computer, one must resolve the difficulties related to:

1. The significant figures and roundoff
2. The discreteness due to the finiteness of the amount of data
3. The numerical techniques
4. The data selection and bad data
5. The choice of mathematical model

The first two constraints are directly related to the finiteness of the computer. Although the last three items must be considered when solving problems in general, if a digital computer is to be used they must be viewed in a special light. For example, experimental data must be selected in such a way that their amount is minimized, and they must be discrete (as opposed to continuous data, for which the measurement is made at all points in an interval).

9-4-1 Significant Figures and Roundoff

As we have seen, numbers can be stored in a computer to only a finite number of significant figures and during an input or computational operation the data or result must be rounded to the number of significant figures accommodated by the computer being used. The number of significant figures depends on whether single-precision or double-precision is being applied. The numbers of significant figures for some representative computers are listed in Fig. 1-8.

The fractional error of a quantity is defined to be the quotient

$$\frac{\text{error}}{\text{quantity}}$$

Estimates of the fractional errors of the results of the arithmetic operations as functions of the fractional errors of the operands are given in Fig. 9-14. (Verification of these fractional errors are requested in Exercise 1.) There are several important points that can be observed from this figure. Since the addition of two numbers of opposite signs is really subtraction, the only unbounded fractional errors occur when two numbers are being subtracted. Fortunately, these large fractional errors are associated with small results, so that the magnitudes of the errors are not necessarily large. However, subtraction is still the most frequent source of appreciable errors. As an example, suppose that the true operands being subtracted are 1.1 and 1.0 and the erroneous operands are 1.11 and 0.99. The operands have fractional errors of approximately 0.01 (or 1%) but the fractional error of the result is

$$\frac{(1.11 - 0.99) - (1.1 - 1.0)}{1.1 - 1.0} = 0.2 \text{ (or } 20\%)$$

Operation	Fractional error		Worst case	Worst case error
Addition	$\dfrac{(a + \epsilon a) + (b + \delta b) - (a + b)}{a + b}$	$= \dfrac{\epsilon a + \delta b}{a + b}$	ϵ, δ opposite signs $b \to -a$	Error $\to \infty$
Subtraction	$\dfrac{(a + \epsilon a) - (b + \delta b) - (a - b)}{a - b}$	$= \dfrac{\epsilon a - \delta b}{a - b}$	ϵ, δ opposite signs $b \to a$	Error $\to \infty$
Multiplication[1]	$\dfrac{(a + \epsilon a)(b + \delta b) - ab}{ab}$	$\approx \epsilon + \delta$	ϵ, δ same signs	$\lvert \epsilon \rvert + \lvert \delta \rvert$
Division[2]	$\dfrac{\dfrac{a + \epsilon a}{b + \delta b} - \dfrac{a}{b}}{\dfrac{a}{b}}$	$\approx \epsilon - \delta$	ϵ, δ opposite signs	$\lvert \epsilon \rvert + \lvert \delta \rvert$
Integer power[3]	$\dfrac{(a + \epsilon a)^n - a^n}{a^n}$	$\approx n\epsilon$	—	$n\epsilon$

a, b — actual values

ϵ — fractional error of quantity a

δ — fractional error of quantity b

$a + \epsilon a, b + \delta b$ — assumed values

[1] Approximation used: $\epsilon \delta \approx 0$

[2] Approximations used: $\dfrac{1}{1 + \delta} \approx 1 - \delta$ and $\epsilon \delta \approx 0$

[3] Approximation used: $\epsilon^i \approx 0$ for all $i > 1$

FIGURE 9-14 *Fractional errors resulting from the arithmetic operations.*

Addition (or subtraction of operands with opposite signs) tends to produce a fractional error that is the average of the fractional errors of the operands. If the true values of the operands were 1.1 and 1.0 and the erroneous values were 1.11 and 1.01, the fractional error of the sum would be

$$\frac{(1.11 + 1.01) - (1.1 + 1.0)}{1.1 + 1.0} \approx 0.01 \text{ (or } 1\%)$$

Hence the fractional error of the result is always in the neighborhood of the fractional errors of the operands.

For multiplication and division the fractional errors of the results tend to be twice those of the operands. If the same numbers are used as those appearing in the addition example, the fractional error of the product would be

$$\frac{(1.11 \times 1.01) - (1.1 \times 1.0)}{1.1 \times 1.0} \approx 0.02 \text{ (or } 2\%)$$

Taking a number to a power by successive multiplications (and perhaps a division) is another potentially serious source of errors. In the other operations, unless the operands are identical, there is a chance that the errors will cancel. This is true even for subtraction. When taking a number to an integer power the factors are all identical, and the fractional error in the result is always very nearly the power times the fractional error of the base. If the true number were 1.0 and the erroneous number were 1.01, the relative error of the number raised to the fourth power would be

$$\frac{1.01^4 - 1.0^4}{1.0^4} = 0.040641 \approx 0.04 \text{ (or 4\%)}$$

How does this discussion relate to significant figures and roundoff? Because there are only a finite number of bits to represent a number inside a computer, there is a built-in guarantee that most numbers are not precisely represented. If a single-precision number is stored to n significant figures, the average fractional error due to the finiteness of the computer alone would be in the vicinity of 10^{-n}. For $n = 6$ the approximate average fractional error caused by roundoff of the input data would be 10^{-6}. This may seem insignificant, but consider the simple program

```
PROGRAM DEMO
READ*, X,Y
Z = (X-Y)**10
PRINT*, Z
END
```

and assume that the values input to X and Y are 1.1 and 1.0. If the computer were to actually store 1.100001 and 0.999999, the difference would be 0.100002 and the fractional error of the difference would be 0.00002. After raising the difference to the tenth power, the fractional error of the result is approximately 0.0002 (or 0.02%).

One might note that the result is still good to almost four significant figures, but many scientific and engineering applications involve millions of computations and if the fractional errors tend to grow with each computation, the final results could be meaningless. The point is that if a problem involves a lot of computations, some attention should be given to the order in which the computations are made and subtractions and powers should be examined carefully. Double precision can be used if there is doubt about the integrity of single-precision results, but for problems involving an extraordinarily large number of computations (e.g., solving 100 equations in 100 unknowns), even double precision may not be adequate and special techniques may be required.

It is not possible to set forth a list of rules for improving accuracy that will apply in all cases, but there are a few hints that can be used often enough that they deserve some attention. Three of the most useful are:

1. When summing a large number of quantities whose magnitudes vary significantly, add the smaller quantities first.
2. When summing quantities with different signs, add the positive quantities, then add the negative quantities, and then add the two sums.
3. Avoid sets of biased quantities by rearranging the computational procedure.

If two numbers whose magnitudes are considerably different are added, most or all of the precision of the smaller number may be lost. For example, on a machine that stores numbers to six significant figures,

$$1000000 + 1 = 1000000$$

By adding several small numbers together before adding them to a much larger number, precision can be preserved. Once again assuming a six-digit machine, adding ten 1's together before adding them to 1 million would give the correct answer. Optimally, the numbers should be added in the ascending order of their magnitudes, but completely sorting the numbers before adding them is usually an unnecessary extreme.

By summing positive quantities, then negative quantities, and finally adding the results, several subtractions could be reduced to a single subtraction. From the discussion of subtraction above it should be intuitively clear that this technique would be advantageous. However, because of possible error cancellations, to prove that improved accuracy is obtained requires the application of the theory of statistics, and such proofs will not be discussed here.

To demonstrate the application of the third hint, suppose that the values of the elements of an array X are between 999.0 and 1001.0 and the following program segment is executed:

```
                REAL X(2000)
                     .
                     .
                     .
                READ*, (X(I), I=1,N)
                     .
                     .
                     .
                Y = 0.0
                DO 10 I=1,N
                    Y = Y+(X(I)-1000.0)**2
           10 CONTINUE
```

Up to three additional digits of accuracy could be retained by inputting the X values less 1000.0 and using the assignment statement

$$Y = Y+X**2$$

in the DO loop. To avoid actually changing the input data (the true values of the elements of X), the input could be done as follows:

```
                DOUBLE PRECISION A(10)
                     .
                     .
                     .
                DO 5 I=1,N,10
                    READ*, (A(J), J=1,10)
                    DO 3 K=1,10
                        X(I+K-1) = A(K) - 1000.0
            3       CONTINUE
            5 CONTINUE
```

This would retain the accuracy of single precision without using double precision for the entire array X.

If the fractional error for addition given in Fig. 9-14 were generalized to a sum of n terms, the outcome would be

$$\frac{\epsilon_1 a_1 + \epsilon_2 a_2 + \cdots + \epsilon_n a_n}{a_1 + a_2 + \cdots + a_n}$$

where the a_i's are the true values of the numbers and the ϵ_i's are their fractional errors. If there were no statistical biasing among the errors, they would tend to cancel and the fractional error of the sum would be much less than the worst-case error (even if all the numbers were to have the same sign).

To discuss errors from a statistical standpoint, let us return to the definition of standard deviation. If the mean of $a_1, \ldots, a_n$ is m, the standard deviation associated with these numbers as individual quantities is

$$\sigma = \sqrt{\frac{(a_1 - m)^2 + \cdots + (a_m - m)^2}{n}}$$

It is seen from this formula that the standard deviation is a measure of the deviation from the mean. The standard deviation for a set of data should be viewed as an abstract entity that indicates the variation of the data from the mean. Therefore, the quantity σ/m would be a measure of the fractional error. It has been shown that for data whose errors are not interdependent, the mean and standard deviation of the sum of n data items which all have mean m and standard deviation σ are nm and $\sigma \sqrt{n}$, respectively. Therefore, the "fractional error" of the sum is $\sigma/(m\sqrt{n})$ and the ratio of the fractional error of the sum to that of an individual datum is

$$\left(\frac{\sigma}{m\sqrt{n}}\right)\Big/\frac{\sigma}{m} = \frac{1}{\sqrt{n}}$$

This gives us the amazing conclusion that the "fractional error" of the sum is reduced to $1/\sqrt{n}$ times that of an individual datum. If there were 100 data items, this factor would be $\frac{1}{10}$.

Although the foregoing discussion is oversimplified and certainly the fractional error could never be less than that mandated by the limitation on significant figures, it does indicate an important point. Roundoff errors that occur while adding numbers do not necessarily build up and result in a large error in the sum. In fact, for errors in the input data that exceed the precision of the computer, there could be an improvement. This is related to the reason for taking a large number of samples when conducting a statistical study. When subtraction is involved (i.e., the signs of the terms may change), the limitation on significant figures is overriding and, as discussed earlier, serious errors can result.

In closing this discussion on significant figures it should be noted that a thorough discussion of the subject would involve complex mathematical concepts that are beyond the assumed background of the reader. For those who are adequately mathematically prepared, a few references that deal with this subject have been included in the Bibliography. The primary purpose of the discussion above, as well as the other discussions given in this section, is to alert the reader to some of the more prominent problems and to give some of the more common and easily understood solutions to these problems.

9-4-2 Discreteness and Numerical Technique

Most physical processes are defined by continuous changes (not a sequence of discrete changes), yet a digital computer must work with discrete data. The location of an airplane or the amount of water in a tank cannot change instantaneously, so in general their values for all times during a time interval cannot possibly be stored inside a computer. As a result, if a computer is to be applied to a scientific or engineering problem, which of the infinity of possible data points should be chosen, and how should they be used to simulate the real world? There is a voluminous amount of printed material attempting to answer these questions and they cannot be answered in this book, but it is worthwhile to consider some of the more central problems.

Usually, the problem of discreteness reduces to deciding how closely the data should be spaced in time or distance (or in terms of some other independent variable), and this decision is based on how "fast" the changes are taking place. For the curve shown in Fig. 9-15(a), it may be adequate to sample y at intervals of length 1, but

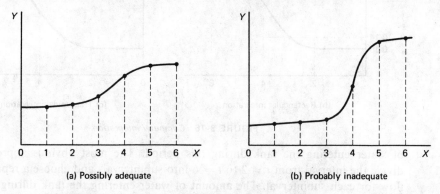

(a) Possibly adequate   (b) Probably inadequate

FIGURE 9-15 *Curves demonstrating the adequacy and inadequacy of spacing.*

for the curve in Fig. 9-15(b) such intervals would probably be inadequate in the vicinity of $x = 4$. Just what is adequate and what is inadequate depends on the accuracy expected. It is sometimes not enough to consider the rate of change, but one may also need to examine the rate of the rate of change, or the rate of the rate of the rate of change, and so on. Graphically, this is related to the sharpness of the bends and the changes in the sharpness of the bends.

Suppose that the curve in Fig. 9-16 represents the flow of water into a tank in liters per second and the total amount of water at $t = 6$ is needed. The amount of water in the tank after 2s is easy to compute because during this time the flow is constant at 0.1 ℓ/s. Obviously, the amount of water in the tank at $t = 2$ is $2 \times 0.1 = 0.2 \, \ell$. From $t = 2$ to $t = 6$ the flow varies and it is necessary to estimate the quantity

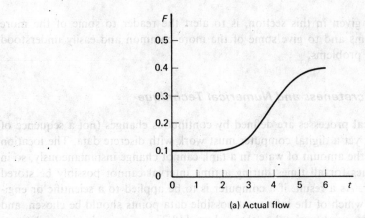

(a) Actual flow

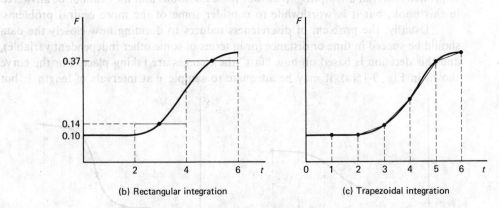

(b) Rectangular integration

(c) Trapezoidal integration

FIGURE 9-16 *Computer integration.*

of water entering the tank during this period. The most obvious approach is to divide the interval from $t = 2$ to $t = 6$ into subintervals and choose a representative flow for each subinterval. The amount of water entering the tank during each subinterval would then be estimated by multiplying the representative flow times the length of the interval. If, as shown in Fig. 9-16(b), subintervals of length 2 are selected and the flows at $t = 3$ and $t = 5$ are used as the representative flows, the total amount of water in the tank at $t = 6$ would be

$$0.1 \times 2 + 0.14 \times 2 + 0.37 \times 2 = 1.22 \ell$$

It is evident that the total amount of water is the area under the curve and the estimated amount is an approximation of this area. Intuitively, one would assume that by making the subintervals shorter, the area could be better approximated. In calculus the subintervals are permitted to become infinitesimally small and the resulting area is called the integral. Because of the finiteness of computers, integrals cannot be calculated precisely and a trade-off exists between the accuracy of the result and the amount of computer time and memory space that is required.

There are choices other than simply making the subintervals shorter. Selected points could be connected by straight-line segments as shown in Fig. 9-16(c), and then the area could be approximated by adding the trapezoidal areas. When this is done the process is called trapezoidal integration. The general formula for trapezoidal integration is

$$\frac{[f(x_1) + f(x_0)](x_1 - x_0)}{2} + \cdots + \frac{[f(x_n) + f(x_{n-1})](x_n - x_{n-1})}{2}$$

where f is the function being integrated and $x_1, \ldots, x_n$ are the abscissas at which the function is sampled. If the sample points are evenly spaced, it can easily be shown (see Exercise 5) that this formula reduces to

$$\Delta\left[\frac{f(x_0)}{2} + f(x_1) + \cdots + f(x_{n-1}) + \frac{f(x_n)}{2}\right]$$

where Δ is the length of the subintervals.

Going a step further, parabolic areas that span two subintervals could be used, in which case the following formula for evenly spaced sample points is obtained:

$$\frac{\Delta}{3}[f(x_0) + 4f(x_1) + 2f(x_2) + 4f(x_3) + 2f(x_4) + \cdots + 4f(x_{n-1}) + f(x_n)]$$

This formula is a generalized form of what is known as *Simpson's rule*. Other integration techniques that are based on higher-degree polynomials are available and their formulae can be found in books on numerical methods. As a general rule, the higher the degree of the approximating polynomial, the fewer the number of required sample points for a given accuracy, but the greater the number of arithmetic computations. Simpson's rule has been found to be a good compromise and is widely used.

The discussion above indicates that two major decisions must be made when using a digital computer to solve a continuous problem:

1. Which sample points should be used?
2. Which numerical technique(s) should be applied?

These decisions are not made independently, but are normally based on interrelated factors.

Another class of problems is demonstrated by the problem of computing the velocity and displacement of a falling object as a function of time. Assume that the force on the object due to the atmosphere is proportional to its velocity, and let m be its mass, g the gravitational pull, and b the constant of proportionality between the velocity and force caused by the atmosphere. If $t_0 = 0$, $t_1 = \Delta$, $t_2 = 2\Delta$, ... are the sample times and $v_i = v(t_i)$ for all i, then the change in the velocity between t_i and t_{i+1} is approximated by

$$v_{i+1} - v_i = \left(-\frac{b}{m}v_i + \frac{g}{m}\right)\Delta$$

Therefore, if the initial velocity v_0 is known, the subsequent velocities can be approximated by the equations

$$v_1 = v_0 + \left(-\frac{b}{m}v_0 + \frac{g}{m}\right)\Delta$$

$$v_2 = v_1 + \left(-\frac{b}{m}v_1 + \frac{g}{m}\right)\Delta$$

$$v_3 = v_2 + \left(-\frac{b}{m}v_2 + \frac{g}{m}\right)\Delta$$

$$\vdots$$

A process such as this in which each new value is produced from the previous value is called a *recursive process*. As with the integration example, the closer the sample points, the more accurately a recursive process can estimate the solution to a continuous problem.

Because for a constant velocity the distance traveled during a time interval is equal to the velocity times the length of the interval, the displacement can also be approximated by recursion using the formula

$$x_{i+1} = x_i + v_i\Delta$$

where x_i is the displacement at time t_i.

The actual solution to the velocity problem assuming $v_0 = 0$ m/s, $m = 1$ kg, $b = 0.1$ newton/s and $g = 10$ m/s per second can be shown to be

$$v(t) = 100(1 - e^{-0.1t})$$

If the initial displacement is 0, the displacement as a function of time can be shown to be

$$x(t) = 100(t + 10e^{-0.1t} - 10)$$

The actual solutions for the velocity and displacement are shown in Fig. 9-17(a) and (b), respectively. Also shown in these figures are the discrete values for computer solutions using $\Delta = 5$ and $\Delta = 10$.

The exact equations for solving problems such as this are called differential equations. As with integration, there are a number of ways of solving differential equations using a digital computer and the various methods have their advantages and disadvantages. The method employed above is the simplest and is called *Euler's method*.

9-4-3 Iteration

Iteration is a computational procedure in which repetition is used successively to approximate a result more and more closely. Iteration was used in the program SQROOT in Fig. 4-13 to find the square root of a number. It involves finding a result, testing the result for accuracy by comparing it with a previous result or some other known value, and either continuing to iterate if the test fails (passes) or exiting

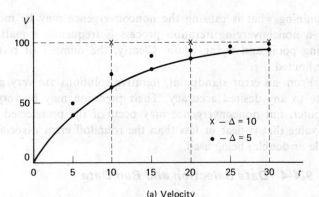

(a) Velocity

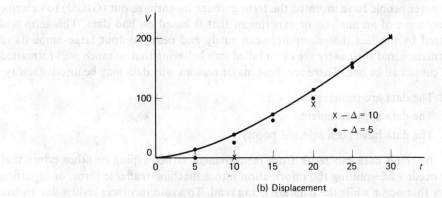

(b) Displacement

FIGURE 9-17 *Recursive solution to a differential equation.*

the iteration algorithm if it passes (fails). In the program SQROOT the test was to compare the square of the result with the original number. If the two numbers were sufficiently close, the iteration process was exited. (More generally, iteration is the primary means of finding roots of a polynomial.) An iterative process is normally implemented using a DO-WHILE or DO-UNTIL control structure.

The advantage of iteration is that if everything goes well, a solution can be found to any preselected degree of accuracy. However, the more iterations, the greater the amount of time that will be required. The major difficulty associated with iteration algorithms is that quite often there is no guarantee that the algorithm will converge (i.e., that it will terminate in a finite number of steps). This means that a counter and an additional test is needed so that the loop will exit after a reasonable number of repetitions. If abnormal exits are included in an algorithm, one must decide on how the abnormalities are to be processed.

Nonconvergence may mean that the iteration process has reached a point where it is *cycling* through a set of values, that the process is diverging (which often causes an overflow), or that there is no solution to which to converge. Providing a test for nonconvergence is usually a matter of limiting the number of iterations, but determining what is causing the nonconvergence may be more difficult. Recovery from a nonconverging iteration process is frequently a matter of choosing a new starting point and trying again. Clearly, the number of restarts would also need to be limited.

From an error standpoint, iterative solutions are very good because they can iterate to any desired accuracy. Their precision may be very close to that of the computer, but nonconvergence may occur if the preselected allowable error is set to a value that is near or less than the roundoff error associated with the precision (single or double) being used.

9-4-4   Data Selection and Bad Data

The results of any study are only as good as the data on which it is based. Computer people have invented the term garbage in–garbage out (GIGO) to describe the outcome of an analysis or experiment that is based on bad data. This term was inspired by the fact that computers can easily and neatly output large amounts of information and their users are often lulled into believing that so much well-formatted data cannot all be bad. There are three major reasons why data may be unsatisfactory:

1. The data are incorrect.
2. The data are incomplete.
3. The data have been selected poorly.

Incorrect data can result from measurement errors, typing or other errors that may occur while putting the information into a machine-readable form, or inputting errors that occur while the data are being read. To avoid incorrect results due to bad input data, the input should be checked carefully and unusual results should always be investigated thoroughly. Although some erroneous input data are obviously wrong, some data errors are subtle and very difficult to find. For large errors and certain types of unusual errors (just what types depend on the application), it is often advantageous to include in the program a subprogram for monitoring the input data. This was the purpose of the subprogram NUMVAL in Sec. 9-3.

To identify incomplete data, the user must thoroughly understand the problem the program is to solve. As was seen from the discussion in the preceding subsections, if the data are to approximate a continuously varying quantity, they must be spaced closely enough that rapid changes are adequately described. If the program is to analyze statistical data, the user must know how much data is needed to produce meaningful results.

On the other hand, quite often there is more data than the computer can analyze in a reasonable period of time, but much of the data is redundant and not needed. The problem is then not one of having an insufficient amount of information, but is one of selecting the significant information. This is particularly crucial when analyzing statistical data. One should never attempt to use a statistical program unless he or she can competently screen the input data and properly interpret the results.

9-4-5 Mathematical Modeling

Mathematical modeling of physical situations can be divided into two major categories:

1. Deterministic modeling
2. Statistical modeling or simulation

Deterministic modeling is used when the physical quantities are known to be described by certain fixed relationships such as scientifically proven formulas. These relationships are almost always used only after making approximating assumptions and, therefore, can produce only approximate results. For example, the equation

$$F = F_0 e^{-at}$$

where F_0 and a are constants, may be used to approximate the flow F of water from a tank as a function of time t, even though the actual flow may be slightly affected by pipe expansion and other phenomena not reflected in the equation.

Statistical simulation is used to solve problems in which at least some of the quantities involved can only be described statistically. Consider the production line depicted in Fig. 9-18. The times needed by the station opeartors to complete their tasks are not fixed, but may vary considerably from one assembly to the next. By statistically studying the times needed by the station operators to do their work, one could write a program to simulate the production flow within the assembly line. At the heart of such a program would be a subprogram called a *random number generator*, which would output the seemingly random numbers that would be used to simulate the random times required by the workers. Because computers follow fixed rules, they cannot produce truly random sequences of numbers, so random number generators are sometimes called pseudo-random number generators. Most computer

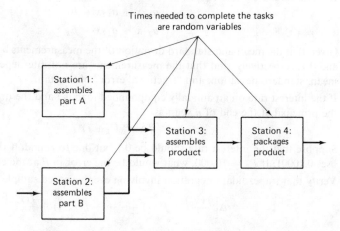

FIGURE 9-18 *Typical process that is described by statistical parameters.*

systems include a random number generator as a system subprogram. A discussion of random number generators, which includes a typical random number generator, is given in Programming Problem 2 at the end of Chap. 6.

Mathematical modeling is obviously very application-dependent and can be extremely complicated. What factors can be ignored and how the random variable distributions should be chosen are questions whose answers are beyond the scope of this book, but which have been introduced because of their fundamental importance. The main point being made is that, even though computers can solve complex problems very quickly, this does not relieve the programmer and the user from the responsibility of thoroughly understanding the problem and the limitations of its solution. In most scientific and engineering situations the user of a program must know enough about the program to quantify the errors in the results. Are the results known to be within 1%, or maybe 10%, or are they known to be within 3% only with a 95% certainty?

EXERCISES

1. Derive the expressions for the fractional errors given in Fig. 9-14.

2. Given that the maximum fractional error in all quantities is 0.000001, determine the approximate worst-case fractional errors of the following expressions.
   (a) $(a - b)/c$
   (b) $a^n b - c$
   (c) $1/a + bc$
   (d) The determinant

   $$\begin{vmatrix} a_{11} & a_{21} \\ a_{12} & a_{22} \end{vmatrix}$$

   (e) The solution to the equations

   $$a_{11}x + a_{12}x = b_1$$
   $$a_{21}x + a_{22}x = b_2$$

3. Given that the mean and standard deviation of the measurements $a_1, \ldots, a_{10,000}$ are 10 and 0.1, respectively, and that the measurements are not interdependent, determine the mean, standard deviation, and "fractional error" of the sum.

4. If the interest rate on an annually compounded loan is i and the original principal is P_0, the principal at the end of n years is

   $$P = P_0(1 + i)^n$$

   Suppose that the interest rate should be 0.1 but due to roundoff the computer actually uses 0.10001. If $P_0 = 10,000$, what would be the error in P at the end of 30 years?

5. Verify that trapezoidal integration involving evenly spaced sample points reduces to

   $$\Delta \left[\frac{f(x_0)}{2} + f(x_1) + \cdots + f(x_{n-1}) + \frac{f(x_n)}{2} \right]$$

6. Assume that the velocity of a rocket is given by the equation

   $$v(t) = te^{-0.1t}$$

and that at $t = 0$ its displacement is $x = 0$. Use rectangular integration and a spacing of $\Delta = 2$ to determine the displacement of the rocket at $t = 10$. Repeat the calculation using $\Delta = 1$, and again using $\Delta = 0.5$. Resolve the problem using trapezoidal integration.

7. Suppose that the change in the amount of a radioactive material between time t_i and t_{i+1} is approximated by

$$w_{i+1} - w_i = -cw_i \Delta$$

where $\Delta = t_{i+1} - t_i$, and, for $i = 0, 1, \ldots$, w_i is the amount of the material at time t_i. For $w_0 = 10$, $\Delta = 10$, and $c = 0.02$, compute the values of w at $\Delta, 2\Delta, \ldots, 40$. Repeat the calculation for $\Delta = 5$, and again for $\Delta = 2$. If the fractional error in c were 0.01, what would be the fractional error in w at $t = 40$ for the case $\Delta = 5$?

8. It can be shown that for certain values of x_0 the solution to

$$x - \cos x = 0$$

can be found by the iteration process

$$x_1 = \cos x_0$$

$$x_2 = \cos x_1$$

$$x_3 = \cos x_2$$

$$\cdot$$

$$\cdot$$

Write a program segment that begins with $x_0 = \pi/4$ and iterates to the solution of the equation. Manually carry out the necessary calculations for solving the equation beginning with $x_0 = \pi/4$; with $x_0 = \pi/2$; with $x_0 = \pi$. Will the iteration process converge for all values of x_0? Manually carry out the same calculations for the equation

$$x - \frac{\pi}{2} \cos x = 0$$

In this case will the process converge for all values of x_0?

9. Consider the problem of averaging 100 grades that are in the interval 0 through 100. Suppose that the true average is 70 but that a grade that is exactly 70 is erroneously input as x. How will the average be affected if $x = 10{,}000$? If $x = 1000$? If $x = 100$? Assume that a subprogram is used to monitor the input data so that a warning message is printed if a grade is less than 0 or greater than 100. If there is no more than one incorrect grade input to the computer, what is the maximum error in the average that can occur without a warning message being printed?

10. The displacement of an electron traveling in the direction opposite to that of an electric field $E = a + bt$ is given by the equation

$$x(t) = v_0 t + c\left(\frac{a}{2} + \frac{b}{6} t\right) t^2$$

where v_0 is the initial velocity and c is a constant of proportionality. For $v_0 = 100$ and $c = 0.01$, plot $x(t)$ between $t = 0$ and $t = 1$ by first assuming that E is constant at 10,000, then plot $x(t)$ on the same interval by assuming that

$$E = 10{,}000 + 10t$$

If the latter is the true solution, what is the maximum error resulting from approximating E by the constant 10,000?

PROGRAMMING PROBLEMS

1. The integer format on most computers can be used only to store integers whose magnitudes are less than 10 digits in length, but sometimes it is necessary to work with integers that contain 100 or more digits. Cryptography is an area in which very large integers are employed. One coding process is to assign combinations of digits to combinations of letters using a table, concatenate the digits to form a number X, and then form a second number $Y = AX + B$, where A and B are secret integers. If the receiving device knows the numbers A and B and the assignment table, it can reverse the process by computing $X = (Y - B)/A$ and applying the assignment table to determine the message. The key to decoding a message is knowing the values of A and B, and, for extremely large values of A and B, being able to guess them is a very remote possibility (even if a computer is used). Assume that a blank is assigned to 10 and the letters are assigned to the integers 11 through 36, respectively,

$$A = 9825017685211076707185131$$

and

$$B = 3921578613001257615921511$$

Using this procedure, the message

HELP ME

is coded starting with

$$X = 18152226102315$$

Write a program that will input a string of up to 50 digits into an integer linear array X (one digit per element), compute $AX + B$ using the normal algorithms for arithmetic, put the result in a linear array Y, and output Y as a string of digits. The numbers A and B should be stored in integer arrays using a DATA statement. Before writing the program, draw a hierarchical diagram. Also, provide a complete documentation package including appropriate diagrams as well as a commented listing of the program. Test your program with the message "I DO."

2. Write a program that will find the area under the function sin x between 0 and π using rectangular, trapezoidal, and Simpson integration. The program is to first read an integer into N. It is to then repeat the following sequence N times: (1) read an even integer into M, (2) use subintervals of length π/M to compute the area using the three integration methods, and (3) print

SUBINTERVAL LENGTH: *(Value of π/M)*
RECTANGULAR INTEGRATION = *(Result)*   ERROR = *(Result − 2.0)*
TRAPEZOIDAL INTEGRATION = *(Result)*   ERROR = *(Result − 2.0)*
SIMPSON INTEGRATION = *(Result)*   ERROR = *(Result − 2.0)*

If an odd value is read into M the program is to print

INVALID NO. OF SUBINTERVALS

and stop. Test the program with N = 5 and M = 2, 4, 10, 20, 100.

3. The Newton–Rhapson method uses the procedure indicated in the following figure to find the roots of a nonlinear expression such as a polynomial:

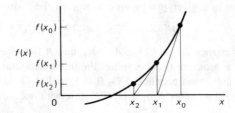

An initial guess x_0 is made and a straight line that is tangent to $f(x)$ at x_0 is used to determine an x_1. Then a tangent line at $f(x_1)$ is used to determine an x_2. The process is repeated until the absolute value of $f(x_n)$ is less than a preselected value. If

$$f(x) = a_0 + \cdots + a_{n-1}x^{n-1} + a_n x^n$$

it can be shown that the Newton–Rhapson method reduces to

$$x_{i+1} = x_i - \frac{a_0 + \cdots + a_{n-1}x_i^{n-1} + a_n x_i^n}{a_1 + \cdots + (n-1)a_{n-1}x_i^{n-2} + na_n x_i^{n-1}}$$

Convergence is not guaranteed, but this method will usually produce the largest root of a polynomial if x_0 is chosen to be larger than this root.

Write a subroutine PROOT that will accept a degree N, a small value E, an initial guess X0, and a linear array A containing the coefficients $a_0, \ldots, a_n$ as arguments and produce a root XR of the corresponding polynomial. The value of XR must be such that the absolute value of the polynomial evaluated at XR is less than E. If the subroutine does not converge in 100 iterations, it is to print

ROOT CANNOT BE FOUND

set a parameter FLAG to 'NO', and return to the calling program. (FLAG is to be set to 'YES' at the beginning of the subroutine.)

Write a main program that will input a degree, a set of coefficients, a value for E, and an initial guess; use PROOT to compute the largest real root of the polynomial; print

ROOT IS = *(Value of root)*

if FLAG = 'YES' and simply stop if FLAG = 'NO'. Test the program by finding the largest root of

$$2x^4 - 2x^3 - 6x^2 + 2x + 4$$

using E = 0.00005 and an initial guess of 10.0.

4. In the design of furnaces or welding processes it is necessary to compute the maximum theoretical flame temperatures. By the conservation of energy the heat energy H_i entering the system plus the heat H_r generated by the combustion must equal the heat H_o leaving the system. It is known that H_o is related to the heat of the exhaust gases by the equation

$$H_o = M_1 H_{o1} + \cdots + M_n H_{on}$$

where the M_is and H_{oi}s are the amounts and heat constants corresponding to the various exhaust gases. It is also known that the theoretical flame temperature T is related to the heat constant of a given gas by an equation of the form

$$H_{oi} = A_{i1}T + \tfrac{1}{2}A_{i2}T^2 + \tfrac{1}{3}A_{i3}T^3 + \tfrac{1}{4}A_{i4}T^4$$

where, for a particular gas i, A_{i1}, A_{i2}, A_{i3}, and A_{i4} can be found in tables.

Write a program that computes the flame temperature T for a propane furnace for which the combustion produces CO_2 (gas 1) and H_2O (gas 2). The A_{ij}'s are to be put into a two-dimensional array A by a DATA statement according to the following table:

	A_{i1}	A_{i2}	A_{i3}	A_{i4}
CO_2	36.11	4.233×10^{-2}	-2.887×10^{-5}	7.464×10^{-9}
H_2O	33.46	0.688×10^{-2}	0.760×10^{-5}	-3.593×10^{-9}

The inputs are to be HI, HR, M(1), M(2), and T0, where T0 is an initial estimate of T. After reading the input values the program is to use the foregoing equations to obtain a fourth-degree polynomial that must equal 0, and then apply the subroutine PROOT in Programming Problem 3 to solve for T. The value for E needed by PROOT is to be 0.1. The input is to be output with appropriate titles and, if PROOT converges to a root within 100 iterations, then

FLAME TEMPERATURE = *(Value of T)*

is to be printed. If PROOT does not converge within 100 iterations, the program is to print

DOES NOT CONVERGE

and stop. Test the program with the data

$$\text{HI} = 7.504 \times 10^4 \qquad \text{HR} = 6.349 \times 10^4 \qquad \text{M(1)} = 79.13 \qquad \text{M(2)} = 158.26$$
$$\text{T0} = 4500.0$$

5. This problem is to utilize the subprograms RANDOM and RANNUM requested in Programming Problems 2 and 3 at the end of Chap. 6. Consider the following assembly line for producing integrated circuits (ICs):

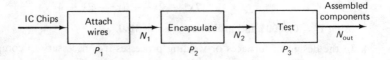

where P_1, P_2, and P_3 are the probability distributions for describing the times needed to complete the respective tasks, N_1 and N_2 are the number of subassemblies waiting for the next task, and N_{out} is the number of devices produced. The distributions have been found to be approximately described by drawing straight-line segments between the points in the following table:

Time(s)	P_1	P_2	P_3
0.0	0.0	0.0	0.0
1.0	0.2	0.1	0.1
2.0	0.5	0.4	0.8
3.0	0.8	0.6	0.9
4.0	1.0	1.0	1.0

Assuming that there are always ICs waiting at the beginning of the assembly line, write a program that uses the subroutine RANNUM to simulate the activity. In particular, the program is to compute N1, N2, and NOUT at M evenly spaced times from T = 0 through T = TMAX. The inputs are to be M and TMAX and the output is to consist of suitably labeled columns containing the values of T, N1, N2, and NOUT. Test the program using

$$M = 101 \qquad TMAX = 1000$$

6. The gravitational force of attraction between two objects is known to be described by the equation

$$F = 6.670 \times 10^{-11}\frac{M_1 M_2}{D^2}$$

where F is the force of attraction in Newtons, M_1 and M_2 are the masses of the two objects in kilograms, and D is the distance between the objects in meters. The motion of an object due to a force applied to it is known to be in the direction of the force and to be described by

$$\text{velocity} = V = \frac{F}{M}T + V_0 \qquad \text{displacement} = Z = \frac{F}{2M}T^2 + V_0 T + Z_0$$

where M is the mass of the object, F is the applied force, V_0 is the initial velocity, and Z_0 is the initial displacement. Consider the following planetary system and approaching spacecraft:

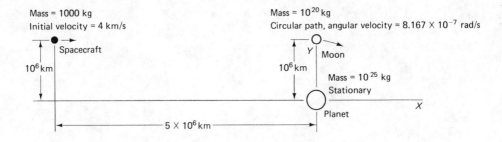

Mass = 1000 kg
Initial velocity = 4 km/s

Spacecraft

10^6 km

Mass = 10^{20} kg
Circular path, angular velocity = 8.167×10^{-7} rad/s

Y Moon

10^6 km

Mass = 10^{25} kg
Stationary

X

Planet

5 × 10^6 km

Assume that the planet is stationary, the moon circles it with a constant angular velocity, and the forces the spacecraft exerts on the planet and moon are negligible (thus the spacecraft's presence does not change their motion).

Write a program that approximates the path of the spacecraft by assuming that the spacecraft travels along N straight-line segments for successive time intervals of length TDEL. The program is to input N and TDEL, print the headings

SPACECRAFT POSITION

X-COORDINATE   Y-COORDINATE

and enter a loop. Inside the loop the program is to compute and print out the position of the spacecraft at the end of I*TDEL, I = 0, . . . , N. Test the program three times, once with each of the following sets of data:

$$\text{Set 1:} \quad N = 5 \quad\quad \text{TDEL} = 400000$$
$$\text{Set 2:} \quad N = 50 \quad\quad \text{TDEL} = 40000$$
$$\text{Set 3:} \quad N = 500 \quad\quad \text{TDEL} = 4000$$

For Set 3, in order to avoid excessive printing, output only every tenth position.

10

DEBUGGING

The term *debugging* as used in this book means the entire process of examining and testing a program for the purpose of finding errors in the program. Although some books have assigned a more precise meaning to debugging, the usage here more closely matches that of the general application of the term. Debugging is an iterative process consisting of repeatedly examining a program, executing it using carefully designed test data, and determining the causes of any erroneous results. The most simplistic type of debugging is to run one set of test data and, after the program is able to run this one set of data, assume that it will perform correctly on all sets of data. The most exhaustive debugging is to run all possible sets of data against the program to prove that it performs correctly with all possible input data. In practice, neither approach is satisfactory since the first approach seldom tests the program adequately and the second approach is either impossible or takes far too much time and is rarely cost effective. A third approach, somewhere between the two just mentioned, is needed to demonstrate that the program performs correctly and to allow debugging to be completed within reasonable time and cost constraints. The purpose of this chapter is to assist the programmer in finding this third alternative.

There are two levels of testing and correcting software. One level involves the debugging of a single program and the other may involve several related programs and is referred to as *systems testing*. Although this chapter is primarily concerned with debugging a single program many of the ideas could be applied to systems testing. This is particularly true of the discussions related to files that are given in the latter part of the chapter.

Planned debugging assumes that bugs exist in the logic of a program and each run is designed to discover as many of these bugs as possible. After each run, the results are analyzed and all recognizable errors are corrected before the next run. Not only are the results checked for accuracy, but the format of the printed output (e.g., the alignment of the results with the column headings) is also checked. Several sets of data are submitted with each run so that the maximum amount of information can be gained from each test. Debugging is complete when all necessary test data are run correctly, preferably in the same run. Generally, only one set of test data is submitted with the first run and the test data are increased with each additional run until debugging is complete.

10-1 DESK CHECKING

One of the best methods of avoiding excessive debug time is desk checking. As indicated in Chap. 4, desk checking involves reading and manually checking the flow of the program as well as the syntax and other details. In a sense the programmer is "playing computer" as he or she checks the variable names, headings, and so on, checks the syntax, and follows the logic of the program to determine if the program is written as intended. This step is especially important after the typing errors have been removed and you are ready to run the program with the first set of test data. Desk checking should also be done after significant rewrites of any part of the program; for example, if a subroutine is rewritten, it should be thoroughly reexamined.

The abbreviated desk-checking list given in Fig. 4-23 can now be extended to encompass the material presented after Chap. 4. This material includes DIMENSION, COMMON, FORMAT, PARAMETER, DATA, and type statements and subprogram calls. Figure 10-1 contains an expanded summary of the items to be reviewed while desk checking before the first run and after each succeeding run.

During desk checking all DIMENSION and type statements should be reexamined and the sizes of all arrays should be recalculated. In programming for a machine with limited memory, the arrays should be examined to make sure that the smallest possible size is specified so that extra space is not used when it is not needed. Also, the type specification of an array should be checked to make sure that it is correct for the array being used. For example, if single-precision numbers would be sufficient but double precision has been specified, twice the required amount of memory will be reserved. This may not be very important for a small array, but in a two dimensional array of numbers that has 100 rows and 100 columns, specifying double-precision may reserve an extra 40,000 bytes of storage. Even a 100 by 10 array may reserve an extra 4000 bytes of storage. (Typically, single-precision and integer numbers occupy one word, or 4 bytes, per array element, whereas double-precision numbers occupy two words or 8 bytes per element. For minicomputers, an integer is sometimes represented by 2 bytes, single-precision numbers by 4 bytes, and double-precision numbers by 6 or 8 bytes, depending on the machine.)

COMMON statements should be checked even more closely than DIMEN-

1. Spelling of variable names.

2. Spelling of all headings, messages, etc.

3. Variable and array types.

4. Sizes of arrays in DIMENSION statements.

5. Sizes of arrays in COMMON statements.

6. Order of variables in COMMON statements.

7. Length of all named COMMON blocks.

8. Availability of a particular named COMMON block
    to a subroutine.

9. Constant names (PARAMETER statements) and
    preassignments (DATA statements).

10. FORMAT statements for:
    a. Column alignment.
    b. Size of field specifications.
    c. Field specification present for every
        variable in the corresponding
        I/O statements.
    d. Rescan points.

11. Program flow:
    a. DO loop initialization and DO
        statement parameters.
    b. Conditions in IF and other statements.
    c. Array limits and DO statement limits.
    d. Usage of flags and codes.

12. Test data for the first test:
    a. Correct values.
    b. Column alignment.
    c. Correct amount of data for the test.

    (a) Before the first run

1. All output:
    a. Printouts for correctness or reasonableness.
    b. Tape or disk files for correctness or
        reasonableness.

2. Errors in the modified areas of the program.

3. Test data for the next run:
    a. Correct values.
    b. Column alignment.
    c. Correct amount of data for the test.

(b) After each run and before the succeeding run

FIGURE 10-1 *Checklist for desk checking.*

SION statements and additional checks should be performed. Remember that common can be either unnamed common or named common. All programs and subprograms can reference unnamed common, but a named common area can only be referenced by the program unit in which it first appears and by any subprograms called either directly or indirectly by that program unit (i.e., any subprogram lower in the hierarchy). The most important aspect of common is that all program units using a common area must list the variables in their proper order. The same names do not have to be specified, but their order and the variable types and sizes must be consistent. For example, if the main program defines unnamed common as

COMMON A(10),B,C,I(20)

and the subprogram defines unnamed common as

COMMON X(10),Y,Z,N(20)

whenever the subprogram references X it will obtain the same data that the main program stored in A. Similarly, B corresponds to Y, C to Z, and I to N. Although the rules of FORTRAN permit arrays to be overlapped and array elements of arrays with different dimensions to be assigned the same location, this practice should be avoided. Note that in the example above the types and array sizes correspond exactly. (For a complete discussion of the rules of COMMON, refer to Chap. 6).

In addition to verifying the items in the common data variable and array list, one should check the common area names. Names that are accidentally mismatched through spelling errors or name changes will usually produce meaningless results. The program may create areas that are not intended or may access the wrong locations.

When using named common, each subprogram that uses a particular named common area must be such that the length of the block is exactly the same as the length in the program or subprogram that first defined the block. The best way to ensure that the lengths match is to use the same subscript limits and types of variables, even if the names are different and even though some variables are not used. Unnamed common does not require that the lengths match.

Another important characteristic of named common is that machines with certain dynamic storage properties assign memory only to the named common between the entering and exiting of the program unit that first defines the named common. Figure 10-2 shows a main program and several subprograms that use the named common areas DATA1 and DATA2. In this figure any subprogram

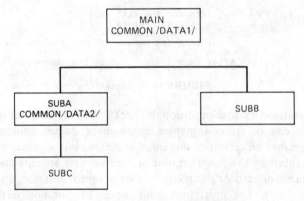

FIGURE 10-2 *Sample program which uses named common.*

(SUBA, SUBB, or SUBC) could reference the data in COMMON DATA1 since they are defined in the program MAIN. The subprograms SUBA and SUBC can reference the data in COMMON DATA2 since they are first defined in SUBA and SUBC is called by SUBA (i.e., DATA2 is present until SUBA returns to MAIN, so it is present during the entire run of SUBA and any subprograms that are called by SUBA). In some implementations of FORTRAN 77, variables contained in DATA2 may be undefined to SUBB.

As a general rule, the variables and arrays in a common area can be referenced faster than those passed as subprogram arguments and, therefore, it is more efficient to use a common area. However, there is a trade-off between arguments and using a common area, because passing arguments is usually less confusing. Also, if a different variable must be passed each time a subprogram is called, a common area cannot be used to pass the variable. (Why?)

An important timesaver in desk checking is to verify that FORMAT statements are set up properly. Make sure that printed results fall in the proper columns and are correctly aligned under their headings. If an output field is made larger to print more digits, make sure that the column heading for that column and all subsequent columns are adjusted accordingly. For example, consider the statements

```
1000 FORMAT ('1',TR5,'COLUMN 1',TR10,'COLUMN 2')
1010 FORMAT ('1',TR7,F5.2,TR13,F6.1)
```

If the F5.2 in FORMAT statement 1010 is changed to F7.2, the TR10 in FORMAT statement 1000 should be changed to TR12 so that the heading "COLUMN 2" remains aligned with its column of numbers.

Checking the format specifications for READ statements can be even more important since an incorrect specification may cause invalid data to be read, and this may invalidate an entire test run. All READ and WRITE statements should also be checked to make sure the *List* items being read into or written from are correct. A final check should be made to ensure that the corresponding FORMAT statements contain the correct types for the variables being read or written (e.g., a REAL variable has a corresponding E, F, G, or D specification) and that there is either a specification for every variable contained in the I/O statement or that the rescan point is correct.

After the typing errors have been removed and while preparing for the first test run, the programmer should read through the entire program and check the general flow of the logic. This is particularly true for programs larger than one or two pages because as one initially writes a program it is easy to lose the logic flow among all the handwritten pages. As mentioned in Chap. 4, one of the checks that should be made is to draw brackets around all DO loops and draw arrows showing all branches. This verifies that the DO loops terminate properly and that the branches are made to the intended points. If a DO loop bracket should cross another such bracket, there is an improperly nested set of DO loops. Make sure that every DO loop and branch statement is terminated with a properly labeled statement.

Another important program flow check is to verify that the subscripts used for the array references do not exceed their ranges and that the subscripts are the ones intended. Check to see that the correct number of arguments is being passed to each subroutine and that their types and order are correct. Program flow should be rechecked after any significant modification to the program to ensure that the modification is correct and that it fits into the general flow of the entire program. One last thing to remember about program flow is that DATA statements can be used to initialize variables, but if these variables are changed, they will contain their new values. Preassignment does not imply that the variables are made constant.

Prior to each test run, the input test data for that run should be checked to verify that they are the correct data and that their position within the record is correct. Do not waste a test run because the test data was off by one column. After each test run, all the output should be checked, not just the output that was expected to be corrected. The previously correct output should be examined to make sure that it was not erroneously changed by the program modification. If the output cannot be checked exactly, at least check that it is reasonable for the test data being used.

A word of warning is that bugs are interrelated. A single syntax or spelling error may cause numerous diagnostic messages or errors in the results, and one should immediately determine if an error in one part of a program is actually due to a bug occurring earlier in the program. On the other hand, do not assume that errors are induced by earlier bugs without examining the situation carefully.

10-2 PROGRAM TESTING

One of the most important questions a programmer must face is how much testing is to be done. When the program is written using top-down design, testing starts with the highest-level program unit and proceeds down through the program hierarchy in a step-by-step manner. Each program unit is tested using very short subprograms, called *stubs*, for all subprograms called by the program unit. A stub may be void of executable statements or may include just enough statements to return correct results for a specific set of input values. As each stub is replaced by an actual subprogram, that subprogram is tested and the bugs discovered are usually in it. Each program unit should be tested thoroughly and the data needed to test each newly added unit should be appended to the previous test data. Using this building block approach, all previous units are retested each time another unit is added and the new unit is tested with the data used in all preceding tests.

A set of test data is called a *test data file*. Test data files may be the data portion of a card deck and/or a mass storage file. For interactive programs some of the test input may be provided through the user's terminal, but for programs requiring a lot of input, one or more test data files are also needed.

With regard to the discussion above it is seen that test data files are expanded as each new program unit is tested. For example, consider the program diagrammed in Fig. 10-3. The program unit MAIN should first be tested using stubs in place of

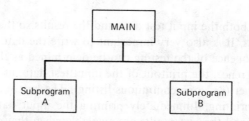

1. Test MAIN by using stubs for Subprogram A and B
2. Test MAIN and Subprogram A using stub for Subprogram B
3. Test the entire program

FIGURE 10-3 *An example of testing a program with two subprograms.*

subprograms A and B. The test data for MAIN are used to build the initial test data file. After MAIN is tested, the stub for A is replaced by subprogram A and the new test data for subprogram A are added to the test data file. The test data file is reprocessed to test subprogram A and, in so doing, MAIN is tested again. When subprogram B is tested, A and MAIN are retested, so that after the testing of B is complete, the whole program has been thoroughly tested. This may sound like overkill, but program bugs have a tendency to interact with each other, and if a program is tested as described above, most of the interactions will be discovered. However, some test data should be included to specifically test the known interactions.

Another question to ask is: When do you start testing? The best answer to this is: When you have something to test. In a top-down design, by using stubs the top program unit can be tested as soon as it is written, and each segment below the top is tested as it is integrated into the overall program. This is a very important benefit of top-down programming since testing is done in parallel with coding (i.e., one can write more code while waiting for a test run). In addition, when a bug is uncovered it is likely to be in the new code, and the location of the problem can be more readily pinpointed. In the older method of programming, called the bottom-up method, program units were written starting at the lowest level (or, more likely, they were written in an arbitrary order to suit the programmer's habits) and were tested using driver programs. These *drivers* were written specifically to test a given program unit and were discarded after the unit had been completely tested and the segment had been integrated into the overall program. With top-down programming, driver programs are no longer needed and time and effort are saved.

Although the emphasis should be placed on top-down testing, there are rare instances in which modules should be individually tested. Some modules may need to be tested extensively and, therefore, running the entire program to test the module may require too much computer time and/or make the selection of the test data more complicated. In such cases, it may be more efficient to write a carefully designed driver and debug the module before inserting it in the program.

As each test run is completed and the results are checked, the output should be dated, identified in some manner, and filed for future reference. It is very important to identify both the input test data and the results so that they can be compared with later results. It is also very important to write the date and time on the printout so that the sequence of the testing can be determined as the debugging progresses. For ease of reference, the printout of the input test data, as well as the results, should be kept together (i.e., one continuous listing). The best way of accomplishing this is to use echo printing. Immediately printing the input data will ensure that both the input data and the test results are available when they are needed and that the programmer will always know exactly what input data produced the results being examined.

As an alternative to creating a test data file, an existing data file may be used. This method has the advantage of saving time, since the test data already exist, but it has the risk that the existing data may not test all the conditions of the program. If the file is large, test runs will become long and costly and the output may be too large to be properly evaluated. One solution to this problem is to process only part of the file. This may be done in several ways, such as processing the first 100 records or by processing every fifth record in the file. Processing the first few records is very easy to implement, but if the file is in some order (e.g., alphabetic), records at the end of that order—which may contain important test conditions—will not be checked. Sometimes this defect can be cured by first copying the first 100 or so records to a second file, and then adding special debug data to the test conditions which are not found in the first 100 records of the original file.

An alternative solution when using an existing file for test data is to build a new test data file from the existing file by extracting every fifth (or tenth, etc.) record. In this manner, every fifth record will be processed and the others discarded. This method usually gets a cross section of the file, but one caution must be observed. If records are grouped such that the contents of the groups are interdependent, groups of records must be selected rather than single records. This type of file could occur, for example, in a student file in which a record containing biographical information is followed by one record for each class the student has taken. For particularly complicated situations it would be best to individually select the records to be processed as test data.

If the program being tested has an unusually large number of possible input combinations, testing may be easier if the test data are created by a program that is written for the sole purpose of creating a test file. This type of program is called a *test-case generator*. Test-case generators are commonly used to test a system of programs but can also be useful for testing a single, large program. Often, the computer system being used to write the program will have a test-case-generator program available for general use. This type of program requires some input to define how the test data are to be created and, after receiving this input, will create any amount of test data desired. For example, if one were to request a test file of 100 records, each having a random number in fields 1 through 5, the input to the test-data generator could be 100, 1, and 5. The contents of each test record may be made to vary according to the input supplied to the test-case generator. Test-case generators will usually allow the specification of alphabetic fields and numeric fields containing nonrandom, random, or sequential values. They will normally allow the person using them to select the range of numbers to be generated.

10-3 OUTPUTTING TEST RESULTS

The most powerful debug tools are the PRINT and WRITE statements. As a program is being written, structured methods should be used to help with the debug process and to help other programmers understand the program. After it is written, desk checking should be used to verify that the program matches the intent of the programmer. Then test data are built to make sure that all of the program will be tested. But after all this preparation, when the test runs begin and the errors come out of the closet, it is the PRINT statement that will rescue the programmer. There are other important tools and the PRINT statement must be used intelligently, but the ability to print data from any point within the program gives the programmer the ability to "see" what is actually happening while the program is running. Although printing as a debug tool can be used from anywhere inside (or even outside) the program being debugged and it can be used to print almost anything the programmer desires, certain uses are more efficient and easier to understand than others. Some of the more common debug printing techniques were given in Fig. 4-23 and a more complete summary is given in Fig. 10-4. In addition to echo printing, milepost

```
Printing intermediate values

Echo printing the input

Milepost printing

Print subroutines (for repetitious printing of
            several variables or arrays)

Outputting debug information to a special debug file

Printing debug data separately versus intermixing
            it with the normal output

Print programs for examining files
```

FIGURE 10-4 *Summary of the principal debug printing techniques.*

printing, and the printing of intermediate values, this summary contains print subroutines, the use of files for temporarily storing test output, and programs for examining files. Because the first three items are discussed in Chap. 4, this section is concerned primarily with the latter items.

In larger programs, where many data values are kept (sometimes in a common area) and updated by various subprograms, PRINT statements to print intermediate variables become quite large. Printing of 20 or 30 variables and sometimes even printing arrays is not unusual. If an identical set of several PRINT statements are needed to provide a suitable output at a number of points within a program, it may become unwieldy to insert the set at as many places as desired. One good solution to this problem is to use a separate print subroutine, written just to aid the debugging process. This type of subroutine becomes even more valuable as the number of variables to print becomes large, and when all or most of the variables are located in common. With this approach, when some of the variables need to be printed at a point within a program, all that is required is the insertion of a CALL statement which calls the print subroutine. Note that when the print subroutine is no longer needed, the program can be returned to its original state by simply deleting the subroutine and the associated CALL statements.

Quite often it is desirable to have the output from a debug print subroutine written to a file that is different from the file used for the normal output. This feature allows the programmer to create the file on disk or tape and print it later only if a problem arises which requires that the data be examined. If the debug data are not needed, one can simply delete the file without printing it, thus saving time and paper. The debug printout for large programs may result in 100, 500, or even more pages of data.

If the debug data are in a different file, some means must be provided to allow the debug data to be related to the input and output data. For example, one may wish to know which input record was being processed when the debug data were printed. The means of relating the two can be provided by passing parameters to the print subroutine and having the subroutine print the parameters together with the debug data.

Another desirable feature when printing debug data is the ability to start and stop the debug printout at various times during the run. For example, if you knew that record 500 of a large file was causing the problem to occur, you might want to turn on the debug printout at record 499 and turn it off again later. When the debug printout is being written by a separate subroutine, this capability is very easy to provide. The print subroutine first checks a flag variable (call it DEBUG) and if it contains the value 'ON', the print subroutine continues to print out the contents of the variables. If, on the other hand, the contents of DEBUG is 'OFF', the print subroutine returns without printing anything.

Figure 10-5 shows a debug print subroutine that is part of a large payroll program. It is used to print the pay, the number of hours worked, the pay rate, the

```
      SUBROUTINE PRTBUG (TITLE, DEBUG)
      INTEGER EMPNUM
      REAL PAY, HOURS, RATE, TAX, DEDUCT, OVRHRS
      CHARACTER*3 DEBUG
      CHARACTER*30 TITLE
      COMMON EMPNUM, PAY, HOURS, RATE, TAX, DEDUCT, OVRHRS
      IF (DEBUG .EQ. 'ON') THEN
            WRITE (9, 100) TITLE
            WRITE (9, 101) PAY, HRS, RATE, TAX
            WRITE (9, 102) DEDUCT, EMPNUM, OVRHRS
      ELSE
      ENDIF
  10  FORMAT (T11, A30/)
 101  FORMAT (T2, 'PAY =', F7.2, TR4, 'HOURS =', F3.1, TR4,
     :            'RATE =', F4.2, TR4, 'TAX =', F7.2)
 102  FORMAT (T2, 'DEDUCTIONS =', F7.2, TR4, 'EMPLOYEE NO. =', I6,
     :            TR4, 'OVERTIME HOURS =', F3.1)
      END
```

FIGURE 10-5 *Debug print subroutine.*

amount of tax, the total amount of deductions, the number of overtime hours, and the employee number. It first checks to see if printing is desired and if not, it returns without printing. Figure 10-6 shows part of a payroll program that uses this debug print subroutine. In setting up the debug calls used in the payroll program, the

```
PROGRAM PAYROLL
INTEGER EMPNUM, RECNUM
REAL PAY, HOURS, RATE, TAX, DEDUCT, OVRHRS
CHARACTER*3 DEBUG
COMMON EMPNUM, PAY, HOURS, RATE, TAX, DEDUCT, OVRHRS
DATA DEBUG /'OFF'/
            .
            .
            .
IF (RECNUM .GT. 100) DEBUG = 'ON'
            .
            .
            .
CALL PRTBUG ('CALLING TAX COMPUTATION', DEBUG)
CALL TXCOMP
CALL PRTBUG ('RETURN FROM TAX COMPUTATION', DEBUG)
            .
            .
            .
END
```

FIGURE 10-6 *Using a debug print subroutine.*

programmer has already determined that the error does not occur until after record 100 and the programmer suspects that the error occurs in the tax computation subroutine. Therefore, debug is turned ON when the record counter exceeds 100 and prints a title showing exactly what is about to occur or has just occurred when the subroutine is called.

In printing debug information the debug data may be intermixed with the normal output of the program or may be written into a different file. Both methods of getting debug output are useful and which method should be used depends on the situation. If the amount of debug information is small, intermixing the debug and normal printout is easiest since no extra identifying information is needed and the debug data do not materially interfere with the placement of data in the normal output. As the amount of debug information gets larger, it starts to interfere with the normal output and causes difficulty in determining whether the normal output is correct and in the correct location. In this case the debug printout should be switched to a separate file. As mentioned earlier, sending the debug printout to a different file also gives the option of not printing it, and this may save time and paper.

For debugging programs that use mass storage files it is sometimes advantageous to write a separate display program that is capable of accessing the files and printing their contents. Such a program could be used to examine the contents of a file both before and after it is processed by the program that is being debugged or, if the program being debugged is run several times, the display program could be applied between the successive runs. The output of a display program is called a *dump* and the process of generating dumps is depicted in Fig. 10-7. Although the figure indicates

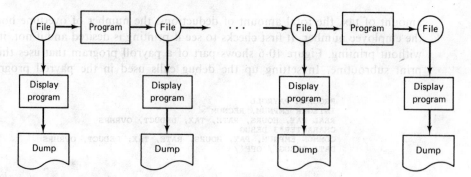

FIGURE 10-7 *Use of a display program in examining a file that is being updated.*

a printed output, the dump could be made to a CRT terminal or even to a mass storage device if immediate feedback is not needed.

A display program could be written to dump the contents of a specific type of file, a general class of files, or files of any type. If the display program is designed to output only one type of file or a narrowly defined class of files, the format of the dump can be carefully designed so that it is easy to read. At the other extreme, if a display program is written to handle any kind of file, the dump must have a general format that may be very difficult to read. Universally applicable programs must dump the information in a format that is directly related to the 0–1 combinations that make up the file on the mass storage device. (They normally output the information using the octal or hexadecimal number system; see Appendix A.) Sophisticated display programs may, through the use of input parameters, allow their users to print only selected portions of the files being examined, designate the type of file to be examined, or dump the information according to a specified format.

10-4 OTHER DEBUGGING AIDS

For large quantities of input data, and for input from mass storage files that cannot be checked visually, it may be advantageous to include a subprogram for monitoring the input for format errors. Editing is also useful and should remain as a permanent part of a program if the expected users are not familiar with computers and therefore do not understand why data have to be in certain columns or why the computer did not "know" the data were wrong.

Editing normally consists of first reading the data characters into an internal file and checking the format before reading the data into the variables. The alternative to editing is to simply read the data, in which case data having an erroneous format will cause an error message to be printed by the operating system and the program to be abnormally ended. All numeric fields should be checked to verify that they contain only numbers, signs, and decimal points; they contain only one sign and only one decimal point; and their symbols are in a valid order. Alphabetic fields should be checked for only alphabetic characters and date fields should be validated for proper month, day, and year. When a data range is known, the data should be checked to verify that they fall within the range, and when an exact range is not known, they should in many cases be checked for reasonableness.

Figure 10-8 shows a logical function NUMRIC which will validate a number entered in F-format or I-format. NUMRIC accepts a character string STRING of

```
      LOGICAL FUNCTION NUMRIC (STRING, LENGTH)
      CHARACTER STRING*(*)
      INTEGER LENGTH, IDEC, ISIGN, INUM
      IDEC = 0
      ISIGN = 0
      INUM = 0
      NUMRIC = .TRUE.
      DO 10 I=1,LENGTH
          IF (STRING(I:I) .EQ. '+' .OR. STRING(I:I) .EQ. '-') THEN
              IF (ISIGN .GT. 0 .OR. INUM .GT. 0 .OR. IDEC .GT. 0)
     :            THEN
                      NUMRIC = .FALSE.
                      GO TO 20
              ELSE
                      ISIGN = ISIGN+1
              ENDIF
          ELSE IF (STRING(I:I) .EQ. '.') THEN
              IF (IDEC .GT. 0) THEN
                      NUMRIC = .FALSE.
                      GO TO 20
              ELSE
                      IDEC = IDEC + 1
              ENDIF
          ELSE IF ((STRING(I:I) .LT. '0' .OR. STRING(I:I) .GT. '9')
     :            .AND. STRING(I:I) .NE. ' ') THEN
              NUMRIC = .FALSE.
              GO TO 20
          ELSE IF (STRING(I:I) .NE. ' ') THEN
              INUM = INUM + 1
          ELSE
          ENDIF
   10 CONTINUE
   20 CONTINUE
      END
```

FIGURE 10-8 *Function subprogram for numeric validation.*

length LENGTH and returns the truth value .FALSE. if an error is found, and otherwise returns the truth value .TRUE. It checks to make sure that the only characters appearing in STRING are "+", "−", " ", ".", and the digits 0 through 9. It also checks for multiple periods and signs and for plus and minus signs that appear after a period or first digit.

Figure 10-9 gives a program segment in which several fields are checked, an error message is printed for each error, and the total number of errors is printed. The program proceeds by reading a line into an internal file and then using the function NUMRIC to verify the formats. If the formats for all the fields are correct, the internal file is read into the proper variables.

In large programs the identification of input data errors and the printing of error messages should be separated into different modules. Then each time an error is detected, an error code could be stored in successive elements of an array. After the error checking is complete, if any errors have occurred, an error print subroutine could be called to print all the error messages. A hierarchical diagram of a program that uses this procedure is shown in Fig. 10-10. In the diagram the subprograms

```
CHARACTER*80 LINE
        .
        .
READ*, LINE
IERR = 0
IF (.NOT. NUMRIC (LINE(1:5),5)) THEN
        PRINT*, 'FIELD 1 NOT NUMERIC'
        IERR = IERR+1
    ELSE
ENDIF
IF (.NOT. NUMRIC (LINE(6:12),7)) THEN
        PRINT*, 'FIELD 2 NOT NUMERIC'
        IERR = IERR+1
    ELSE
ENDIF
IF (.NOT. NUMRIC (LINE(20:25),6)) THEN
        PRINT*, 'FIELD 3 NOT NUMERIC'
        IERR = IERR+1
    ELSE
ENDIF
IF (IERR = 0) THEN
        READ (LINE, FMT = '(I5,F7.3,TR7,F6.2)'), I,X,Y
    ELSE
        PRINT*, IERR,' ERRORS FOUND'
ENDIF
```

FIGURE 10-9 *Example of checking input data for incorrect formats.*

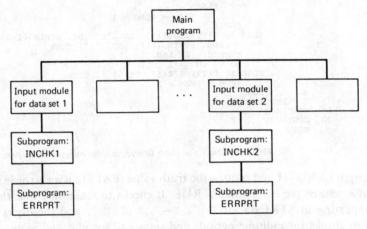

FIGURE 10-10 *Use of an input data, error-printing subprogram.*

INCHK1 and INCHK2 are for verifying the input data and the subprogram ERRPRT is for printing the results. This technique is used for three reasons:

1. To improve program modularity.

2. To prevent duplication of error-printing statements.

3. To group the input data error messages together within the printout so that they can be readily found in the printout. (Indiscriminate intermixing of error messages with normal output makes the messages harder to notice and increases the chance that they will go undetected.)

In addition, by properly coordinating the data-checking and error-printing sub-programs, the quantity of error messages may be reduced. For example, the checking subprogram could count the numbers of errors of each type and then the error-printing subprogram could include these counts in the error message, thus avoiding repetitive printing of error messages. This same concept could, of course, be extended to errors other than input data errors.

When using programming methods that involve an iterative solution, steps should be taken, particularly in the early debugging stage, to gurantee that the itera-tive process terminates. If there is a bug in the program and the process is not con-verging, excessive computer time will be used and very little knowledge will be gained. One method of ensuring that the process terminates is to insert a counter in the process and allow only a limited number of iterations. Remember also that in the test which determines when the iterative process should be terminated, the com-parison should not be made for exact equality, but for the difference being very small. For example, in comparing the numbers A and B,

```
                    IF (ABS(A-B) .LT. EPS) THEN
```

where EPS is a preselected small number, should be used instead of

```
                    IF (A .EQ. B) THEN
```

In the early stages of debugging or at any time a problem seems to be related to the subscript limits of an array, it is a good idea to put checks into the program to verify that array subscripts are within their limits. Quite often the check can be placed just before the array reference, and if an out-of-bounds condition occurs, the array name should be printed together with the problem subscript and any other data that would be helpful in determining the error.

As discussed in an earlier chapter, when the data are too large for the output field, FORTRAN puts asterisks in place of the data. To avoid this problem, assume that all the numbers involved in the calculation to create the output will be worst case (i.e., the largest possible value) and provide sufficient output space to print the largest possible number. Another alternative is to use the G-format so that some output will always be present even if the numbers are not in their desired formats.

Tracing is the process of printing the statement numbers or subprogram names each time they are executed. Often the translator or computer system will provide this facility and the programmer simply has to tell the translator or computer system when to provide the trace output. Tracing facilities are very powerful debug tools, but they usually produce large amounts of printout with each run. Because of the amount of printout, the use of tracing is time consuming and costly and should not be used except for bugs that are unusually difficult to find. When tracing is necessary, read the translator reference manual carefully and make the best possible use of the facilities. Usually, the trace capability can be turned on and off from inside the program (just as we turned the print subroutine on or off) and this capability should be used freely to reduce the amount of output. If the translator or computer system does not provide tracing, the programmer can create a form of tracing by using the milepost printing techniques discussed in Chap. 4.

Another method of determining what is wrong inside a program is to examine a memory image dump. The dump may be provided by the computer system whenever a very severe error occurs, although the programmer normally has to request that a dump be printed. To use the memory image dump the programmer must be familiar with how variables, constants, and arrays are stored in memory, and must know how to locate these areas in the dump printout. It is usually helpful also if the programmer is familiar with the machine language of the particular computer. Because memory image dumps consist of the contents of memory printed in octal or hexadecimal, the ability to use these dumps is limited to experienced programmers.

One of the most helpful debug aids is the diagnostic messages that the computer system prints whenever a severe error occurs. For example, if a program attempts to read beyond the end of a file, most systems will print a message telling the programmer of the error, and usually the system will identify the program or subprogram that was running at the time of the error. Quite often the system also prints the line number where the error occurred. The programmer should always look for these messages—they are usually output after the program's normal printout—and determine what the message means. If the message is not self-explanatory, find the translator or computer system manual which has an explanation of the message.

One mistake less experienced programmers often make is to "sit" on a problem too long without seeking help from others. Frequently, the programmer is too familiar with the program and tends to overlook even obvious errors. Someone who is not familiar with the program can only read what is written and cannot unconsciously correct the errors without seeing them. Also, explaining a program or program segment to someone else forces the programmer to rethink the details of the program. Often this allows the programmer to see the errors without the other person actually understanding the program. However, before taking a problem to someone else the programmer should be well prepared and all of the pertinent information should be readily available.

10-5 INTERACTIVE DEBUGGING

Interactive debugging is the process of debugging in an interactive environment with a terminal being used to run the programs on command rather than having them run in batch mode. When debugging on an interactive system, several new facilities may be available and the debug methods discussed earlier may be easier to use and even more powerful.

The print facilities are more powerful when used from an interactive terminal because, by sending the debug printout directly to the terminal, the programmer is able to find problems more quickly. If while observing the output on the terminal the programmer finds that the program is producing no useful output, he or she can terminate execution of the program immediately.

Tracing can be used more often when a CRT is used to display the output because paper is not being wasted. Trace data can be examined more easily if they are written to a disk file and then displayed using the text editor. The text editor can be used to search trace files for specific subroutine calls or for specific line numbers, making this information much easier and faster to locate. When the desired information is found, most text editors allow you to print only the information you need rather than the entire trace file.

Some or all of the test data can be input directly to the program from the terminal keyboard so that at least some of the data can be easily tailored for each run. When a problem appears, different test data can be entered to help isolate the exact module or line that is in error. This allows test results to change dynamically as bugs are found and corrections are made. One should, however, beware of one, possibly very serious, drawback to interactive debugging. Since test data can be changed so easily, programmers fail to plan the test data adequately and can end up wasting both their time and the computer's time.

Often, the computer system or translator will provide additional facilities for use during interactive debugging sessions. For example, some systems include commands that permit the programmer to GO TO any statement number in the program before continuing program execution, or to display the contents of variables or arrays at any time during the execution of the program. Some systems provide the ability to "single step" the program (i.e., to stop after each statement) while allowing the programmer to display certain variable contents between statement executions. Interactive facilities can be very powerful and the programmer should become familiar with the capabilities of the system being used.

PROGRAMMING PROBLEMS

1. Derive a complete set of test data for the memory cost program in Fig. 6-8 and then debug this program.

APPENDIX A*

NUMBER SYSTEMS

It should be emphasized at the outset that the definition of a number has nothing to do with the symbology used to represent it. Numbers are abstract mathematical entities that are defined from fundamental assumptions called postulates. Historically, several systems have been employed to write these numbers. The discussion in this section will be restricted to nonnegative integers and will open by describing the usual way of representing them (i.e., using decimal digits).

From elementary arithmetic it is known that any nonnegative integer may be written in the form

$$a_n 10^n + a_{n-1} 10^{n-1} + \ldots + a_1 10^1 + a_0 10^0$$
$$= a_n 10^n + a_{n-1} 10^{n-1} + \ldots + a_1 10 + a_0$$

where $a_n, a_{n-1}, \ldots, a_1, a_0$ are integers in the range 0 through 9. Normally, the powers of 10 and the plus signs are deleted, leaving the abbreviated form

$$a_n a_{n-1} \ldots a_1 a_0$$

The integers $a_n, \ldots, a_0$ are called *digits* and the notation is further facilitated by using single symbols to represent them. There must be 10 of these symbols and the standard symbols used for these integers are, of course, 0, 1, ..., 8, 9. As an example, the number

$$6 \times 10^3 + 2 \times 10^2 + 3 \times 10 + 5$$

is conventionally written 6235. Although the algorithms for performing the arithmetic operations are derived using the expanded form, once they are known they may also

*This appendix has been reprinted from Glenn A. Gibson, and Yu-cheng Liu, *Microcomputers for Engineers and Scientists*, Englewood Cliffs, N.J.: Prentice-Hall, Inc., 1980. Copyrights reserved.

be reduced so that the powers of 10 and the plus signs need not appear. As a result, the expanded form never appears in ordinary arithmetic.

The question is: Can the same notation be applied to the 1/0 combinations that the computer is required to use? The restriction is that only two symbols are available because the computer is limited to two-state combinations. Ten symbols were required in the foregoing notation because powers of 10 were used. Could powers of 2 be used? The answer is "yes"; in fact, powers of any positive integer greater than 1 could be employed as long as an equal number of symbols is available. The general form is

$$a_n x^n + \ldots + a_1 x + a_0$$

where the positive integer x is called the *base* (or *radix*). If the base is 10, the resulting notational system is called the *decimal number system* and the associated arithmetic is referred to as *base* 10 *arithmetic*. If the base is 2, the notational system is called the *binary number system* and the associated arithmetic is referred to as *base* 2 *arithmetic*. The digits in the binary number system are sometimes called *bits* and the standard two symbols used to represent the bits are 0 and 1. An example of a binary number is

$$1 \times 2^3 + 0 \times 2^2 + 1 \times 2 + 1 = 1011$$

There are two other number systems that frequently appear in computer related discussions: they are the *octal number system* (*base* 8) and the *hexadecimal number system* (*base* 16). The commonly used number bases and their symbols are summarized in Fig. A-1. The binary equivalents of the decimal, octal, and hexadecimal numbers are given in parentheses. Note that for the hexadecimal system, symbols beyond those utilized by the decimal number system must be found to represent the integers 10 through 15. Because they conform to our writing habits, the letters A through F have been chosen to fill this need.

Although the computer cannot work directly with the numbers in the octal and hexadecimal systems, these systems have a simple relationship to the binary system that is useful in reducing notation. In the binary example above, a sequence of four digits was needed to represent the number eleven. Eleven would be written with only two digits (13) in octal and only one digit (B) in hexadecimal. The savings in digits is even more pronounced as the integers get larger.

It is seen from Fig. A-1 that, where possible, the same symbols are used in all four number systems. This leads to the obvious problem of determining which system is being used to represent a number. Is 1101 the integer thirteen or the integer one thousand one hundred and one? If a discussion is centered on a single number system and that system is easily understood from the context, there is no difficulty; but if several systems are mixed in a discussion, the need to extend the notation so that it designates the base is apparent. The most common method of denoting the base is to subscript the number with the base written in decimal; for example, 1101_2 would indicate the integer thirteen and 1101_{10} would indicate one thousand one hundred and one. If no subscript is given, the intended base should be evident from the context.

	Binary	Octal	Decimal	Hexadecimal
	(Base 2)	(Base 8)	(Base 10)	(Base 16)
	0	0 (000)	0 (0000)	0 (0000)
	1	1 (001)	1 (0001)	1 (0001)
		2 (010)	2 (0010)	2 (0010)
		3 (011)	3 (0011)	3 (0011)
		4 (100)	4 (0100)	4 (0100)
		5 (101)	5 (0101)	5 (0101)
		6 (110)	6 (0110)	6 (0110)
		7 (111)	7 (0111)	7 (0111)
			8 (1000)	8 (1000)
			9 (1001)	9 (1001)
				A (1010)
				B (1011)
				C (1100)
				D (1101)
				E (1110)
				F (1111)

Note: Binary equivalents are given in parentheses.

FIGURE A-1 *Commonly used number systems.*

Because people think in terms of decimal numbers and computers work with binary numbers, there is an immediate need to convert numbers from one system to another. First consider the conversion from binary to decimal. This is accomplished by using the decimal system to carry out the computation indicated by the expression

$$a_n 2^n + a_{n-1} 2^{n-1} + \ldots + a_1 2 + a_0$$

One way of performing this computation is to simply compute the necessary powers of 2 and sum those whose coefficients are 1. Figure A-2 is a tabulation of the powers

$$2^0 = 1$$
$$2^1 = 2$$
$$2^2 = 4$$
$$2^3 = 8$$
$$2^4 = 16$$
$$2^5 = 32$$
$$2^6 = 64$$
$$2^7 = 128$$
$$2^8 = 256$$
$$2^9 = 512$$
$$2^{10} = 1024$$

FIGURE A-2 *Powers of 2 from 0 to 10.*

of 2 from 0 to 10. (These numbers are referenced frequently and should be memorized.) The decimal equivalent of the binary number 110101 can be found as follows:

$$1 \times 2^5 + 1 \times 2^4 + 0 \times 2^3 + 1 \times 2^2 + 0 \times 2 + 1$$
$$= 32 + 16 + 0 + 4 + 0 + 1 = 53_{10}$$

A more systematic way of performing the same computation is to use *Horner's rule*, which states that

$$a_n x^n + a_{n-1} x^{n-1} + \ldots + a_1 x + a_0 = ((\ldots (a_n x + a_{n-1}) x \ldots) x + a_1) x + a_0$$

For example,

$$1 \times 2^5 + 1 \times 2^4 + 0 \times 2^3 + 1 \times 2^2 + 0 \times 2 + 1$$
$$= ((((1 \times 2 + 1)2 + 0)2 + 1)2 + 0)2 + 1$$

This suggests the procedure

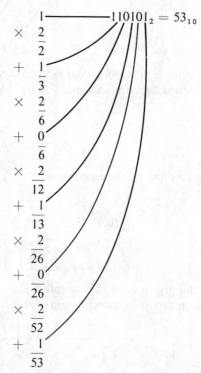

Horner's rule can also be used to find the binary equivalent of a decimal number. To understand how this is done, note that

$$\frac{((\ldots (a_n x + a_{n-1}) x \ldots) x + a_1) x + a_0}{x} = (\ldots (a_n x + a_{n-1}) x \ldots) x + a_1 + \frac{a_0}{x}$$

The quantity

$$(\ldots (a_n x + a_{n-1}) x \ldots) x + a_1$$

is the quotient and a_0 is the remainder. By repeating the operation on the quotient, the equation

$$\frac{(\ldots(a_n x + a_{n-1})x \ldots)x + a_1}{x} = (\ldots(a_n x + a_{n-1})x \ldots)x + a_2 + \frac{a_1}{x}$$

is obtained. This time, a_1 is the remainder. Clearly, repeated divisions will successively produce the coefficients a_0 through a_n. The method is demonstrated as follows:

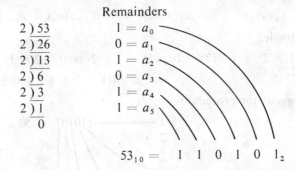

$$
\begin{array}{r l}
& \text{Remainders} \\
2\,)\,\overline{53} & 1 = a_0 \\
2\,)\,\overline{26} & 0 = a_1 \\
2\,)\,\overline{13} & 1 = a_2 \\
2\,)\,\overline{6} & 0 = a_3 \\
2\,)\,\overline{3} & 1 = a_4 \\
2\,)\,\overline{1} & 1 = a_5 \\
0 &
\end{array}
$$

$$53_{10} = 1\ 1\ 0\ 1\ 0\ 1_2$$

To convert from octal to binary it is necessary only to convert each digit and then place the resulting bit combinations side by side as follows:

$$
\begin{array}{c}
7\ \ 5\ \ 2 \\
\overline{1\ 1\ 1}\ \ \overline{1\ 0\ 1}\ \ \overline{0\ 1\ 0}
\end{array}
$$

This procedure is justified by the equation

$$
\begin{aligned}
7 \times 8^2 + 5 \times 8 + 2 &= (1 \times 2^2 + 1 \times 2 + 1)2^6 + (1 \times 2^2 + 0 \times 2 + 1)2^3 \\
&\quad + (0 \times 2^2 + 1 \times 2 + 0) \\
&= 1 \times 2^8 + 1 \times 2^7 + 1 \times 2^6 + 1 \times 2^5 + 0 \times 2^4 \\
&\quad + 1 \times 2^3 + 0 \times 2^2 + 1 \times 2 + 0
\end{aligned}
$$

To convert from binary to octal it is simply a matter of grouping the bits by threes and converting each group to its octal equivalent: for example.

$$
\begin{array}{c}
\underbrace{1\ 1\ 0}\ \underbrace{1\ 0\ 1}\ \underbrace{1\ 0\ 0}\ \underbrace{1\ 1} \\
3\ \ 2\ \ 6\ \ 3
\end{array}
$$

The conversions between binary and hexadecimal can be performed similarly, except that the grouping is done by fours instead of threes:

$$
\begin{array}{cc}
\begin{array}{c}
9\ \ A\ \ 1 \\
\overline{1\ 0\ 0\ 1}\ \overline{1\ 0\ 1\ 0}\ \overline{0\ 0\ 0\ 1}
\end{array}
&
\begin{array}{c}
\underbrace{1\ 1\ 0\ 1}\ \underbrace{0\ 1\ 1\ 0}\ \underbrace{1\ 0\ 1\ 0\ 0} \\
6\ \ B\ \ 4
\end{array}
\end{array}
$$

The algorithms for carrying out the arithmetic operations in the binary number system are the same as those used in the decimal number system but are somewhat easier to execute because of the simplicity of the addition and multiplication tables. These tables are given in Fig. A-3. An example of each of the four operations is given

	0	1
0	0	1
1	1	10

(a)

	0	1
0	0	0
1	0	1

(b)

FIGURE A-3 *Addition and multiplication tables for the binary number system:* (*a*) *Addition;* (*b*) *Multiplication.*

in Fig. A-4; each example is accompanied by the equivalent decimal calculation. Carrying, borrowing, and shifting are done exactly the same way as if the operands were decimal numbers. Note that multiplication involves only shifting and adding because multiplication by a single bit is a matter of writing an intermediate result (multiplication by 1) or shifting without writing the intermediate result (multiplication by 0). Similarly, division consists of shifting and subtracting.

```
  110101        53             101101        45
 +10010        +18            -100110       -38
 -------       ----           -------       ----
 1000111        71               111         7
```

(a)   (b)

```
  10110         22            10001              17
 ×1011         ×11       110 )1100110        6 )102
 ------        ----           110               6
  10110         22            -----             ---
 10110          22            00110             42
10110          ----            110              42
------          242           ----             ---
11110010                         0               0
```

(c)   (d)

FIGURE A-4 *Examples of the four arithmetic operations using both binary and decimal arithmetic:* (*a*) *Addition;* (*b*) *Subtraction;* (*c*) *Multiplication;* (*d*) *Division.*

Performing the arithmetic operations in octal is more difficult than in decimal because people are generally unfamiliar with the octal addition and multiplication tables. In hexadecimal, they are even more difficult to perform because these tables are so large. Although it is worthwhile to learn how to add and subtract in these number systems, very few people learn how to multiply or divide in them. If a product or quotient is needed, one can convert the operands to the decimal system, perform the operation, and then convert the result back to the original system.

Because the storage capacity of a computer's memory and control circuitry is finite, it is necessary to group the bits it operates on into finite sequences. This means that once the size of a group of bits is decided upon, there are only a finite number of integers that can be represented by the group. If there are n bits in a group, the number of possible combinations of 0's and 1's is 2^n. If the bits are used to represent nonnegative integers, the integers 0 through $2^n - 1$ can be represented (e.g., 8 bits can represent the integers 0 through 255).

Quite often the groups are large and n may be 24, 32, 64, and so on. There are tables available that give these high powers of 2 exactly, but it is usually not necessary that they be known exactly. Normally, one needs only an estimate of the powers of 2 greater than 10, and such an estimate can be quickly obtained from Fig. A-2 and the approximation

$$2^{10} = 1024 \approx 10^3$$

To see how this is done, suppose that an approximation of 2^{36} is desired. Then

$$2^{36} = 2^6 \times 2^{30} = 2^6 \times (2^{10})^3 \approx 2^6 \times (10^3)^3 = 64 \text{ billion}$$

One undesirable aspect of the finiteness of the groups of bits is that the result of an operation may not fit into the number of bits reserved for it. When this is the case, an *overflow* is said to occur. The magnitude of the result of an addition or subtraction require one more bit than either of the operands, and the product of two numbers may require twice as many bits as is reserved for the numbers being multiplied. Although the division of two integers never yields a quotient that needs more bits than is reserved for the dividend, it is usually desirable to also store the remainder. Therefore, to conserve space and minimize the circuitry, it is common to reserve a fewer number of bits for the quotient than would be needed to accommodate all possible cases. The end result is that all four arithmetic operations may cause overflows and the size of the bit groupings is an important consideration when designing a computer.

APPENDIX B

COMPARISON OF VERSIONS OF FORTRAN

This appendix consists of a table that provides a comparative summary of the more important versions of FORTRAN. The first column gives the statement type, the second column gives the section(s) in which the statement is discussed, and the third, fourth, and fifth columns contain comparative comments about the statement for FORTRAN 77, WATFIV-S, and FORTRAN IV, respectively. Many entries include the statement "Not included in the standard." Although the standard does not require the presence of the feature being considered, the feature may be included in enhanced versions of the level of FORTRAN indicated by the column heading.

Statement type	Section(s)	Full FORTRAN 77	WATFIV-S	1966 Standard FORTRAN
PROGRAM	2-1-4	Included.	Included.	Not included in standard.
STOP	2-1-4	Included.	Included.	Included.
END	2-1-4	Also performs a STOP.	Also performs a STOP.	Standard FORTRAN does not perform a STOP.
CONTINUE	2-8	Included.	Included.	Included.
List directed I-O PRINT *	2-3-1	List may include expressions, string constants, arrays, and implied DO loops.	Same as FORTRAN 77 except that asterisks are deleted.	Not included in standard. Limited unformatted PRINT in extended versions such as WATFIV.
READ *	2-3-2	List may include variables, array elements, arrays, and implied DO loops.	Same as FORTRAN 77 except that asterisks are deleted.	Not included in standard. Limited unformatted READ in extended versions such as WATFIV.
Formatted I-O PRINT	7-1	Format specification may be FORMAT statement label or character string. List is same as for PRINT *.	Same as FORTRAN 77 except that format specification must be a statement label.	Not included in standard.
READ (without control list)	7-1	Same as for PRINT except that input list is limited as with READ *.	Same as FORTRAN 77 except that format specification must be statement label.	Not included in standard.
WRITE	7-4	Control list may include unit, format, record, status, error, and end specifiers. Internal file capability. Format specification and list same as PRINT.	Same as FORTRAN 77 except that format specification must be a statement label. Specifiers are system-dependent. Internal file called core-to-core transfer.	Standard only requires unit and format specifiers. Format specification must be a statement label.
READ (with control list)	7-4	Same as for WRITE.	Same as for WRITE.	Same as for WRITE.
FORMAT	7-2-2	Does not include H format code, must use single quotes.	Includes Z format code for hexadecimal. Does not include BN, BZ, TR, TL, S, SP, or SS format codes.	Includes H format code, but single quotes cannot be used for string constants in standard. Does not include BN, BZ, TR, TL, S, SP, or SS format codes.

OPEN and CLOSE	8-3	Included, but rules are system-dependent.	System-dependent.	Not included in standard.
INQUIRE	8-5	Included, but rules are system-dependent.	System-dependent.	Not included.
BACKSPACE, REWIND, and ENDFILE	8-2	For sequential files.	For sequential files.	For sequential files.
Assignment	2-2	Permits logical, string, and mixed-mode arithmetic expressions (including complex expressions). Substrings and concatenation of strings are included.	Same as FORTRAN 77 except that string expressions and substrings are not included.	Mixed mode is not standard but can be done with most translators. Character string expressions and substrings are not included. Complex arithmetic not included in standard basic FORTRAN.
Subscripts	2-10	Subscripts may be denoted by integer expressions.	Subscripts may be any real or integer expressions.	Subscripts must be integer expressions of the form Const.*Var. $\pm$ Const.
Branching GO TO	2-4	Assigned GO TO is included.	Same as FORTRAN 77.	Same as FORTRAN 77 except that assigned GO TO is not standard.
IF Logical	2-4	Used primarily for exits.	Same as FORTRAN 77.	Used for all IF-THEN-ELSE structures since IF blocks are not included. Operators .EQV. and .NEQV. not standard.
Arithmetic	4-3	Included, but should not be used.	Included, but should not be used.	Included, but should not be used.
IF blocks IF-THEN-ELSE	4-1	Used for IF-THEN-ELSE structures.	Same as FORTRAN 77.	Not included.
ELSE IF-THEN	4-3	Used for CASE structures.	Same as FORTRAN 77.	Same as FORTRAN 77.
Computed GO TO	4-3	Included, but not normally used. Defaults to next statement.	Same as FORTRAN 77.	Default is not in standard. Used for CASE structures.
Cases	4-3	Implemented using ELSE IF-THEN.	Implemented using ELSE IF-THEN or DO-CASE blocks.	Implemented with computed GO TO.

Statement type	Section(s)	Full FORTRAN 77	WATFIV-S	1966 Standard FORTRAN
Looping				
DO	2-9	Index may be integer or real. Initial value, limit, and increment may be integer or real expressions. Increment may be negative.	Index must be integer. Initial value, limit, and increment must be positive integer constants or integer variables.	Index must be integer. Initial value, limit, and increment must be positive integer constants or integer variables.
DO-WHILE	4-2	Not included in FORTRAN 77 standard.	Denoted by WHILE and terminated with ENDWHILE.	Not included.
DO-UNTIL	4-2	Not included in FORTRAN 77 standard.	May be formed using LOOP, ENDLOOP, and QUIT statements. Some versions such as WATFIV V220 include an UNTIL statement.	Not included.
Exits	3-2	Normally done using logical IF statements.	Loops with exits may be formed using LOOP and ENDLOOP statements, then QUIT statements provide escape-type exits.	Normally done using logical IF statements.
Type declaration				
INTEGER, REAL, DOUBLE PRECISION, LOGICAL, and COMPLEX	5-1	May be used for dimensioning.	Same as FORTRAN 77.	COMPLEX not included in standard.
CHARACTER	5-1-3	Must be used to designate character string variables and arrays. May be used for dimensioning.	Same as FORTRAN 77. Other types of variables and arrays may also be used for storing character strings.	Not in standard basic FORTRAN. Character strings are put in other types of variables and arrays.
IMPLICIT	5-1-5	Included.	Included.	Not included in standard.
Naming constants and preassignment				
PARAMETER	5-2	Included.	Not included.	Not included.
DATA	5-2	May include implied DO loops and repeat factors.	Same as FORTRAN 77.	Implied DO loops not included in standard.

SOCIAL EFFECTS OF COMPUTERS

Feature	Reference			
Storage allocation DIMENSION	2-10 5-4	Up to seven dimensions. Limits may be any integers. Subprograms may use variable dimensioning.	Same as FORTRAN 77 except that lower subscript limit must be 1.	Up to three dimensions. Lower subscript limit must be 1. Variable dimensioning not included in standard.
COMMON Unnamed Named	6-9	Included. Included.	Included. Included—rules are system-dependent.	Included. Not included in standard basic FORTRAN.
EQUIVALENCE	5-5	Included.	Included.	Included.
Subprograms CALL, SUBROUTINE, FUNCTION, RETURN, ENTRY, EXTERNAL, INTRINSIC, SAVE, and BLOCK DATA	Chap. 6	All of the listed statements are included.	Same as FORTRAN 77 except that INTRINSIC and SAVE are not included.	Same as FORTRAN 77 except that ENTRY, SAVE, and INTRINSIC are not in standard.
Intrinsic functions	2-2 5-1	Includes generic intrinsic functions.	No generic intrinsic functions. See Cress reference in Bibliography.	No generic intrinsic functions. Standard intrinsic functions are limited. See Organick reference in Bibliography. Not included in standard.
Statement functions	6-12	Included.	Included.	Included.

BIBLIOGRAPHY

SOCIAL EFFECTS OF COMPUTERS

ADAMS, J. M., AND DOUGLAS H. HADEN, *Social Effects of Computer Use and Misuse*. New York: John Wiley & Sons, Inc., 1976.

ARBIB, MICHAEL A., *Computers and the Cybernetic Society*. New York: Academic Press, Inc., 1977.

KRAUSS, LEONARD, AND EILEEN MACGAHAN, *Computer Fraud and Countermeasures*. Englewood Cliffs, N.J.: Prentice-Hall, Inc., 1979.

LYNCH, ROBERT E., AND JOHN R. RICE, *Computers: Their Impact and Use*. New York: Holt, Rinehart and Winston, 1977.

SANDERS, DONALD H., *Computers in Society*, 2nd ed. New York: McGraw-Hill Book Company, 1977.

COMPUTER SYSTEMS

CASSEL, DON, AND MARTIN JACKSON, *Introduction to Computers and Information Processing*. Reston, Va.: Reston Publishing Company, Inc., 1980.

KINDRED, ALTON R., *An Introduction to Computers*. Englewood Cliffs, N.J.: Prentice-Hall, Inc., 1976.

BINARY NUMBERS

GIBSON, GLENN A., AND YU-CHENG LIU, *Microcomputers for Engineers and Scientists*. Englewood Cliffs, N.J.: Prentice-Hall, Inc., 1980.

KRUTZ, Ronald L., *Microprocessors and Logic Design*. New York: John Wiley & Sons, Inc., 1980.

FORTRAN 77

DAVIS, GORDON, AND THOMAS HOFFMAN, *FORTRAN: A Structured, Disciplined Style*. New York: McGraw-Hill Book Company, 1978.

FRIEDMAN, FRANK L. AND ELLIOT B. KOFFMAN, *Problem Solving and Structured Programming in FORTRAN 77*, 2nd ed. Reading, Mass.: Addison-Wesley Publishing Company, 1981.

HUME, J. N. P., AND R. C. HOLT, *Programming FORTRAN 77: A Structured Approach*, 2nd ed. Reston, Va.: Reston Publishing Company, Inc., 1981.

MEISSNER, LOREN, AND ELLIOTT ORGANICK, *FORTRAN 77: Featuring Structured Programming*. Reading, Mass.: Addison-Wesley Publishing Company, 1980.

NICKERSON, ROBERT C., *Fundamentals of FORTRAN Programming*, 2nd ed. Cambridge, Mass.: Winthrop Publishers, Inc., 1980.

PAGE, REX, AND RICH DIDDAY, *FORTRAN 77 for Humans*. St. Paul, Minn.: West Publishing Company, 1980.

SCHALLERT, WILLIAM F., AND CAROL CLARK, *Programming in FORTRAN*. Reading, Mass.: Addison-Wesley Publishing Company, 1979.

WAGONER, JERROLD L., *FORTRAN 77: Principles of Programming*. New York: John Wiley & Sons, Inc., 1980.

WATFIV-S

CRESS, PAUL, PAUL DIRKSEN, AND J. W. GRAHAM, *Structured FORTRAN with WATFIV-S*. Englewood Cliffs, N.J.: Prentice-Hall, Inc., 1980.

DYCK, V. A., J. D. LAWSON, AND J. A. SMITH, *Introduction to Computing: Structured Problem Solving Using WATFIV-S*. Reston, Va.: Reston Publishing Company, Inc., 1979.

OLDER VERSIONS OF FORTRAN

BOGUSLAVSKY, BORIS W., *Elementary Computer Programming in FORTRAN IV*, 2nd ed. Reston, Va.: Reston Publishing Company, Inc., 1980.

BOILLOT, MICHEL, *Understanding FORTRAN*. St. Paul, Minn.: West Publishing Company, 1978.

CHATTERGY, RAHUL, AND UDO W. POOCH, *Top-Down Modular Programming in FORTRAN with WATFIV*. Cambridge, Mass.: Winthrop Publishers, Inc., 1980.

COOPER, LAURA, AND MARILYN SMITH, *Standard FORTRAN: A Problem Solving Approach*. Boston: Houghton Mifflin Company, 1973.

GOTTFRIED, BYRON S., *FORTRAN IV Programmer's Reference Guide*. New York: Quantum Publishers, Inc., 1973.

ORGANICK, ELLIOTT, AND LOREN MEISSNER, *FORTRAN IV*, 2nd ed. Reading, Mass.: Addison-Wesley Publishing Company, 1974.

PROGRAMMING AIDS

BOHL, MARILYN, *Tools for Structured Design*. Palo Alto, Calif.: Science Research Associates, Inc., 1978.

BOILLOT, MICHEL, GARY GLEASON, AND L. W. HORN, *Essentials of Flowcharting*, 2nd ed. Duboque, Iowa: William C. Brown Company Publishers, 1979.

HUSKELL, RICHARD E., *FORTRAN Programming Using Structured Flowcharting*. Palo Alto, Calif.: Science Research Associates, Inc., 1978.

PROGRAM DESIGN

JENSEN, RANDELL W., AND CHARLES C. TONIES, *Software Engineering*. Englewood Cliffs, N.J.: Prentice-Hall, Inc., 1979.

MYERS, GLENFORD J., *Software Reliability*. New York: John Wiley & Sons, Inc., 1976.

NUMERICAL METHODS AND MATHEMATICAL MODELING

ARDEN, BRUCE, AND KENNETH ASTILL, *Numerical Algorithms: Origins and Applications*. Reading, Mass.: Addison-Wesley Publishing Company, 1970.

CARNAHAN, BRICE, AND JAMES O. WILKES, *Digital Computing and Numerical Methods*. New York: John Wiley & Sons, Inc., 1973.

DYM, CLIVE, AND ELIZABETH IVEY, *Principles of Mathematical Modeling*. New York: Academic Press, Inc., 1980.

FAGEN, RICHARD, AND SUSAN BROSCHE, *FORTRAN Computer Programming for Statistics: A Manual*. Englewood Cliffs, N.J.: Prentice-Hall, Inc., 1979.

MALCOLM, M. A., C. B. MOLER, AND G. E. FORSYTHE, *Computer Methods for Mathematical Computations*. Englewood Cliffs, N.J.: Prentice-Hall, Inc., 1977.

ENGINEERING AND SCIENTIFIC
APPLICATIONS OF FORTRAN

DORN, WILLIAM, AND DANIEL MCCRACKEN, *Numerical Methods with FORTRAN IV Case Studies*. New York: John Wiley & Sons, Inc., 1972.

GEAR, C. WILLIAM, *Applications and Algorithms in Science and Engineering, Module A: Introduction to Computers, Structured Programming, and Applications*. Palo Alto, Calif.: Science Research Associates, Inc., 1978.

SCHICK, WILLIAM, AND CHARLES MERZ, JR., *FORTRAN for Engineering*. New York: McGraw-Hill Book Company, 1972.

INDEX

INDEX